RETHINKING CHURC

Edited by David Lyon and Marguerite Van Die

Ambitious in scope, *Rethinking Church, State, and Modernity* considers some central concepts in the sociology and history of religion and explores how Canada's religious experience is distinctive in the modern world. The contributors to this volume challenge the institutional approach that stresses a strict division between 'church' and 'state,' which seems increasingly inappropriate in late-modern and post-modern society and instead, favour a more fluid interpretation.

Canada, which stands somewhere between a largely secularized Europe and the relatively religious United States, is well situated as a testing ground for the leading conceptions of the fate of religion in modern and postmodern societies. The book focuses mainly on Christianity, looking at what is distinctive about Canadian situations, and discusses the concomitant decline of some religious groups and the ongoing vitality of others in an increasingly multifaith and globalized society. The emergence of constitutional rights and identity politics has contributed to the changing concepts about the relationship between church and state. The contributors to this volume pay special attention to the political and social attitudes of religious groups and to the consequences of these attitudes. Subjects covered include the role of religion and references to God in the Canadian Constitution; anglophone religious leaders' responses to the referendum crisis of 1995; evangelical subcultures in Canada and the United States; and specifically postmodern topics such as the body and consumerism.

DAVID LYON is a member of the department of sociology at Queen's University.

MARGUERITE VAN DIE teaches in the departments of history and theology, Queen's University.

Rethinking Church, State, and Modernity

Canada between Europe and America

Edited by David Lyon and Marguerite Van Die

UNIVERSITY OF TORONTO PRESS
Toronto Buffalo London

© University of Toronto Press Incorporated 2000
Toronto Buffalo London
Printed in Canada

ISBN 0-8020-4408-5 (cloth)
ISBN 0-8020-8213-0 (paper)

Printed on acid-free paper

Canadian Cataloguing in Publication Data

Main entry under title:

Rethinking church, state, and modernity : Canada between Europe and
America

Includes bibliographical references and index.
ISBN 0-8020-4408-5 (bound)   ISBN 0-8020-8213-0 (pbk.)

1. Church and state – Canada.   2. Church and state – United States.
3. Religion and state – Canada.   4. Religion and state – United States.
I. Lyon, David, 1948– .   II. Van Die, Marguerite.

BR570.R47 2000   322.1′0971   C00-931688-4

University of Toronto Press acknowledges the financial assistance to its
publishing program of the Canada Council for the Arts and the
Ontario Arts Council.

University of Toronto Press acknowledges the financial support for
its publishing activities of the Government of Canada through the
Book Publishing Industry Development Program (BPIDP).

In memory of our friend and colleague
George Rawlyk
1935–1995

Contents

PART FIVE: IDENTITY, GENDER, BODY

Acknowledgments

We are very grateful to the Pew Charitable Trusts for a major grant that enabled us to work on the research project, 'Religion and Politics in the United States and Canada' of which this book is one product. We also wish to thank Queen's University for its support, our colleagues who have encouraged us in the task, and graduate students – especially Eric Piché and Shelley Z. Reuter in sociology, and Doug Hessler, who played important parts in the production of this volume. abi lyon prepared the index. The dedication to George Rawlyk, of Queen's history department, is also an expression of thanks. Our joint research grant application, following his death, was intended as one means of maintaining some momentum in the religious research for which he had become so well known in Canada and beyond.

Contributors

Gregory Baum, emeritus professor of sociology and religious studies, McGill University, Montreal, Canada.

Peter Beyer, associate professor of religious studies, University of Ottawa, Canada.

Kevin J. Christiano, associate professor of sociology, University of Notre Dame, United States.

George Egerton, associate professor of history, University of British Columbia, Vancouver, Canada.

Andrew S. Grenville, senior vice-president, Angus Reid Group, Toronto, Canada.

Danièle Hervieu-Léger, Directeur d'études, École des Hautes Études en Sciences Sociales, Paris, France.

Harry H. Hiller, professor of sociology, University of Calgary, Canada.

William H. Katerberg, associate professor of history, Calvin College, Grand Rapids, United States.

David Lyon, professor of sociology, Queen's University, Kingston, Canada.

David Martin, professor emeritus at the London School of Economics and Political Science, and honorary professor at the University of Lancaster, England.

Nancy Nason-Clark, professor of sociology, University of New Brunswick, Fredericton, Canada.

Roger O'Toole, professor of sociology, University of Toronto, at Scarborough, Toronto, Canada.

Sam Reimer, assistant professor of sociology, Atlantic Baptist University, Halifax, Canada.

David Seljak, assistant professor of religion, St Jerome's University, University of Waterloo, Waterloo, Canada.

John H. Simpson, professor of sociology, University of Toronto, Toronto, Canada.

John G. Stackhouse, Jr, Sangwoo Youtong Chee Professor of Theology, Regent College, Vancouver, Canada.

Marguerite Van Die, associate professor of history, Queen's University, and Queen's Theological College, Kingston, Canada.

RETHINKING CHURCH, STATE, AND MODERNITY

Introduction

DAVID LYON

For many decades the concepts of 'church, state, and modernity,' have helped historians and sociologists to come to grips with what is going on in the realm of 'religion and society' in the twentieth century. 'Church' refers to religious organizations whose presence and significance were taken for granted in Canada until well after the 1960s. 'State' is a shorthand for government activities that were assumed to be sovereign and self-contained in a geographical territory. And 'modernity,' the most recent addition, speaks of that cluster of social and cultural phenomena associated with liberal democracy, industrial capitalism, high technology, spreading urbanism, and a belief in progress as an article of cultural faith. By placing these three together one could effectively organize the pertinent patterns of interactions between significant events, processes, and personalities.

No more. All three concepts are now contested, with good reason, and the result is that the conceptual terrain suddenly appears as treacherous as quicksand, with apparently no firm place to stand. What is 'church' when attendance rates plummet but personal declarations of faith remain buoyant? What is the 'state' when significant spheres of government jurisdiction are overridden by decisions of transnational corporations? And what is 'modernity' when some of its key early twentieth-century features – such as political commitment to progress or a growing blue-collar sector – are losing their clear outline or are shrinking?

These are some of the tides and currents that must be taken into account in understanding the present. They immediately connect the debate over church, state, and modernity with wider questions of social and cultural transformation. These include disturbances in the delicate patterns of geopolitical forces, new cultural contacts enabled by communication and information technologies, the fracturing and fragmenting of old alliances and stable social networks, and a concomitant quest for identity, whether ethnic, sexual, national, or religious. Such social sea-changes have stretched the capacities of old concepts and theories to explain what is going on, and have generated a quest for new ones.

To comment on only one of the above, in contemporary Canada the Christian monopoly on religious identity no longer obtains. There always were pockets of difference, but today many faith traditions are found in Canada. This important fact is acknowledged but not elaborated in this book. For purposes of continuity of argument – other faith traditions deserve proper treatment in their own right – and coherence of analysis between contributors, we chose to focus primarily on changes within Christianity. On the one hand, in rethinking concepts it helps if at least one variable – in this case 'church' – is held constant. On the other, to do justice to all religious groups in Canada today would make a very unwieldy book indeed!

Of course, questions couched as 'church, state, and modernity' can easily become matters of abstract speculation, particularly at a time when conceptual uncertainty is general rather than specific. By examining these debates in relation to concrete Canadian situations, which is the burden of this book, the character and extent of contemporary cultural and social change may better be gauged. In Canada, what Grace Davie (1994) calls 'believing without belonging' is a phenomenon that is rapidly on the rise. While less than a quarter of the population actually attends a place of worship, almost two-thirds retain a strong sense of conventional Christian commitment, seeing the death and resurrection of Jesus as central for personal forgiveness (Angus Reid 1996c). In Canada, most 'church-and-state' issues, such as who should control educational institutions, still reflect the unique history of this country with its twin 'shadow establishments' – Protestant and Roman Catholic – despite the emerging influence of other faith traditions and political commitments to multiculturalism. And in Canada, with its heavy dependence on communication and information technologies, and its tilt towards consumer capitalism, the classic features of industrial society are very much in question, with the result that networks and identities are now at least as important as the social classes and institutions once characteristic of modernity (see Castells 1996, 1997, 1998; Lyon, 2000).

Questions of religion-and-society in Canada, as elsewhere, are best understood through comparative study. American sociologist Seymour Martin Lipset's advice is well known, that 'knowledge of Canada or the United States is the best way to gain insight into the other North American country' (1990). But as his compatriot, historian Mark Noll (1992) observes, this reveals a paradox which begs further questions for comparative analysis: of the two, Canada seems to qualify best as a 'Christian' country in the nineteenth century, or rather, as '*two* Christian nations, Catholic and Protestant.'

The only way to grasp this is to make another comparison, this time with Europe. British sociologist David Martin (a contributor to this book) proposes that, religiously, Anglo-Canada was, in its early modern development, a type of Protestant pluralism but with an informal religious establishment that placed it 'half way between England and the U.S.A.' (1978, 35). Quebec, on the other hand, was a distinct 'sub-society' that put certain restrictions on Protestant hegemony, particularly until the 1960s, after which religion-and-society relations experienced some seismic readjustments. The result, in a sense, is that two secularizations – understood as de facto disestablishments – have occurred in Canada. This sets the scene, then, for what follows. In this book, Canadian situations are used as case studies for testing new theories of social and cultural change that centre on what were once thought of broadly as issues of church-and-state.

What an Opinion Poll Can Tell Us

Some general clues about the direction of change may be gleaned from opinion polling, which is why in 1996 the editors approached the Angus Reid Group to run a survey entitled *God and Society in North America*.[1] This provides valuable soundings about the professed religious and political beliefs and practices of a cross-section of Canadians and Americans, and shows, among other things, that being actively religious continues to have significant implications for social involvement even in so-called secular Canada. The survey is discussed in a number of chapters in this book, including those of Andrew Grenville, Sam Reimer, and John Simpson. No one pretends that self-reported statements about belief and behaviour tell anything like the whole story of faith and commitment, but these statistics do yield some helpful clues about key trends. Such survey results also cast doubt on the usefulness of standard social science concepts, such as 'church' and 'state,' but also of others, such as 'secularization' and, of course, 'modernity.'

The 1996 survey confirmed what has been evident, at least from opinion polling, for some time: many Canadians believe without belonging. Although less than 25 per cent attend church more than twice per month, 85 per cent believe in God (15 per cent more than in the United Kingdom or New Zealand, who also attend a little less, for example) and around 30 per cent would define their Christianity in very orthodox ways. This contrasts with the United States, where an even higher belief rate is also reflected in almost 45 per cent attending church twice monthly. (Italians believe less but attend more; Northern Irish believe the same but attend more.) There is plenty of piety well beyond the pews.

But does the believing make any difference in, say, social and political life? Canadians vary considerably when asked whether religion is important to their political thinking. Regionally, the rate is highest in Manitoba and the Maritimes (28 per cent) and lowest in Quebec (9 per cent). Whether or not religious background is significant (as opposed to stated opinion) is an empirical question. As far as attendance is concerned, whereas in Canada 48 per cent of weekly churchgoers believe religion is important to their political thinking, only 12 per cent of occasional attenders think so (the U.S. figure drops from 61 per cent to 25 per cent). Yet 46 per cent of Canadians think it essential that 'traditional Christian values' should play a major role in Canadian politics (compare this with 56 per cent in the United States). So in a generalized way, almost half the Canadian population seems to want 'Christian values'; less than a quarter think their faith affects their politics, but this reflects mainly the view of churchgoers, not unattached believers. It would be a mistake to assume from this, however, that religiosity is of diminishing significance for social involvement and political activity in Canada. All the above data show is how conventional modes of religiosity have become less significant, in some cases, for conventional political action, especially voting. Canadian Christian political identities are constructed, it seems, in ways that need not make direct reference to church or party.

One thing is very clear: Canadian hopes for 'Christian values' do not translate directly or unambiguously into an identification with the

'Christian right' a fact that is picked up by John Simpson in his chapter. Only 18 per cent of Canadians would align themselves thus, compared with 34 per cent of Americans. Committed evangelicals are more likely than other religious groups to identify with the Christian right, although it is still the case that a larger proportion of evangelicals vote Liberal than Reform. Mainline Protestants identify less with the right, and Catholics are least likely so to identify themselves. Regionally, the Maritimes have the biggest concentration of the 'Christian right' (32 per cent), followed by the Prairies (27 per cent), Alberta (22 per cent), Ontario and British Columbia (both 20 per cent), and with Quebec showing only a tiny proportion (10 per cent). Part of the reason for this difference, compared with the United States, lies in the organization of political support. In the United States, non-party political action committees (PACs) allow funding directly to specific interest groups, and without such groups the impact of the American Christian right would have been far smaller. In Canada, by contrast, funding goes directly to political parties.

The political priorities of religious groups have to do with raising moral standards – this is a shared aim among different groups – and promoting the family, where they differ. Committed evangelicals and Catholics place the family above building a strong economy, which mainline Protestants, with the majority of all Canadians, put first. General Canadian priorities differ markedly from American at this point. Canadians put strengthening the economy (32 per cent) before promoting the family (20 per cent), whereas Americans reverse the order (13 per cent, 31 per cent). Higher unemployment rates in Canada than in the United States, and higher crime rates in the United States than in Canada would, of course, help to explain where the perceived social problems would be most acutely felt. Canadian evangelicals could be said to be closest to the general American population in the shared aim of promoting the family. The ties would appear even stronger if one compared the Maritimes with, say, the Southern States.

The desire to express faith in voluntary activity shows up strongly. A number of American observers, including, notably, Robert Putnam (1995a), have argued that in the United States community involvement has declined, and that this constitutes a danger for democratic participation. Although this so-called social capital debate has not yet become so important in Canada, many suspect that similar trends exist here, too (on the United States, see Edwards and Foley 1997; on Canada, Piché 1999). Yet the evidence in both countries suggests that the matter is

more complicated, and that religious participation is a crucially significant variable (Post-Modernity Project 1996, n3; Ammerman 1997a, 362–
7). While 47 per cent of Canadians (to the United States 54 per cent) are
members of voluntary organizations and associations, 68 per cent of
such members attend church weekly, curiously enough, just *more* than
in the United States (65 per cent). In both countries, the likelihood of
involvement increases with age and education levels, and varies with
region.

What then, constitutes the barriers to proper understanding in this
field? If the survey evidence throws up such interesting correlations
and connections, then why is more not known about the contemporary
religious cultures of Canada and their social significance? This book
suggests some answers to those questions, answers that take us beyond
political party and religious denomination, and beyond secularization
as a master narrative.

Beyond Party and Denomination

A once prominent and conventional method for examining the social
significance of religious belief was to look at denominational background and voting preferences, an area of study that has fallen into
relative neglect in recent years. This does, however, yield some interesting background to today's situations. For well over a century religion
and politics in Canada were deeply intertwined. In anglophone Canada
nationality itself was interpreted using evangelical referents, and political life was shot through with religious colouring. An alliance between
Protestantism and British civilization was expressed in the hope of
some that Canada would be God's Dominion, and was manifested in
the Anglo-Protestant hegemony that lasted until the Second World War.
Both Roger O'Toole and George Egerton comment on aspects of this in
the present volume. The Anglo hegemony contained diverse features
from Tory Anglicanism to Baptist and Methodist Social Gospellers. A
different hegemony existed in Quebec, which developed a distinct
society that was the product not of the state, but of the Catholic Church,
and where anglophone ultramontane Catholics, too, succeeded in having their institutions – particularly educational ones – supported and
protected. Despite the overt antagonism between evangelical and ultramontane positions, together they ensured that religion deeply influenced Canadian public life. This occurred not only before and after
Confederation, but right up to the postwar waves of immigration that

would alter profoundly the Canadian demographic profile (Clarke 1996, 357–9; see also Baum, Beyer, Hiller, and Seljak in this volume).

Despite those waves of new immigration that produced a much more culturally diverse Canada, and reduced the frequency of overt religious references in political life, the religion-and-politics relation did not simply disappear. The strong connections between religious allegiance and voting patterns, for instance, were still seen to be highly significant in the late 1970s and early 1980s. In the mid-1970s Mildred Schwartz could claim that 'religion is the greatest source of polarization for political parties' in Canada (1974, 579). Catholics tended to vote Liberal; Protestants, Conservative. During the following decade the connections blurred somewhat, and the debate centred on the issue of how newcomers – non-inheritors of some already existing political tradition – made a difference to voting outcomes (for example, see Johnston 1985; Irvine 1985). Yet the religious connection with party choice persisted, even when actual policy choices were detached from religious preference, against all expectation. As Johnston puts it, 'Canadians are typically astounded when told that religion is the most powerful predictor of their party preferences' (1985, 99).

Because of this astonishment, perhaps, media and scholarly analysts tend to ignore what is still a very significant factor in Canadian politics: religion. The Catholic and non-Catholic cleavage remains a predictor of voting choices, even though this seems to be diluted when, for instance, Catholics are more exposed to media accounts (Mendelsohn and Nadeau 1997). Both these factors – ignoring the religious dimension and its being highly significant – were strikingly apparent in the Quebec referendum in 1995. While media attention focused on Jacques Parizeau's blaming 'money and the ethnic vote' for the narrow defeat of the 'Yes' side, other evidence pointed towards committed francophone Catholics playing a much greater role. No less than 60 per cent of Catholics who attend mass weekly – 13 per cent of the francophone population – voted 'No' (Grenville and Reid 1996, A9). Grenville and Reid argue that these people are both more accepting of differences, and they view separation as a threat to religiously valued community.

Beyond Secularization

By and large, the idea that religious commitments affect public life is scarcely raised today in most Canadian media and academic accounts. One major reason for this is that another idea has taken root successfully – that secularization has severed such links. Secularization, in its most vulgar guise, refers to the steady decline of the religious in modern societies, as seen, in Canada, in the evacuation of the churches, and the loss of religious referents in cultural and political life. This is not to deny that mainline denominations are indeed depopulating, or that God is seldom mentioned in Parliament or the press. Nor is it to deny that a long-term process of splitting apart, or uncoupling, of church-and-state occurs in most modern societies.

The point is that secularization, understood as religious decline, deflects attention from ways that the religious impulse is being relocated, and religious activities restructured. It may also obscure the peculiar paths that the uncoupling of church-and-state take in specific social settings. The dangerous thing about secularization is not so much that it is false, as that it has taken root as a taken-for-granted, unproblematic assumption of much academic and media analysis, which makes it one of the most misused and abused concepts in history and sociology today.

Debates over secularization in Canada have often been polarized, or else the participants have talked past each other, dealing, as they are, with different phenomena. This may be seen, for instance, in the controversy of describing and dating the process. While some historians – such as Nancy Christie and Michael Gauvreau (1996) – argue that the social influence of the churches reached its zenith in the years up to and including the Second World War, and thus that secularization began relatively late in Canada outside Quebec, others argue that precisely this social involvement marks a departure from what is religiously central. From this latter viewpoint, on their own evidence, Christie and Gauvreau should date secular decline much earlier than they do.

According to David Marshall (1992), for example, the secular rot set in as social concerns began to undermine theological belief. As the emphasis shifted from the 'spiritual' to the 'social' among Christian clergy, from Victorian times, this intellectual movement paradoxically preceded a diminishing social and political impact. By abandoning the transcendent for the immanent in a highly social gospel, Ramsay Cook concurs, the mainstream churches of Canada 'set off down the path to the secular city' (1997, 11; cf 1985). It is hard to see a way out of the impasse, thus defined. Rather than pursuing the debate in this way, a good starting point for rethinking secularization is to look at ways in which the religious is restructured and relocated, instead of seeking indices of general decline, or moments of doctrinal transition.

This is just what British sociologist David Martin does in his 'general theory of secularization.' For him, secularization has everything to do with the altering relations between church and state in modern times. He assumes that modernity has affected religious institutions, tending to erode them in particular ways and on certain indices. He also assumes that social differentiation – where 'successive social spheres are released from ecclesiastical control' (1996) – and individualization – whereby a public structure of belief and a sense of collective religious obligation is attenuated – are its cognate features. However, none of this is inevitable or irreversible. The interesting thing is what happens when these processes pass through particular historical and cultural filters. In France, the church–state clash was major and prolonged, with final separation in 1905. In England, the clash was minor and separation slow and incomplete. As far as differentiation goes, in the mid-twentieth century practice was low in England, though church and state were connected, whereas in France practice was higher even though they were disconnected.

In the case of the United States and Canada this account is most telling. Martin has now pulled back from the conventional view that North America was an exception to European secularizing trends, and that Europe might now appear as an exception to more global trends. But the Canadian case intersects in significant respects with both European – in the cases of the United Kingdom and France – and American religion-and-society relations. The unique, dominantly Catholic situation of Quebec gives additional nuance (still) within the Canadian ambit. Martin's questions about Europe – the shift of religion's location from state to civil society, social capital, religion and nationhood, and globalization – could also be asked, with profit, of North America.

Another European sociologist whose work is highly pertinent to the Canadian situation is Danièle Hervieu-Léger (who contributes here). She also deals with the relation of religion and modernity in ways that are critical of secularization theories and that point to opportunities for a much more nuanced sociology of belief. In her *Vers un nouveau Christianisme* (1986) she carefully discards received secularization theory while also problematizing 'modernity.' She argues that the logic of modernity actually opens spaces for the religious, even while it apparently closes down others. For Hervieu-Léger, secularization is 'the process of permanently reorganizing the work of religion in a society structurally powerless to fulfil the expectations that it has had to create in order to exist' as a modern society' (1986, 227; my translation).

Like Martin, Hervieu-Léger deals not only with the fate of religious institutions, or of religious functionaries (the focus of Marshall's [1992] Canadian study) but also with how religiosity is manifest in high modern times (which is what Peter Beyer, among others, does here). In her *La religion pour mémoire* she argues that 'modern religion is written entirely under the sign of fluidity and mobility, at the heart of a cultural, political, social, and economic universe dominated by the massive reality of pluralism' (1993b, 239; my translation). Though this sounds 'postmodern' Hervieu-Léger distances herself from such terms, preferring Anthony Giddens's or Alain Touraine's 'high' or 'late' modernity. This approach shifts the central focus from religious elites, and gives analytical voice to the expression of popular religiosities. Applying this outlook to Protestant Christian contexts, this would mean caution about generalizing about religion in Canada from the views of certain mainstream denominational theological seminaries or the *Globe and Mail* newspaper, and a willingness to listen to persons from one of the prairie Bible colleges or to read stories in, say, the evangelical periodical *Christian Week*, and to talk with the diverse clientele of Christian bookstores.

Interestingly enough, such judgments on the relocation of belief are not far removed from the analysis of American sociologist, Robert Wuthnow. His argument about the 'restructuring of American religion' is both critical of linear models *and* proposes that secularization be thought of in terms of 'qualitative changes in the character of religion' (1988, 297). Wuthnow uses the idea of 'restructuring' in the fashion of evolutionary theories, yet without succumbing to the fallacies associated with some varieties of such theory. He also calls for careful historical work in order to interpret 'religious characteristics in relation to elements of the broader social fabric' (ibid., 307). Thus religious organizations, such as the denomination, may in circumstances of a more general organizational transition lose some of their sacredness and popular appeal. This could, rather as Emile Durkheim foresaw, also be seen as part of a shift towards more individualized religiosity, perhaps even the sacralization of the self and not necessarily to an overall diminution of the religious dimension. It may also lead to new alliances, such as those noted by Nancy Nason-Clark in this volume, that would be hard to predict within a crude secularization frame.

In important ways, these more subtle secularization theses are connecting with mainstream cultural and social analysis – not least in the focus on consumption and consumerism. William Katerberg discusses this in his chapter. If the deregulation of religion offers a larger range of choice, then one might expect more evidence of an individualistic, pick'n'mix approach to the religious sphere. In Canada, the work of Reginald Bibby (e.g., 1993) is well known for its focus on the commodification of religion and the emergence of a spiritual supermarket. To some, Bibby's understanding of this is more sanguine than the rather acidic treatment of the same theme by the late George Rawlyk, for whom the privatizing of some evangelicalism is a turn to another 'gospel of narcissistic, therapeutic self-realization underpinning North American consumerism' (1997, xvii).

Of course, the ways in which the so-called spiritual supermarket works are as yet far from fully understood. How and why apparently conflicting beliefs or attitudes can be held by the same person, or, more importantly, what social processes produce proclivities to certain kinds of belief combinations, and social-political stances, have yet to be explored (although in Europe, Hervieu-Léger has made a good start). This is where links must be made with the cultural analyses of the *Theory, Culture and Society* group, especially Mike Featherstone (1995) and Arjun Appadurai (1986). Rather than seeing the consumer approach to religion as private, passive, or atomic, we could do worse than following their urging that consumption – including the crucially significant consumption of *symbols* – be seen as profoundly social, relational, and active (Featherstone 1995, 24).

Secularization, then, only helps us as a general framework for understanding contemporary situations. The complex 'mixed economy' pattern of Canadian secularization, which allowed churches to continue profoundly to influence public life until after the Second World War (and even later in Quebec as both Baum and Seljak show in this volume) may also have contributed to the more decisive dismissal of such influences in the decades that followed the 1960s. This process produced not 'no religion' but rather, deregulated, reshaped, relocated, and restructured religion, as discussed by all the contributors to this book. It is highly misleading to use 'secularization' as proxy for more detailed analysis of what is actually happening today. This is why contributions for this book were assembled: to initiate a fresh discussion that goes beyond standard concepts in understanding some of the patterns of belief and practice in contemporary Canada.

The Shape of This Book

In what follows, this exploration is clustered under a number of related headings, as various authors approach from different angles the task of rethinking church, state, and modernity. At the most general and comparative level, of 'patterns and flows,' David Martin situates the Canadian religious scene in the broad sweep of secularization. Canadian shadow establishments yield a distinctive character to the picture (much as in Australia) and fairly high levels of participation in religious institutions persist until quite late compared with Europe. How centres relate to peripheries, how the balance between religious life in Quebec and the rest of Canada is maintained, and how migration alters the religious face of the country are discussed in terms of the varied patterns of openness to the world, or the degree of accommodation to modernity. However, Martin also suggests that to watch the changing fortunes of social influence is also to watch the mutating content of what the churches teach, a topic that remains vital for an adequate sociology of religion.

What goes on in Canada may be seen within a wider span of globalization. As well as having its distinct features, Quebec also occupies a place on a continuum of societies deeply influenced by Roman Catholicism, with the long-term result that prospects for organized religion in that part of Canada may now relate as much to external forces as to internal conditions. Roger O'Toole sees similar trends in the rest of Canada, although his focus is more on the ways that Canadian religious groups have come to terms with modernity. Rejecting for the present at least the notion of postmodernity as a cultural watershed, O'Toole discerns buoyantly viable ongoing projects as well as time-honoured heritages among Canadian believers. Thus, paradoxically perhaps, both modernity and the religious life are alive and well in Canada, and may yet contribute to their *mutual* modification, even though each must now be viewed in more nuanced and multifaceted ways.

If continuity is a strong theme in O'Toole's chapter, it is reinforced further in Danièle Hervieu-Léger's detailed and provocative argument about modern religious individualism. So far from seeing modes of individualized belief and practice as merely a reflex of late-modern individualism, she argues that the former may actually antedate and anticipate the latter. Among other things, this raises in a fresh way the question of how much weight should be placed on approaches that stress above all the fortunes of social institutions such as churches.

Again, this stance does not deny that modernity requires rethinking, along with modes of religiosity and social participation, but it underlines again the long-term tendencies of religious life, the advent of what Hervieu-Léger thinks of as 'late modernity' notwithstanding. This strand of thought weaves itself into later chapters (particularly those of William Katerberg and Andrew Grenville).

How do patterns and flows translate into actual alignments and alliances between the so-called church and state? This can be traced both formally, in constitutional debates and statements, and in terms of everyday realities of its citizens. George Egerton follows 'the career of God' in the Canadian constitution, and ponders a future in which that constitution, though maintaining some residual references, in practice displaces references to God. But beyond the legal limits, insists Kevin Christiano, lies another world, at least of equal interest to analysts. Here we find the modern pressures, felt keenly in everyday life, that push the church–state question out into the open, and where 'indistinct boundaries between the two often heighten the heat of conflict.' Then if one examines specifically Christian groups that have set out to bring their influence to bear upon the public sphere, as John Stackhouse does in his chapter, it is noteworthy that the agendas are varied, changeable, and sometimes not easily predictable. New kinds of transdenominational and even interfaith linkages have become evident, and the range of issues touches everything from pipelines to public prayer or condoms to the constitution.

Compare this with Quebec, however, and yet another landscape is revealed. In what might be called the tensions between civic and civil religion, Gregory Baum explores the meaning of two highly significant responses to rapid if not cataclysmic secularization in Quebec after the 1960s. The Dumont Commission, dating from that period, accepted the new secular situation, but argued that the church should find its voice as social critic, as well as putting its own democratic house in order. The LaRochelle Report, on the other hand, recommended that in light of the imminent collapse of the church, radical steps would have to be taken, moving quite away from certain key traditional stances. What has actually happened? David Seljak suggests that, in relation to the 1980 and 1995 referenda, the churches have carved out new niches for themselves, giving voice to carefully argued positions on a variety of issues, that neither echo an old conservatism, nor embrace a new liberalism. Meanwhile, although Canadians outside Quebec may not grasp what has been going on in these terms, this does not mean that they are uninterested or unconcerned. In a striking study of religious responses to the threat of Quebec separation in 1995, Harry Hiller demonstrates how many people mobilized *in religious ways*, particularly with prayer vigils, to indicate their commitment to an inclusive Canada. 'Could this be evidence of a civil religious undercurrent unique in Canada?' asks Hiller.

Other patterns of practice also call for careful study and often demand fresh approaches. Peter Beyer nods towards Durkheim in commenting on 'modern forms of the religious life,' suggesting that in Canada, unlike the United States, national identity has been linked with particular religious groupings – although much of this is what might be called 'invisible religion' – in both segments of the country. This means, strikingly, that the pattern of change in Canada is as distinct from that of the United States and its denominations as it is from Europe and its older churches. The invisible, or privatized forms of faith are also considered by Andrew Grenville, who concludes from survey evidence that contemporary religiosity in Canada (as elsewhere) is a 'complicated reality,' not easily discerned with simple tools such as vulgar secularization theory. Among other things, this means that church and denomination are at least 'less salient' than they once were to understanding the religious sphere. While 'committed churchgoers may still don their Sunday best for church, at the other end of the spectrum "private theists" sport shorts and T-shirts as they ponder the majesty of the stars.' Of course, those same stars shine south of the border, and each of the studies just mentioned looks at the United States as well as Canada. Sam Reimer follows this with a more specific look at evangelical cultures in those two countries, clearly demonstrating that while globalizing tendencies help produce a more generic style of evangelicalism, differences between the two countries persist, though perhaps in more muted forms.

If religiosity is being individualized, and if free choice is even promoted, for instance, by the LaRochelle Report in Quebec, then how is this expressed in actual religious-political issues? For Nancy Nason-Clark, an unexpected alliance has grown between church-based helping agencies for victims of wife abuse, on the one hand, and 'secular' transition houses, on the other. The spiritual journeys of women touched by such abuse have not taken them only to transition houses, as standard secularization theory might lead one to expect. Choices offered to such women are not necessarily polarized between 'family values' (that might keep them in the abusive context) and 'feminist principles' (which some who are committed to 'family values' might eschew). They are often creatively combined in new ways that defy such easy categorization. Similarly, argues John Simpson, when it comes to abortion and homosexuality, religious involvement in body politics challenges simplistic analyses. Since the 1960s, the human body decisively became part of the 'self-project,' and the 'somatic society' was born. Responses to body controversies have softer edges in Canada than in the United States, insists Simpson, because sectarianism is less marked in the former than in the latter. In Canada, the lower level of polarization around body politics may be seen for instance *both* in the liberal stance taken on homosexuality by the United Church *and* in the recommendations by Citizens for Public Justice to the House of Commons Standing Committee on Human Rights (Citizens for Public Justice 1996) that legal equality be granted to gay and lesbian couples, *without* confusing these relationships with 'marriage.'

It is no accident, however, that the stress on 'choice' in these and other cases coincides with the tremendous growth of consumerism in Canada as elsewhere. William Katerberg argues that while religious identity has itself become increasingly a matter of consumption, this occurs differently in the United States than in Canada. More open than some other contributors to the designation of Canada as 'postmodern,' Katerberg offers evidence from the worlds of electronic media and multiculturalism, while simultaneously resisting the view that this reduces everything to mere 'private choices.' Indeed, he shows that other notions, such as 'public and private,' also require rethinking, alongside church, state, and modernity.

To invite 'rethinking' church, state, and modernity is risky. On the one hand, one does not wish to exaggerate change. After all, nation-states, churches, and the central institutions and outlooks of modernity persist and will continue to do so for some time to come. In Canada national sovereignty is still intact, despite the action of corrosives. The churches still represent by far the largest single repository of the religious life (as Reginald Bibby rightly reminds us from his series of major national surveys, 1987, 1993). Rational dependence on science and technology, and on the processes of democracy, still inform decisively the economic and political directions taken in Canada. On the other hand, striking change is nonetheless under way. The signs suggest that these concepts – church, state, and modernity – are losing their ability adequately to comprehend what is going on, at the same time as new forms of – mainly Christian-derived – religiosity continue to inform the lives of a large proportion of Canadians. If their implications for 'Canadian life' are properly to be grasped, the varieties of modes for expressing religious and political commitments must be understood in fresh ways.

At the outset, it must be remembered that both the 'state' and the 'church' in their modern forms tend to organize life in terms of bureaucratic definition. The categories, structures, and boundaries thus generated seem to appear increasingly alien, problematic, or simply irrelevant to the everyday life-paths of many people (Albrow 1996, 167). Selves and social relationships are negotiated, constructed, and altered in exploratory rather than regimented fashion. Processes of globalization serve, through consumerism and new communications media, both to make the world into one place *and* to relocalize social and cultural life (Robertson 1995). The nation-state, as 'society' within a territory, and the churches, as modes of organizing and regulating the religious life, are both vulnerable to the fluidity and flux that is catalyzed by these processes. What has been less analysed is the human capacity to revitalize dormant forms or seek fresh forms of relationship that maintain sociality beyond the bounds of conventional circumscription.

It may be that the structural uncertainties and indeterminacies of globalized modern life actually put a greater premium on faith and on commitment. Such allegiances, however, tend to be articulated with other social and cultural processes and institutions than previously was the case. The centrality of selves and of bodies, the significance of communities of memory and of feeling, these are the phenomena that spill over the edges of older cultural containers to produce new patterns of attitude and of action. In Canada, believers who belong to religious organizations are still more politically influential than those who do not. But believers who do not belong are not necessarily the privatized, apolitical creatures who appear in some accounts of civic decline and fragmentation. The search for spiritualities and for new modes of social connection and political expression in Canada may well take us beyond church, state, and modernity. But it will do so in ways that are channelled and filtered by distinctive Canadian cultural and historical experiences.

NOTES

Earlier drafts of this chapter were read at the Canadian Sociology and Anthropology Association Meeting in St John's, Newfoundland, June 1997, and at the

Society for the Scientific Study of Religion / Religious Research Association Conference in Montreal, November 1998. Thanks are due to those whose comments have helped improve it, and especially to Peter Beyer, Will Katerberg, John Simpson, and Marguerite Van Die.

1 In 1996 David Lyon and Marguerite Van Die received a major grant from the Pew Charitable Trusts in Philadelphia for a research project on 'Religion and Politics in North America,' the first phase of which was the Angus Reid Group survey, *God and Society in North America.*

Part One

PATTERNS AND FLOWS

chapter one

Canada in Comparative Perspective

DAVID MARTIN

Clearly, someone from outside Canada asked to comment on religion inside Canada has no new data to offer not already better known to Canadian scholars. The only tactic available to the outsider is a novel theoretical perspective or else comparisons with other countries. My particular tactic depends on those comparisons in particular as they are informed by the perspective of my *A General Theory of Secularization,* published just two decades ago.

Most of my comparisons will turn on about a dozen key questions, but there is a prior question to be asked about which countries offer the most fruitful comparisons. My first supposition is that comparisons arise most obviously in relation to those societies recently settled by people of mostly European descent in the ambit of Anglo-American culture: Britain, Canada, Australia, New Zealand, and the United States. At one end of the spectrum presented by these societies is Britain (the original source with Holland of voluntarism) with a residual state church and regular practice in the region of 10 per cent. At the other end is the United States, with no state church and regular practice in the region of 40 per cent. Canada and Australia with their history of shadow establishments have figures of about 30 per cent and 20 per cent regular practice respectively, though I am surprised to see how very high Canadian practice is in the first half of the twentieth century. That raises a question about the different times at which the Victorian boom in religion ceased in each of those countries. Or, to put it another way: why did the boom end first in Britain?

Apart from these five closely related societies there are two other sources of comparison I want to deploy. One is found in those north-western European states, notably, Holland, Germany, and Switzerland, where there are two (or three) main religious traditions, each rooted in different parts of the country. The other is found in former British colonies, such as Jamaica, which reproduced variants on the British pattern. Jamaica exhibits a residue of the Anglican establishment and a large sector of what was once called 'nonconformity,' but that sector has been inundated with Pentecostalism. It is from these societies that I draw the bulk of my comparisons.

I begin with a group of questions, roughly hanging together, which have for the most part only to be raised in relation to Canada to be answered. Are there founding cultures and what is their relative size, power, and territorial distribution? Clearly, in the group of Anglo-American societies initially cited earlier, Canada is the only one with two, or possibly three, founding cultures, of which one has a demar-cated territorial base. The nearest comparison here would have been South Africa, which also had two or three, indeed several, founding cultures, each with territorial linkages; but in other respects South Africa is too different to deploy. Of course, in the northern European set both Protestant and Roman Catholic cultures have territorial bases, although in the case of the Catholic culture it is much more demarcated. That in itself is suggestive: where a Catholic culture has a territorial base in a Protestant society it is more clearly bounded and internally integrated. It is marked out in a way the Protestant culture is not, either because the Protestant culture does not need to be or because Protes-tantism produces a less organic connection. Moreover, such Catholic cultures have invariably retained a higher level of practice for longer into the modern period, until going into sudden crisis in the 1960s. There is a world of comparison to be exploited here, above all between the crises in Dutch and Québécois Catholicism; this is worth further consideration before going on to the next question.

Catholic practice has been higher in Protestant countries where Catho-lics are a minority than where they are a majority and politically and/or socially dominant. That is because they form a carefully defended subculture, defining identity over and against a state perceived as alien or, at any rate, as populated by non-Catholic elites. In such situations Catholics seek parity of esteem and may sometimes align themselves with other movements that seek to displace those elites. However, once that is achieved or is well in train, the religious bonds and boundaries that helped bring it about are more constricting than enabling. At that point it only needs a rupture somewhere in the protective dyke of symbolic practices for major parts of the culture to give way and the level of pressure behind the dyke to fall dramatically. Furthermore, minorities often latch on to aspects of their distinguishing characteristics so as to define them as essential – in these cases all the paraphernalia of the sacerdotal system. Once the Second Vatican Council shifted some of the markers of difference, many of the other markers collapsed at the same time. There was, therefore, a crisis in mass-going and above all a crisis in vocations. In Quebec and in Catholic Holland this was greater than in England, Australia, or the United States, because a territorial base created the sense of a complete subsociety. Everything was thrown into turmoil, and not just the sector of everyday living defined as religious. Religion then became a cultural colouring and ritual recollection rather than a militant practice, and in Quebec that role was carried by politics and language as much as by faith. It might also be that the extension of the welfare state pre-empts the role of the Church more comprehensively where the Church has been standing in for a complete subsociety (or stateless nation).

The next related question has to do with the degrees of dominance achieved numerically and/or socially by the founding cultures in particular areas, which may be provinces such as Alberta, but might be larger, like the Atlantic region of Canada, or smaller. The reference point here is Britain, or rather England and Scotland, since both England and Scotland have had churches that were numerically and socially dominant, although neither has been as socially dominant as Catholicism in French culture or as numerically dominant as Catholicism in Irish culture. What we have then in Canada are residues of Scottish and English established religion, free from the anchors of social and numerical dominance, but still bearing status and vaguely connected with overall 'Anglo' cultural dominance in North America, and specifically in Canada. That diminishing aura stands over and against a French Catholic tradition deprived of its original anchor in the prerevolutionary French state, and the Irish Catholic tradition set free from direct English political hegemony to encounter a vaguer cultural hegemony. (Of course, the two Catholic traditions are as incompatible as the Irish and Italian, Polish, and German Catholic traditions were in the United States.)

What one would expect to happen is something as follows. The Catholic Irish and Catholic French struggle between themselves, but are united in their ultramontane devotion to Rome, which is the linchpin of their several identities. The Anglican Church, without the social supports of its home base, faces a vigorous Methodist movement competing for the same ethnic constituency. This Methodist movement runs parallel to American Methodism, though unaided by the desire in America to desert a church associated with the prerevolutionary colonial power. Anglicanism thus inevitably becomes a minority, though not as small a minority as in the United States, and its established pretensions lack a sufficient numerical base, even in Newfoundland.

In any case, the Scots are relatively numerous and in some of the western provinces are the closest approximation to a numerical or social establishment. However, the approximation is not all that close, and in any case the two ex-establishments of England and Scotland are often mixed rather than segregated as in Britain, and so cancel each other out to some extent. So the Scots do as they do in England: gravitate towards their nearest Protestant neighbours, notably the Methodists and Congregationalists, and the bulk of them eventually formed the United Church in 1925. In this respect Canadian developments parallel Australian ones, including the emergence of a largish residue of conservative Presbyterians reluctant to merge their theological (and social?) identity. This pan-Protestant sector then becomes the largest single group within the more or less dominant Protestant culture. (I presume this argument, if correct, might apply also to the Scots-Irish, who had their own local dominances early on, for example, in Toronto.)

At this juncture some comparisons need to be made with the United States, Australia, and New Zealand. Of course, in all four countries there are local dominances, but in the United States they are checked by the total separation of church and state, and by a genuine federalism that assists continuous fragmentation as well as making the voluntary association normative. Thus, in the United States the initial dominance of two or three Protestant founding cultures (English, Scots, Scots-Irish, and Dutch) fragments into cultural variants, each counterbalancing the other even where one or the other is relatively more numerous. The increased opportunity for subcultural formation and maintenance, and the relative weakness of state provision, makes for a very wide range of competitive religious agencies operating across the board. In Canada, by contrast, there remain shadow establishments rather as in early New England, on the 'mosaic' model rather than on the 'melting pot' model. No doubt that standard contrast of mosaic with melting pot can be pushed too far, but it presumably retains some leverage. In other words, in Canada there are identifiable, though modest, hegemonies that have a link to distinct institutional churches rather than to an overall Protestant tone. Of course, in both societies the culture most strongly attached to a distinct church is the Catholic one, but that is not initially well placed to combine institutional presence with social dominance, except in Quebec, and (to some extent) in New Orleans.

If we turn from the comparison with the United States to the Australian and New Zealand comparisons there are, once again, local concentrations of socioecclesiastical power, for example, Anglicans in Christchurch, South Island, and Presbyterians in Otago and Dunedin, South Island. The differences between Australia or New Zealand and Canada seem to lie in the relatively greater number of Anglicans in the former two societies (about one in four), and in New Zealand the greater number of Presbyterians (about one in five). Thus, in New Zealand there has been a dual shadow establishment institutionally defined: practice is about 15 per cent. In Australia there is a greater degree of pluralism, and a Catholic Church which even in bare numbers, let alone practice, is marginally larger than the Anglican Church. Practice there is about 20 per cent. The net result of this is that if we were to abstract Quebec from Canada then the three societies are strikingly similar, apart from the smaller proportion of Anglicans in Canada.

All three societies have experienced declines since the 1960s, roughly along the same lines, with the Catholic Church and the liberal Protestant Anglican churches taking the main impact and the conservative evangelical churches (or evangelical sectors of other churches) holding their own or expanding. However, this relative evangelical success does not place evangelicals on a par with co-believers in the United States, where, by comparison with all the other societies, there is a higher degree of overall practice within a totally voluntary system, which is further associated with a proportionately much larger evangelical sector, able to take advantage of the opportunities for subcultural institution building. Britain, in particular England, is at the other end of the spectrum, with relatively little opportunity for subcultural institution building, although even in England the evangelical sector is the most lively.

Here perhaps is the right place to introduce the Jamaican comparison, with a sidelong glance at South Africa. Jamaica offers a massive contrast with all the other societies cited, in that a combination of Anglican 'emplacement,' indicated by a central location in townships, with adjacent Methodist and Baptist churches, has been overtaken by a Pentecostal inundation of about one person in three. Likewise in South

Africa, Pentecostally derived churches may account for up to one in five. By contrast, Pentecostalism in Canada and Australia, though expanding, only accounts for some 1 per cent. Plainly, societies like those in the West Indies, Sub-Saharan Africa, and Latin America are much more open to Pentecostal inundation, though one would expect charismatic manifestations of various kinds to emerge from the Roman Catholic fallout in Quebec. Indeed, in Quebec one has an interesting combination: quite high levels of serious alienation and of Pentecostalism.

The next question is a very important one, although not permitting a clear answer, and it has to do with the role of elites, especially those in the so-called knowledge class, concerned with the manipulation of symbols. What strikes one in the United States is the inability of this class, though clearly dominant in the upper echelons of education and in the TV media, to overwhelm and erode the religious subcultures. Perhaps this is because there are so many elites in the United States, and so much fragmentation of control. By contrast, in England the elite has substantial levers of control and successfully radiates out secular impulses. It is as if the monopolistic power once invested in the Church has been transferred to secular elites. Presumably, Canada and Australia exist somewhere in between on the spectrum, between the United States and Britain.

Of course, one of the most important subcultures in the United States is the South, and that represents a defeated nation whose identity is nourished in evangelical faith. One might describe the South as a vast periphery larger than most autonomous states. Canada, however, has no equivalent (unless there is a partial analogy in Quebec), but it does have a relatively isolated and relatively practising region – in the east. That generates the obvious question as to where resistant peripheries lie in relation to centres, and what are the relative strengths of peripheries *vis-à-vis* centres. Clearly, in Britain the peripheries are weak, just as the subcultures and religious counter-elites are weak, whereas in the United States peripheries, subcultures, and counter-elites are strong and can defend their own space. Once again Canada, Australia, and New Zealand have their resistant peripheries, and also, in the past, have been peripheries of Britain and the United States, with the balance of power slowly slipping from the former to the latter. (I have never forgotten the symbolism in Canberra of a set of British bells placed symmetrically over against an American eagle.) At any rate, London is a strong centre, whereas Canberra, Ottawa, and Washington are weak centres when considered against their vast hinterlands.

There is one further question that this time sets the United States and Britain (or rather England) together against Canada and Australia, and that is the strength and coherence of the national myth, as New Israel and New Jerusalem as well as the socially progressive Light of the World, and as New Athens, and New Rome. England passed her messianic and millenarian myth over to the United States, and both nations mingled Christian light with secular enlightenment, Providence with destiny. Caught between such powerful grand narratives Canada, Australia, and New Zealand have struggled to create secondary variants. Canada seems to have generated the idea of 'His Dominion' in awkward lock step with French Catholic projections, and that seems to have mutated towards a social gospel of international good works alongside the innocence claimed by Scandinavia. It is almost as if a post-Protestant virtue wells up in the everlasting pine forests and the vistas of virgin snow. Yet there is not enough 'dynamic density' to support it, especially in a nation strung out along the longest undefended frontier in the world. It follows that a 'civil religion' is a possibility frequently canvassed but not achieved. Order and continuity and a scepticism towards expansive revolutionary enthusiasms of the American kind characterize an upright nation, but you cannot make fire out of driven snow.

Two other questions are inevitable in any comparative analysis of religion and culture. They concern, first, the pattern of migration and, second, the distribution of Native peoples or peoples of another colour likely to be exposed to prejudice, forced segregation, or coercive assimilation. With regard to the pattern of migration it has not yet converted Canada from a bicultural to a multicultural society. The arrival of Asians in British Columbia, or of Ukrainians in Ontario, or Greeks in Quebec does not in that respect add a new dimension – yet – beyond maybe giving a further thrust to the privatization of Christianity.

If Protestant and Catholic Christianity possess both a public face and a political voice, the emergence of a significant non-Christian sector hastens the occlusion of face and voice. In the United States that is coped with by adding one more voice to numerous other voices. In Canada, however, the Christian voice spoke for a community nearly coextensive with active or nominal Christian identity, and when that ceases to be the case the voice is muted or else fixated on intercommunal relations. The greatest problem is likely to emerge where a foreign religious body, such as Greek Orthodoxy, inserts itself in the heartland of a culturally 'integral' Quebec. The majority community suspects a logic whereby all of the out-groups ally together to counterbalance the in-group. That is an obvious source of interreligious tension that is rooted in ethnic tension. Here I make a tentative query about a contrast between Quebec and Ontario. The exuberant ethnic and religious variety characterizing Toronto seems not a problem, whereas major increases of minorities in the heartlands of Québécois nationalism and semi-monopoly Catholicism might well become so.

With regard to Native American or Inuit peoples a rather similar consideration applies in that tension arises where they claim large segments of a territory also claimed by an embattled nationalism. However, this again is much more an ethnic and cultural tension, and only marginally religious. In large parts of Latin America subordinate Native peoples have been disproportionately drawn to Protestantism, but in Canada there seems little disposition to find counter-definition through a distinctive faith. In any case, conditions are relatively benign. (In Russia, where they are not benign, militant paganism is a real option.) Proportions of Native peoples in the region of 1.5 per cent in both Canada and Australia have not been large enough for massive tension, although recent political events in Australia illustrate how volatile such situations can become. By contrast, a population of about 10 per cent of Maori descent in New Zealand now represents a serious political problem.

A final set of comparisons relates to those northwestern European countries with a bipolar religious difference rooted in a (very rough) north-south territorial split. All of these have similar characteristics to Canada in that the Catholic areas are more practising and Catholic voters likely to support parties well disposed to Catholic and regional interests, for example, the Christian Social Union in relation to Bavaria. However, the Catholic minorities have not shown any inclination to support a separated nationalism such as from time to time emerges. Perhaps the lack of a linguistic reinforcement for Bavarian or South Dutch distinctiveness has something to do with this. The nearest analogue may be Czechoslovakia, now the Czech Republic and Slovakia. Here the difference was between Catholicism in Slovakia and indifference in the Czech Republic, and in the upshot, the resentments in Slovakia over supposed Czech misdemeanours in relation to economic assets led to a separation in which the Slovak politicians were exerting more pressure than the population was for independence. Nevertheless, it went through without violence, and such a scenario may be quite possible for Canada.

Perhaps one might conclude by a brief comparative glance at the problems of the United Church, as these compare with the problems of the parallel body in Australia, and comparable denominations elsewhere. Here it is not possible to say much that adds to work done by Roger O'Toole and others, but it is worth underlining widespread similarities across several societies. If we take England first it is abundantly clear that denominations like the Methodists and (to a lesser extent the Presbyterians) are prone to ecumenical unions and that these in no way seriously bolster their resistance to decline. In England the Methodists and the United Reformed Church, both products of earlier unions, have continued a steep decline. Many of those who have 'ceased to meet' have relocated themselves in the Church of England, and perhaps most dramatically in its ministry. Decline breeds decline, both in terms of the possibility of living a full life within the group, including marriage partners in the same denomination, and in terms of lowered morale. That situation also characterized the United and Uniting churches in Canada and Australia respectively, although both are larger than their British counterparts and can still pull themselves round. The Methodist and Presbyterian churches in the United States have declined, and the Methodists (and even the Baptists) of Jamaica have also done so. So this is a widespread phenomenon clearly illustrated in Canada. It is as if the voluntary bodies, whose ethos has been so congruent with (and so productive of) democratic and participatory modes in the Anglo-American world, have no resistance to their environment and simply leak into it. By the early years of the twentieth century they were shifting towards liturgical styles and social service, and their distinctive call for the circumcision of the heart and complete revision of life was blunted. The latent power built up by evangelical fervour was now being expended without renewal so that conversion was translated into decency. Insofar as they adopted formal styles of worship and its furnishings there were others to whom that came more naturally, and insofar as they no longer preached for a decision, there were others who moved into the vacated space, notably the Pentecostals. The institutions they helped create for education and welfare were gently secularized, leaving only an aura of piety, and their functions were replicated or improved upon by state provision. They provided the motivation for innumerable conscientious citizens who staffed the social and educational services and were active in good causes, yet somehow this credit account with society at large was almost invisible. Their children acquired mobility through these virtues but felt no special religious call to stay in the institutions that had fostered them. In Canadian society or English or Australian society they were simply part of unnoticed normality, the religious form of the good character of the culture.

Moreover, the increased openness to the world, especially the world of education and social service, meant that the cultural wars that emerged in those worlds flooded back into the Church. The result was that churches that helped form the image of a caring service for others and of mutual help were themselves reformed in the image of what they created. The churches divided into politicized and evangelical wings tugging in contrary directions under the aegis of leaderships and teachers in denominational colleges for whom political correctness was as salient as Christian values, and who indeed saw little difference between the two. The churches were ripe for demythologization and the emptying out of the original generating power into what used to be called, in Christian parlance, 'the world.' The world used up their virtues of duty, service, and commitment to others, and then proceeded along its own calculating and utilitarian course, while every now and then regretting the loss of social capital, because it was so inconvenient. Only their decline in Anglo-American societies makes clear the nature of the contribution that the churches made to the social and political fabric.

Perhaps (in the cultural context of Ontario where Methodism has been important) I can conclude by a programmatic extension, still focused on the problems of a liberalized evangelical Christianity in Anglo–North American society as illustrated throughout the century so nearly passed. I have already mentioned the failure of this kind of religion to hold on to the institutions it initially inspired, whether we are talking about the Young Men's Christian Association (YMCA) or universities with religious foundations or large associations for youth work, such as the Methodist Association of Youth Clubs in England. Those who founded and initially ran such institutions had a vision rooted in faith to which they gave social and charitable form, but the justification they offered for God became, in time, the good consequences of their own activity: a sort of social works righteousness. The New Testament became a charter selectively deployed to legitimate and motivate that activity, but there was no particular reason why those they served should share those motivations. Again, all kinds of agreeable and harmless social interactions could occur within the ambit of the church, but their connection with the Church was quite contingent.

The drama committee of the Wesley Guild and the Epworth Choral Society, let alone the Badminton Club, were simply moderately equipped competitors for people's time.

In approaching this slackening of the specifically religious as it embeds and embodies itself in social activity, I suspect we need to integrate our sociology, and our social history of institutions with what people feel able to say about God and Jesus and what selected aspects of the Christian gospel they feel able to preach. In other words we need to integrate the kind of social history dealing with the local evolution of religious institutions with the content of Christian messages and especially teachings about God and redemption. The decline of preaching presumably has something to do with a diminishing stock of things to say. What brought about the collapse of the great preaching stations in this tradition? Or to put it another way: why should people seek out a folksy psychotherapy in the context of hymn singing on Sunday mornings? What powerful interpretation of the wider culture, its directions, events, and concerns, could this subculture offer out of its own unique resources? Why should the cosmopolitan world and its media listen to analyses more professionally available elsewhere?

To ask that last question is ultimately to raise the question of content and thus the presentation of the nature of God and the role of Christ. Thomas Jenkins, in his *The Character of God* (1997), analyses that presentation in Protestant culture over the past century and a half in such a way as to challenge sociologists to integrate it with their empirical analysis and social historians to incorporate it with their accounts of institutional change. The question is: what follows from an uncertainty about sin, redemption, and the meaning of the cross as it plays into an etiolation of the vocabulary and of the phraseology of faith as well as into the emptying of God into politics, communal celebration, and history? The question that Jenkins raises relates to our quest for sociological understanding: what roles have the churches assigned to Christ, what emphases and what silences about the peculiarity of the gospels, what characterizations of the agency, being, and character of God?

chapter two

Canadian Religion: Heritage and Project

ROGER O'TOOLE

The following investigation attempts to exploit the current *fin de siècle* or millennial mood by juxtaposing past and present in an effort to ponder the future. In seeking to adjust the 'horizon of expectation' (Gadamer 1985, 269; Toulmin 1990, 1–2) surrounding contemporary Canadian religion it employs sociological and historical insights in order to examine the intricate religious encounter with modernity and the ways in which this encounter interweaves social-scientific and popular knowledge. My impressionistic assessment of the contemporary mood of mainstream religion triggers a journey into the *past* and provokes meditation on the theme of religious memory while simultaneously urging contemplation of the *future* of organized religion in the coming century. In suggesting that the nexus between the elusive categories of religion and modernity is less antagonistic and deterministic than is often believed, this inquiry concludes on a somewhat different note than might be expected by many social scientists and religious practitioners. In lifting the severe sentence imposed by secular forms of predestination doctrine, this conclusion confronts the gloomier sections of religious opinion with the current insights of a wide range of sociologists for whom religion remains both heritage and project (Commission d'étude sur les laïcs et l'église 1971).

Religion and Modernity

Any attempt to explore the links between religion and modernity is faced by a double definitional difficulty, as these are among the most contentious, value-laden, and troublesome terms in the sociological and philosophical lexicons. No attempt will be made to define 'religion' here, as the focus of discussion will be *organized religion* in the conventional Western societal sense. It seems advisable to sketch the parameters of 'modernity,' however, in order to indicate both its wide resonance and confusing variations. A concept that is regarded by some writers as the *central* concept of contemporary sociology and by others as obsolete and irrelevant merits careful scrutiny. Thus, while Jeffrey Alexander (1995, 5) correctly regards modernity as 'a linguistic signifier of the greatest import,' it is no easy task to determine precisely what the term signifies either in the context of scholarly discourse or in the wider realms of public opinion and popular culture. In this respect, an instructive parallel may be drawn with David Martin's classic (1965) dissection of the (closely related) concept of *secularization*, a term which, despite the valiant efforts of Martin and others, remains notoriously lacking in precision and overburdened with ideology in many accounts. Just as, in some quarters, secularization has attained the status of a 'myth,' modernity too exhibits a mythical character that is not necessarily confined to its vernacular variants (Lyon 1985).

Although it is hardly possible to speak of a consensus regarding the meaning of modernity, it is a useful strategy to try to separate its core and peripheral aspects. Thus, in attempting to specify the distinctiveness of the most general frameworks of ideas, sentiments, and social relationships that make life modern, James Beckford (1992, 12) isolates 'a faith in the power of reason and reliable knowledge to generate order, purpose, progress, efficiency and growth even if the costs include fragmentation of communal or personal identity and constant change.' In like manner, Charles Davis (1994, 30) associates modernity with 'a fundamental shift in human culture which can be roughly circumscribed with key words – freedom, science, rationalization, differentiation' and which thereby generates an autonomous self-consciousness. Furthermore, in an extended critical review of the 'orthodox' or 'received' notion of modernity, Stephen Toulmin (1990, 11–17) identifies its key features as secular culture, scientific revolution, new method in philosophy, the power of reason or rationality, technology, and the sovereign nation-state. All of these, by definition, involve a rejection of tradition and superstition as elements in a saga that, in his view, is one-sided, over-optimistic, and self-congratulatory.

Within the social sciences, modernity has had a colourful history, a fact that is unsurprising since, in most accounts, social-scientific thought emerged in direct response to the impact of the modern. As a central concept of mid-twentieth-century functionalist orthodoxy, modernity (and more specifically 'modernization') fell on hard times in response to the sociological fashions of the 1970s and 1980s, only to re-emerge triumphantly more recently just as postmodernism was dictating its obituary (Alexander 1995, 42–3; Tiryakian 1991). Whether contemporary society is best described in terms of postmodernity or high (or late) modernity is not at issue here. What is undeniable is that the concept of modernity has been resuscitated (if not resurrected) by some of its former critics (Giddens 1990, 1991). At the present time, most sociologists would probably identify 'classic' modernity with science, rationalization, industrialization, democratization, individualism, capitalism, the nation-state, secularization, differentiation, organization, efficiency, growth, and dynamism in various combinations and degrees. Modernity in its current phase is likely to be depicted in terms of such concepts as discontinuity, doubt, risk, reflexivity, globalization, disembedding of social institutions, postindustrialism, pace, and scope of change, institutions of surveillance, autonomy, and sequestration (Alexander 1995, 11; Giddens 1990, 1991, 1994).

Of course, attitudes to modernity have varied and altered over time. Since Nietzche especially, what Weber called the 'rosy blush' of the Enlightenment has faded notably so that modernity is portrayed unflatteringly as a monster, a cage, or a virtually uncontrollable juggernaut by some writers (Weber 1958, 182; Giddens 1990, 137–51). Nonetheless, the idea of modernity continues to impress and inspire in the popular global arena, while the concept of the modern defies all cries for its abandonment. The greatest source of strength in modernity as an *idea* is its greatest defect when it is utilized as a social-scientific concept. As an *idea* it has a mythological quality; it is a grand narrative (Lyotard 1984) packed with such notions as progress, providence, teleology, historicism, determinism, inevitability, and fatalism, all underscored by a triumphalist scientism. As a *concept* its usefulness is seriously impaired by such ideological elements, for the 'hubris of linearity' (Alexander 1995, 42) and nomological conceit have too frequently attended its social-scientific application. The roots of much self-consciously modern thought in secularized adaptations of Christian doctrine (what Herbert Butterfield termed 'lapsed Christianity') have frequently been exposed (Toulmin 1990, 20–1; Ferguson 1997, 26). In this tradition, Alexander (1995, 14) rightly notes that the 'discourse of modernity bears a striking resemblance to metaphysical and religious salvation discourse.' It must, therefore, be handled with the greatest caution and circumspection in a scholarly, sociological context.

Indicating the profound disagreement concerning 'the features that constitute modern society as distinctively modern and about the defining characteristics of religion,' Davis (1994, 39) comments: 'If we do not agree on what modernity means and on what religion means, how can we relate the two?' The difficulty of articulating a clear and unequivocal connection between religion and modernity is made evident by even the most cursory inspection of sociological opinion on this topic (Beckford 1992, 1996; Lyon 1996; Bruce 1992; Davie 1994, 189–204). The orthodox and, in many quarters, still dominant view is that modernity (to some extent by definition) necessarily and inevitably sounds the death-knell of religion. Modern religion is thus, at worst, a contradiction in terms and, at best, a matter of prolonged death agony less tragic than trivial. This is the perception of classic 'secularization theory' whose most subtle contemporary exponent is Bryan Wilson (1966, 1975, 1982, 1985, 1992). It is also the assumption, from a very different sociological standpoint, of the German critical theorist Jürgen Habermas (1976, 80; Davis 1980, 138–41), who regards the 'project of modernity' as leaving no room for religion. Irretrievably obsolete and dismantled beyond repair, religion is a remnant superseded by a philosophy of communicative practice.

The extinction of religion is not, however, anticipated by all sociologists. Some extol its capacity for resistance and its ability to ride the tide of modernity. Others proclaim that the modern condition itself generates religious consciousness and activity whether in widely diffused, esoteric, traditional, experimental, organized, ethereal, enduring, or ephemeral form. In Weberian fashion, Talcott Parsons (1951, 1960, 1963, 1968) stresses the extent to which religious institutions (specifically those of Protestant Christianity) have been essential prerequisites of modernity, generating those values and norms vital to the structure and process of dynamic modern social systems. It is ironic that, while the central core of recent secularization theory lies in his notion of *social differentiation* (Martin 1995, 295), Parsons himself insists that the progressive separation of religious institutions from the wider society actually enhances religion's importance. Far from implying or requiring secularization, differentiation encourages religious involvement in the creation of core values supportive of modernization. Thus, modernity is both a product and perpetuator of religion.

Assessing the prospects of religion under conditions of high or late modernity, Anthony Giddens (1991, 202–8) refers to a 'sequestration of experience' which modernity imposes on major areas of life, most notably those provoking existential or moral questions. The stifling of such concerns by systematic marginalization is, however, far from successful. In the void of doubt, insecurity, identity crisis, and personal meaninglessness, which lie at the heart of modernity in its latest phase, Giddens detects spiritual stirrings. Indeed, he believes that high modernity creates a need for answers to new moral and ethical questions so intense that recourse to religion in some form is inevitable. Paradoxically, high modernity's reorganization of time and space, its disembedding of institutions, and its thoroughgoing reflexivity, which ought to seriously reduce religion's chances of survival, produce precisely the opposite effect. They generate a 'religious resurgence' on two fronts for, in such circumstances, a 'return of the repressed' assumes both traditional and innovative religious forms. People may draw upon residual traditions that have survived the modernist onslaught or they may turn to 'new forms of religious sensibility and spiritual endeavour' in their attempts at the 'remoralizing of daily life.' The significance of such resurgence should not be minimized for both inherited and experimental forms of religion constitute, in Beckford's (1996, 36) words, 'integral aspects of modernity's dynamism: not just freak shows on the side.'

In a similar appraisal, Danièle Hervieu-Léger (1986, 1990, 1993a) also perceives modernity's paradoxical role in the preservation and perpetuation of religion. Her fundamental argument has been well expressed by Grace Davie (1996, 103): 'By their very nature, modern societies sap the strength of traditional religions. Thus the notion that there exists a structural incompatibility between the demands of modern societies and the prosperity of traditional forms of religion is correct to a considerable extent. On the other hand, modern societies cannot exist without some form of religiosity. They require, and so generate, innovative expressions of religious life without which they could not continue in their present form.' Acutely sensitive to the ambiguities of religious evidence, Hervieu-Léger nonetheless forcefully rejects an interpretation of the revival or return of religion in various forms as an indication of the collapse of modernity. Attributing special significance to what she calls the 'religion of emotional communities,' she underscores the compatibility between modern society and myriad forms of traditional and non-traditional religiosity. Emotional communities and other contemporary manifestations of the religious impulse are, in fact, the products of a continuous, open-ended process of modernity that is highly attuned to religious sensibility (Hervieu-Léger 1994).

The difficulty of formulating a definitive version of the relation between religion and modernity is demonstrated most clearly in the writings of Peter Berger (1967, 1974, 1977), whose viewpoint has altered radically in response to religious developments in the past quarter-century. In his early work, Berger assumes that modernity, rationality, and technology wreak havoc on religious life and pose profound threats to its persistence. While accepting the apparently overwhelming evidence of secularization, however, he denies that the disappearance of religion is, by any means, inevitable. Not unappreciative of the positive aspects of modernity, he nonetheless portrays religion (particularly in its prophetic mode) as a potent, or at least potential, source of resistance to the modern erosion of identity and meaning. In the conflict between modernity and religion, the latter faces the formidable, though not impossible, challenge of mitigating the worst aspects of the modern condition. More recently, Berger (1997, 974) has finally abandoned his old argument by decisively rejecting the notion that modernity is intrinsically hostile to religion: 'I think that what I and most other sociologists of religion wrote in the 1960s about secularization was a mistake. Our underlying argument was that secularization and modernity go hand in hand. With more modernization comes more secularization. It wasn't a crazy theory. There was some evidence for it but I think it was basically wrong. Most of the world today is not secular. It's very religious.' There is, thus, no sociological consensus on the nature of the ties between religion and modernity and it is difficult to avoid Beckford's (1992, 14) conclusion that, in the hands of authoritative sociologists, 'modernity is given the appearance of being, variously, constitutive of religion, ambivalent towards religion or exclusive of religion.'

This is an important caveat for the social-scientist or religious practitioner seeking to examine the links between modernity and religion in specific situations. Ambiguities abound even when, for purposes of systematic analysis, the broad *idea* of the modern is displaced by a more precise *concept* of modernity. Thus, conceptual clarification must involve close scrutiny of the more inclusive frameworks, paradigms, worldviews, or ideologies within which particular conceptual discourses are embedded. What is abundantly clear from the complex varieties of necessity and contingency evident in sociological articulation of the interplay between the religious and the modern is that *the orthodox association of modernity and inevitable religious decline is a strongly contested*

opinion. There is no social-scientific consensus to this effect, and powerful scholarly conviction to the contrary.

The Religious Past

The interweaving of social-scientific and popular culture is often mer-
curial and always labyrinthine, and frequently displays the phenomenon of cultural lag. Thus, the fact that sociological opinion is seriously
divided on matters of modernity, secularization, and religion seems, so
far, to have made little impression on wider public sentiment, particularly within organized religion. More crudely, this means that news that
the death sentence imposed on religion by orthodox modernity has
been commuted by a significant segment of social-scientific scholarship
has been slow to reach the religiously committed. Although such news
might encourage optimism or at least curb pessimism, there have been
few signs of improving morale in Canadian organized religion in recent
years.

Impressionistic characterization of the current mood of mainstream
religion is a hazardous venture, but few would deny the existence of a
sense of serious concern within both the leadership and the rank and
file of Canadian churches and denominations. This concern, centred on
the prospects of religious belief and practice, is well founded. For
nearly four decades, organized religion has experienced such significant and largely unbroken decline that 'secularization' has become a
key term in congregational vocabularies. Reginald Bibby (1987, 271;
1993, 314), the sympathetic sociological chronicler of this continuing
crisis, offers little comfort but some encouragement in his assertion that
'the recognition of religion's poverty can lead to the rediscovery of its
potential.' However, his growing frustration is palpable as each new
survey documents the failure of mainstream churches to meet his challenge 'to bridge the gap between the churches and the culture.' While
the situation he documents is grim indeed, it is the churches' response
to this reality that Bibby appears to find truly discouraging from a
religious standpoint.

Bibby's perception converges with broader stereotypical conceptions
of mainstream religion as experiencing failure of nerve, a sense of
fatalism, and a mood of resignation in the face of modernity and secu-
larity. This is most obvious when, in describing the inadequacy of
'experimental' and 'traditional' responses to the present crisis, he
concludes that the wider, secular culture 'calls most of the shots' (Bibby

1987, 253). Whether they attempt to embrace it, ignore it, or resist it, religious organizations, in his view, effectively concede the triumph of the modern and the secular. They attempt to make the most of this situation but they do not aspire to *change* it. It is tempting to discern, in this restricted religious horizon of expectation, intimidation by notions of inevitability derived from a popularly interpreted secularization myth and an antiquated but still influential grand narrative of modernity. Moreover, to the extent that it reluctantly regards a secular future as a foregone conclusion (Bernstein 1994), organized religion is complicit in a self-fulfilling prophecy.

Expansion of Canadian religion's horizon of expectation is best begun by turning to the past rather than to the present or future. Retrieval of the religious past as a prelude to the recovery of religious memory is essential if the poverty of historicism (Popper 1957) in its current guise is to be exposed and confronted. No period of Canadian history casts more doubt on notions of inevitability and inexorability than the Victorian era, for during this time the fate of religion proved very different from what it ought to have been according to the orthodox idea of modernity. According to the script of the Enlightenment project and some contemporary theories of modernity, the period in which Canada forged its way to political independence and economic success should have proved a classic case of religious decline in the face of rapid industrialization, rationalization, differentiation, technological change, and state expansion. In fact, the new nation witnessed a remarkable growth and intensification of religious activity that constituted nothing less than a *success story*. More than half a century ago, the American sociologist W.G. Sumner (1933) wrote an essay entitled 'The Bequests of the Nineteenth Century to the Twentieth.' Consideration of nineteenth-century bequests at the turn of another century ought, in a Canadian context, to include the clear demonstration that organized religion is capable of adapting to the challenge of modernity with energy, ingenuity, and a high degree of accomplishment.

Although threatened and altered considerably by the multifaceted encounter with modernity, Canadian churches and denominations exerted a vigorous reciprocal influence. Far from capitulating to secular forces, they succeeded in making social, economic, political, and constitutional concerns a part of their spiritual project to an extent that ensured that a depiction of Canada as a 'fundamentally religious nation' was a sober and exact sociological assessment (Clark 1968, 182; Kilbourn 1968, 7; Crysdale and Montminy 1974, vii; Noll 1992, 546–7).

In the years leading up to Confederation, the ending of the rancorous debate over the Anglican establishment created a system of 'legally disestablished religiosity': an informal separation of church and state in which the influence of religion on politics and secular life was *intensified* by the absence of church establishment (Moir 1967, xiii–xix). Free from state influence or control, organized religion secured such profound importance in the new nation that it is impossible to comprehend the expansion of the Canadian state and economy without reference to it.

While the achievement of Confederation is conventionally depicted as a saga of political and economic destiny, its important religious component was signified in the choice of the term 'dominion' and the motto *A Mari usque ad Mare* (both drawn from Psalm 72) in the official symbolization of the body politic. This transformation of 'a disparate collection of superfluous British colonies into a prosperous, integrated, and modern society' was, in fact, heavily indebted to a millenarian vision of a new form of community where 'the dominion of the Lord' would supersede a 'wilderness of sin and injustice' (Westfall 1976; 1989, 3–4; Noll 1992, 246). The intimate association of religion and politics this implied bred in religious elites a deep sense of national responsibility that culminated in a crucial role in the creation of the nation. As H.H. Walsh (1956, 7; Grant 1977) commented: 'Both in the formation of a federal constitution and the extension of the original four provinces westward, Canadian churches have played a conspicuous role. From the very beginning of Confederation they helped to give a substantial reality to an artificially contrived nation by fashioning their own indigenous church structures in accordance with the new national boundaries that began to take form after 1867.'

Consolidation of state, economy, and religion went hand in hand. Faced by materialism, commercialism, industrialism, land clearance, immigration, settlement, rapid population growth, and their attendant social problems, organized religion responded remarkably. Whether in social reform movements, voluntary societies, educational ventures, charitable trusts, or the missionary effort to win the West for Christ, churches and denominations skilfully adapted to modernity, led the search for a national identity and enhanced their public presence significantly. Indeed, as Phyllis Airhart (1990, 99; Noll 1992, 547) observes, Christians in British North America 'demonstrated even more public religiosity' than their American neighbours. By their endeavour to 'create a spiritual refuge within a secular society' and to forge a

TABLE 2.1
Religions of the population of Canada (%)

Year	Canadian Total (N)	Methodist	Presbyterian	Anglican	Baptist	Roman Catholic
1871	3,689,257	15.4	14.8	13.3	6.7	40.4
1881	4,324,810	17.2	15.6	13.3	6.9	41.4
1891	4,833,239	17.5	15.6	13.4	6.2	41.2
1901	5,371,315	17.1	15.7	12.7	5.9	41.5
1911	7,206,643	15.0	15.5	14.8	5.3	39.3

Source: *Census of Canada.*

'moral pathway through the hazards of a materialist world,' religious organizations grew greatly in numbers, strength, and influence. In a Protestant context, this process was intensified (in a climate of interdenominational pluralism and relative tolerance) by a series of alliances, mergers, and unions that consolidated numerous branches of Christianity at an accelerating pace and paved the way for the church union movement of the next century (Westfall 1989, 6; Walsh 1963, 1956; Grant 1963). The degree of consolidation occurring in this 'churching of Canada' (Finke and Stark 1992) may be gauged by examination of basic census figures from the last decades of the nineteenth century and the first decade of the twentieth (see Table 2.1). In a forty-year-period, in which the Canadian population doubled and in which an overwhelming majority of the population professed allegiance to a religious organization, it is notable that more than 90 per cent of Canadians consistently claimed to belong to one or other of *five* major denominations. This point may, perhaps, be made more strongly, given the relatively small number of Baptists, if it is stated that nearly 90 per cent of Canadians claimed affiliation with one or other of *four* major denominations.

Paralleling the high degree of political and economic consolidation in the nation during the first decades of its existence, organized religion vigorously pursued a moral and spiritual alternative to money, machinery, and materialism in a decidedly modern manner. By means of well-organized and highly efficient involvement in the secular world, religion undoubtedly assisted in the modernization of Canada, changing its own form accordingly (Walsh 1954, 78; O'Toole 1982; Noll 1992, 283–4). In the process, however, its impact on both the character of the nation and Canadian character was so immense that it is no exaggeration to say that 'in few countries in the western world has religion exerted as great an influence on the community as it has in Canada' (Clark 1968, 168). The strongly religious quality of Canadian life remained evident, even to unsympathetic observers half a century after the death of Queen Victoria. Thus, in the years immediately following the Second World War, the sociologist S.D. Clark (1968, 171; Stackhouse 1990, 200–5) could still write: 'The influence of organized religion in this country has perhaps never been stronger ... even where emancipation from religious controls has extended furthest a sharp limitation has been placed upon activity of a purely secular character. Canada has been and remains a fundamentally religious nation. No great political or social upheaval has served to break the close ties with a past which placed a great emphasis on religious values of life.'

In retrospect, Clark's reluctant eulogy to religious relevance has more the ring of an elegy. Depicting 'a time, not long ago ... when religion was a major and even decisive factor in the lives of Canadian individuals and communities,' it evokes a situation so remote and unfamiliar that it seems 'either a projection of nostalgic fantasy or a truism that can only be stated but no longer imagined in concrete detail' (Grant 1973b, 1; Stackhouse 1990, 234). Since the 1960s a process of radical social upheaval has broken many religious 'ties to the past' and stretched others to their limit. Ironically, in circumstances where the contemporary encounter with a new phase of modernity has severely tested religion's capacity to react, adapt, and respond to its demands, knowledge of an earlier, highly successful collision with the modern has faded rapidly from religious memory. Moreover, to the extent that it has forgotten its Victorian heritage, Canadian mainstream religion has deprived itself of a salutary, historically grounded parable whose clear message is: *in the meeting of religion and modernity, the ruin of the former is by no means an inevitable result.*

Contemporary Religion

As measured by the familiar litany of shrinking membership, declining participation, reduced vocations, ageing congregations, dwindling funds, and increasing marginalization, the past four decades have undoubtedly been lean ones for Canadian religion (Bibby 1987, 1993, 1995). In such circumstances, an initial consequence of heightened attention to the past is likely to be an acute awareness of the gulf that separates contemporary religious life from the vigour and vitality of its Victorian counterpart. Closer scrutiny of the religious past, however, also reveals the extent to which the current religious situation still *closely resembles* that of the nineteenth century. The imprint of the Victorian experience is visible in both content and form: in its Christianity and its denominationalism.

The persistently *Christian* character of Canada, in a broad sense, is an important legacy of this past century and a frequently underestimated fact of considerable sociological interest. Despite the impact of secularization, an apparent crisis of religious commitment and a rapidly expanding non-European presence, Canada remains decidedly Christian. Although less than a third of the population regularly attends religious services, an overwhelming number of Canadians describe themselves as Christians, and significant minorities of these subscribe in varying degrees to specific doctrinal beliefs and articles of the Christian faith (Maclean's 1993; Bibby 1993, 152–68; 1987, 86–110; O'Toole 1996, 120–2). Moreover, a recent expansion of numbers of those embracing religions other than Christianity together with an increase in those professing no religion has not altered this state of affairs to any significant degree. Canada remains 'a society where Christian traditions with historical roots in Britain and Western Europe dominate the demography of religious identity from Newfoundland to British Columbia' (Simpson 1988, 351).

As a direct result of its nineteenth-century heritage of consolidation, contemporary Canadian religion exhibits a distinctively concentrated denominational structure differing from both U.S. and European patterns. Thus, if employment of the currently fashionable market paradigm conjures an image of the United States as an arena of religious free-competition, all indicators north of the border signal circumstances of protracted religious oligopoly. The history of religion in Canada is, in large part, the story of conflict, competition, and accommodation among Anglicans, Roman Catholics, and the groups that formed what is now the United Church (notably Methodists and Presbyterians). Furthermore, the 'domination of churches and denominations,' especially these so-called Big Three, is still arguably the paramount characteristic of organized religion in this country (Simpson 1988, 351; Nock 1993, 47–53; Bibby 1987, 48–9).

At present, therefore, approximately two-thirds of Canadians still identify themselves as members of the Roman Catholic, Anglican, or United churches. While this proportion has eroded considerably over the past century and has diminished notably in the past thirty years, it remains a striking statistic. Equally significant is the fact that, of the more than 80 per cent of Canadians who define themselves as Christian, approximately 80 per cent proclaim allegiance to one or other of these three major denominations. Of further interest is the tendency (somewhat in contrast to the U.S. situation) for denominational affiliation to be remarkably stable over generations so that most people remain loyal to the denomination of their forebears (Statistics Canada 1993a; Maclean's 1993; Bibby 1987, 49–61, 1993, 152–68).

The persistent ability of tripartite denominationalism to retain the professed allegiance (in some sense) of a large majority of Canadians, despite low levels of church attendance and religious activism, presents an intriguing sociological puzzle. This does not seem to be merely another case of 'belief without belonging' (Davie 1994), a form of religiosity increasingly apparent in modern societies. On the contrary, a sense of belonging albeit derived, in many cases, from a passive, perceived identification with a particular organization, appears to be important in the Canadian context. Remarkably few Canadians are content, in fact, to describe themselves simply as Christians no matter how inclusive their religiosity or nominal their supposed affiliation. This suggests that the Victorian affirmation of denominational membership as a central pillar of personal identity lingers on through the generations. Whether it does so as a residual reflex emerging intermittently from the margins of consciousness or as the half-forgotten inheritance of an imaginary community unearthed in troubled times is an issue in which organized religion has a significant stake. The degree to which an inherited denominational structure languishes as a relic of the past or flourishes as a resource for the future may depend, even in an ecumenical age, on the ability of religious bodies to rediscover, recapture, and recreate the rationale for their existence as distinct traditions and communities of faith for the benefit of even their most nominal adherents. In this endeavour, the recovery of lost or repressed religious memory appears to be of prime importance.

Religious Memory

Although the topic of *collective memory* has attracted considerable historical and social-scientific interest in recent years (Middleton and Edwards 1990; Fentress and Wickham 1992; Nora 1996), it has been surprisingly under-utilized by students of religion. This is surprising given that the originator of the term, the French Durkheimian sociologist Maurice Halbwachs (1950, 1992), paid special attention to the role of memory in the adaptation of religious institutions to social change. When advancing 'into unknown territory,' Halbwachs believed, religion must avoid complete rejection of the past (even if this merely involves preservation of some of its 'forms') and must attempt to enframe new elements 'in a totality of remembrances, traditions, and familiar ideas' (1992, 86).

Fortunately, the significance of memory in a religious context has not gone entirely unrecognized. Stressing that communities 'have a history' and are 'constituted by their past,' Robert Bellah and his colleagues (1985, 152–5) insist that a *real* community is a 'community of memory' which refuses to forget its past or dishonour its tradition and which is involved in a continual retelling of its story or 'constitutive narrative.' While necessarily backward-looking, these 'communities of memory that tie us to the past also turn us to the future as communities of hope.'

Applying Bellah's concept to U.S. religious denominations, Robert Wuthnow (1993, 47–8) suggests that the weakening of ties to the past in most areas of contemporary life has strengthened a broad public perception of the church or denomination as a significant community of memory charged with a special mission to preserve the past and carry on a particular tradition. Interestingly, while its other functions progressively erode, the religious denomination's role in the preservation of memory is relatively enhanced. Its perpetuation of the past by 'telling stories that bring the past into the present' is, in Wuthnow's opinion, an undertaking of 'the utmost significance,' not least because narratives of the past are prerequisites of an ability to fantasize about the future. For a denomination to live up to its mandate as a community of memory means facing history squarely, 'redeeming what is unique about its own past,' and, in the process, strengthening its ability to encounter modernity with ingenuity, creativity, and success (ibid., 49).

For Hervieu-Léger (1993b, 1994), the fitness of specific religious traditions (in the form of churches and denominations) to meet the threat of secularization depends precisely upon their ability to undertake the demanding task of *reinforcing or reinculcating social memory*. This struggle for memory pits religious organizations against a modernity which, in her interpretation, endangers existing religion while simultaneously nourishing new forms of spontaneous religiosity. The notion of a *tradition* (an inherited and shared system of belief) is central to Hervieu-

Léger's very definition of religion. In her conception, religion requires a believing community in the form of either a concrete group or an imaginary genealogy that stretches backward and reaches forward: 'The crucial point to grasp is the *chain* which makes the individual believer a member of the community – a community which gathers past, present and future members – and the tradition which becomes the basis of legitimation for this religious belief. From this point of view, religion is the ideological, symbolic and social device by which both individual and collective awareness of belonging to a particular lineage of believers is created, maintained, developed and controlled' (Davie 1996, 110; Hervieu-Léger 1994, 126–7).

At the present time, however, religion is forced to undergo a more or less permanent process of reconstruction and reinvention as it reacts to an unceasing barrage of sociocultural transformations. Under conditions of such enduring discontinuity, its memory and its ability to memorize are both seriously impaired. Religious memory is endangered because *all* memory is problematic in modern societies, and such societies appear increasingly unable to produce meaning systems based on a chain of believing or to sustain 'a living, collective memory as a source of meaning both for the present and for the future' (Hervieu-Léger 1994, 125–6).

In a climate of collective amnesia, the difficulty of preserving religious traditions through the reinforcement or reinculcation of social memory is intense, as Hervieu-Léger demonstrates in her empirical investigations. If regular attendance at religious services, repetition of liturgies, and contact with religious functionaries are crucial to memory retention, then increasing numbers of nominal Protestants and cultural Catholics are cause for concern. In this regard, her documentation of explicit efforts by the Roman Catholic Church to rescue and restore core memories before they fade away altogether is worthy of note. Thus, in an age when the 'impact of the constant acceleration of history ... erases the present by precipitating successive events into the past at an ever-increasing speed,' Hervieu-Léger's intriguing investigation of modern memory mutations and the formation of 'lines of believers' undoubtedly offers a 'productive approach to the analysis of religious modernity' (Hervieu-Léger 1994, 125–6).

Although, in recent decades, many innovative, experimental, and uninstitutionalized varieties of religious experience have emerged in modern Western societies, mainstream religiosity appears likely to retain its traditional organizational forms for the foreseeable future. Thus,

Martin (1995, 302) argues that 'religious bodies including traditional churches will not succumb to privatization, but contribute vitally to the generation of new values and to the debate over civil society.' In a similar vein, Wuthnow (1993, 10, 16, 24, 28) vehemently denies that denominations 'are a thing of the past,' asserting that they 'are likely to remain influential in the religious politics of the future.' It might be said, more accurately, that denominations are definitely things of the past in terms of their *heritage* but that they also represent, in the opinion of many commentators, *projects* for the future that offset the need for particularity and roots against the increasing and, in many ways, desirable claims of universalism (Davis 1994, 133; see also Beyer in this volume). In this respect their past and future are inextricably linked.

Whether denominationalism in its concentrated Canadian form will prove a boon or a burden, an asset or an obstacle in efforts to preserve, propagate, and perpetuate religion in the coming century remains to be seen. What is already apparent, however, is that the *recovery of memory* must play a significant part in denominational preparations to meet the challenges ahead. Apart from its importance in the restoration of community, a serious attempt to rekindle the embers of memory within the Canadian religious mainstream can provide the opportunity for religious organizations to learn from their own past (Bibby 1987, 3–6; 1993, 152–68; Walsh 1954; Grant 1955; Clifford 1969; Moir 1983; McGowan 1990).

Historical underscoring of nineteenth-century religious success, while significant in itself, may also reveal the notable degree to which present problems represent an unintended and ironic consequence of that very success. In particular, the consolidation and expansion of state institutions, which Victorian churches and denominations worked so diligently to ensure, has resulted in a fundamental paring back of religious functions (Beyer 1997; Zylberberg and Côté 1993). In responding to this situation either by remaining within present limits or attempting to recapture lost ground, religious bodies may benefit from historical application of an insight of Hervieu-Léger (1986; discussed in Davie 1996, 108). Contemplating her conclusion that the most successful contemporary institutions are those that *both accept and resist modernity*, Canadian denominations will likely recognize this strategy in their investigations of the religious activities of their nineteenth-century forebears. Moreover, in formulating precise policies of selective acceptance and resistance, they may well seek precedents through the scrutiny of specific Victorian case studies. Finally, detailed investigation of the depth and breadth of religious influence on Victorian political life may stimulate reinterpretation of recent denominational incursions into the public sphere, whatever their long-term significance (O'Toole et al. 1991; Hewitt 1993, 257–9; Rawlyk 1990b; Casanova 1994). As the collective memory of organized religion is restored, current ventures into the realm of 'public religion' may look less like radical experimentation and more like a return to core denominational tradition.

Conclusion

The future of Canadian religion may be problematic and precarious, but it is not a foregone conclusion. Prediction must not be confused with predestination and sociological legitimacy must only be accorded to visions of the future that are sufficiently 'open-ended' to allow counterfactual possibilities (Ferguson 1997). As Davis (1980, 30) observes: 'It is when we grasp past and present as openness to the future that we understand them as history not nature, as the realm of human freedom not of natural necessity.'

Noting correctly that 'most of the scenarios once envisioned for the grand ballroom of history have been set aside by serious students of social theory,' Wuthnow (1993, 15–16) suggests that the 'future is now something like ourselves that we think of in nuanced and multifaceted terms.' To peer into the future then, is indeed to 'see through a glass darkly.' While a sociological perspective that stresses human creativity rather than societal determinism (Wallace and Wolf 1995, 6–8; Davis 1994, 124; Giddens 1976) is not necessarily predisposed to perceive a brighter future for religion, it does underscore the reality that churches and denominations are not inevitably imprisoned by external secular forces. Thus, though clearly disappointed with the performance of Canadian organized religion, Bibby (1993, 313–14) emphasizes the fact that its fate is, to a significant extent, in its own hands: 'The gods may become known through today's churches, perhaps outside of them, perhaps not at all. But let no one minimize what can be done ... The churches and the country may yet be awakened to the identity of the unknown gods. It may not happen. But, then again, it can.'

From this point of view, both modernity and religion are unfinished projects (Habermas 1981; 1987, ix) that allow for a wide range of speculation and differing measures of optimism and pessimism. In recovering its memory, critically contemplating the present, and articulating a strategy of selective espousal and repudiation of modernity, Canadian mainstream religion might begin to glimpse a better future. It would be a boon indeed if, in the process, it were to echo the past by exploding the notion that modernity is an inescapable 'iron fate' that spells doom for religion and by publicly identifying 'what is great in the culture of modernity, as well as what is shallow or dangerous' (Taylor 1991, 98, 120–1). By such means, religion might, ironically, assist in the salvation of modernity envisaged by so many social theorists (Casanova 1994, 234; Taylor 1991, 93–108; Kolakowski 1990, 10–13; Küng 1988, 6–10; Habermas 1987, 302–3; Berman 1988, 5–12; Kumar 1995, 173–8; Toulmin 1990, xi, 175–209).

chapter three

Individualism Religious and Modern: Continuities and Discontinuities

DANIÈLE HERVIEU-LÉGER

All European and North American empirical studies of contemporary forms of religiosity show that the religious landscape of Western societies is characterized by an irresistible movement towards individualization and subjectivization of belief and practice. This widespread finding amply explains why the question of individualism has become a recurrent theme of all sociological reflection on religious modernity. It would be quite misleading, however, to conclude that religious individualism is a novel reality associated only with modernity. It would be more accurate to speak of religious individualization as originating in the differentiation between two forms: ritual religion (which requires of the faithful careful observation of prescribed practice) and inner religion (which requires, either mystically or ethically, the personal and permanent appropriation of religious truths by each believer). In all the great religious traditions this distinction, in its various forms, was evident well before the emergence of modernity. From this perspective one could read for instance the whole history of Christian mysticism as a history of the formation of the religious individual. In the case of Canada, this may readily be illustrated by the place of Ignatian and other expressions of counter-Reformation spirituality in the 'heroic age' of pre-Conquest Roman Catholicism, and the distinction between the religion of order and the religion of experience in early nineteenth-century Protestantism (Murphy and Perin 1996, 4–30, 136).

But it is a paradoxical story! From the perspective of Christian

Translated by David Lyon and Marguerite Van Die

mysticism, the quest of union with God occurs through a task of self-deprivation, through the renunciation of the passions, interests, thoughts, sentiments, and representations in which the singularity of the individual is inscribed. Yet this same deprivation, this uprooting of the individual from the particular defining characteristics of one's life, also becomes a way of access to the inner self, for those who choose this journey. It offers, moreover, the fullest possible form of self-consciousness: the kind that comes precisely from the experience of union with the One. Already in the third century, Plotinus, whose experience was shot-through with neo-Platonic influences, and who shaped decisively the entire tradition of Christian spirituality, wrote of this 'negative affirmation' of the believer: 'Often,' he wrote, I awake to myself by escaping my body, a stranger to everything; deep within myself, I see the most marvellous Beauty. I am utterly convinced that I have a higher destiny; my activity is a peak experience; I am united with the divine being.'

On the one hand, then, the way of mysticism, deployed throughout centuries of Christian history, constitutes a path of extreme individualization of religious experience, reserved for a small number of virtuosi, bearers, as Max Weber put it, of a 'mystic charisma.' On the other hand, it is through the 'rational and methodical shaping' of the individual life (Weber 1996, 431) that the moral way transforms the believer. Calvinism has taken furthest – in Christian contexts – the moral logic of religious individualization, by developing the idea that each individual must be assured of personal salvation in all aspects of daily life, and especially within his or her vocation. In the absence of any human mediation between the individual self and God, the believer is thus confronted, in a radically individual fashion, with the question of personal salvation.

So, what is the connection between religious individualism, whether mystical or ethical, and modernity? There is no need to insist on the classical Weberian thesis that stressed the connection between this-worldly asceticism of Calvinistic Puritanism and the infant spirit of modern capitalism. But it would be misleading to deduce from this that the Christian trajectory of religious individualization, which found its most radical instance in Calvinism, anticipated in a seamless and linear fashion the emergence of modern individualism. Establishing an unbroken continuity between ethical or mystical religious individualism and modern conceptions of the individual is as absurd as the opposite position that turns religious individualism into a new product of modernity. For religious individualism differs from modern individualism on at least two counts. First, it consists of an individual forsaking self to trust in God. Second, it devalues completely the worldly realities that impede union with the divine. This double difficulty is not simply characteristic of an other-worldly conception of the mystical and ethical, such as that developed by the Roman Catholic tradition. It is equally present in the this-worldly conception of ethics that were promoted during the Reformation. This is why the German theologian and sociologist Ernst Troeltsch reacted so critically against the idea that an inner-worldly religious individualism, springing from the Reformation, prepared and ushered in the modern concept of the individual, thus opening the way for democracy.

Troeltsch certainly insists on the fact that Luther's valorization of the secular calling paved the way for a practical ethic appropriate to capitalist development. But he stresses at the same time that this ethic was in contradiction with a modern ethic that recognizes and amplifies the autonomy of earthly realities. Luther is still located in the neo-Platonic outlook that devalues worldly realities. In an even clearer way, turning to Calvin, Troeltsch challenges the notion that in developing his doctrine of predestination and pushing to its limit the logic of *sola gratia*, Calvin catalyzed the process of modern individualization. For Calvin, to be elect is not the same as to be valorized as an individual: saved by pure grace, the believer finds meaning only in service of God's kingdom. If the believer engages intensely in mundane tasks, this engagement is exclusively for the glory of God and because the world is itself willed by God. But on its own, this activity has no meaning. It neither allows the individual assurance of salvation nor offers value in personal achievement. Calvinist individualism denies the autonomy of the individual and, from this point of view, remains in contradiction with the positive and rationalist individualism springing from the Enlightenment. 'Calvin,' wrote Troeltsch in the *Soziallehren*, 'did not allow human liberty. It is excluded in both theological and social systems. God's kingdom is not offered as a matter of free choice; it is undoubtedly established by persuasion, but just as much also by the repression of all rebellion, by constraint. For Calvin, God's honour is maintained when humans bow before the law, in an attitude of free or forced submission' (Troeltsch 1912, 635). The Calvinist demand for submission is fundamentally opposed to the modern conception of the autonomous individual. But it also sets apart the Calvinism of the Puritan sects, insofar as these demanded of their followers free and voluntary membership.

In fact, if there is a 'protestant modernity' it is found primarily, according to Troeltsch, in the pietistic neo-Calvinist and Puritan streams, and it originates in large part from the political conflicts that led these communities to claim liberty of conscience, to promote communal organization founded on universal free will, and to affirm their independence by generalizing the practice of electing their own pastors. In reaction against the tutelage of the churches and their ritual formalism, such communities radicalized the Lutheran problematic of the ethical interiorization of one's relation to God. They developed at the same time a separateness from the world that in fact recognized its autonomy. The sectarian spirituality of the radical Reformation maintained, from this perspective, positive elective affinities with modern individualism. But Protestant spirituality, Lutheran and Calvinist, remained confined, for the most part, within a logic of negative affirmation of the individual, characteristic of premodern religious individualism.

Religious individualism no more produced modernity than modernity invented religious individualism. What characterizes the contemporary religious scene is not religious individualism as such; it is the absorption of religious individualism into modern individualism. The modern mutation of religious individualism: the case of the 'mystical-esoteric.'

Nowhere is the modern version of religious individualism as obvious as among the ensemble of spiritual groups and networks that orbit around the publishing houses, bookstores, and workshops that together form the 'mystical-esoteric.' What unites these groups is a religiosity entirely centred on the individual and his or her personal fulfilment. This is evidenced for example in the 'self-spirituality' of the New Age movement, described so well by Paul Heelas (1996), which in the Canadian case can best be seen in its West Coast manifestations in 'Lotus Land.' The absorption of religious individualism into modern individualism may find specific focus in the New Age, but it is also diffused more generally, and may be found as an emphasis within some conventionally religious groups, including conservative Christian ones (see Bibby 1993, 48–52; Burkinshaw 1995).

The description given by F. Champion (1993) situates well the main tendencies of what I call the mystical-esoteric. This religiosity is characterized first of all by the primacy accorded to personal experience, which leads each along his or her own path. It does not aim to discover or connect with a truth existing beyond the self: it is a matter of experiencing – each in his or her own way – personal truth. No authority can, in spiritual matters, impose on the individual some sort of external obligation to conform. The ultimate aim is self perfection, that does not aim for moral perfection of the individual, but rather for the individual's access to a superior state of being. This self-perfection is accessible through mind and body practices that borrow a whole gamut of techniques fine-tuned from the great spiritual and mystical traditions. But the recourse to these techniques occurs within a decidedly optimistic vision of human ability to reach full self-realization, depending on which path is responsibly chosen.

Salvation aimed at through this process of self-perfection is not only invested in this present life, it aims to reach, unaided, and in as complete a fashion as possible, the objectives that modern society offers as possible for all: health, well-being, vitality, beauty. Such a strictly this-worldly idea of salvation is part of a monist conception of the world: it challenges all dualisms (such as human-divine or natural-supernatural). At the same time it puts in question the fragmentation of knowledge and practice that shipwrecks the modern ambition of collective and personal progress. Such a view of the spiritual reunification of individual and collective life must ensure the rule of an 'ethic of love' that shows the convergence of ways of truth explored by these individuals. It implies equally a fresh alliance with modern science. Indeed, the objective of power over nature, which it pursues, meets the goal of empowering the physical and psychic capacities of the individual who guides the spiritual quest. Hence, the importance that a number of these ways of thought accord to extraordinary realities (out-of-body experiences, time-travel, communication with spirits or with extraterrestrials, and so on). The fact that a person can reach this by developing her or his own spiritual capacities does not contradict the scientific project. On the contrary, it completes it, because it is at root a way for the individual to enter into the earthly knowledge and power project that modern science develops in other ways.

If these mystical-esoteric groups and networks, in spite of the relatively unobtrusive character of their development (at least in France), constitute an analytic tool for understanding contemporary religious realities, it is because they advance in all their results tendencies that are equally present in the renewal movements generated by the historic religions: the quest of personal authenticity, the importance attached to experience, the rejection of closed meaning systems, an inner-worldly concept of salvation thought of as individual self-perfection, and so on. These different tendencies illustrate very exactly the phenomenon of the absorption of religious individualism into modern individualism, under the sign of the valorization of the world, on the one hand, and the affirmation of the autonomy of the believing subject on the other. 'Religious modernity' is fundamentally a product of this process.

Accessible God, Distant God: Two Poles of the Mutation

Obviously, this raises the question of the historic stages through which this mutation occurred. One might think that it started at the same time as modernity made itself felt, in social, political, and cultural contexts, a modernity that defined itself as the fulfilment of an order of reason, opening up the ambition of a methodological conquest of nature and establishing the autonomy of individuals capable of exercising collectively their political sovereignty. The cultural and political direction of the eighteenth century opened, in both aspects, the possibility of the recombining religious with modern individualism. Logically it even demands this recomposition, to the extent that the advent of modernity did not absorb, to any degree, all the metaphysical and spiritual questions of persons confronted with the uncertainty and finitude of the human condition. Clearly, a thoroughgoing historical inquiry would be required to back up this proposition adequately. To carry it through, one would have to engage particularly in a study of spiritual movements that preceded and accompanied the Enlightenment. Since I cannot do this here, I shall limit myself only to underscoring certain key features.

Modern religious individualism is characterized, as we have already noted, by the accenting of the individual's personal fulfilment, but equally by the recognition accorded to worldly realities in which such individuals conduct themselves autonomously. One could hypothesize that if premodern Christian individualism was able to achieve its transformation into modern individualism, this is because it is itself facing two ways at once: on the one hand, putting God within human grasp, and on the other, radically distancing God from the sphere of human activity. The first movement displaced the quest of self-surrender to achieve union with the divine in favour of emotional experience of the divine within oneself. The second, in reducing the plausibility of divine intervention in the world, unleashed the individual's autonomous power.

Thus formulated, the hypothesis is clearly somewhat terse. It remains to be tested, and caveats given. But various indices, occurring here in the French context, but which are replicated in various ways in North America, suggest that it may be justified. The spirituality of the seventeenth century is specifically characterized, for Catholics as for Protestants, by the emergence of a strongly emotional piety. These movements favoured the emotional nearness of God rather than the absence of a God with whom the faithful only connect at the price of a relentless self-denying asceticism. For Canada, one has only to recall as examples the intense spirituality of Ursuline Marie de l'Incarnation, in the seventeenth century, and the Protestant evangelical Henry Alline in the eighteenth century. Here lies one of the keys to the success of that which was experienced by a large lay public, in the stream known as the 'French school of spirituality.' This stream, connected most notably with the 'devout humanism' inspired by St François de Sales, has contributed to the spreading of a more gentle and humane spirituality than the heroic mysticism of the great Spanish saints to which it witnesses: a spirituality that at all times puts the believer not in a desperate effort to escape the conditions of life, but rather in a peaceful contemplation of Christ in each of his 'states of humanity.'

In a general sense, the different streams of spirituality that proliferated in France in the seventeenth century were less concerned to achieve the extinction of the individual in God, than in access through prayer and meditation, to achieve a humble feeling of the divine presence. This ordinary form of contemplation requires an inner receptiveness, a 'loving contemplation,' a 'singular and personal attentiveness to divine things,' but it does not necessarily entail a frantic asceticism. In proposing a spiritual path centred on the peaceful and overwhelming inner presence of God, the French mystics opened up at the same time – at least potentially – a way for a large number of believers. It was a question of coming single-mindedly before God to 'enjoy and to get used to his divine company, speaking humbly and conversing lovingly with him at all times, at each moment, without rule or limit.'

This orientation was not reserved for virtuosi with exceptional vocations. Because of this it suggests – even though it still remains contained in the mystical problematic of annihilating the self within God through the renunciation of desire and fear – the possible road of a spirituality that is easy, accessible, positive, in which the individual can find a personal path of fulfilment. It presents a friendly God, a God 'close to the heart,' caring about human need, who offers intimate conversation, a representation which the spirituality of the nineteenth and twentieth centuries would develop later in various ways.

The insistence that the Catholic spirituality of the seventeenth century placed upon the felt presence of God and on the emotional experience that a believer can have suggests a parallel with the rediscovery of emotional experience as the living source of faith, central to the pietist movement, in seventeenth-century German Protestantism. Challenging simultaneously the formalism of dogmatic statement and the chilliness of a routinized Christian practice, this movement undertook to create 'communities of the awakened,' and the publication by Jacob Spener of the 'Pia Desideria, ou désir sincère d'une amélioration de la vraie vie évangélique' (1675). He held up an inner piety and stressed strongly the affective dimension of personal spiritual experience. This outlook dominated European and North American Protestant theology until the middle of the eighteenth century and, along with a profound renewal of church life, gave birth to myriad Protestant initiatives in medical, educational, social, and artistic fields.

The parallel with French spirituality during the seventeenth century appears all the more valid because pietism is also characterized by a concern to renew the religious life of the people, and not only through the exploration of a way of religious virtuosity reserved for a few. In a more general sense, one may ask if these fresh spiritual springs of the seventeenth and eighteenth centuries do not have some similarity, at least indirectly, with the first appearance of a modern individualism that valorizes psychological self-fulfilment. Certain significant connections between a spiritual problematic of tranquillity before God and the unification of the self in God, and the views that flourished in the eighteenth century on the nature of human happiness on earth justify, in a way, this investigation. The 'peaceful rest,' which, according to Marmontel, results from the silencing of the passions and complete stillness, or again the Rousseau-like notion of happiness as the 'self-reconciliation' that coexists, says the author of the *Reveries*, with the search for intensity and for the elation associated with heightened consciousness, suggests such a parallel.

For that matter, does the Rousseau of *La profession de foi du Vicaire Savoyard* not bring to mind a God 'felt-in-the-heart'? The literature, which in the eighteenth century made the heart and the feelings the way to truth (and at the same time the way to self-fulfilment), is echoed, in certain respects, in the spiritualities that make emotional experience the moment par excellence of the divine encounter. The centrality accorded by pietism to individuals and their feelings, the place it gave to introspection – a place demonstrated by the importance of letter writing and intimate journals – have in any case left a profound trace in the German pre-Romantic and Romantic literary imagination. Such parallels and influences must be treated with care. But it can at least be asked if a diversified problematic of spiritual-personal cannot be found in these different currents, which goes beyond the premodern mystical problematic of the erasure of the individual in God.

Over against a movement that pictures a friendly, nearby God, manifesting intimately the divine presence in the human heart, the culture of the Enlightenment appears to be distinguished by a totally opposite tendency to push God into a far-off sky to be left there. This spirituality of a divine distance permeated in an explicit fashion, the different currents of deism. Originating across the English Channel, at the core of the Anglican and the nonconforming Protestant churches, it had no better apostle in France than Voltaire, whose attempt to promote a religion-without-a-church, capable of overcoming the limited particularity of different revelations: a religious way rooted in the natural religion that forms the universal religion of humanity (Dupront 1996, 137–230).

Voltaire (who, contrary to a widespread notion, was never an atheist) sought throughout all his long and turbulent life the means of replacing clerical religion with the 'true' religion that is 'the worship of the supreme Being, without any metaphysical dogma.' God is the power of unity and eternity in the universe, God who reigns through natural law, God the geometrician 'who has arranged everything in order, and assigned weights and measures,' but who never intervenes at all in human life. Voltaire accepts the idea of a creator and father God. On the other hand, he takes exception to any idea of an incarnate God, who interacts with humankind and with whom one can have a personal relationship. In the Voltairean outlook God is merely present in human life to the extent that he is the foundation, according to Dupront, of a collective bond: that of the community of brothers and sisters in the universal human family. 'I understand by natural religion,' wrote Voltaire, 'the principles of a common human morality.' The desacralization of religion is, in this perspective, a necessary condition for the advent of a universally shared ethical religion.

It is interesting to dwell on Voltaire's religion, from the viewpoint of the connections between modernity and spirituality, because it most explicitly shapes a much broader movement that developed both before and after him. Eighteenth-century deism is the vehicle of a radical critique of clerical Christianity. It at the same time blames the Church for holding onto a mythical sacred reality, the source of 'prejudices and superstitions,' and for not recognizing, by absolutizing the revelation to which it appeals, the existence of a universal religion beyond space and time, a common human religion, present across the diversity of the historic religions. English deism, the intellectual mysticism of Spinoza, the masonic conception of a great Architect of the universe that spread from the eighteenth century throughout all enlightened Europe, each in their way, developed this theme. The deist movement of the Enlightenment originated out of a critique of traditional religion, but retained the reference to God and sought to establish it, throughout the century, as a positive religion. Above all, in deism, God is present, but without communicating with humans. It is the final movement, according to Dupront, of a religious evolution that developed in three stages:

1 In the medieval religion of the Christian world, the supernatural and the natural were co-participants with God, and all theodicy of salvation, and of common salvation; the modes of communication were at the same time natural as well as eschatological.
2 With the crisis of the Reformation, there was a separation of God and humanity, or at least a growing distinction; communication became individual; this is the religion of Deus Solus.
3 The third phase is our own: between the two worlds, the human and the divine, there is a silent coexistence.

Deism thus takes its place, in the religious experience of the modern West, as the 'evidence of the exhaustion of a traditional religion of common salvation and of a society's fear to agree to all the consequences of a religion uniquely concerned with individual salvation' (Dupront 1996, 210–11). In other words, it marks the transition between the universe of traditional religion and that of religious modernity. Whether in the thought of l'Institut Canadien in mid-nineteenth-century Quebec or in the social reform concerns of Protestant 'regenerators,' aspects of this deist critique, though late in coming, did not pass by Christianity in Canada either (Murphy and Perin 1996, 224–301; Cook 1985).

To summarize: the spirituality of the Enlightenment placed itself between two poles that can be defined ideal-typically, the one by the discovery of the friendly and intimate proximity between humans and a God knowable within the heart, the other by the establishment of an indifferent coexistence between human beings and God, a coexistence that assures and affirms human autonomy. From the first pole come Christian spiritual currents of the seventeenth century, but also Jewish Hassidism, originating in the eighteenth century in Poland, that flourished by opposing the intellectual aridity of rabbinic Judaism with an emotional, joyful, and enthusiastic piety, strongly marked by cabalist influences. Deism in its diverse variants has a strong affinity with the second pole: a nearby God on the one hand; a distant God on the other. The closeness of a God with whom communication is possible, easy, and emotionally gratifying, turns God progressively into the personal agent of individual personal growth.

The distance of a God whom one worships from afar and whom one does not expect to intervene in human life gives earthly human activity its full head. These two spiritual configurations place themselves at the juncture of the traditional religious world governed by the heteronomous authority of Revelation and of the modern world, where individual autonomy rules. At the same time as the distance between these worlds is accentuated, the spiritual density of each pole becomes progressively weaker: deism, confronted by the rationality of modern scientific thought, rapidly exhausts itself; Roman Catholic mysticism as well as pietism throughout the eighteenth century experience a decline that contrasts with the spiritual vitality of the preceding century.

All along the way, the two movements, which seem contradictory, show that they are in fact inseparable from each other, and mutually reinforce each other. The affective interiorization of the divine presence within the self makes it possible to face up to the experience of a world where God no longer acts, and sharpens at the same time the sense of emptiness that marks the entry into modernity. The two images in tension – that of an intimate and of a distant God – together shape the transition in which religious individualism came to terms with a modern individualism that at the time was in the process of imposing itself on Western culture. If the movement of growing intimacy of the relation with God is pushed to its ultimate conclusion, it will leave behind nothing but a purely inner piety, subjective and private, less and less capable of expressing itself in a shared communal faith, a piety that by the same token has no place for any vision of a God who is actively present in day-to-day reality. This very intimate God is also, in this scenario, a God who is very far away. The spiritual valorization of the emotional proximity of the divine lends itself to a theological justification for the withdrawal of God from a world that has become decisively secular. The recognition of this absence henceforward becomes a legitimate faith-stance.

The perspective is developed in the thought of Italian philosopher Gianni Vattimo, for whom the incarnation of Christ becomes the basis for a 'friendly Christianity' ('I do not call you servants, but friends') that eradicates, in principle, all the transcendant, ineffable, and mysterious qualities of the sacred. God's intimacy with humanity constitutes, according to Vattimo, the very core of the secularization that Christianity brings about. This 'friendly Christianity' implies and supports the modern revolution caused by the affirmation of a believer, capable of thinking for himself as an equal partner in a community of friends; capable equally of autonomous action in a world freed from the cumbersome presence of the sacred. A fresh face of religious individualism has here emerged: that of modern religious individualism that flourishes in the most contemporary forms of spirituality.

Modern Religiosity and the Search for Power:
The Quest of the New Alliance with Science

The collection of heterodox spiritualities that immediately preceded and encapsulated the Enlightenment watershed presaged, in yet other ways, the defining features of contemporary religiosity, identified particularly in the manifold currents of New Age spiritualities. To put the whole in perspective, one must sketch the shape of a third component, found extensively and directly in these currents. I am speaking here of those forms of esoteric mysticism, which draw attention to numerous ways of searching for an individual spiritual practice that provides access to knowledge and a new approach to the world. There is a practice equally capable of giving the individual mastery over all the forces at work in all aspects of reality – natural, social, and psychic – and enabling such achievement in hope of a more authentically human society. In the eighteenth century, the spiritual currents that developed this creative will to power were nourished from various sources. The Jewish cabal, whose teachings were diffused by the Christian cabalists of the Renaissance and their successors in diverse theosophical schools had assured the diffusion across Europe and in every social strata, offered them inexhaustible resources. The richness of this mine in the spirituality of many groups searching for a primordial wisdom summarizes the totality of knowledge and the traditions in an important thread showing the continuity, over two centuries, between the spiritual effervescence of the Enlightenment century and the new contemporary spiritual culture. Prerevolutionary Lyon gives us a sense of this abundant compost. The search for power associated with the development of new knowledge saturates, for instance, the martinism of Martinès de Pasqually, whose *Traité de la réintégration des êtres* combines a theosophical reading of the universe and a doctrine of 'emanation': the divine unity originally contains all things; it expands constantly through the emanation (the emancipation by the Creator) of 'emanated' being to which God gives free will, that is, liberty and autonomy. The doctrine of Villermoz, derived from Pasqually's theories, presents itself as a Masonic crypto-Catholicism that emphasizes at the same time the union of the churches, the quest for communication with the spiritual world, and the requirement of moral purity. Pasqually's other disciple, Claude de Saint-Martin, founder of the great mystical movement called martinism, proclaimed the complete universality of revelation – all people without exception have received the divine word – and defines religious life as an individual quest for communication. His 1782 work, entitled *Tableau naturel des rapports qui existent entre Dieu, l'homme et l'univers,* develops an individualistic spiritual theology, capable of satisfying simultaneously the Enlightenment spirit and the pre-Romantic impulses that were beginning to appear at the time. The development of these movements (one could cite many others) that proliferated in France at the dawn of the Revolution are forerunners of the search for a connection – a fusion even – between the spiritual quest and the project of scientific knowledge and technical mastery over the world that has often been identified as a distinguishing feature of more contemporary spiritual currents. Spiritual experience as a means and expression of the power which an individual can exercise over self and the world, without any involvement in a particular church: that precisely is an essential aspect of the reordering of religious individualism which its absorption into modernity infers.

The study of the different configurations of the relationship between modernity and spirituality since the seventeenth and eighteenth centuries would, we repeat, call for reflection much deeper than what I have sketched here. This recapitulation is however indispensable for putting into perspective the contemporary development of 'new religious movements,' whose novelty is frequently overestimated by sociology. In fact, the specificity of these movements is that they push to the extreme the logic of subsuming the spiritual quest within a psychological modernity characterized by individual concern for self-fulfilment. In sum, the tendencies constantly emphasized by empirical research towards the subjectivization of traditional religious belief, at the expense of transcendent truths, along with the tendencies towards the valorization of the authenticity of the spiritual journey that each is expected to follow according to individual temperament and interests, are all indicators of this movement, on a more general level.

Part Two

ALIGNMENTS AND ALLIANCES

chapter four

Church and State in Institutional Flux: Canada and the United States

KEVIN J. CHRISTIANO

It is curious that the United States, Canada, and the British Isles, with a shared heritage in which so many common elements are acknowledged, have generally been dismissed as essentially dissimilar in one important aspect of their histories: the relations of church and state, of religious belief and public life. In this sphere historical interpretation has largely managed to refrain from anything approaching a comparative view.

E.R. Norman (1968, 1)

In Canada, no less than in the United States, they do things a bit differently out west. Consider Glen Clark, the former premier of British Columbia. Although in a bygone era a student in Roman Catholic schools, Premier Clark claimed to sustain no strong religious convictions of his own. Nevertheless, extracurricular reading on the implications of religious values for public policy (Wallis 1994) piqued Clark's interest. To learn more, the premier in 1998 issued invitations to some three dozen leaders of religious organizations from around the province to join him in Vancouver for two hours of dialogue behind closed doors.

What was discussed among the premier and officials of British Columbia's churches could be divined only indirectly, from press interviews with several participants outside the room and after the session had ended (see Todd 1998a, 1998b, 1998c; cf Fotheringham 1998). According to a report published the following day in the *Globe and Mail* (Matas 1998, A3), Premier Clark received 'plenty of suggestions urging that the government pursue justice and mercy' – appeals that it is hard to imagine any politician, let alone a New Democrat, dismissing out of hand. Indeed, those in attendance resolved to reunite and to continue their talks on ethics at a later date.

What is more significant, however, than the content of the premier's conversations with the clergy and other religious authorities is, first, that the session occurred at all,[1] and, second, that it produced so balanced and relatively moderate a reaction. Both aspects, I submit, point to important differences between Canadians and Americans in their attitudes towards relations between churches and actors for the state. For the most part, public figures in the United States step willingly but warily onto religious terrain, eager to collect indices of good morals and stable character but reluctant to leave the impression that values born of faith will dictate or substantially influence official decision making. By way of contrast, in Canada, as its 'national newspaper' (*Globe and Mail* 1998, A22) editorialized about Clark, 'politicians sometimes find religion; they rarely go out looking for it.'

Moreover, few voices, it seems from published analyses of this event, are raised in alarm or panic if a Canadian officeholder should actually discover the religious guidance that he or she seeks. 'New forays are being made into the zone that separates church and state in this country,' commented the *Globe* with perhaps unwitting precision in its morning-after editorial. The vocabulary of this description is apt. One bequest to the United States from the private correspondence of Thomas Jefferson is the metaphor of a 'wall of separation' between church and state (Jefferson 1987, 79). A wall divides territory, and positions are located on one side or the other; there is no 'in between.' For Canadians, a divergent history and a different law have staked out a 'zone' of conjunction between the two institutions, an image that suggests the possibility (if not the lasting comfort) of assuming an intermediary stance on questions of church and state.

Farther down its columns, the *Globe*'s editorial asks, 'Is this a trend that we should welcome?' Instead of ruling religious ideas out of contention by virtue of an inherited symbolism, the editors endeavour to weigh the benefits and risks of activity that news organs not a great distance to the south might classify, summarily and pejoratively, as 'entanglements' of the state with churches. 'It could be helpful,' the editorialist indicates with becoming modesty: 'Useful insights can be obtained from the place where the electoral meets the ethical. Religious leaders are uniquely positioned to play a part in political issues that delve into morality. Politicians, when they get in touch with religious debate, are tapping into vital communities of interest within their constituencies.' This is a positive appraisal of religion's role in public life, but the writer issues a number of cautions as well. Believers who enter the political domain should expect to yield at times to immediate circumstances; the wheels of politics are greased with compromise. Authoritative interpreters of faith should be hesitant to broadcast political decrees from the pulpit as if from on high; they are just so many more singers in the cacophonous chorus of democracy. Finally, churches should inspect carefully parties whose apparently humble overtures smack of 'political stuntsmanship': 'Religion is a calling,' sayeth the *Globe*; 'politics is for the called-upon.'

Without making too much of a single example, the response of the *Globe and Mail* to Premier Clark's parley strikes me as worthwhile, constructive, and above all practical. It shuns ideology (except for reservations about the left-leaning economic statements of the Canadian Catholic bishops), it avoids taking sides (apart from a parenthetical swipe at the tolerant-to-a-fault United Church of Canada), and it draws its few tentative lessons directly from experience. It qualifies, in other words, as a typically Canadian treatment of the problem. In derivation the opinions are empirical, not theoretical; in expression they are sober, not shrill.

This essay will contend that a distinctive pattern of political and social development in Canada is the source of these traits. In particular, a Canadian record of church–state interaction that occupies a middle ground between the stolid establishments of Europe and the strict separation espoused in the United States, I will argue, is more reasoned, more flexible, and more sociologically realistic than the principles applied elsewhere in North America. Close examination of these Canadian interactions, I believe, offers to Americans valuable instruction in understandings of church and state that rely less on legal formalities and more on concern for a common good. At the same time, however, convergence in Canada on an essentially American model of individual interests, and the rights necessary to defend them, gives rise to an uncertain and potentially more conflict-laden relationship between the two institutions in the future.

Constitutional Legacies

It would be difficult to exaggerate the visibility with which the political and legal cultures of the United States bear the marks of their eighteenth-century origins. 'The United States,' reflected the literary theorist Northrop Frye (1976, 321), 'found its identity in the eighteenth century, the age of rationalism and enlightenment.'

With only minor mediations and modifications, the American state and the constitution that underlies it descend from arguments over human nature and social experience that predominated throughout most of the intellectual West more than two hundred years ago. From these universal disputes was distilled a local ideal of the American as a novel kind of personality: a committed citizen but also a free individual; a person with values but without history, with clarity of vision but without clear antecedents, on a mission yet lacking any dispatchers to whom account would be returned except Nature and Nature's God.

Even if a war had not been fought to secure their independence, Americans would always remain revolutionaries at heart. The eighteenth-century American proposed a fresh start for philosophy, for government, and for the whole of humanity (Handy 1987, 204–6). In the language of religion, the Revolution had inaugurated for the erstwhile colonists the next dispensation in history, 'a new order for the ages' (*Novus ordo seclorum*). Frye emphasizes the sacred connotations of constitutional tradition in the United States, a legacy, he explains, 'which still functions much as the Torah does for Judaism.' His elaboration of this tradition echoes the words of the Bible: 'In the beginning the Americans created America, and America is the beginning of the world. That is, it is the oldest country in the world: no other nation's history goes back so far with less social metamorphosis. Through all the anxieties and doubts of recent years one can still hear the confident tones of its Book of Genesis: "We hold these truths to be self-evident." At least a Canadian can hear them, because nothing has ever been self-evident in Canada' (Frye 1976, 322–3).

'Canada had no enlightenment and very little eighteenth century,' Frye continues (cf Frye 1982, 65; Grant 1973a, 345–6; Handy 1976, 260; 1987, 209–10). How had the northern reaches of the continent been so neglected? Frye condenses a wealth of historical detail in his answer: 'The British and the French spent the eighteenth century in Canada battering down each other's forts' (Frye 1976, 323). The difficult though less lethal labour of constitution-making was not undertaken until another hundred years had passed, and then the dedicated efforts of the Fathers of Confederation were motivated more by practical necessity than by political inspiration. They were not so much building a nation as they were trying, through the agency of the state, to blunt the most menacing effects of the one situated immediately to their south. Thus, in the phrase of a prominent student of Canadian federalism, 'Confederation was born in pragmatism without the attendance of a readily definable philosophic rationale' (Black 1975, 4).

The majority of the historians and political scientists who have scrutinized Canada's founding period concur with this understated view. A recent assessment (Bazowski and MacDermid 1997, 231), for example, casts Canada's original constitution, the British North America (BNA) Act (1867), as 'a decidedly utilitarian constitution famously deficient in explicitly philosophical statements.' Former Prime Minister Pierre Elliott Trudeau, in a chapter published the year that he abandoned an academic career teaching law and plunged as a candidate into federal politics (see Christiano 1994, 74–8), asserted that the BNA Act was remarkable for 'its absence of principles, ideals, or other frills.' Historical circumstances had required that the Fathers of Confederation accommodate their plans to the needs of a divided country under external threat, a land that had literally outgrown its government. 'The Canadian nation,' Trudeau observed, 'seems founded on the common sense of empirical politicians who had wanted to establish some law and order over a disjointed half-continent' (1965a, 29–30; cf Grant 1988c, 244–5).

Of course, a pragmatism that barely addresses problems of the moment hardly satisfies the hope for a national ideology. A more critical evaluation of Confederation's pedigree comes from the political scientist Philip Resnick. The Fathers, he complains, 'did not speak the language of the Rights of Man or of life, liberty, and the pursuit of happiness.' Because Confederation foreshadowed the construction of an east–west railroad, unity for Canada would consist not in rights of citizenship and ties of personhood, but in rights-of-way and ties of wood. All the same, Resnick laments, 'It is hard to get excited about the handiwork of railway buccaneers and their kept lawyers' (1984, 16).

Dealing with Diversity

With the crucial asset of a national ideal at their disposal, Americans could react to diversity in their midst with appeals to unity at ever-higher levels of abstraction, the most general of which being the concept of 'Americanism' itself. Citizens of the United States are able to transcend difference because what makes them distinctive as a people is thought to reside at a level above their differences as persons. Americans, then, are neither a race nor an ethnic group – nor, for that matter, a nationality in the customary sense of that noun. Rather, they may be likened to adherents to a lofty creed. The country's Latin motto *E pluribus unum* ('out of many, one') is thus more than a pious prayer; it is a depiction of the course of national self-definition. Significantly, *A mari usque ad mare* ('from sea unto sea'), the national motto of Canada, defines the outer extremes of Canadian territorial sovereignty but, unlike its American counterpart, says nothing about what in theory happens within those boundaries.

Canada possesses several founding peoples, but few foundational principles. Therefore, history has left it free to deal with the diversity of its population with little more than 'proceeding by hunch and feeling,' to use Northrop Frye's words (1976, 327). Though somewhat more formal, the Canadian scholar Edwin R. Black (1975, xi) admits much the same insight: 'We have worried more about how to get along and how to continue doing public business with each other in a mutually satisfying way than we have about ideal forms of governance for mankind.'

The contrast between the two countries in how they manage diversity is perhaps better illustrated with a geographical analogy. In a thought-provoking essay on Canadian–American relations, Northrop Frye invites readers to 'consider the emotional difference' between an approach to the shores of the United States aboard a ship from England and a comparable voyage to Canada. As transatlantic passengers, we notice that the American coastline is well-defined and symmetrical. But the near edges of Canada present quite a different sight: 'One enters Canada through the Strait of Belle Isle into the Gulf of St Lawrence, where five Canadian provinces surround us, with enormous islands and glimpses of a mysterious mainland in the distance, but in the foreground only sea and sky. Then we go down the waterway of the St Lawrence, which in itself is only the end of a chain of rivers and lakes that starts in the Rockies. The United States confronts the European visitor; Canada surrounds and engulfs him, or did until the coming of the airplane' (Frye 1982, 58).

In a similar manner, the United States encounters diversity straight ahead and attempts effectively to hurdle it. In contrast, Canada seems to enfold and to absorb difference, the better to handle it. American culture aspires to overcome difference, while Canada strives in politics to guide its passage and in law to control its effects. The Canadian system *ing*ests diversity without really *dig*esting it. The former process is an unavoidable fact of modern life; the latter is as unnecessary to

Canada's political survival as it is dangerous to the national self-image.

These variations in styles, both official and unofficial, for accommodating pluralism have evident relevance for comparisons between the United States and Canada with respect to the place of religion in each society (see Westin 1983, 33). In the United States, a relatively doctrinaire division between the institutions of church and state is a natural concomitant of an overarching national unity, the maintenance of which is not the exclusive responsibility of one denomination or interchurch coalition. The sociologist David Martin contends that in the American case 'the total break between an institutional church and the state' permits 'religious symbols to remain a major part of the common vocabulary of legitimation' (1978, 116). In this way, 'a pluralistic religion-in-general' can be enlisted 'to buttress the higher level legitimations of American society' (ibid., 70; cf Beckford 1992, 16).

Canada, for its part, can claim no such immunity from the most burdensome implications of religious diversity. In Canada, more than in the United States, religion lays down a line of social division around which a perpetual negotiation, as delicate as it is important, has taken place. As John H. Simpson (1988, 352–3) notes in his overview of the Canadian churches, 'Canada more than many other societies is characterized by ongoing processes of complex and intricate adjustment between significant groups and regions under the tutelage of relatively fragile centralized authority.' It is to this constant negotiation that Kenneth Westhues (1976b, 221) is referring when he speaks of Canadian social organization as the outcome of the 'legitimate and overt bargaining of corporate actors.'

Like the United States, Canada has a religiously diverse population, and this fact alone weakens the ability of the state in either locale to act in the traditional place of the churches. But in Canada, the lack of a collective ideology that might transcend difference, or of an effective vehicle for national aspirations other than the government, offsets some of the mutual antagonism that church and state would experience as institutional competitors. Canadians hence have come to depend on a more universally active state, and do not shy from cooperation in voluntary initiatives that are consecrated towards service of the common good, whether that elusive goal is formulated in public or private terms (Grant 1973a, 348; Handy 1976, 229).

While both societies abide by a separation of church and state, the meaning of that structure changes when one crosses the international boundary. If a 'wall of separation' can be said to exist for Canadians, church historian John Webster Grant (1988c, 243–4) proposes, 'they have been prepared to allow chinks in it that most Americans would regard as unthinkable.' Their justification for this seeming laxity inheres in a historical reluctance in Canada to 'drawing with any precision a line between areas in which the state has a legitimate interest and those that ought to be left to voluntary activities of the churches.' As a consequence, Grant believes, 'few Canadians find "separation of church and state" an acceptable description either of their situation or of their ideal for it' (Grant 1973a, 341; cf Lipset 1990, 80–2; Noll 1992, 161; Pangle 1993, 3). No theoretical absolutes control their thinking in that area. Rather, Grant (1988c, 244) argues, 'Canadians have shown a disposition to approach issues of church and state somewhat pragmatically' (see also Handy 1976, 259–60; Moir 1968, 258; Westhues 1976b, 218–21).

Canadian Accommodations

Canadian law incorporates a variety of provisions pertaining to religion that also prevail in the United States. As in the United States, these include protections from governmental interference in religious practices, broad supports for freedom of conscience, and special, though limited, accommodations to existing churches. Examples that would qualify in this description are the privilege for communications between lay persons and religious ministers, removal of liability for payment of certain types of taxes, and, under specific conditions, exemptions from compliance with government regulations or the obligation to render military service (Doyle 1984a). But law in Canada contains in addition privileges for religions that were written into a succession of constitutional documents in testimony both to the demands of the day and to what has been characterized as a 'permissive and pragmatic relationship' between church and state (Moir 1968, 247) that effected a 'practical recognition' of religion (Grant 1988b, 234).

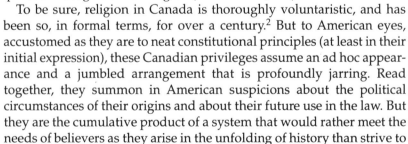

To be sure, religion in Canada is thoroughly voluntaristic, and has been so, in formal terms, for over a century.[2] But to American eyes, accustomed as they are to neat constitutional principles (at least in their initial expression), these Canadian privileges assume an ad hoc appearance and a jumbled arrangement that is profoundly jarring. Read together, they summon in American suspicions about the political circumstances of their origins and about their future use in the law. But they are the cumulative product of a system that would rather meet the needs of believers as they arise in the unfolding of history than strive to shape those people and their history in the pattern of a predetermined vision (Grant 1988c, 244). Canadians, John Webster Grant has observed, 'take for granted the existence of a plurality of religious groups but have never found it necessary to articulate a consistent theory of religious pluralism. They enjoy the same freedom as Americans to belong to religious denominations of their choice but are inclined to think of their groupings more as communities given to them in their history than as voluntary associations created for particular purposes' (Grant 1973a, 346).

Measures for the Mennonites

Prime examples of accommodation to the special expectations of a religious group resident in Canada are the measures that the federal government sponsored in the nineteenth century to induce the immigration and orchestrate the settlement of thousands of Mennonite families from Europe. Once established, these measures have continued for much of the nation's history to cement the attachment of Mennonites to their adopted land and to improve their fortunes for new lives in Canada.

The first Mennonites to reach Canada travelled north from the newly independent colonies starting in 1786. In Canada they claimed the identical rights that had been extended to them under British rule in America. For even in the years before mass migration to North America, British imperial law made important concessions to the Mennonites and to other dissenting sects. In Upper Canada, for example, the Militia Act of 1793 contained a passage that exempted them by name from any obligation to serve in local units of the army: 'And it be further enacted,' read the legislation, 'that the persons called Quakers, Mennonists, and Tunkers, who from certain scruples of conscience, decline bearing arms, shall not be compelled to serve in the said Militia, but every person professing that he is one of the people called Quakers, Mennonists, or Tunkers, and producing a certificate of his being a Quaker, Mennonist, or Tunker, signed by any three or more of the people (who are or shall be by them authorized to grant certificates for this or any other purpose of which a pastor, minister, or preacher shall be one) shall be excused and exempted from serving in the said Militia' (quoted in Epp 1974, 100–1; and in Janzen 1990, 12, 163).[3]

The government exacted a price for its indulgence, however, in the form of special taxes (or 'commutation money') that were levied upon all who obtained the exemption. Those who would not pay tribute to the state with their time and possibly their blood, then, would pay with grain, livestock, and household or personal goods. What is more, the amount of the levy escalated sharply in times of hostilities. Persons who resisted imposition of the tax, or whose individual assets were insufficient to pay it, saw their property confiscated. To many pacifists, the taxes amounted to support for the military through a different means, and so they were religiously objectionable. To others, they seemed a fine for scrupulous adherence to religious principle, and so they were politically wrong. After petitioning the legislature, the various peace churches were able to have the taxes repealed in 1849 (Janzen 1990, 164).

Foreign Mennonites, who as 'free peasants' colonized the steppes of southern Russia (now Ukraine), looked towards North America as a political haven when, after 1870, the czar embarked on a program to eradicate their German-speaking culture. In this process, privileges that had been granted to them between 1800 and 1803 were to be ended, and the czar gave opponents of the changes ten years to emigrate. More than seventeen thousand Mennonites, about one-third of their total population within the borders of Russia, took advantage of the opportunity to relocate. Coincidentally in 1870, Canada exerted control of the lands in the Northwest that the Hudson's Bay Company had administered. The first members of the Russian group landed at Quebec four years later and headed west to Manitoba. All together, a total greater than one-third of the mobile proportion of Russian Mennonites ultimately moved to Canada in that decade (Ens 1994, 11, 21, 231; Francis 1955, 28; Janzen 1990, 13, 166; Loewen 1993, 61–5, 263, 270 n1).

Before the Mennonites left Russia, they were careful to follow their practice of negotiating a *Privilegium*, or an agreement concerning their treatment, with the authorities in their new country (Francis 1955, 47–9; Loewen 1993, 9, 14). Some provisions in this agreement addressed practical and material considerations. For instance, the Mennonites sought from the Canadian government assistance to compensate for the expense of their migration, in addition to land for farming free of charge – or at low prices and with loans for the purchases on easy terms of credit. They wanted, as well, an exemption from the normal requirement that homesteaders actually live on the land that they intended to cultivate. In order to preserve their communities, Mennonites preferred as an alternative to live adjacent to one another in self-governing townships and to share a common pasture. So-called block settlement by virtue of a 'hamlet privilege' was more feasible in Canada than in the United States, making the former country a more appealing stop (Ens 1994, 14, 38, 94–5; Epp 1974, 192–4; Francis 1948, 145–6; 1955, 46–7; Janzen 1990, 12–13; Loewen 1993, 76–7).

Much more crucial, however, was the possibility for accommodations to the migrating Mennonites that would enable them to maintain their religious faith and the cultural institutions that transmitted it to new generations. The Russian group requested and received commitments that the Canadian government would allow it to continue the use of its language, grant it the right to operate its own schools, accept affirmation of oaths instead of swearing, and – most critical of all points – recognize an exemption for the Mennonites from all military service. This last exception already had ample precedent in British and Canadian law.[4]

A series of letters of understanding from Canadian officials and orders-in-council dispatched from Ottawa (reprinted in Ens 1994, 237–40; and in Francis 1955, 44–5) assured the Mennonites that this guarantee would prevail in times of both peace and war, and that it could not be revoked (Ens 1994, 12–21, 172–3; Janzen 1990, 12–13, 164–5). An invitation from 1873, for example, promised that 'The fullest privilege of exercising their religious principles is by law afforded the Mennonites, without any kind of molestation or restriction whatever' (quoted in Epp 1974, 338; and in Francis 1955, 45). Not that the typical Mennonite would easily relax his spiritual vigilance. Any immigrant farmer who applied for naturalization in Canada was confronted on the form with a pledge that he defend 'His Majesty the King ... to the utmost of my might.' Deferring to a Higher King, one Mennonite candidate wrote into the space beside the declaration of loyalty an addendum: 'in so far as it does not go against Christ's teaching' (quoted in Ens 1994, 39).

Mennonite would-be settlers historically had shown a habit of dealing directly with the highest authorities in their host countries; repeatedly they relied on personal assurances of safety and security that they received from these figures (for example, see Ens 1994, 20, 46; Loewen 1993, 83–4). This had been true in Russia for the century between when Catherine II pledged to the Mennonites 'eternal' protection and when the imperial regime of Alexander II set out to assimilate them. They had also seen the efficacy of this approach in the warm welcome that was extended officially to the Swiss Mennonites who in the eighteenth century had taken up residence in Pennsylvania, then under British colonial rule (Epp 1974, 42–3).

The British embraced minorities like the Mennonites not out of any philosophical preference for pluralism, but because, as one Mennonite historian (ibid., 1974, 43) phrased it, 'they were useful' in peopling vast parcels of land at the farthest ends of the Empire, and bringing them within administrative control and under productive cultivation. In Canada especially, 'paper jurisdiction over the huge prairie region with its 1,500-kilometre undefended border meant little without a settled population occupying the land' (Ens 1994, 12).[5] But regardless of its motivations, 'the new British tolerance for dissent made such a deep impression on the Mennonites on both sides of the Atlantic that they would seek refuge under its wide umbrella again and again – eventually in Canada – in the years to come' (Epp 1974, 43). So was the trust of Russian Mennonites transferred in the 1870s to officials of England, and through them to representatives of the British Crown in Canada. A descendent from their migration registered thanks to Queen Victoria, for 'it was through her that the way for the Mennonites from Russia to Canada was opened, and just as Empress Catherine of Russia had once appeared as the saviour of the Mennonites, so the Queen of England now appeared in almost the same way' (quoted in Ens 1994, 20).

Mennonite leaders were convinced that their people, a small and insular minority, had less to fear from a favourable if paternalistic monarch and the colonial governments that were ultimately answerable to her than from the majoritarian tendencies of a popular democracy, as the United States had become – this in spite of written law and constitutional guarantees. Noted one Mennonite delegate who had scouted new locations for settlement from Manitoba down to Texas, Canada was the superior destination for his group because 'the English government would be more liberal' in bestowing exemptions on the German-speaking pacifists. His contingent chose Canada, according to another member, 'because it was under the protection of the Queen of England; and we believed that our freedom from military service would survive longer there and also that church and school would remain under our own jurisdiction' (quoted in Ens 1994, 20; and in Epp 1974, 183). These considerations sufficed for many immigrants to suppress their real doubts about the arability of Canadian soil and opt for the northern country over the United States (Epp 1974, 195; Loewen 1993, 74). What better a fit for the Tory tradition in Canada than these unlikely if dependent monarchists!

The affection of the transplanted Mennonites for the British Crown was promptly and fully reciprocated. Lord Dufferin, as governor general the Queen's representative in Canada, travelled to Manitoba in 1877 to encourage the Mennonite pioneers and to invite them, without entirely relinquishing their particularity, to participate completely in the civic life of their new nation (Francis 1955, 78–9). In a long-remembered speech, he acknowledged the hard work and perseverance of the Mennonites under harsh conditions, and he expressed his 'unmitigated satisfaction' with the progress that they had made subduing the frontier.

Lord Dufferin then praised the settlers for their fidelity to their religious convictions in the face of enormous sacrifices. He reiterated the government's commitment not to pressure them to abandon pacifism, and urged them instead to apply their abundant energies to 'a war, not against flesh and blood, a task so abhorrent to Mennonite religious feeling' but 'against the brute forces of nature' (quoted in Epp 1974, 217–18). 'The battle to which we invite you is the battle against the wilderness,' he assured his listeners. 'You will not be required to shed human blood' (quoted in Epp 1974, 370; cf Ens 1994, 38; Janzen 1990, 171; Loewen 1993, 84).

✳ Besides easing fears of the newcomers and exhorting them to continued effort in their labours, Lord Dufferin's visit, a bare three years after their entry into Canada and a mere decade after Confederation, brought a further message to the Mennonites. He insisted that, just as the immigrants had availed themselves of plentiful land on the Canadian prairie, so should they accept the 'liberties and freedom' that were the right of the Queen's subjects around the world. 'Beneath the flag whose folds now wave above us, you will find protection, peace, civil and religious liberty, constitutional freedom and equal laws,' he said (quoted in Epp 1974, 218).[6]

On his return trip east, the governor general paused in Winnipeg, where his address to a banquet in his honour lauded the combination of 'Mennonite industry and British benevolences' (Epp 1974, 218). Lord Dufferin remarked on how quickly the barren lands of the West had been put to the plough and made fruitful, leading to a growth in wealth and comfort for the Mennonite farmers in which he took a vicarious pride. Yet, he boasted to the prominent urbanites in his audience, he was 'infinitely prouder in being able to throw over them the aegis of the British constitution, and in bidding them freely share with us our unrivalled political institutions, our untrammelled personal liberties' (quoted in Epp 1974, 218; and in Loewen 1993, 84).

Confidence among Mennonites in the comparatively greater reliability of Canadian promises moved some branches of the church to organize a clandestine migration of young men north from the United States when conscription was adopted there to raise troops for the First World War (Francis 1955, 190; Juhnke 1989, 233; Loewen 1993, 258–9). 'These crossings,' according to one account (Teichroew 1971, 230), 'involved rendezvous with anonymous buggy drivers or sympathetic Mennonites from the border areas who transported nervous Mennonite youths across unguarded portions of the North Dakota and Montana borders in the dark of night.' Although the numbers of such flights were not large, the wartime administration in Ottawa, concerned about the sentiment of its newly mobilized ally, definitely did not approve. Nevertheless, Canada persisted as an attractive refuge for young American Mennonites because it 'provided in practice what could not be promised as a public statement': namely, relatively free (if bureaucratically complicated) access to exemption from compulsory military service (Teichroew 1971, 229). Historian William Westfall would conclude much later that Canada's willingness to respond affirmatively to American dissidents was 'clearly valued much more highly than were the more abstract guarantees of freedom of religion and freedom of speech which, in theory, enjoyed full constitutional protection in the United States' (1997, 191).

Admittedly, Canada has not in every instance distinguished itself as a haven of safety for religious minorities. One need only examine the treatment that the federal and provincial governments afforded the Jehovah's Witnesses (see Botting 1993; Doyle 1984b, 420–7; Kaplan 1989; Mol 1985, 138–43) to detect the darker impulses of state power at work. In the province of Quebec especially, reaction to ceaseless and sometimes obnoxious proselytizing by this small sect took the form of an unapologetic campaign of persecution (Mol 1985, 139; Sarra-Bournet 1986). For fully seven years, Premier Maurice Duplessis conducted what he trumpeted as 'a war without mercy' (quoted in Black 1977, 386) against the Witnesses. During that period, some sixteen hundred cases against Jehovah's Witnesses occupied Quebec's courts (Black 1977, 388). Only the courageous intervention in the 1950s of Canadian constitutional jurists and civil libertarians (the lawyer and poet F.R. Scott comes to mind)[7] eventually thwarted the wish of Duplessis to drive the Witnesses into oblivion.

So every nation, Canada not excepted, has at times failed to defend vigorously the liberties of its citizens, and particularly those rights belonging to members of religious minorities. My argument is simply that the Canadian state, for its own reasons, could grant to many of these groups at an early hour and without great conflict a degree of latitude in action that in the United States they would acquire only much later, and often after tense confrontations or as the result of protracted litigation.

Limits of Liberalism

To ascertain changes between the nineteenth and twentieth centuries in attitudes within the expanding Canadian state towards religious difference (Beyer 1997, 284–5; Zylberberg and Côté 1993), the Mennonites again act as a helpful example. In the 1970s, one hundred years after their mass migration from Europe, several branches of the Mennonite church in Canada petitioned the federal government to be relieved of the portion of their taxes that funded participation in the Canada Pension Plan, the country's universal and obligatory social insurance program for old-age beneficiaries. As part of their lobbying effort, a delegation of leaders paid a visit on the incumbent prime minister, Pierre Trudeau.

In the end, Trudeau rebuffed them, as had Cabinet ministers and officials previously, with the insistence that no exceptions to the plan could be contemplated without seriously weakening it. The Mennonites could not grasp how their forced contributions were not an infringement upon freedom of religion, so they pressed the prime minister for an explanation of his stand. Trudeau replied: 'Religious freedom exists, I take it, when people are free in their conscience and they can exercise their beliefs freely within the country, belong to a church of their choice, and so on. But, in some cases, if the morals which flow from their metaphysics – if I can put it that way – are not morals accepted by the community in which they live, it is unfair to say that preventing those moral precepts from applying is an attack on religious freedom ... when the government adopts laws which are good for the majority, I don't think that freedom of religion permits people from opting out' (quoted in Janzen 1990, 262).

Trudeau premised his brief and impromptu answer on a conception of religion that is simultaneously intellectualized and individualized. Religion, in this view, inheres in what a person believes in the privacy of his or her conscience. At least in this quite circumscribed respect, Trudeau's thinking is a match to that of the American founders. Where he differs is in his estimation of what society owes to the individual believer. As a Canadian, he is more willing than American authorities to mingle productively the functions of church and state, but apparently less disposed to remove the government from places in society where it may conflict with individual liberty. For the former prime minister, one would guess, religious freedom in this case reliably reigns over the space inside each person's head and in the private behaviours planned there, but nowhere else.[8]

Commentators have made much of the perception that, aided by small-*l* liberal leaders like Trudeau, the values of the Canadian and American legal systems are converging. For ages, the paradigmatic question for American constitutionalists has been, 'What does this legal arrangement do *to* ones among us?' The approach is overwhelmingly pragmatic, but at the same time it assumes the stability and longevity of the society as a whole and concentrates its concern on the condition of rights-bearing individuals. It thus illustrates the penchant in the United States for elevating battles of interests into contests of principle, for privileging contrary attitudes and the social conflict that they often produce. Hence there has grown in America an immense legal infrastructure at practically every level of life, constantly at the ready to fend off the incursions of a pervasive government or the majoritarian abuses of popular opinion. This is 'The American Way,' and it is unlikely to change substantially; perhaps it should not.

In contrast, the salient constitutional question across Canadian history has been, 'How do we make this legal arrangement work *for* us?' This, too, reveals a pragmatic thrust, but it is one devoted to tending and mending the rends in the national fabric, under the assumption that such a chore precedes and indirectly addresses the needs of individuals. Thus, in Canada, identifiable social groups possess rights under law along with the persons who compose them (Bender 1983; McDonald 1988, 182), and even the highly individualistic Charter of Rights and Freedoms (reprinted in McKercher 1983b, 247–55) guarantees the fundamental liberties of Canadians within 'such reasonable limits prescribed by law as can be demonstrably justified in a free and democratic society' (Section 1, 248). Indeed, many Canadians – and nearly all Québécois and Québécoises – would concur with Michael McDonald's self-described 'provocative' suggestion that 'it is a mistake to adopt a normative view that treats individuals apart from their groups, in particular those groups that provide for the individuals in question a horizon of meaning and a focus of identity' (McDonald 1988, 187; see also Glendon 1991, 38–9; Taylor 1992).

By almost all accounts, the Constitution Act of 1982, and the Canadian Charter of Rights and Freedoms that leads off its text, has pushed Canada abruptly away from a traditional and collectivist legal culture and towards a liberal individualist law in the American mode (Lipset 1990, 101–10, 116, 225–6; Nelson 1995, 27; Noll 1992, 453; Rawlyk 1990b, 256; cf Bazowski and MacDermid 1997, 242–5). Such a legal code is based on commitments to the dignity, autonomy, and equality of all persons regardless of social background; the integration of groups into society; open avenues to political participation; and governance according to the will of the majority. Individuals alone hold rights, and the state exists to facilitate their unimpeded though reasoned exercise through assertion of the rule of law (Janzen 1990, 2, 301–5; Nelson 1995, 26–30; Taylor 1992, 440–2; Tushnet 1992, 317–22).

The incompatibility of these assumptions with the ends of the Canadian system as it has operated until the recent past ought to be clear. 'Inevitably,' political analyst William R. McKercher (1983a, 16) warned, 'Canadian federalism will be altered by the Charter, perhaps in ways that cannot now be foreseen.' His fellow political scientist, the eminent Donald V. Smiley (1983b, 220), was much more blunt: 'The coming into effect of the Charter,' Smiley predicted contemporaneously, 'will be the most radical break ever made in a constitutional and legal tradition hitherto characterized by continuity and incremental change.' Smiley is furthermore sceptical that, over time and with greater public familiarity, the old assumptions of Canadian politics will harmonize with the Charter. 'Nobody has ever become a convert to Christianity through reading the Apostle's Creed,' he quipped during an academic discussion (Smiley 1983a, 105).

What of the status of religion amid these major changes? The legal scholar Mark Tushnet has argued that with liberalism at its foundation, American society cannot 'now provide the support needed for a concept of politics into which religion would comfortably fit.' The United States would benefit, he writes, from 'a view of the law that affirms the connectedness that religious belief mobilizes and that liberalism denies' (Tushnet 1992, 289). But customary legal thinking propels understanding in the opposite direction.

In the past, Canadians integrated religious groups into their national experience through accommodations that rested 'not so much on broad principles of political theory as on the fact that, historically, British and Canadian governments had given them a broad liberty' (Janzen 1990, 270). Charles Taylor, the distinguished Canadian philosopher, has gone as far as to profess that 'In a way, accommodating difference is what Canada is all about' (1992, 445). The Charter may have altered this course permanently.

Did the twentieth-century citizens of Canada in consequence develop a space for religion in their society that abandons the most practical features of their old system and borrows the least suitable elements of the American one? Has legally sanctifying the private place of religion effectively deprived it of public import? The function of religion, says the Canadian psychoanalyst Charles Levin,

> has been taken over by legalistic liberalism, the rule of law, and the entrenched principles of habeas corpus, due process, freedom of conscience, freedom of communication, equal opportunity, and so on. To a variable extent, liberal democracies both create and reflect this novel circumstance of social relativity. Under these conditions, religion like everything else must be satisfied to compete in a game which has no final winner. In functional terms, it is now just another commodity, another social or political trend, another 'lifestyle choice' to be wondered about and polled and televised and marketed but never absolutely embraced because – thank God – we are now protected by Constitutional Law even from our own deepest wishes. (Levin 1998, 12)

Paradoxically, the more that legal thinking infects the entirety of the public sphere, if Levin is correct, the less useful it is to conceive of church and state primarily as legal (as opposed to social) actors.

Conclusion

On initial inspection, a call for considering church and state in all their actual overlap, instead of according to the provisions of theories that were composed in the throes of modernity (but for wholly other purposes), may seem itself to incline towards a postmodern conclusion. As the British sociologist James A. Beckford (1992, 19; see also Lyon 1994b; 1996, 19) has noted, a rejection of received rigidities, a tendency to combine elements that had heretofore been held in isolation, and a concession that grand perspectives may not supply the answers to persistent questions, are all hallmarks of a postmodern sensibility.

Yet, in place of this superficial similarity of criticisms, one could insist that the mere continuation and extension of trends long recognized as modern (Beckford 1996, 34) fairly demand a more genuinely sociological analysis of church–state relations. If during the modern age simple social practices and small-scale patterns of human behaviour succumb to differentiation and institutional complexity, if broadly based social functions are incorporated into multipurpose arrangements with specialized parts, if cultural diversity abounds and fragmentation of identities ensues, if vast systems of social action render us ever more interdependent, and if old traditions are blurred but not obliterated under modernity, then every social scientist is now a modernist – or better, a commentator on modern matters. These types of sweeping changes, whether welcome or not, are exactly what sociology developed in the first instance to address. Declares Beckford (1992, 12), 'It is virtually a truism to say that all the formative contributions towards classical sociology were preoccupied with trying to understand modernity.'

With the spread of modernity arrived a process through which core meanings of religious belief and devotion are herded into the private sphere (Beyer 1990, 373–6). Nevertheless, 'there are certainly grounds for suggesting,' writes Beckford (1992, 16), 'that the anticipated privatization of religion is at least being paralleled by a process whereby religion is also becoming more publicly visible and controversial.' Thus, in its latter stages, modernity has fostered an attraction of popular attention to religion's remaining public presence in institutions like denominational organizations and especially in the state (Lyon 1996, 20–1). Yet law is not the sole social force (nor on many occasions the most powerful one) to constrain and channel their interaction. Still the contest of church and state for standing and influence in the present day unfolds in the open, where the very notion of 'religion' is subject to competing claims, and where indistinct boundaries between the two institutions often heighten the heat of conflict.

It makes little sense, however, for scholars of church and state in North America to recoil from the elevated temperature in this poorly insulated space purely to maintain in an unaltered condition definitions that were enacted to vindicate rights under law (Glendon 1991, esp. 14), and not to describe social reality as it already exists. In the prelude to their study of religion and politics in a mid-sized American city, N.J. Demerath III and Rhys H. Williams remark that, in addition to conforming to the letter of the law, legal conceptions of church and state emit a 'spirit' that 'is also haunting.' The result is that 'a wide range of customs and developments lurk around the edges of civic politics and religion like ghosts from the past and harbingers of the future. Finding them requires a search that goes beyond the law books themselves ...

Indeed, rather than restrict our attention to only those church-state
relations mentioned in constitutional legacy, we have sought out broader
issues not only of religion and politics but of culture and power'
(Demerath and Williams 1992a, 5, 7).

A more inclusive focus, such as that which Demerath and Williams
recommend, ought to lead to an entire series of what Beckford (1992, 11)
would term 'more sociologically interesting questions.' Another sociologist, Nancy T. Ammerman, obviously agrees with the newer habit of
viewing religion not through the lenses of prescriptive categories, but
alternatively as it presents itself in the everyday world: 'By asking new
questions about the popular, the embodied and practiced, we may see
our old answers in a whole new light. Rather than worrying about the
plausibility of religious ideas, we may ask ourselves about the presence
of an infrastructure for the distribution of religious goods. Rather than
worrying about the relationship between church and state, we may see
sacred and profane in non-institutional and less separated terms'
(Ammerman 1997d, 290; see also Ammerman 1997b).

NOTES

1 In fact, news accounts archived on the World Wide Web (Beatty 1997; Kines
   1997) reveal that Glen Clark conferred collectively with Canadian leaders of
   church and parachurch organizations at least once before, during the
   previous summer. An article in the evangelical publication *Christian Week*
   (Mackey 1997) reports positively on a meeting attended by Clark and
   approximately thirty religious representatives in Victoria, British Columbia,
   on 8 July 1997. A view of the same meeting from the perspective of Mam-
   mon (Palmer 1997) is less complimentary.
2 See, among other analyses: Beyer (1997, 273, 278–9, 286); Doyle (1984b,
   416–7); Grant (1988b, 85–100, 135–51, 233–4); Handy (1976, 245–8); Kenney
   (1933, 443); Moir (1959, 27–81; 1968); Mol (1985, 214); Norman (1968, 9,
   48–74); O'Toole (1982, 183–5); and Westfall (1989, 82–6).
3 Comparable language appeared in succeeding militia laws, including those
   passed in the united Canadas in 1841 and 1855, and the new dominion's
   Militia and Defence Act of 1868 (see Ens 1994, 38, 47n4, 172; Epp 1974, 193,
   367; Francis 1955, 46; Janzen 1990, 164–5).
4 The Canadian government conferred a similar range of accommodations on
   other militantly pacifistic sects, such as the Doukhobors, who ventured
   from Russia to Saskatchewan, and then to the interior of British Columbia

(Handy 1976, 373–4; Janzen 1990, esp. 10–12, 166; Mol 1985, 107–8); and the Hutterites, who sojourned through central Europe to North America before settling in colonies across the prairies on both sides of the Canadian–American border (Handy 1976, 373; Janzen 1990, 166; Mol 1985, 93–7).

5 Howard Palmer (1990) furnishes a similar explanation for the reception that met American members of the Church of Jesus Christ of Latter-day Saints (Mormons) who migrated to southern Alberta beginning in 1887. 'Mormons were not the first persecuted religious minority seeking asylum,' writes Palmer (1990, 109), and with such prior groups as the Mennonites 'the federal government had already shown it was willing to have a pluralistic West to achieve its goals.'

Federal authorities greeted the Mormons, some of whom were fugitives from American justice for having contracted plural marriages south of the border, with enthusiasm. In particular, Canada valued these immigrants for their fluency in spoken English, for their reputation for sobriety and industry, and most of all for their knowledge of hydraulics that they could call upon to irrigate the semi-arid Canadian soil as they had their old farms in Utah and the rest of the Intermountain West (Palmer 1990, 110–17). Reports of local journalists and visiting inspectors glowed with compliments about how the Latter-day Saints could 'convert [a] barren soil into one of fruitfulness' because they 'thoroughly understand prairie farming.' They were, claimed a vice-president of the Canadian Pacific Railway, 'the most efficient colonizing instruments on the continent' (quoted in Palmer 1990, 119, 111).

6 Ironically, passage in Manitoba of two 'patriotic' laws would contribute to a partial exodus of the province's Mennonite population to Latin America (Handy 1976, 373; Mol 1985, 91). The Manitoba Flag Act of 1908 ordered schools to fly over their grounds the Union Jack – 'a military banner' in the eyes of many Mennonites (quoted in Loewen 1993, 246; cf Francis 1955, 174–6). The School Attendance Act of 1916 required those same institutions to employ English as their language of instruction (Francis 1955, 183–6).

Throughout the 1920s, approximately six thousand Canadian Mennonites departed for new homes in Mexico and Paraguay (Francis 1955, 187–8; Janzen 1990, 3, 98; Loewen 1993, 247).

7 The best biography of this extraordinary Canadian, with consideration of both the political and the cultural angles of his work, is by the literary scholar Sandra Djwa (1987).

8 Elsewhere (Christiano 1989, 1994), I have attempted to assess the political advancement as well as the threats to Canadian stability that flowed from Pierre Trudeau's support for a legal philosophy of liberal individualism. Also consult the contribution by George Egerton in this volume.

chapter five

Trudeau, God, and the Canadian Constitution: Religion, Human Rights, and Government Authority in the Making of the 1982 Constitution

GEORGE EGERTON

Whereas Canada is founded upon principles that recognize the supremacy of God and the rule of law ...

Preamble to the Canadian Charter of Rights and Freedoms, 1982

I don't think God gives a damn whether he's in the constitution or not.

Pierre Trudeau, Liberal Caucus, April 1981

In the settlement of 1982, which saw the success of Prime Minister Pierre Trudeau's program to patriate the Canadian Constitution with a Charter of Rights and Freedoms, thereby bringing to an end the anomaly of Britain's long-term, reluctant custody of the British North America (BNA) Act, the Charter contained the brief confessional preamble, 'Whereas Canada is founded upon principles that recognize the supremacy of God and the rule of law.' By including this divine referent, Canada joined a group of some forty other states whose constitutions make an explicit acknowledgment of God, Allah, or the Creator ('Constitution Finder' 1998).[1] Moreover, this marked some constitutional innovation for Canada, in that the BNA Act had no reference to God, neither did the unwritten British constitution, nor the American – although the royal title stipulated rule 'by the Grace of God,' and the royal motto was *Dieu et Mon Droit*, while the authors of the American Declaration of Independence proclaimed as self-evident truths that all men are 'endowed by their Creator with certain unalienable Rights' and appealed to the 'Supreme Judge of the world,' while proceeding 'with a firm reliance on divine Providence.' Canada's motto, *A Mare usque ad Mare*, after Psalm 72, 'He shall have dominion also from sea to sea,' expressed the religious sentiments of Leonard Tilley and other Fathers of Confederation.

It is doubtful if the Canadian political elites of 1982 were as firm as the patriarchs of 1867 in their devotion to the supremacy of God. Indeed, the language of the preamble seemed somewhat anachronistic in an increasingly secular age that had witnessed the retrenchment of religion in public life, and where Trudeau and his constitutional advisers had started out with the intention to separate politics from religion.[2] Trudeau's views on this issue were clearly expressed in the *Globe and Mail* of 25 April 1981, which quoted the prime minister as stating that he thought it 'strange, so long after the Middle Ages that some politicians felt obliged to mention God in a constitution which is, after all, a secular and not a spiritual document' (p. 12).

F.R. Scott, famed Dean of Law at McGill University and, as Canada's foremost constitutional scholar, mentor to Trudeau, argued in his *Essays on the Constitution* (1977, ix) that changing a constitution 'confronts a society with the most important choices, for in the constitution will be found the philosophical principles and rules which largely determine the relations of the individual and cultural groups to one another and to the state.' It is the intention of this chapter to examine the philosophical principles contending in the political process and discourse leading to the patriation of the Canadian Constitution in 1982. The analysis focuses on the dialectic of religion and politics in both formal and informal constitutional debate, as Canadians attempted to identify and legislate the fundamental principles, values, rights, institutions, and procedures by which they wished to be governed. It is argued that the records generated by constitutional debates and decisions, and especially the seminally important quest to define and constitutionally entrench human rights, illuminate most clearly the historic shifting in Canada from a Christian to a post-Christian political culture – with the secularization of the state and privatization of religion as favoured by the liberal-pluralist jurisprudence of Pierre Trudeau.[3]

Although the analysis is informed by sociological theories of secularization, the approach is historical, privileging the roles and intentionality of major actors while attempting to describe and explain why things happened the way they did in changing circumstances.

God first received statutory status in Canadian legislation in the preamble to the Canadian Bill of Rights, which was passed under the

Diefenbaker government in 1960:

> The Parliament of Canada, affirming that the Canadian Nation is founded
> upon principles that acknowledge the supremacy of God, the dignity and
> worth of the human person and the position of the family in a society of
> free men and free institutions;
>   Affirming also that men and institutions remain free only when free-
> dom is founded upon respect for moral and spiritual values and the rule of
> law;
>   And being desirous of enshrining these principles and the human rights
> and fundamental freedoms derived from them, in a Bill of Rights ...

This brief preamble both signifies many elements in the historical
relationship of religion and politics in Canadian history and indicates
salient themes for the future. It had been more than a century since the
Canadian pattern of church–state relations had been settled, with the
Anglicans losing the struggle for establishment over the endowments
of the clergy reserves. Although the Canadian church–state relationship
was distinct from the separationist model of America, the establish-
mentarianism of England, and secularism of republican France, what
the retreat from state confessionalism amounted to was a quasi-establishment of the major denominations, or 'national churches,' which, in
the Canadian experience, included Roman Catholicism. Despite the
differences in the formal constitutional patterns of Britain, America,
and Canada, viewed in larger perspective the historical development of
relationships between politics and religion in these countries showed
more significant similarities than differences. As Edward Norman (1968)
has argued, Britain and the United States, together with the British
North American provinces, despite differences in chronology, were
undergoing similar social and cultural transformations, which resulted
by the mid-nineteenth century in basically similar revisions in church–
state relations. Denominational pluralism had made the working of an
exclusive national church establishment and endowment politically
impossible, in Britain as well as in America. The religiosity of the
peoples of these countries, however, guaranteed that the concept of a
state completely neutral in religious matters, or strictly secular as in
French republican theory, had but negligible support. What evolved in
each of these political cultures was a rather anomalous, but nevertheless popular and durable, constitutional mixture of vestigial state
confessionalism and religious denominationalism.

In the British North American provinces, where disestablishment occurred informally rather than constitutionally, the remaining linkages between church and state remained strong, reflecting the hegemonic Christian pluralism of Canada's religious demography. In its relationship with the state, the dominant function of denominational religion in Canada, Protestant and Catholic, has been 'priestly': to legitimate governmental authority and law, while serving as chaplain to public institutions. A secondary function has been the 'prophetic' call for moral reform and social justice, finding its most passionate expressions in temperance crusades and in the social gospel movement of the 1920s.

If the inequities of capitalism inspired the prophets of the League for Social Reconstruction, Catholic cooperative movements, and the social democratic Co-operative Commonwealth Federation (CCF), the two world wars of the twentieth century and the following cold war, evoked and reinforced the priestly functions of Canadian religion, while maintaining the vision held by both religious and political elites of Canada as a Christian, liberal democracy.[4] The struggles against Fascism, Nazism, and Communism could therefore be portrayed by these elites as just crusades in defence of Christian and democratic values.

Equally, Canadian participation in post-1945 attempts to define and protect human rights, both internationally in the United Nations Universal Declaration of Human Rights of 1948, and domestically in the several parliamentary committees set up under Prime Ministers Mackenzie King and Louis St Laurent (Parliament 1948; Senate 1950), always manifestly grounded human rights in a religious framework. Protestant human rights spokesmen reflected the teachings of the World Council of Churches (1949, 93–9), while their Catholic counterparts mirrored the Thomist tradition of natural law communicated in papal and episcopal documents (Arès 1948, 1949a, 1949b, 1949c).[5] The parliamentary committee drafting the Diefenbaker Bill of Rights had seen powerful transdenominational consensus behind the religious confessionalism of its preamble, with Catholic Liberals such as Paul Martin, Catholic Conservatives Noel Dorion, Paul Martineau, and Justice Minister Fulton, and Baptist John Diefenbaker agreeing as they had on few other issues (Fulton 1983; Commons 1960).

The Canadian Bill of Rights, despite the hopes of Mr Diefenbaker and his supporters, did not mark a watershed in Canadian jurisprudence, as few substantial human rights cases came under its purview. Nor did the declared 'supremacy of God' herald a new era of faith in Canadian society. Indeed, as of 1960 Canadian jurisprudence and religiosity were on the verge of several decades of radical change that would transform the status and functions of religion in Canadian political culture (see Bibby 1987, 1993). From our vantage point at the end of the century, we can see that the 'religious revival' of the postwar era was but a temporary respite and brief counter-trend to the deeper cultural and social correlates of late modernity. The language used by political and religious leaders leading to constitutional recognition of the supremacy of God as the foundation for state authority and human rights would soon be widely viewed as triumphalist, exclusivist, and patriarchal, if not worse, in a culture of liberal pluralism. By the time that God would return to haunt the renewed Canadian constitutional discourse directed by Pierre Trudeau as justice minister and then prime minister after 1968, Canadian public life and rhetoric would be in a process of rapid secularization – which, in the context of Canadian cultural tradition, meant de-Christianization.

The larger dimensions of this story can but be alluded to in this chapter. Certainly, the Canadian experience forms part of a process of modernization shared with, and influenced by, Britain, the United States, and all industrialized societies. From Britain came the recommendations of the Wolfenden Report (Great Britain, Parliament 1957)[6] – that criminality and morality should be separated in such matters as homosexuality and prostitution and that the state should confine itself to the proscription and punishment of behaviour that was manifestly harmful to society, while protecting the freedom of the individual, even if the choices indulged socially harmless 'sinning.' These themes would spark a profound debate in jurisprudence on the proper relations of religion, morality, and law, a debate that attracted powerful antagonists in both Britain and the United States, most notably Professor H.L.A. Hart (1963) and Lord Patrick Devlin (1965; also see Mitchell 1967). Canadian legal journals addressed the new criminology, while the philosophy of the Wolfenden Report found a sympathetic hearing in liberal Canadian quarters.[7]

Concurrently, from the United States the integration of politics and religion was most clearly challenged by a series of Supreme Court decisions that asserted a strict wall of separation between church and state in matters of public education. In the benchmark decisions of *Engel* v *Vitale* (1962) and *Abington School District* v *Schempp* (1963), the Court ruled that the First Amendment's proscription of the establishment of religion extended to laws instituting public prayers and devotional Bible readings in public schools. The judicial activism of the Supreme

Court, most notable in the 1973 decision of *Roe* v *Wade* legalizing abortion, alienated and mobilized the Protestant religious right and Catholicism, while the Vietnam War and the nuclear arms race estranged many on the religious left from government, drawing them into the peace movement. Concurrently, the civil rights struggle for racial justice politically mobilized African American Christians in alignment with the mainline religious left. The previously benevolent church–state relationship would be turned into a battle zone of bitter cultural warfare, with human rights often framing the agenda and rhetoric for conflict.

While these radical transitions in jurisprudence received earlier and more heightened philosophical delineation in Great Britain and the United States, the Canadian experience has had the special merit of coinciding with the making of a new constitution – a project that focused in large measure on the question of protecting human rights. The Canadian constitutional drama, moreover, was driven by a philosopher-king, Pierre Trudeau who, as prime minister after 1968, made the constitutional entrenchment of a charter of rights his own political mission, seeing it through to success in the constitutional settlement of 1982.

When in 1967 Trudeau became justice minister in the Liberal government of Lester B. Pearson, the concurrent celebrations marking the centennial year of the Canadian confederation were troubled, at least latently, by a diffuse sense of social malaise as to national purpose and identity. With the crises of the Great Depression and war receding into generational memory in an era of unprecedented prosperity and comparative international détente, the country found itself faced with not only the manifest challenge of resurgent Québécois nationalism but also a 'Quiet Revolution' that was eager to challenge the traditional cultural privileging of religion well beyond Quebec Catholicism. In the germinating legitimation crisis, which attended the drift, scandals, and confusions of the last years of the Pearson government, it was the genius of Trudeau's politics to project updated themes of classic liberal ideology: federalism to confront the separatist aspirations of Quebec nationalism; pluralism to accommodate and contain cultural assertion and ideological conflict; civil libertarianism to enshrine protection for individual rights in a revised constitution; and secularism to disentangle a modernized Canadian legal order from its religious constraints. Each of these themes resonated with Canadian mass culture in the latter half of the 1960s, and appealed deeply to academic, cultural, and media elites, offering renewed government purpose and legitimation while at the same time rejuvenating the Liberal party.

When the project to modernize Canadian law and liberate it from its religious framework addressed itself first to divorce legislation, Trudeau instructed Parliament on the seminal themes of the new jurisprudence: 'We are now living in a social climate in which people are beginning to realize, perhaps for the first time in the history of this country, that we are not entitled to impose the concepts which belong to a sacred society upon a civil or profane society. The concepts of the civil society in which we live are pluralistic, and I think this parliament realizes that it would be a mistake for us to try to legislate into this society concepts which belong to a theological or sacred order' (Commons 1967, 5083).

It is clear that while Trudeau's principal political engagement was to renew the constitutional bases of federalism to contain Quebec nationalism, this political struggle was fought within a sophisticated philosophical and ideological framework that entailed radically altered relationships between religion and politics. Educated in the classical college system of Catholic Quebec, Trudeau, although personally retaining a privatized and modernized Catholicism, rebelled against the religio-politico nexus of the Duplessis era which he saw as corruptive of both the personal faith of Catholics and the cultural and political life of Quebec. In his polemical and theoretical writings of the 1950s, Trudeau was animated principally by the quest to bring the classic themes of Enlightenment thinking and British liberal theory to the retrograde political atmosphere of Quebec (Trudeau 1970).[8] Central to this engagement was the argument that government authority could no longer be legitimated by reference to the now thoroughly corrupted natural law framework of traditional Quebec Catholic political theory. Trudeau's conception of a civil society based on the sovereignty of the rational individual, possessing 'inalienable rights, over and above capital, the nation, tradition, the Church, and even the State' (Trudeau 1970, 205), contrasted sharply with the dominant, if latent, conservatism, statism, and regionalism of Canadian tradition. It also marked a radical departure from the traditional Liberal conception of Canada as a Christian society.

That the rights and freedoms of the individual would provide the animus for a comprehensive modernization and liberalization of Canadian law was evident not only in Trudeau's approach to the issue of divorce law, but also in the initiatives he undertook regarding other 'morality' issues, such as lotteries, birth control, homosexuality and deviant sexual behaviour, and abortion – all of which contained potentially explosive intersections of religious and legal principles. After legal study of several of these issues within the Justice Department, and after comprehensive public hearings on the issues of birth control and abortion conducted by the House of Commons Standing Committee on Health and Welfare, Trudeau combined these morality issues with a series of other changes in the criminal law code into an Omnibus Bill which was given first reading in the Commons on 21 December 1967.

By the time the Omnibus Bill was passed in 1969, Trudeau had captured the leadership of the Liberal party and led it to electoral triumph in 1968, assisted by the powerful, if transient, appeal of 'Trudeaumania.' The political and religious discourse generated by the divorce and omnibus bills demonstrated that the traditional Canadian church–state relationship was being fundamentally altered. The prime minister, in appealing explicitly to replace 'theology' with 'intelligence' in politics (Head 1972, v), and, as the *Globe and Mail* reported on 22 December 1967, to get the state out of the bedrooms of the nation, not only struck a sympathetic chord with public opinion, he also received the eager support of the mainline Protestant church leaders for liberalization of laws governing birth control and abortion (Commons 1966–8), as well as divorce (Parliament 1966–7; see also Commons 1967–9, Omnibus Bill). Justice Minister John Turner repeatedly appealed to the principles of jurisprudence deriving from the Wolfenden Report in advocating separation of the spheres of crime from sin, thereby widening the realm of private liberty and moral choice (Commons 1969a, 4723; Commons 1969c, 171–3). Put sociologically, in face of cultural pluralism the Liberal government was facilitating a process of differentiation whereby religion would be divested of its former role as arbiter of public morals, with churches being transformed from the 'conscience of the nation' to privatized suppliers of spiritual services to consumers.[9]

While the mainline Protestant church hierarchies were seemingly eager to adapt to the rules of pluralism and privatization, and give support to the new jurisprudence, Catholic and evangelical church representatives were troubled by the separation of Christian morality and law. Catholic spokesmen were willing to make the distinction between the morality that would be required of the faithful and legislation 'for the common good' on such issues as birth control and divorce. When it came to abortion, however, the bishops refused to make this distinction and opposed any legislation that did not protect human life from conception onward. Liberal Catholic legislators, including John Turner (1993), nevertheless claimed the freedom to legislate for the common good on this issue as well, even as they remained personally opposed to abortion.

In these seminal political debates, the voice of traditional Christian morality and jurisprudence no longer was expressed by the elites of the major national parties. From the Conservative side it was left to Walter Dinsdale, Salvation Army officer and MP from Brandon-Souris, Manitoba, to articulate the minority views of evangelical Protestantism, while traditional Quebec Catholicism could no longer speak through the Liberal party, having to rely for expression on the Créditistes. It was Léonel Beaudoin, Créditiste member from Richmond, Quebec, who spelled out the opposition of the Catholic bishops to the abortion legislation before Parliament (Commons 1969b, 5402–70).

If traditional religion was recessing to the private domain before the liberal pluralism of Trudeau's jurisprudence, God's name was still invoked in the prayers that opened each day of Parliament's business. God was also added, in 1967, to the revised version of 'O Canada!' and called upon to 'keep our land glorious and free!'[10] God remained supreme but largely ignored in the Diefenbaker Bill of Rights, while the cause of human rights was advanced as the federal government and most of the provinces adopted human rights codes and established human rights commissions during the 1960s and 1970s. As well, Canada's ratifications of the International Covenant on Civil and Political Rights (together with its Optional Protocol) and the International Covenant on Economic, Social, and Cultural Rights went into force in 1976, while the government joined in other U.N. ventures to define and defend human rights concerning children, women, minorities, and refugees. The Law Reform Commission, established in 1971 by Justice Minister Turner, undertook a series of extensive studies scouting the terrain of a new liberal-pluralist jurisprudence. It remained to see how God would fare in the prime minister's long-standing passion to entrench a Charter of Rights in the patriated Canadian Constitution.

A friend and protege of F.R. Scott, Trudeau had advocated a constitutionally entrenched charter of rights from the early 1960s (Trudeau 1965b, 371–93),[11] as attempts at constitutional innovation had deadlocked repeatedly on the central dilemma of provincial agreement to an amending formula, despite the near successes of Justice Ministers Fulton and Guy Favreau. It would be the amending formula again which frustrated the first Trudeau round of constitutional conferences, when Premier Bourassa removed Quebec's support for the Victoria Accord of 1971. The constitutional proposals for an entrenched charter generated by Trudeau and his advisers contained no religious or divine referent, but rather expressed the core themes of liberal pluralism that the protection of human rights and freedoms represented the fundamental purpose of democratic government and that 'individual fulfilment is the fundamental goal of society' (Canadian Intergovernmental Conference Secretariat 1969, 4–6). The election of the Parti Québécois in 1976 with a sovereigntist agenda rekindled the constitutional crisis, as Canadians awaited the referendum promised by Premier René Lévesque, while Trudeau and the provincial premiers engaged in a renewed, complex series of constitutional manoeuvres.

Trudeau's invocation of the War Measures Act in October 1970 to suppress separatist terrorism in Quebec both demonstrated the perceived fragility of state authority and shocked civil libertarians that one of their own would go so far. If Trudeau's determined leadership had contained the legitimation crisis of Canadian liberalism, clearly by the time of the defeat of the Liberal government in 1979, followed by the brief Conservative interregnum under Joe Clark, the foundations of the Canadian federation were again facing fundamental challenge. Trudeau's seeming resurrection in 1980, after his announced retirement, and the subsequent Liberal election victory of February that year, followed by the defeat of Lévesque's proposed sovereignty-association in the Quebec referendum a few months later, in May 1980, served to refuel the constitutional flame. The result, after further tortuous failed negotiations with the provinces, was the unilateral federalist constitutional resolution launched by Trudeau in October 1980, which entailed a final British amendment of the BNA Act and patriation with an amending formula and an entrenched charter of rights. There then followed a year filled with further constitutional manoeuvring, appeals to the courts, committee hearings, parliamentary confrontation, culminating in the brilliant, if machiavellian, success of the prime minister in breaking up the premiers' 'gang of eight,' isolating Lévesque, and then committing the English-speaking premiers to the constitutional package of 5 November 1981. Patriation of the Canadian Constitution, with its amending formula and entrenched Charter of Rights and Freedoms, would follow in April 1982, after a final act passed by the British Parliament.

In the all-absorbing constitutional struggles that engulfed Canadian politics through 1980–2, the question of God's standing in the document seemed a relatively minor issue compared with the central place in the constitutional discourse played by such themes as the amending formula, the provincial–federal division of jurisdictions, the language guarantees, the asymmetry of Quebec's status, and the rights claimed by lobbies representing women and Aboriginal peoples. Trudeau's constitutional draft of June 1980, perhaps anticipating the salience of this point with restive religious conservatives, asserted in its preamble that the Canadian people 'shall always be, with the help of God, a free and self-governing people.' But this symbolic allusion to God disappeared, along with the draft preamble, in the unsuccessful bargaining with the premiers in September which, in turn, resulted in the government's constitutional resolution of October 1980.

The government, under criticism for its unilateralist challenge, had referred its October resolution for hurried study to a Joint Committee of the Senate and the House of Commons, chaired by Liberal Senator Harry Hays and Serge Joyal, Liberal MP from Montreal, while dissident premiers attempted to halt Trudeau's agenda by testing its legality in several provincial courts. It was in the intensive hearings of the Hays-Joyal Committee that religious questions returned to constitutional discourse as, along with the criticisms mobilized by civil libertarian, Native, and women's groups, the religious lobbies also made their opinions known, while the Conservative members of the committee were given a major opening to redress the 'Godlessness' of the Liberals' proposed charter (Parliament 1981).

Catholic leaders worried that the draft charter's concentration on individual rights could diminish group rights, particularly the rights enjoyed in several provinces to publicly funded confessional schools whose trustees could maintain Catholic teaching and discipline. Moreover, the amending formula might allow denominational school rights to be removed from constitutional protection by a simple majority in a referendum.[12] Liberal member of the committee Bryce Mackasey responded by repeating the government's emphatic assurances that the charter would not in any way diminish the rights of denominational schools (Parliament 1981, session 19, 4 December 1980). Catholic bishops and pro-life groups were concerned also that the Charter failed to give adequate protection to the unborn and would be used by pro-choice groups and the courts to widen grounds for abortion. When government leaders pledged that the Charter would not be construed as diminishing existing restrictions, Cardinal Emmett Carter, as reported in the *Globe and Mail* on 25 April 1981, dropped his opposition to the Charter, 'though [he was] still not satisfied with the protection accorded the unborn' (p. 7).

The submissions and witnesses from the Protestant mainline denominations gave their strong support to protection of human rights in the Charter, but were anxious to see its provisions extended to cover the concerns of civil libertarians, Native peoples, and women. Clarke MacDonald, moderator of the United Church, emphasized the justice themes that were the central concerns of his church in the constitutional struggle, underlining the church's support for Aboriginal peoples and workers, and stressing the rights of all minorities, including the right of Quebec to self-determination. He also recommended the inclusion of 'sexual orientation' in the list of categories to be protected by the Charter against discrimination (Parliament 1981, session 29, 18 December 1980). Anglican Primate Edward Scott also gave priority to the protection of Native people's rights, while speaking of the grounding of Canadian values and human rights in God who, as creator and sustainer, had made all people in His own image. Scott called for a consensual rather than an imposed, unilateral process of constitutional change, thereby allowing for a new era of justice for all of Canada's marginalized peoples (Parliament 1981, session 33, 7 January 1981).

The Anglican and United Church briefs shared a positive approach to the pluralist jurisprudence of the Liberals, while pressing to extend rights and entitlements for the underprivileged as the principal justice issue. Neither of the official briefs suggested that a reference to God should be restored or included in the Charter's preamble (Parliament 1981, session 57, 13 February 1981).[13] The Conservative members on the committee knew, however, that this issue was emerging as central to the concerns of evangelical Christian communities across Canada. Jake Epp, Conservative MP for Provencher, Manitoba, and Conservative constitutional critic, queried Scott and MacDonald whether they favoured a reference to God in the Charter's preamble. Both Protestant leaders responded positively, if reservedly; moreover, they made it clear that this was their personal choice, not the official position of their churches.

Beyond the Catholic and Protestant mainline churches, another religious constituency was emerging quickly by the time of the Hays-Joyal hearings – a loose coalition of evangelical, fundamentalist, and pentecostal Christians, drawn mainly from evangelical denominations, but also from the evangelical and charismatic (or neo-pentecostal) sections of the mainline churches. For some time these religious communities had sensed increasing estrangement from Canadian political culture as transformed in the secularist jurisprudence of the Trudeau era, while at the same time experiencing their peripheralization in the political and legal processes that had generated radical changes in the fields of divorce, family law, abortion, sexual permissiveness, public education, and human rights. They had also witnessed the emergence of the American 'new religious right' in the late 1970s and its powerful role in the election of Ronald Reagan as president in 1980.

Although there would be no equivalents to Jerry Falwell and his 'moral majority' in Canada, David Mainse, Pentecostal host of *700 Huntley Street*, had attracted a large national television following (*Faith Today* 1986, 58), while Ontario Baptist Ken Campbell had worked at building a Christian 'moderate majority' under the banner of 'Renaissance Canada.'[14] More politically significant was the emergence of the Evangelical Fellowship of Canada (EFC) as an effective and articulate lobby, embracing the spectrum of evangelical Christian Canadian churches, organizations, and believers. The EFC had been founded in the mid-1960s, but it was primarily the challenge of legal and constitutional revisions of the early 1980s that served to transform its leadership and role in Canadian public life (Stiller 1984; see also Stackhouse 1993).[15]

Through 1980–1, each of these Christian organizations would attempt to mobilize their constituencies: *Huntley Street* organized a cross-Canada tour culminating in a nationally televised 'Salute to Canada' on 20 June 1980, at which both Pierre Trudeau and Joe Clark addressed the country's spiritual heritage (Knowles 1982, 9–11);[16] Ken Campbell launched Renaissance Canada on a 'crusade for Faith, Freedom, and the Family'; while the EFC, along with these other organizations, pressed the government to honour Canada's Judaeo-Christian heritage. The principal objectives shared in the evangelical Christian agenda during the culmination of the constitutional struggle entailed seeking clear protection for the rights of religious believers and institutions, the traditional family, and the unborn. Most important, evangelical leaders were anxious to see an explicit reference to the supremacy of God stipulated in a preamble to the draft charter.

The Conservative members of the Hays-Joyal committee were happy to champion the items desired by evangelical Christians. Several of the Conservative members, especially Jake Epp, had close personal ties to the evangelical lobbies, while other Conservative members, such as David Crombie, were effective in portraying the religious concerns of the evangelicals in the context of traditional Conservative philosophy on government and human rights. Crombie argued that it was necessary to set out in a preamble the 'fundamental principles' that gave legitimacy to the specific rights to be included. A reference to God, the dignity inherent to the human person, and the moral and spiritual basis of law would make it clear that rights that derived from God, tradition, and history were merely 'affirmed' and maintained by governments – not 'given.' To affirm the privileged position of institutions such as the family and property would also provide guidance to subsequent rulings by courts and judges (Parliament 1981, session 41, 20 January 1981; session 43, 22 January 1981). It was Jake Epp who moved the amendments on 20 January 1981, which incorporated the principal evangelical themes. Epp did this by taking the language of the preamble to the Diefenbaker Bill of Rights and moving its insertion at the beginning of the new Charter:

> Affirming that the Canadian nation is founded upon principles that acknowledge the supremacy of God, the dignity and worth of the human person and the position of the family in a society of free individuals and free institutions,
>   Affirming also that individuals and institutions remain free only when freedom is founded upon respect for moral and spiritual values and the rule of law. (Parliament 1981, session 41, 20 January 1981; session 42, 21 January 1981; Epp 1981)

Svend Robinson, New Democratic Party MP from Burnaby, British Columbia, protested to the committee that such a preamble violated Canadians' right to 'freedom of conscience' and the essential 'respect for plurality' that had evolved in Canadian society since the 1960 Bill of Rights. For Robinson, who would soon emerge as Canada's leading gay politician, respect for pluralism meant that 'we do not entrench one particular religion; indeed we do not entrench any religion at all.' Robinson made it clear, however, that he was speaking personally, not giving the policy of the NDP on God. His NDP colleague, Catholic priest Bob Ogle, expressed NDP support for a constitutional reference to God, which would entail no disrespect for the rights of non-believers (Parliament 1981, session 42, 21 January 1981; Johnston 1981; Robinson 1981).[17]

Liberal leaders resented the Conservatives' attempt to pre-empt the high ground concerning a divine referent in the constitution. Robert Kaplan, solicitor general, explained again to the committee that the Liberals had included a reference to God in their original draft, but it was the premiers who were responsible for dropping the preamble. The present resolution and Charter represented just the first stage of constitutional renewal; once the constitution was patriated there would then be the necessary time to write fundamental Canadian values into a full preamble to the new constitution (Parliament 1981, session 41, 20 January 1981).[18] The Liberals therefore blocked the Conservative amendments, and the constitutional resolution in the committee's report to Parliament of 13 February (Parliament 1981, session 57) contained no preamble, nor any reference to God.

The political horse-trading on God deeply offended evangelical Christian leaders, who now rekindled their efforts. David Mainse of *Huntley Street* appealed to his television followers to join with other evangelicals in writing their MPs and government leaders to press for the reference to God, while Ken Campbell mounted a major newspaper campaign, taking out full-page ads in leading dailies.[19] Leaders of the Evangelical Fellowship of Canada directly petitioned the prime minister, making explicit their reasons for wanting a constitutional reference to God: 'The acknowledgement of one Supreme God to whom we as a nation are answerable gives ground for legislation bearing on all matters human. To omit any such reference only leaves the door open for substitution of other less worthy grounds – utilitarianism, naturalism, secularism, etc. – since legislation cannot escape growing out of presuppositions. Moreover, human rights though recognized by the state in a democratic society are a sacred endowment from God not bestowed but administered by the state. (Resolution 1981, 2)[20]

While Conservatives kept up their attack in Parliament against the Liberals' omission of God, there were several Liberals themselves who had close connections with the growing evangelical lobbies – notably Liberal Deputy House Leader David Smith, MP from Don Valley East; Garnet Bloomfield, MP for Middlesex, Ontario; and Senate Liberal Leader Ray Perrault from British Columbia. When the constitutional battle in Parliament culminated in April, David Smith (1981, 1982) assembled a brief for Trudeau and his key advisers that called for immediate Liberal action to restore the reference to God.[21] Smith's brief summarized polling and political reporting on the moral majority phenomenon in the United States, and demographic data on recent Canadian religious trends that held political salience. Beyond the figures on Canadian denominational affiliation and attendance, which compared the increase of conservative Christianity with the declining numbers of mainline churches, Smith underlined what he saw as the most significant trend for the future – the major numerical advantage that evangelical and pentecostal Bible schools and colleges had over the mainline seminaries in the training of students and leaders (Smith 1981, 3–4).[22] As well, Smith noted the remarkable new convergence of evangelical Protestantism and charismatic and traditionalist Catholicism in many points of theology, as well as political attitudes on such issues as abortion, drugs, homosexuality, and capital punishment. These religious and political reconfigurations broke with the old denominational barriers and political alignments; for instance, even on the 'French factor' and language issues, Smith believed that the theological convergence between evangelical Protestants and devout Roman Catholics could 'break down those ancient barriers.' Sharing basic beliefs with Catholics on such fundamental doctrines as the deity of Christ, the inspiration of the Bible, the virgin birth, and salvation, according to Smith, gave evangelical Protestants in this emerging coalition 'far greater common ground' with former religious enemies 'than with non-evangelical bleeding heart United Church activists worrying about California grapes, Noranda mines in Chile, abortion on demand and civil rights for gays' (Smith 1981, 1–7).

Smith identified the question of reference to God in the constitution as the foremost issue that concerned Canadian conservative Christians and their leaders:

- This is virtually an 'instant' issue but it is so simple and straightforward that quite frankly it is the *only* aspect of the Constitutional debate some evangelicals understand
- Many view our reaction to it as a litmus paper test on whether our collective leadership, but particularly the P.M., place a high value on spiritual matters and are prepared to recognize the sovereignty of God
- To evangelicals the *only* position that is satisfactory is *inclusion*
- There are no explanations for its' [*sic*] exclusion that will wash, particularly blaming the premiers
- In fact at the 1st Ministers' conference in Sept. none of them referred to or objected to the inclusion of God in the draft preamble. Quebec didn't like the preamble for other reasons. No one in Canada is convinced we care too much about what the gang of 8 think about anything and they don't really believe us when we try to pin this one on them. (Smith 1981, 5)

Smith's recommended 'Strategy for Improved Rapport between

'Evangelicals' and the Government' warned that if the Liberals failed to put God in the constitution, they would 'pay for this politically for years' (Smith 1981, 8).[23]

The political considerations raised by David Smith and other Christian Liberals were convincing for the prime minister (Smith 1982),[24] and the Liberals inserted their own reference to God in the amendments to the draft constitution which went through the Commons on 23 April, and the Senate the next day. The Conservatives voted against the Liberal amendments, prompting Trudeau's criticism that they were 'hypocritical and detestable' for playing politics with God, and claiming that they were inspired more by fear of the electorate than fear of God. Although, as noted, Trudeau thought it strange 'so long after the Middle Ages that some politicians felt obliged to mention God in a constitution which is, after all, a secular and not a spiritual document,' he also genuflected to the electorate, claiming, as reported in the *Globe and Mail* of 25 April 1981, that it was his personal preference to include the reference. Privately, Trudeau told the Liberal caucus that he did not think 'God gives a damn whether he was in the constitution or not' (Smith 1982).

The Canadian Charter of Rights and Freedoms would henceforth include the following preamble: 'Whereas Canada is founded upon principles that recognize the supremacy of God and the rule of law.' This would remain through the dramatic events of the fall of 1981, when the Supreme Court made its ruling on the constitutionality of the government's unilateral strategy, and as Trudeau, in early November, was successful in seducing René Lévesque away from the 'gang of eight' with the offer of a constitutional referendum, then abandoning him once the other premiers were drawn into support of the compromise resolution that would go to the British Parliament in December. The patriated constitutional would then receive royal proclamation when Queen Elizabeth II visited Ottawa for a signing ceremony on 17 April 1982, held on Parliament Hill. Canada thereby joined the group of states whose constitutions have paid homage to God. What does this signify to us with regard to the religious dimension of the constitutional struggle and, more broadly, the relations of church and state in late-twentieth-century Canadian political culture?

At first glance, the inclusion of the reference to God represented a signal success for the evangelical Christian lobbyists, working effectively through sympathetic parliamentarians, especially David Smith and Jake Epp, and demonstrating an ability to mobilize impressive public support. Jean Chrétien would claim that the government received more mail on this issue than any other (Commons 1981, 9938; Page 1993b).[25] Without this mobilization there would have been no 'sacred canopy' (Berger 1967), however small, erected over the new constitution. The brief confessional preamble also erected a barrier against future pressures, feared by conservative Christians, to remove all public functions and privileges of religion in the construction of a completely secular state.[26] Subsequently, the Evangelical Fellowship of Canada, under the energetic leadership of its new executive director, Brian Stiller, would be developed into a highly effective ecumenical Christian agency for monitoring Canadian public life, assisting evangelicals in understanding the religious dimensions of current events, and representing the interests and values of its constituency before legislatures, courts, and the media.

The constitutional success, however, did not mean that the deeper cultural tides of de-Christianization or secularization had been reversed or that the traditional role of religion in Canadian political history had been restored.[27] The constitutional reference to God had come as a result of tactical political calculations, not from any conversion on the part of Trudeau or the Liberals to the philosophical or theological convictions expressed by Conservatives such as Jake Epp and David Crombie, let alone the Evangelical Fellowship of Canada. If Trudeau's desire to remove theology from politics had suffered a temporary reverse, the Charter itself would serve to launch a new era of liberal-pluralist jurisprudence in Canadian political culture. Indeed, similar to the patterns of jurisprudence through the post-1960s decades in Britain and the United States, the Canadian church–state relationship would be transformed as the Christian religion would see the state largely divest itself of religion's traditional 'priestly' functions of legitimating government authority and law, and delineating national purpose.

The story recounted in this essay, then, confirms central themes in sociological theory of secularization: differentiation and specialization of social and cultural institutions in industrialized, modernized states; diminished social and cultural salience for traditional religious institutions; privatization of religious belief and behaviour; pluralization of religious values; attenuated religious belief, affiliation, and participation; and religious competition with ideological rivals – notably liberal pluralism in the experience of English-speaking Canada. Indeed the ideology of liberal pluralism has supplanted traditional religion in defining public purpose for political and legal institutions, while the courts, in many ways, have replaced the church as 'the conscience of the nation.'

What are the principal elements and dynamics of Canadian liberal-pluralist ideology? As this chapter has suggested, these can be identified most clearly in the modernization of Canadian law on divorce, sexual behaviour, and abortion directed by Trudeau as justice minister, and in the constitutional discourse which culminated with his victory, as prime minister, in the Charter and settlement of 1982. Although Trudeau's ideas owed much to his wide-ranging studies in European, British, and American political theory, it was his genius to refract the classic liberal tradition to serve the vision of a modernized Canadian constitution and polity. It was a vision of democratic citizenship in a state that gave priority to protection of the freedom and rights of the individual, in a federalist constitutional order that mediated the relationships among a plurality of individuals, social groups, and institutions. Although Canadian liberal-pluralism in the 1960s would make major attempts to accommodate bilingualism and biculturalism (and soon multiculturalism), as the previous religious dualism of Catholicism-Protestantism gave way to secular distinctions of language and culture, for Trudeau the rights and freedoms of the individual always deserved priority over the rights of any group – whether based on religion, ethnicity, province, region, class, or sex. And it was in the protection of human rights and legal order, with a vastly expanded jurisdiction for the courts and human rights tribunals, that modern democratic government found its principal purpose and legitimation.

The ideology of liberal pluralism has attracted much powerful support from the elites of Canadian political culture: the major federal political parties; the media; the arts and entertainment sectors; the professional organizations, notably the Canadian Bar Association, the Canadian Medical Association, and provincial teachers' organizations; the students and university intelligentsia of English-speaking Canada; the feminist lobbies; and the principal labour organizations. The voices of mainstream liberal Protestantism have also given full blessing to liberal-pluralism, bilingualism, multiculturalism, and human rights; and the various pollings and analyses of core Canadian values demonstrate wide-ranging popular support (see Sniderman 1988).[28]

This ideological and social conversion of Canadians to liberal-pluralism has not, however, been without impediments and contradictions. Even in English-speaking Canada, studies and polling of Canadian political attitudes in the 1990s indicate comparatively high levels of dissatisfaction with political institutions, together with an unwillingness to accord ruling elites much by way of honour, respect, or even legitimacy. This was a central finding in 1991 of the Citizens' Forum on Canada's Future, chaired by Keith Spicer, which captured the bitterness and disunity of Canadians after the failure of the Meech Lake Accord (Citizens' Forum 1991). The comprehensive defeat of the Charlottetown Accord in the October 1992 referendum, despite its endorsement by federal and provincial political governments and elites, also seemed to indicate a pervasive malaise in Canada regarding its governmental institutions, processes, and leadership – in other words, a continuing legitimation crisis.

Moreover, liberal-pluralism's warmest champions among the political lobbies for feminists, Aboriginal peoples, gays, immigrants, educators, artists, and civil libertarians generate strains on the capacity of governments to grant and arbitrate inflating claims for rights. The shared values necessary to the maintenance of communal identities and national purpose tend to erode in the competition for ever-expanding entitlements.

The principal ideological and political challenge to the dominant liberal-pluralism of the Canadian federation has been Québécois nationalism. Indeed, it was the challenge of this nationalism that first evoked the Liberal response of bilingualism and biculturalism, and thrust Trudeau into his role as champion of liberal-pluralist federalism against what he labelled the new 'tribalism.' The enduring appeal of the sovereigntist idea to Québécois through several failed constitutional accords and referenda has served not only to demonstrate the degree to which nationalism has supplanted Catholicism as the source of Québécois collective identity, but also how the concurrent de-Christianization of the Canadian state has compounded the dilemmas of Canadian unity – as the Christian religion was one of the few bridges that traversed the two solitudes. In 1995 the Canadian state would survive another referendum on sovereignty in Quebec. But the narrow margin of support for federalism further eroded confidence in the resources of government and political leaders. It remains to be seen whether the ideology of liberal-pluralism will continue to generate sufficient political legitimation to sustain the Canadian state through future challenges of Québécois nationalism.

The capacity of modern democratic governments to perform successfully without religious legitimations has a very brief and untested history. Equally, it remains to be seen if religion will remain within the peripheralized and privatized spheres assigned to it in liberal-pluralist jurisprudence. If the mainline national churches of Canada have been demographically diminished and politically marginalized, the reconfigurations and realignments of religious conservatives from Protestantism, Catholicism, Pentecostalism, and Orthodoxy, in Canada and internationally, perhaps herald something new in church–state relations for the next millennium.

NOTES

1 In a listing of some 130 contemporary state constitutions, 40 make an explicit reference to God or the Creator ('Constitution Finder' 1998).
2 For Trudeau's early anti-clericalism and commitment to separating church and state, see Trudeau (1968b, xx).
3 Leading sources for the author's sociological theory of secularization would include Berger (1967), Wilson (1966), and Martin (1978). The definition of secularization used in this article, put briefly, would entail processes of both 'functional' and 'substantive' change that result in the decline in the social 'functions' for traditional religion (Christianity in Canada) through differentiation and specialization, and reduction of the cultural salience of religious ideas and belief.
4 For the role of Canadian churches in the Second World War, see Faulkner (1975).
5 Canada's policy on the Universal Declaration is documented in Department of Foreign Affairs (1991, 350–66).
6 The report was named after its chairman, Sir John Wolfenden.
7 For a traditionalist Catholic analysis of the forces generating change in Canadian jurisprudence, see de Valk (1974).
8 In a series of articles published during 1958 in *Vrai*, a journal edited by his friend, Jacques Hébert, and republished in Trudeau (1970), Trudeau challenged the religious foundations of Quebec political culture and propounded the themes of his democratic political philosophy. For Trudeau's liberalism, see Remple (1975, 24–39), Whitaker (1980, 5–31), and Hiemstra (1983). Trudeau's religious development and the influence of Emmanuel Mournier's Catholic 'personalism' are treated in Clarkson and McCall (1991).
9 For theory on differentiation, see Martin (1978, 68–82).

10 It would take until 1980 for Parliament to adopt 'O Canada!' as the official national anthem.
11 For Trudeau's own review of his constitutional development, see Trudeau (1968a, 1–9).
12 This brief by the Canadian Catholic School Trustees Association had the support of the Canadian Conference of Catholic Bishops. See also the testimony of the Ontario Conference of Catholic Bishops (Parliament 1981, session 33, 7 January 1981).
13 The author is indebted to Eugene Morawsky of the House of Commons Committees Branch for making the written submissions available for study.
14 As of 1983, Campbell claimed that Renaissance Canada had some 5,000 financial contributors to an annual budget of about $250,000, and a mailing list of some 50,000 in Canada and another 6,000 in the United States (Campbell 1983; see also Campbell 1980). Jerry Falwell came to Canada in the summer of 1979 to visit Campbell and Renaissance Canada, and wrote the preface for *No Small Stir.*
15 Stiller was executive director of the Evangelical Fellowship of Canada from 1983 to 1997.
16 The speeches of 20 June delivered by the prime minister and the leader of the opposition were both written by Dr Donald Page, then deputy director, Historical Section, Department of External Affairs, and chair of the Public Service Christian Fellowship, an ecumenical association of evangelicals (Page 1993a). At the time of the author's interview Dr Page was vice-president for academic affairs, Trinity Western University.
17 Maureen Johnson was assistant to Father Bob Ogle.
18 Liberal Senator Jack Austin put it less delicately: 'The Conservatives are trying to downgrade God and we will put him in his right place at the right time' (Parliament 1981, session 56, 9 February 1981).
19 For the scope of Campbell's campaign see his periodical, *Encounter*, vol. 10 (Spring 1981).
20 This resolution was adopted by the Evangelical Fellowship of Canada at its biennial meeting convened in Toronto, 25 February 1981.
21 The brief consisted of a ten-page executive summary by Smith, 'The Evangelicals,' which detailed demographic data on Canadian and American religiosity assembled for Smith by the Library of Parliament, and a selection of letters to Smith from religious leaders and constituents. I am grateful to David Smith for giving me a copy of the brief. Smith was a member of Yorkminster Baptist Church, Toronto. His father, C.B. Smith, had been a prominent leader in the Pentecostal Assemblies of Canada.

22 The brief showed over 6,300 full-time students in ministerial training at evangelical and pentecostal colleges, as compared with 649 Protestant mainline seminarians.

23 Other items in Smith's recommended strategy included: Central Mortgage and Housing Corporation (CMHC) loans to assist the building of Bible college residences and church–operated seniors homes; Canadian International Development Agency (CIDA) funding for church–operated educational and medical facilities overseas; tax breaks for religious schools, restoration of Renaissance Canada's tax status as a religious charity; and appointment of an evangelical staffer to the prime minister's office. Smith thought that formal recognition of evangelical leaders in a lunch at 24 Sussex Drive would be *pure gold.*

24 Smith claimed it was the figures on training of future evangelical leaders that were most persuasive for Trudeau.

25 The justice minister reported 7,000 to 8,000 letters.

26 The confessionalism of the preamble would presumably preclude strict 'no establishment' arguments that have emerged in U.S. Supreme Court rulings against any role for, or privileging of, religion in public life.

27 For a good overview of census and polling data of the 1980s illuminating trends in Canadian religious behaviour, see Baril and Mori (1991, 21–4).

28 Sniderman gives the most comprehensive survey assessing Canadian attitudes in this area. The survey is interpreted, with an emphasis on the salience of 'value pluralism,' in Sniderman et al. (1988).

chapter six

Bearing Witness: Christian Groups Engage Canadian Politics since the 1960s

JOHN G. STACKHOUSE, JR

'The government has no business in the bedrooms of the nation.' Former federal Justice Minister Pierre Elliott Trudeau thus notoriously sought to justify sweeping changes in the Criminal Code of Canada in 1968 that made divorce easier for unhappy couples and homosexual activity legal for certain happy ones. Trudeau was obviously wrong about this, of course, and for at least two reasons. First, governments affect bedroom conduct by staying out of them just as much as by going in. The incidence of rape, child molestation, bestiality, and other unusual sexual activities likely would change if governments resolutely turned a blind eye towards them. And second, Trudeau's remark is untrue to history: at least some of such behaviours have been seen by most societies, and thus most governments, as matters of considerable state interest.

Trudeau's remark, and the legislation it was intended to justify, awoke many Canadian Christians from political complacency. Historian John Webster Grant remarked that 'Canada emerged late from the Victorian period,' and well into the 1960s many Canadian Christians believed they lived in a Christian country and could count on its institutions, especially its governments, to uphold Christian values (1988a, 180). But the social changes of the 1960s, of which the Quiet Revolution in Quebec was only the swiftest and most obvious, made clear to increasing numbers of Canadians that their assumption of Christian hegemony was unjustified. As multiculturalism became an official policy of the Canadian government, as a new individualistic Charter of Rights and Freedoms became law in 1982, and as a wide range of legislative stories played out – perhaps most obviously the failure of Parliament to decide on a law regarding abortion in the early 1990s – many Canadian Christians realized that Canada was no longer a Christian country in any formal or substantial sense of the term.[1] Indeed, for many Christians Canada seemed to be increasingly anti-Christian. And some of them, at least, decided to respond directly in the political arena.[2]

The major denominations of Canadian Christianity played their part through their designated leaders. The Canadian Conference of Catholic Bishops, for example, startled many within and without its communion by criticizing governments especially for their treatment of the poor. The hierarchies of the United and Anglican churches, by far the two largest Protestant denominations in Canada, also issued press releases and commissioned a variety of studies that offered advice; on as a 1998 United Church statement put it, 'a wide range of current social issues from lotteries to climate change, to land claims for Native peoples' (United Church of Canada 1998). Much smaller groups, such as the Salvation Army and the Pentecostal Assemblies of Canada, occasionally spoke to matters of particular concern to them, whether relief of the poor in the former case or religious education and sexual issues in the latter (VanderVennen 1991; Williams 1984).

Increasingly, however, Canadian Christians since the 1960s spoke through other channels than denominational leaders and councils. Instead, Christians engaged politics through what American sociologist Robert Wuthnow calls 'special purpose groups,' alliances of Christian individuals or groups that form to meet particular challenges and to advance particular agendas – and particularly to respond to unwelcome governmental initiatives (Wuthnow 1988, especially chapter 6).[3] Wuthnow contends that the explosive growth and considerable influence of such groups is the most important feature of what he calls the 'restructuring of American religion' in recent times. I contend that the rise of such groups is important in recent Canadian history as well. But when it comes to political engagement in particular, a survey of Canadian Christian special purpose groups shows some patterns that differ considerably from those of their American counterparts.

Denominations

The Roman Catholic Church is Canada's largest Christian denomination, with almost every second Canadian (47 per cent) claiming some affiliation with it in the 1991 census. Catholic responses to government varied greatly through the course of Canadian history depending on which policy was being discussed or enacted in which part of the country. Sometimes Catholics supported government initiatives (such as separate school systems enjoying a measure of tax-funded support), sometimes they acquiesced after mild protest (such as the opening of businesses on Sundays), and sometimes they resisted vociferously (as in the case of the legalization of abortion).

Since 1943 the main public voice of Canadian Roman Catholicism in political matters has been the Canadian Conference of Catholic Bishops (CCCB). The CCCB marks the first time that the English- and French-speaking hierarchies joined in a national organization. The group originally focused on pastoral work in the dioceses, but the Second Vatican Council (1962–5) opened up the episcopal agenda to issues of ecumenism, liturgical reform, and social issues. At the same time, as a result of the Quiet Revolution the Church in Quebec no longer enjoyed the traditional close relations with government and society as a whole, and federal and provincial legislation on social matters elsewhere in the country prompted an increasingly critical stance by the bishops.

This stance was most evident in the 1983 statement by the CCCB's Social Affairs Commission, *Ethical Reflections on the Economic Crisis*, which was followed up by a submission to the Macdonald Commission on the Economic Union and Development Prospects for Canada. Such public pronouncements were viewed both within and without the Church as evidence of a new activism among the Catholic clerics, with a new and decidedly leftward tilt. Since that time, some observers believe they have traced a retrenchment of such critical activism, with Archbishop (and, recently, Cardinal) Aloysius Ambrozic as Exhibit A of the theological and political conservative.[4] But the CCCB continued to promote the well-being of the Canadian poor (as in its 1994 statement questioning *Will the Poor Have the Most to Fear from Social Security Reform?*) and Canada's Indians and Inuit (*Let Justice Flow Like a Mighty River*, a brief presented in 1995 to the Royal Commission on Aboriginal Peoples).

Hierarchies of Canada's major Protestant denominations, notably the United and Anglican churches (which together drew the nominal allegiance of every fifth Canadian in 1991), also have a history of speaking to governments on behalf of their own welfare and that of others as well. The basic pattern is strikingly imaged by the United Church's Roger Hutchinson: 'Rather than "whispering in the ear of the King" and articulating the reigning consensus, the churches confront the King's representatives with moral imperatives and information based on grassroots contacts' (Matthews and Pratt 1982(?), 20–1). Domestic and international economic issues (from welfare reform to the toleration of foreign sweatshops) and human rights concerns (whether Aboriginals at home or prisoners of conscience abroad) dominated the social agendas of these churches throughout this period (Greene 1990).

Smaller, evangelical denominations were much less audible in such debates, but occasionally a group made its concerns known on matters close to its heart. The Salvation Army, for example, broke its normal silence to speak out on behalf of the rights of Aboriginal peoples in the Mackenzie Valley Pipeline debate of the 1970s (Williams 1984, 15–28; see also Hutchinson 1992), and the Pentecostal Assemblies of Canada and of Newfoundland forthrightly resisted the recent successful attempt of the Newfoundland government to change the denominationally based school system in that province – a change that entailed an actual amendment to the Canadian Constitution (Fieguth 1997).

Special Purpose Groups

Since the 1960s, however, the most visible expression of Christian political concern – aside from the occasional headline-scoring proclamation from denominational leaders – has been special purpose groups. Most of these have been interdenominational or transdenominational groups. (By 'interdenominational' I mean groups that enjoy the official sponsorship of more than one denomination; by 'transdenominational' those groups that profess no denominational allegiance per se and are supported by members of more than one denomination.) Such groups receive most of the attention in this survey.

The unique cultural situation of Quebec, however, gives pause on this matter, as on so many others.[5] Since the Quiet Revolution, the Roman Catholic Church in Quebec has allied itself with a variety of groups, including labour unions, educational institutions, and groups concerned for international relief and development. Catholic Action in its various forms, le Centre de pastorale en milieu ouvrier (CPMO), and the Canadian Organization for Development and Peace (Développement et paix, in Quebec) are just some of the more prominent groups in a wave of such organizations linking the Roman Catholic church with allies in the community at large focusing on this or that social or political issue.

Outside Quebec, however, the interdenominational or transdenominational model has predominated. The Canadian Council of Churches has sometimes been the vehicle for such political concerns, but more typically mainline Protestant activity has been devoted to the special purpose groups known as interdenominational coalitions, alliances formed around this or that particular issue.

The short-lived Coalition for Development, which emerged out of a Catholic–Protestant conference on poverty at Montreal in 1968, was the first of these. Among the most conspicuous have been the following: the Interchurch Consultative Committee on Development and Relief (ICCDR); the Interchurch Committee for the Promotion of Justice in Canada, better known as PLURA after its sponsoring denominations (Presbyterian, Lutheran, United, Roman Catholic, and Anglican); the Taskforce on the Churches and Corporate Responsibility; the whimsically named GATT-Fly, a group focused on international trade that drew its name and mandate from the conviction that 'the church is called to be a gadfly, a radical questioner of the status quo';[6] the Inter-Church Committee on Human Rights in Latin America (ICCHRLA); and Project North, the Inter-Church Project on Northern Development (as of 1988, the Aboriginal Rights Coalition).

All of these were products of the 1970s. Most were ad hoc responses to particular government initiatives and were fuelled in part by the bracing experience of Catholics and Protestants working together in the heyday of Canadian mainline ecumenism.[7] Most of these groups continued into the 1990s, with the annual budgets of those engaged directly in public policy matters ranging from about $125,000 to $300,000 (the largest was that of ICCHRLA).[8]

More energetic in later decades, perhaps, and increasingly visible were groups that emerged out of Canada's smaller denominations and the transdenominational networks of evangelical Protestantism (Rawlyk 1996; Stackhouse 1993). Best known of these was the Evangelical Fellowship of Canada (EFC). Founded in 1964 as a support group of Toronto-area pastors, the EFC began to address governments programmatically only since the hiring of Brian C. Stiller as full-time executive director in 1983. Since that time, the EFC presented a steady stream of briefs and declarations to various levels of government and the courts, although mostly at the federal level, representing what it saw to be the convictions of Canada's two-million-plus evangelicals and its two dozen constituent denominations. Abortion, euthanasia, homosexuality, Christian education, and other family-oriented matters were predictably at the top of the list of concerns, but the EFC also expended considerable energy in studying and speaking out on Aboriginal rights and the revision of Canada's Constitution in the light of the 1990 Meech Lake Accord, among other issues.[9] In 1996, the EFC opened its Office of National Affairs in Ottawa with full-time staff devoted to cultivating influence at the federal level of politics and the courts.[10]

A more recent group, founded in 1983, Focus on the Family (Canada) ('Focus') grew up alongside the EFC and frequently stood at its side in the courts and in presentations to governments and the media. Unlike the formal coalition of denominations, churches, other organizations, and individuals that made up the EFC, Focus was a free-standing organization governed only by its own board and affiliated with its parent organization led by founder James Dobson in the United States. By 1998 it had grown to employ a staff of fifty-three utilizing a budget of more than $7 million, thus dwarfing every other transdenominational institution in this survey (Sclater 1998c).[11] The EFC, by comparison, had a budget of about $3 million, and the others for which budget numbers were available had less. But the amount Focus actually devoted to public policy matters was less than 5 per cent of its total budget: about $350,000 per year, which still was more than any public policy-centred interchurch coalition, but also somewhat less than the budgets of other groups to be mentioned presently – and less than the $500,000 to $600,000 the EFC was devoting to public policy activity by the mid-1990s (Walsh and Clemenger 1998).[12]

Focus did not have the public profile of the EFC: Brian Stiller himself was much better known than any of the Focus staff members in Canada. But it did present briefs to government and the courts, as part of its broader campaign to revive a 'traditional' Christian understanding of the family: television violence, homosexual rights, euthanasia and, of course, abortion, all drew particular attention (Sclater 1998a, 1998b). And, like most of these similar groups, it published its concerns to its members and other interested readers, both informing about, and encouraging a particular view on, this or that issue.

Other groups straddled the theological 'liberal-conservative' and ecclesiastical 'mainline-evangelical' divides – divisions that were never absolute in Canadian Christianity anyhow (Stackhouse 1995a). The Citizens for Public Justice (CPJ) emerged out of post–Second World War Dutch Calvinism in Canada, a tradition whose heritage of social and political engagement went back to the Netherlands and the career of former Dutch Prime Minister Abraham Kuyper. As part of the multiple fronts of the Christian Reformed community in Canada that included Christian schooling from the elementary to postgraduate levels and

Christian labour unions, CPJ spoke out on a wide range of issues, notably, since the 1980s through its director Harry Kits and its best-known activist, Gerald Vandezande. Its first area of concern was justice in Canadian energy policy in the mid-1970s, particularly in regard to Aboriginal peoples. Since then it addressed international and domestic human rights, refugee regulations, international trade (including the recent Multilateral Agreement on Investment), abortion, and rights for homosexuals, among other issues (Kits 1988, 1989). It did so with a viewpoint that was, in typical Calvinist style, painstakingly worked out from theological premises. CPJ was generally left of centre in its views, but not always: to select two 'hot-button' issues, CPJ was conservatively pro-life, while cautiously supportive of increasing certain rights and benefits for homosexual couples without morally endorsing homosexuality per se.

As if to balance such a voice with a somewhat more conservative – even 'neo-conservative' – accent, in the 1990s a group of concerned Christians (both Protestant and Catholic) founded the Centre for Renewal of Public Policy in Ottawa.[13] The centre commissioned and published a series of article-length critiques of social and political trends in Canada: 'values' versus 'virtues' education in schools (reminiscent of Alasdair MacIntyre and William Bennett's concerns in the United States); the courts as de facto legislatures (Charter challenges have become the method of choice for those who have little chance of obtaining political support for their positions); political correctness in the academy and judiciary; health care matters (especially those connected with a 'pro-life' agenda such as abortion and euthanasia); and the overarching conviction that Canadian society was unclear as to how to truly accommodate a pluralism of ideological convictions without taking either extreme option of radical relativism or implicit secularist hegemony (Centre for Renewal 1998, 6).[14] The centre represented its concerns to government through its full-time staff and other members in Ottawa. Its spokespersons, notably lawyer Iain Benson and pediatrician John Patrick, addressed various political, educational, and ecclesiastical fora across the country, including conferences sponsored by the centre itself. And, starting in June 1997, it informed its constituency regularly about its interpretations of high court decisions through the faxed newsletter *Lex View*. By 1998, the centre had an annual budget approaching two-thirds of a million dollars – slightly larger than CPJ's half-million – and was ambitiously seeking funds to double its work over the next year (Centre for Renewal 1998, 8–9).

In all of these organizations, Christians worked with Christians. In an increasingly pluralized Canada, however, interfaith, as well as interdenominational, alliances began to form. One of the more conspicuous of these was the Ontario Multi-Faith Coalition for Equity in Education (OMCEE). Founded in 1993, OMCEE brought together representatives of Christian, Islamic, Sikh, and Hindu religious communities in order to press the Ontario government – which provided funding to public and Roman Catholic separate school systems – to provide more options in the public school system. OMCEE sought not only religious education in existing schools, but also religion-based schools operating under public school boards. This committee made its case to the Ontario Royal Commission on Learning (Ontario Multi-Faith Coalition 1993, 1994), intervened in various court cases, and finally lost its case before the Ontario Court of Appeal in 1997. An appeal to the Supreme Court of Canada was denied early in 1998 (Harvey 1997; Small 1998). Multiculturalism would continue to be officially confined to whatever educational structures the provinces allowed. In Ontario's case those structures would continue to be public or Roman Catholic, just as they were a century before.

Other such groups formed, such as the Interfaith Social Assistance Review Committee (ISARC), active since the late 1980s, to address questions of social assistance by the Ontario government. ISARC included representatives of the Ontario Conference of Catholic Bishops; mainline Protestant groups such as the United Church of Canada, the Anglican Church of Canada, the Evangelical Lutheran Church of Canada, and the Presbyterian Church in Canada; the Disciples of Christ and Society of Friends (Quakers); Unitarian Fellowships; and also the Canadian Council for Reform Judaism and the Toronto and Region Islamic Congregation. A more diverse group was the Interfaith Working Group on Canada's Future that mobilized to respond to the constitutional debates in the late-1980s and 1990s. This ad hoc group brought together CPJ, EFC, Catholic and Protestant denominational leaders, and leaders in the Islamic, Hindu, and Buddhist communities (Citizens for Public Justice 1997, 10–11). Clearly, the changing face of Canadian culture – both the increasing numbers of adherents of other faiths and the increasing sense of concern about various governmental initiatives – was driving Canadian Christians to establish new alliances in response.

Observations

It is difficult, of course, if not impossible, to gauge the effect of any or all of these organizations on Canadian political life, or on Canadian religion either. It is evident that some of these groups represent a flowering of concern regarding the public sphere, an efflorescence perhaps most obvious among evangelical Protestants. It is also clear that the decline of some interchurch coalitions stands as another mark of the general waning of mainline Christianity in Canada. Still, however, it is no fault of the salt if its preservative work is difficult to assess with any precision, especially given the complexity of the social forces involved.

Several other observations, however, are easier to make. First, the sphere of social and political engagement shows that it is only somewhat helpful to use terms such as 'mainline' and 'evangelical' as if they defined well-differentiated groups in Canadian Protestantism. In particular, it is not as if social concern was the exclusive province of the larger, pluralistic denominations, while the smaller, more homogeneously evangelical groups confined themselves to matters of personal and ecclesiastical piety – as the agenda of the EFC, with its two dozen constituent denominations of this sort – attests.

Second, it is striking to see Roman Catholics and Protestants working together in several of these groups, whether in formally interdenominational terms as in the mainline coalitions, or in transdenominational groups such as CPJ and the Centre for Renewal of Public Policy. Given Canada's history of alternating periods of conflict and bemused tolerance among these groups, the relatively recent rapprochements, even alliances, across the Catholic-Protestant divide are remarkable. I understand this to be the result of an interplay between changing theologies (in both liberal and conservative variants on both sides that are more appreciative of others' Christian integrity) and the increasing need for a united front in a culture that is less and less publicly or deeply Christian. (The charismatic renewal movement – which also crosses the Protestant–Catholic divide – seems not to have played an important part in these social and political alliances.)

Third, this passing reference to the charismatic movement, a transdenominational grassroots movement, raises the awkward and important question as to just how much of this organized political activity represented the concerns and interests of people in the pews, rather than the leaders in the pulpits and conference rooms. What Lee Cormie asserts about his own church, the Roman Catholic, might well have been true of other traditions as well: 'With a few happy exceptions there has been too little emphasis on educating and mobilizing people in the pews concerning these issues and the need to respond. There has been a tendency toward institutionalizing social justice activity in the churches in the hands of a few who define the issues, decide on the appropriate response, and generally manage the strategy of the churches in this regard' (Cormie 1991, 83).[15]

I have argued elsewhere that several of the leading evangelical organizations could claim at least a good measure of grassroots support, funded as they were by relatively many and small donations, rather than one or a few major supporters (Stackhouse 1993, 201–2). But the question of just who the leaders of each of these groups actually speak for is one that deserves more careful investigation.

Fourth, it is impressive to consider that the leaders generally speak on behalf of more than their own groups. In the case of the Ontario Multi-Faith Coalition for Equity in Education, the call was made to let the various religious communities 'do their own thing,' ideologically speaking, in elementary and secondary education. But in most of the other cases surveyed here, the groups seek the welfare of others as well as of their own kind. It is not just Roman Catholic and evangelical abortion that is opposed, but all abortion. It is not simply the rights of Christian Aboriginals that are supported, but of all Aboriginal peoples. It is not merely the relief of Christian poor people that is sought, but of all Canadians afflicted with poverty. Thus, these groups participate in the public policy conversation not only to defend their group's rights and privileges, but customarily, if not universally, to commend principles to govern the common life of all Canadians.

Some of this sort of agenda can be read as an antimodern attempt to re-establish religious hegemony. But most of the language and arguments used by these groups, instead, are resolutely public, rarely narrowly specific to the originating community, and thus modern – or perhaps, better, 'postmodern' – in the assumption that politics in contemporary, multicultural Canada must be worked out with recognition and tolerance of various points of view, not by the championing of one tribe's values over everyone else's. It is noteworthy, then, that even though some nostalgia for Canada's Christian past has been evident here and there, no major Canadian religious group involved in public discourse has explicitly campaigned for a return to a Christian Canada. Among the several parallels between the conclusions of this study and that of David Seljak (in this volume) regarding Catholics in Quebec and elsewhere, it is striking that the Assemblée des évêques du Québec, among other Catholic groups, has not called for a return to the days before the Quiet Revolution.

Fifth, when one looks southward for comparison, one is struck by the fact that not one of these Canadian Christian groups is aligned with a political party. Indeed, the history of most of these groups is of freely criticizing, and suggesting positive change to, the party in power, whatever its political label and orientation. As if to provide the exception to prove this rule, a tiny group calling itself the Christian Heritage Party has in recent years attempted to pursue political ends by this sort of direct action. It has failed, however, to garner significant support from any sector of Canadian Christians (Mackey 1987, 36–7).[16] Indeed, it is difficult to sustain any simple 'left-right' typology for most of the groups in this brief catalogue. (The mainline Protestant coalitions are the most consistent as they have typically hewed to a left-of-centre position.)

Surveys have shown that not only are the mainline churches politically diverse, but the so-called evangelical groups are politically diverse as well. The common journalistic linkage of evangelicals with political conservatism (as that is currently understood in Canada and the United States) simply will not endure serious scrutiny (Bibby 1987, 193–201). In fact, evangelicals have been politically diverse throughout the history of Canada, as several scholars have argued (Gauvreau 1990, 86–92; Phillips 1996). This should scarcely surprise anyone familiar with the reality of evangelicalism as a transdenominational impulse focused on a few spiritual convictions about God, salvation, the Bible, and evangelism, with no obvious and definite implications for political engagement. Given the diversity of evangelicals through the centuries, one should expect a diversity of political philosophies today (Stackhouse 1995b).

Sixth, and carrying on this point in the light of the foregoing, there is no organized religious right in Canada that wields significant and obvious political power in the electoral process – nor any religious left or centre, for that matter. None of these groups has attempted to marshal votes through direct mail and 'voter's guides'; none has organized Christian candidates through the formal political system; none has seriously claimed to 'deliver' support for this or that leader or party.

Finally, in regard to secularization theory per se, this survey of Canadian Christian engagement testifies only ambiguously to the importance of some of the typical 'carriers' of both modernity and secularization.[17] *Pluralization*, for example, is evident in the apparent mushrooming of such groups since the 1960s. There seem to be more, and of more variety, than previously in Canadian history, although hard data on this question has not been gathered to date.[18]

Individualization is also increasingly pronounced. Many observers of the North American religious scene have remarked on what seems to be an erosion of denominational loyalties. Usually this observation is made in terms of denominational 'switching,' the leaving of one denomination for another in search of meeting individual or family preferences. In Canada, Reginald Bibby has served up several discussions of the 'circulation of the saints.' He has also maintained, however, that denominational loyalties remain perhaps surprisingly strong (Bibby 1987, 1993). When one looks at the data from, say, Statistics Canada regarding the self-identification of Canadians with this or that denomination, Bibby's point seems well founded (Statistics Canada 1993a). The larger religious groups over the past century have stayed larger, the smaller have remained smaller, with the occasional exception (such as the burgeoning Pentecostal Assemblies) to prove the rule.[19]

Yet another phenomenon – characterized by Bibby in Canada as 'religion à la carte' and by American Robert Bellah and his associates in its most extreme form as 'Sheilaism,' what we might call 'do-it-yourself religion' – qualifies the question of denominational loyalties on at least two different planes (Bibby 1987, chapter 4; Bellah et al. 1985, 221). First, if someone calls herself an Anglican, but believes in reincarnation and astrology, rarely attends church, and cannot name half of the Ten Commandments or recite the Apostles' Creed, one might have good reason to question the depth of her Anglican identity while allowing her yet to identify herself as 'Anglican.'

But the question of special purpose groups, such as those in focus in this chapter, adds a second level to this point whether or not one is an orthodox, church-going, knowledgeable believer. One might be all those things, and still place most of one's interest, and money, and time in a set of special purpose groups not especially, or even at all, related to one's denomination. Consider now an Anglican who would meet anyone's test of Anglican fidelity but whose younger children attend Pioneer Clubs, whose older children belong to the InterVarsity Christian Fellowship chapter at university, whose charitable giving goes largely to World Vision, and whose political concerns are channelled through Citizens for Public Justice. Between denominational identity and full-blown do-it-yourself 'Sheilaism' lies this Christian version of 'religion à la carte,' in which individual Christian identity and participation connects with the groups and causes one chooses for oneself within the range of Christian – and even interfaith – options. The whole idea of denominational identity is so radically qualified here in terms of what people believe and say and spend their time and money on as to require a reconsideration of denomination as the primary category, let alone the exclusive one, of religious identification – and, indeed, to challenge any attempt to lump large groups of people together on the basis merely of professed denominational affiliation without acknowledging and exploring other, perhaps more basic, loyalties and identities manifested in support of these other groups.[20]

Differentiation has not advanced to the point of each issue having its own special interest groups, as most of the groups surveyed here (except the explicitly concentrated mainline coalitions and Focus on the Family) have dealt with a wide range of issues, from constitutional revision to abortion, from religious education to international trade. Still, it is remarkable that the Christian church has responded to the differentiation of Canadian society – seen in most classic secularization theory as a threat to religion – not by merely retreating to the private sphere, but by differentiating itself at least partly in order to continue to influence public life. (The question remains, of course, whether Christianity is thereby strengthened or not.)[21]

Thus, the *privatization* of religion seems something much less than absolute in Canadian society when one attends to the political conversation. Whether or not such Christian groups can point to particular successes in this or that political discussion, they have been at least frequently, even normally, present at the public table when a very wide array of matters has been up for debate, including such 'public' issues as immigration policy, free trade, and Aboriginal land claims. Indeed, there seems to be no time in Canadian history in which large proportions of the Christian church retreated from, or simply remained separate from, public life.[22]

The Canadian model (including francophone Quebec, or so I conclude from the scholarship of Baum, Seljak, and others) therefore seems impressively uniform: Christian groups speak to political leaders about their concerns without attempting to wield power directly through the electoral process. Despite the variation in political outlook and preferred outcome on this or that matter, this wide range of Christian groups – which, at least formally, represents the vast majority of Christians in Canada – sticks to the task of bearing witness.

NOTES

I gratefully acknowledge the assistance of the editors, the Pew Charitable Trusts, and the Social Sciences and Humanities Research Council of Canada.

1 Bill C-43 passed in the House of Commons in May 1990 by a vote of 140 to 131. It was defeated by a tie vote of 43 to 43 in the Senate in January 1991. On the larger question of a 'Christian Canada,' see Stackhouse (1992).

2 Thus, the plotline for such Christians is not a story of 'deprivatization' of religion, as José Casanova (1994) puts it. Instead, it is one of Christian cultural dominance, followed by erosion of that dominance *without recognizing it*, and then both recognition and resurgence of public involvement. At no time, that is, does Canadian Christianity or any major group within it consciously abandon the public sphere. Casanova tries to stretch 'deprivatization' to cover this sort of plot line as well, but acknowledges that this is not an accurate use of his own term: 'The descriptive connotation of the term is somewhat misleading since we are not dealing so much with a move from the private to the public sphere as with a change in the type of publicity. The descriptive connotation of the term deprivatization is properly speaking only appropriate for cases such as the public mobilization of [American] Protestant fundamentalism or the public interventions of the American Catholic bishops, both of which represent a move by religion from the private to the public sphere' (ibid., 221).

3 Casanova echoes Wuthnow's assertion that the growth of such groups was prompted especially by increasing encroachment of governments: 'What seems to precipitate the religious response are different types of state intervention and administrative colonization of the lifeworld and the private sphere' (Casanova 1994, 227).

4 Observations of the Roman Catholic Church in Canada during this period include the following: Westhues (1976a), Baum (1986), Kroeker (1986; see also responses by Gregory Baum and Roger Hutchinson that follow, pp. 19–22), Cormie 1991; and the essays by Baum and Seljak in this volume.

5 As with many generalizations about Canadian society, consideration of Quebec prompts important qualification. To be sure, some Quebeckers (including francophone Quebeckers) are represented in some of the groups that are discussed below. But important linguistic and cultural differences have kept many francophone Quebeckers from joining in the predominantly anglophone and Ottawa-focused organizations surveyed in this brief study, while much activity similar to what is described in the present

essay for Canada as a whole has taken place in Quebec focused on the challenges peculiar to that province. See Baum (1992), Seljak (1995), and the article by David Seljak in this volume.

6 Canadian Council of Churches – Canadian Catholic Conference Brief to the Senate Poverty Committee (quoted without further reference in Hutchinson 1992, 348). For more on GATT-Fly, see Ruttan (1985). In 1990 GATT-Fly changed its name to the Ecumenical Coalition on Economic Justice.

7 Anti-apartheid was one cause that galvanized interdenominational concern (see Pratt 1997). For a fascinating glimpse into the workings of such groups see Matthews and Pratt [1982?].

8 For sketches of these groups, see Lind and Mihevc (1994). Recent budget figures were reported to the author by Irene Ty, administrative assistant to the Coalition Priorities and Administrative Committee, Toronto (telephone conversation, 5 May 1998).

9 On the latter issues see Van Ginkel (1992).

10 For an introduction to the Evangelical Fellowship of Canada, see Stackhouse (1993, chap. 12). Stiller made his own views known in various EFC writings, some of which were published in Stiller (1994), and Stiller with Guenther (1997).

11 James A. Sclater is vice-president of public policy for the Focus on the Family (Canada) Association.

12 Gary Walsh is president of EFC and Bruce Clemenger is the group's Ottawa office director.

13 The Centre has eschewed any facile identification as 'right-wing' (see Benson n.d.). And the listing of the late George Rawlyk, a noted democratic socialist, on the advisory council of the centre supports Benson's assertion. Still, from my reading of centre materials, I think its general flavour relative to CPJ is complementary in the way I have suggested. The presence of notable American conservatives Richard John Neuhaus, Paul Vitz, and Russell Hittinger on centre programs encourages this interpretation. Still, the centre's forthright concerns for the relief of poor Canadians is more typical of centrist and left-of-centre Canadian politics, giving support to the centre's express concern to remain non-partisan.

14 Quotation is from Centre for Renewal (1998, 6). As perhaps further indication of the centre's agreement with William Bennett's agenda, this statement articulates the centre's intention to begin compiling an 'Index of Leading Cultural Indicators' (p. 5) – a project along the lines of Bennett's American counterpart of the same name.

15 This view is echoed in Hewitt (1993, 261–4).

16 A few years later, ironically, Canada's only other officially Christian party, the Social Credit Party, voted to remove a clause from its constitution calling for adherence to 'Christian principles' (see Revision 1990, 1129).

17 For fundamental treatments of this question, see Berger (1967), Martin (1978), and Lyon (1985). See Casanova (1994) for a revision of these treatments; and for a recent sample of the ongoing debate, see Bruce (1992).

18 Even the Canadian Council of Christian Charities, according to its director, Frank Luellau, despairs of sorting out which among the tens of thousands of charities registered with Revenue Canada can be called 'religious' (Luellau 1998). According to data offered by the Voluntary Sector Roundtable (accessed by the author from their website, www.pagvs.com, on 26 May 1998), there were well over 25,000 'places of worship' registered as charities with Revenue Canada in 1994, constituting 35 per cent of total registered charities. Under the separate category of 'Religion,' which included monasteries, convents, and missionary organizations, about 4,000 were listed, making up 5.6 per cent of the total.

19 Steve Bruce contends that British figures resemble Canadian ones: 'A consistent finding ... is that a very high proportion of people in Europe assert some confessional or denominational identification. In Britain, generally less than a quarter of respondents in a variety of surveys claim "no religion"' (1996, 33).

20 José Casanova (1994, 54) wonders whether this pluralization of religious special purpose groups is, ironically, the 'triumph of the denominational principle.' But the functional, not just the theological, distinction remains important here between a special purpose group and a congregation (not a denomination) that is a full-fledged religious community integrating worship, fellowship, and mission from cradle to grave. No special purpose group, in the nature of the case, can substitute for the holistic community of the typical church.

21 Thus, Casanova's distinction between secularization-as-differentiation and secularization-as-threat-to-religion is endorsed here, while leaving open the question as to whether in fact the one does entail the other in some normative, theological sense. Is a Christian Church deployed into so many disparate and disconnected forms in some normative sense thereby falling short of an ideal of organizational coherence?

22 Monastic Catholicism and sectarian Protestantism, obviously, seem to be counter-cases. But neither were utterly isolated from public life in Canada, as the work of monks and nuns in Roman Catholic education and the influence of sectarian Protestants on prairie politics – whether Social Credit or CCF – demonstrate. For this theme see Rawlyk (1990c) and Stackhouse (1992).

Part Three

CIVIC AND CIVIL RELIGION

Resisting the 'No Man's Land' of Private Religion: The Catholic Church and Public Politics in Quebec

DAVID SELJAK

In his book *Public Religions in the Modern World* (1994), José Casanova argues that, contrary to the models *described* by dominant modernization theories and programs *prescribed* by liberal political theories, there are new forms of participation in public debates by religious communities which do not represent a regression to premodern religious practices or a rejection of modern values. *Modern* public religions do not violate the consciences of individuals, the autonomy of political society and the state, or the democratic norms of pluralism and liberty. Instead, they protect those very values when they participate as actors in important ethical debates at the level of civil society. They do not reject modernity but offer a moral critique of 'specific forms of institutionalization of modernity' (p. 221). Casanova labels these new forms of public activity the 'deprivatization of religion,' since they resist the 'privatized role to which they were being relegated by secularist modernization theories and by liberal political theories' (p. 221).

Following David Martin's theory of secularization, Casanova argues that the decline of religious mentalities and the privatization of religion predicted by dominant theories of secularization has not occurred. Only secularization as a function of differentiation has been proven to be a 'structural trend' in modernizing societies. This process encourages agents and institutions to operate in their own specialized spheres according to the logic of their own rational operations, free from barriers imposed by 'irrational' religion, custom, and tradition (Casanova 1994, 40). Public religions challenge the claims of the enormous rational bureaucracies created by the modern state and market to operate solely according to the inherent logic of their distinct spheres. In doing so they challenge the dominant cultural division of society into neat realms of 'public' and 'private,' where the public sphere is dominated by so-called universal reason and the private by ethnic and religious particularisms. While affirming the separation of church and state and of religion and politics, proponents of modern public religions argue that moral and cultural values, spirituality, and ethics must not be relegated to the 'private' realm of individual experience, family, ethnic community, and parish. By introducing ethical criticism into questions of public policy, which technocratic elites claim must be solved only in rational or instrumental terms, Casanova argues, modern public religions serve to protect the integrity of 'civil society,' that public arena dominated by neither state nor church which serves as the heart of a modern democracy.

The Quebec Experience: From Civil Religion to Public Denomination

The participation of the Catholic Church in the 1980 and 1995 referenda on Quebec's sovereignty is an interesting illustration of Casanova's thesis. Examining the Church's public reaction to this new nationalism is a particularly effective measure of its successful 'deprivatization' as a *modern* public religion, because before 1960 the Catholic Church enjoyed a privileged position in Quebec society, what Casanova calls a position of 'social establishment.' While the state and political parties were officially secular, Catholicism provided the basic elements of French Quebeckers' 'civil religion.' The Church controlled virtually all education, health care, and social services for French Quebeckers, who formed the majority of the population. In 1958, 99 per cent of the French-speakers (more than 85 per cent of the entire population) were Catholic and more than 88 per cent of all Quebec Catholics reported attending Sunday Mass regularly (Bibby 1993, 6, Table 1.1).[1] Both Quebec society and the Church were highly clerical; in 1961, more than 45,000 nuns, priests, and brothers oversaw the Church's massive bureaucracy (Hamelin 1984, 173, Table 13). Quebec culture and nationalism legitimated this semi-established status and public presence by uniting a conservative Catholicism with French Canadian ethnic identity. As David Martin has shown elsewhere, this relationship was not unique.[2]

During the Quiet Revolution of the 1960s, the Church rapidly lost control over Quebec's social bureaucracy to the new interventionist state. The rapidity with which secularization overtook Quebec society and political culture was staggering. One illustration will serve to make the point: before 1960 every important nationalist movement or party had also been Catholic. Twelve years later not a single significant movement or party was openly so. The political modernization of Quebec, according to sociologist Marcel Rioux (1976), meant an explosion of the rational, critical spirit in a culture dominated by custom, religion, and traditional authority. In the early 1960s, both substantive and instrumental issues were subject to critical reason. Within the Liberal party and its offshoot the Parti Québécois, groups raised ethical questions about the very structure, values, and goals of Quebec society. However, according to Paul-Marcel Lemaire (1993, 17–18), by the end of the 1960s 'un certain pragmatisme d'allure typiquement nord-américaine' took over, relegating deeper ethical debates to the margins. In the 1970s, it was the agents of the interventionist state bureaucracy, capitalist institutions, and the militantly secular intelligentsia who claimed to represent the forces of reason and progress.[3] Public Catholicism was identified with the discredited Duplessis regime even though privately French Quebeckers remained faithful to their heritage. In mainstream culture, Catholicism became almost wholly privatized as a religion of rites of passage and a cultural touchstone (Milot 1991).[4]

In the 1980s, with the rise of neo-conservatism (called more accurately *néolibéralisme* in French), the non-interventionist state and market institutions claimed that they now represented the forces of reason. Neo-conservatives saw in the laws of the market *natural* laws which, like the laws discovered by physics and chemistry, are immutable and beyond human control. They argued that any intervention in this 'natural' process is an inevitably self-defeating violation which could only lead to injustice and harm for the very people the intervention sought to help (for example, generous social programs harmed the poor by discouraging economic growth and personal responsibility). Finally, neo-conservatives argued that the market was the only necessary basis for social organization; they believed that other large-scale institutions which operated according to a logic other than the rational laws of the market harmed society, hence their mistrust of the state (Sharp 1995, 232). This belief in the market's ability to create spontaneously the most just social order meant that neo-conservatives mistrusted 'ideological' or 'political' solutions (that is, all alternative models) and offered no other social project than adaptation to the reality of market laws. They suspected anyone who disagreed with their rational analysis and program of having a 'political agenda' or representing a 'special interest group.' Consequently, they relegated social projects inspired by particular values, ethics, or ethnic or religious traditions to the private sphere.

According to Charles Taylor (1991, 109–10), this obsession with the maximization of market efficiency closed down all ethical debates. People's attention was turned to instrumental questions of how to produce more rather than substantive questions about the common good. Societies organized around a 'single principle' (either on the left or right) precluded ethical debates and consequently stifled freedom. All debates were flattened out and reduced to a calculus of individual or collective material self-interest.

In Quebec, neo-conservatism had become an increasingly important guide for government policy during the second administration of René Lévesque's Parti québécois (PQ) from 1981 to 1985, the tenure of Robert Bourassa's Parti libérale du Québec (PLQ) from 1985 to 1994, and Jacques Parizeau's PQ government from 1994 to the referendum in 1995. This shift led to the privatization of Crown corporations, reduction of government spending on social programs, and the creation of a pro-business environment by encouraging investment and limiting the powers of labour unions (ibid., 341–423). In all of these initiatives, the governments of Lévesque, Bourassa, and Parizeau limited or rolled back the involvement of the state in the capitalist economy (McRoberts 1988, 358–423). This represented a major shift in the political culture of Quebec which, since the Quiet Revolution, was dominated by the idea that government intervention in the economy was the most important strategy of national and social development.[5]

While the Church reacted to the secularization of Quebec society with relative serenity,[6] at each stage of this two-step process it protested the privatization or 'folklorization' of Catholicism. This reaction, as Gregory Baum argues elsewhere in this volume, must be understood in the context of the Second Vatican Council, which redefined the position of the Church to modern society, accepting the autonomy of political society and the state, affirming the rights of individual consciences in political matters, and calling Roman Catholics to participate in the important political and social debates of their societies (Casanova 1994, 71–3). In Quebec, the decisions of the council rendered unworkable the conservative nationalism of traditionalist Catholic groups, allowed liberals and radicals to be critical of the old Church and the old Quebec while remaining Catholic, and inspired Catholics to redefine the public role of the Church (Seljak 1996). The Catholic hierarchy established a Royal Commission-style public inquiry into the Church's relationship to the new society in 1968. In 1971, the Dumont Commission published a multivolume report which closed the door on the old-style semi-established religion but also rejected the privatization of Catholicism which it labelled a religious 'no man's land' (Commission d'étude 1971, 83). The Church had a public role in the new society, the commission concluded, even if this role would be radically different from its earlier one (pp. 129–37).[7] In the 1970s, the Church's new public role was most visibly defined by its social teaching on a wide variety of justice issues, ranging from the rights of Aboriginal peoples, immigrants, welfare recipients, and women to economic inequality, workers' rights, and the environment (Rochais 1984).

The 1980 Referendum and Catholic Social Teaching

Elected in 1976, less than eight years after its formation, the PQ scheduled a referendum for 20 May 1980 to give the government of Quebec a mandate to negotiate with the federal government to establish a new relationship of 'sovereignty-association,' that is, some form of political sovereignty with strong economic ties to Canada (McRoberts 1988, 301–10). While most Quebeckers defined the issues in the 1980 referendum in political and economic terms, groups within the Catholic Church also defined the whole debate as a spiritual and ethical decision, touching upon Catholic values such as the common good, solidarity among citizens, and social justice. As such, they felt, the Church had to participate in the debate as a public actor. The bishops, Catholic journals, and social action groups had learned to become effective public pressure groups, and they applied the techniques learned in the 1960s and 1970s to the new situation.

The decision to participate in a public and highly politicized debate put the Church in an awkward position. While the 'Yes' and 'No' committees were officially non-partisan, it was clear that the PQ government and official opposition Liberals were closely identified with each respectively. For the episcopacy or Church leadership to come out in favour of one side or the other was clearly unacceptable since this would have resurrected the spectre of the *grande noirceur* of the 1950s. During the referendum campaign, the bishops took pains to ensure that the Church was not identified with either side. Members of the clergy were allowed to take sides, but they could not present their own opinions as Church teaching (Martel 1980; Béliveau 1980b).[8] As the Assemblée des évêques du Québec (AÉQ) argued in its first pastoral letter on the 1980 referendum, the gospels could inspire certain values, attitudes, and concerns, but neither sovereignty-association nor federalism could be defended as directly dictated by Christianity.[9] Individuals, however, were allowed to make their own decisions (Assemblée des évêques 1984b, 144). Neither the bishops nor Catholic leaders assumed that they spoke for all Quebeckers or that they could tell Catholics how to vote. The pastoral letters and other gestures were offered as ethical reflections on a pressing political question from members of an important institution with historical ties to Quebec society. While Catholic groups, journals, and public figures did publicize their choices in both referenda, they consistently distanced their political options from direct identification with the Gospel message.

Catholic Values and Quebec Political Culture

However, the bishops did take firm positions on more fundamental ethical matters. The first was their defence of the right of Quebeckers to determine their own future through a democratic process. The bishops defined 'the people of Quebec' as members of the francophone majority, the anglophone community, the ethnic communities, and the Aboriginal peoples. Together, these citizens of the territory of Quebec had the right to negotiate the terms of their political alliance with the rest of Canada (Commission d'étude 1971, 140–1).[10] Nationalism, so far as it promoted the rights of people to self-determination as defined in the 1966 Covenant of the United Nations and the 1971 World Synod of Bishops' document *Justice in the World*, was ethically acceptable.[11] The right of Quebeckers to self-determination was given its most articulate defence in the pages of *Relations*, the journal of a group of Montreal-based Jesuits engaged in social questions. There, Père Irénée Desrochers (1978c; 1979c) defended the right of Quebeckers to decide their fate as a moral principle which preceded the whole referendum debate. Most engaged Catholics did not defend Quebeckers' right to self-determination; they simply assumed it. This position was shared by both of the major political parties and even by the leaders of the 'No' campaign. Quebeckers were understood as a people and not as an ethnic minority (Desrochers 1979a).

Because, in the Church's social teaching, every right is balanced by a responsibility, Catholics did not understand this right to a national identity as absolute. In their second letter on the 1980 referendum, the Quebec bishops argued that the right to national self-determination was circumscribed by the duty to promote the common good, solidarity among nations, and social justice (Assemblée des évêques 1984a, 146–8). Nationalism could not be defined in narrow ethnic terms, nor could it fixate on preserving the past. The bishops outlined their vision of a just society without supporting any specific political parties or policies. To make specific recommendations would again identify the Church too closely with either the social democracy of the PQ or the liberalism of the Liberal party. The bishops' vision of a just society was based on five 'grandes orientations' defined by Catholic social thought in the 1970s: (1) the responsibility of citizens to participate in public policy decisions; (2) the balancing of rights and duties of persons in light of the common good; (3) an equitable distribution of goods and responsibilities; (4) a serious concern for the spiritual and cultural elements of society; and (5) solidarity among peoples (ibid., 145–6).

Finally, the bishops argued that the democratic process of the referendum itself was an important step in the maturation of Quebec political culture. In their 1979 and 1980 pastoral letters on the referendum, the bishops warned that Christians were obliged to support the democratic process, respect their opponents, and continue to serve the community whatever its choice (ibid., 145–6; 1984b, 139). Two weeks before the referendum, Msgr Grégoire issued a brief statement entitled Le référendum: avant et après in English and French. The letter, which was reprinted in Le Devoir, stated that the Christian faith demanded that people respect the truth, recognize the limits of their own positions, and refuse to demonize or maltreat their opponents in the debate. It also demanded that Christians become fully aware of the question and the stakes in the debate, make a rational and sincere decision, and then participate fully in the name of that decision. Catholicism did not allow indifference or apathy on important social questions (Grégoire 1980). The bishops argued that without these basic Christian values, the democratic process itself would collapse. These sentiments were seconded by the progressive Catholic press. Particularly important to the Catholic left was the consciousness-raising of ordinary Quebeckers. In the May 1980 editorial of Relations, Albert Beaudry wrote that the referendum was a historical event, 'non seulement parce qu'il représente un exercice authentique de liberté démocratique, mais par la prise de conscience collective dont il devient l'instrument' (Beaudry 1980, 131).

Sovereignty as a Social Justice Issue

Some Catholics felt that the bishops did not go far enough in their analysis of the sovereignty issue as a question of social justice. In his 1979 book, *Une foi ensouchée dans ce pays*, Jacques Grand'Maison (1979, 26–30) blasted the bishops for their 'stratospheric absenteeism' on injustices committed against the French Canadian community in Quebec. In *Relations*, Desrochers complained that the bishops' first pastoral letter on the referendum implied that the constitutional status quo was morally acceptable. While Gospel values did not dictate a 'Yes' vote in this referendum, he argued, the Gospel message of justice for all did preclude the continuation of the current situation (1979b, 266–8). Confederation, according to these Catholics, had two purposes: to formalize the national oppression of French Canadians in Canadian federalism and to assure the oppression of all workers in oppressive capitalist structures. Still, they argued, one had to maintain a critical distance between the Gospel and any specific political project. The PQ project of sovereignty-association, they argued, was limited by the *petit bourgeois* nationalism of its artisans, its affirmation of the free market, and its bureaucratic orientation which centralized decision-making power in the new middle class of technocrats rather than in the workers. The demands of social justice required a much more radical restructuring of Quebec society, and independence was just the first step in this revolutionary project. This *'oui, mais ...'* (yes, but ...) position was also adopted by the Réseau des chrétiens politisés, the Quebec incarnation of Christians for Socialism and the editorial team of *Dossiers 'Vie ouvrière,'* the journal of the Centre de pastorale en milieu ouvrier (CPMO), Jeunesse ouvrière catholique, and the Mouvement de travailleurs chrétiens (MTC). Some Catholics even helped to form an ecumenical coalition called the Comité chrétien pour le oui during the referendum debate to publicize this 'yes, but ...' position (Seljak 1995, 472–502).[12]

The Church's support of the right of Quebeckers to self-determination, the democratic referendum process, and the values and virtues which sustain a democratic political culture were met with public approval. The entire texts of the bishops' letters were carried in all of the daily newspapers and editorialists generally welcomed their participation (*Montreal Gazette* 1979; Lachance 1980; de Lagrave 1979). They did not see the participation of Catholics – *as* Catholics – in public debates as a demand for special privileges or a threat to pluralism or democracy. Of course, the more radical position taken by progressive independentists raised more objections. Claude Ryan, the leader of the Liberal party and head of the 'No' committee, charged progressive Catholics with replacing a clericalism of the right with a clericalism of the left. He denounced the Comité chrétiens pour le oui as false priests and false brothers who were dragging the Gospel into a purely secular, political, and rational debate (Bouchard 1980; Béliveau 1980a). Marcel Adam (1980), the editor of Quebec's largest daily newspaper *La Presse*, sharply criticized the committee's introduction of Christianity into the referendum debate as a throw-back to *duplessisme*, that unholy ideological alliance between Catholicism and French Canadian nationalism. But members of the Catholic left defended their participation in public debates. Members of the Comité chrétien pour le oui replied to Ryan's attacks claiming that it was he who manipulated latent Catholic conservatism and its identification with the political status quo (Bouchard 1980; Béliveau 1980a). Indeed, polls showed that church-going Catholics tended to reject independentism more readily than other French Quebeckers (Nevitte 1978). Still, most Quebeckers seemed to accept the public participation of the Church in the referendum debate.

Neo-Liberalism and the 1995 Referendum

Having established its new public role through its social teaching in the 1970s and its participation in the 1980 debate, the Catholic Church had a tradition – however short – on which to draw in the 1995 referendum. Indeed, the Church did not alter the nature of its public performance; the only difference in the Church's position was the context now defined by the shift to neo-conservatism. Groups who wanted to carve out a public Catholicism tended to define the 1995 referendum debate as a battle against neo-conservatism, which they saw as the dominant ideology in Canada and the world. They argued that this new orientation was reflected in the proposed bill on Quebec's sovereignty, which was the subject of the referendum. The bill, composed of a preamble and seventeen articles, did not mention any socioeconomic rights or project for a more just society. Catholic critics of the bill – even those who supported sovereignty – argued that this absence of a social project stemmed from the government's neo-conservative assumption that the market-place would define the social reality of an independent Quebec (Baum 1995, 13–14).

It was not surprising that Catholic groups in Quebec would find this approach unsatisfactory on two counts. First, the referendum debate, they argued, was structured to preclude ethical issues. Both sides argued that their option offered Quebeckers the most advantageous position in the new global economy. Second, the most vocal groups had consistently opposed even Keynesian liberalism in the 1970s, and neo-conservatism was even less interested in addressing issues of inequality and exploitation. Inspired by the criticism of world capitalism expressed in papal and ecclesiastical documents such as Paul VI's *Populorum progressio* and *Octogesima adveniens*, the 1971 World Synod of Bishops' *Justice in the World*, and John Paul II's *Laborem exercens*, a number of important Catholic groups, including the Assemblée des évêques du Québec, adopted a radical critique of liberal democracy and the capitalist economy. Despite a general collapse of the left in Quebec after 1981, the bishops and some important Catholic groups had remained committed to their criticism of liberal capitalism and promoted models of development based on social democracy or a more decentralized participatory democracy.[13] For example, in 1994 a group of bishops, along with economists, labour leaders, and business people, created a document entitled *Sortons le Québec de l'appauvrissement* which criticized the neo-conservative philosophy of the Liberal government and suggested alternative economic strategies based on cooperatives, job-sharing, worker management, and local initiatives (*Sortons le Québec* 1994). Along with other Catholic groups the bishops have supported the province-wide anti-poverty movement Solidarité populaire Québec (SPQ), a coalition of popular movements, small cooperatives, labour unions, and other community groups formed to fight the dominant neo-conservative orthodoxy (Baum 1995, 13). Consequently, it was not surprising that Catholic groups would be uncomfortable with a project for Quebec sovereignty which did not address their demands for a blueprint for a more participatory, egalitarian, and solidarity-oriented society. Jean-Marc Biron and Dominique Boisvert published an open letter in *Le Devoir*, arguing that because the referendum question did not address a social project, it could only divide Quebeckers along ethnic lines (Baum 1995, 14).

The Catholic Critique of Neo-Conservatism during the Referendum

Eight months before the 1995 referendum, the executive committee of the Assemblée des évêques du Québec released a pastoral letter entitled 'Le référendum sur l'avenir du Québec.' In it, the bishops affirmed the position which they had adopted during the 1980 referendum concerning the right of Quebeckers to self-determination, the liberty of individual consciences and the autonomy of political society, the legitimacy of the democratic process, and the Christian values of honesty, openness, cooperation, and tolerance. The letter ended on an optimistic note, observing that Quebeckers have not abandoned all of their ethical and cultural values to the demands of the market. According to the bishops, Quebeckers insisted that their politicians solve the problem of the deficit and reform social programs without blaming the poor or placing the burden squarely on their shoulders (Comité exécutif de l'Assemblée des évêques 1995, 104–5).

Despite this implicit criticism of neo-conservatism, the 1995 pastoral letter was much more restrained than the bishops' 1990 submission to the Bélanger-Campeau Commission, established in the wake of the failed Meech Lake Accord by Bourassa's Liberal government. In their earlier report entitled 'Les chemins de l'avenir,' the bishops argued that neo-conservatism promoted the material welfare of certain individuals over the solidarity of the entire community and justice for the poorest members of society. Moreover, they complained that neo-conservatism tended to reduce all human relations to market relations. Consequently, so-called rational economic values automatically excluded cultural, ethical, and religious values in all questions of public policy. Such an approach, the bishops argued, promoted an economic fatalism, a resignation to the allegedly natural laws of the market. In opposition to this fatalism, the bishops insisted that Quebeckers seek out an ethical project which would reform society. They underlined the need for constitutional reform not only as a question of national integrity but also as a way to ensure social justice for the more than one million poor people in Quebec and the impoverished regions of the province. They affirmed the distinct society position outlined in the Meech Lake debate, the priority of French as the public language, the greatest autonomy possible for the First Nations, respect for the rights of minorities, the decentralization of powers towards the regions, the responsibility of Quebeckers for the welfare of francophones outside of Quebec, and the creation of a participatory democracy founded on values of equality and mutual responsibility (Assemblée des évêques 1991). In their February 1995 letter, the final position was much more restrained (Biron 1995). Perhaps the relatively vague nature of the letter may be explained by the episcopacy's policy of maintaining a posture of political non-partisanship. Again the bishops were very careful to avoid having the Church identified with any one political party by openly criticizing the PQ law on sovereignty.

Two days after the referendum, the executive committee of AÉQ released a second pastoral letter entitled '*Le référendum et l'évolution de la société québécoise*' calling for calm, tolerance, and a renewed commitment to the development of a more just society. The referendum vote, they argued, did not settle the constitutional issue nor did it move Quebec society towards a consensus on a *projet de société*. Because the aftermath of the referendum was marked by division and disorientation, responsible citizens were called to adopt 'the Gospel-inspired attitudes of respect and dialogue, rigorous quest for truth and justice, acceptance of our diffferences [sic] and attention to the weakest members of our society' (Assemblée des évêques 1995, 1).[14] The solution required a commitment to the collective good and an openness to others. The bishops lamented the fact that the proposed sovereignty bill and the debate led by the major players did not address important social issues. Still, the tone of their letter was optimistic; they warned against cynicism. The referendum was not a 'useless exercise' but an expression of political maturity and of a democratic culture. It encouraged people to reflect on every aspect of their political, economic, cultural, and social lives instead of short-term issues of economic self-interest (p. 2). This in itself was a protest against the economic fatalism which dominated Quebec political culture in the 1990s.

For the writers of *Relations* as well, the nationalist movement and referendum process were exciting expressions of democratic participation. Joseph Giguère applauded the fact that community-based groups had succeeded in transforming the regional and national commissions on Quebec's sovereignty into opportunities of civic participation and direct democracy. In contrast to the discourse of the PQ, the participants tied Quebec national identity to 'la démocratisation de la société civile, la justice sociale, l'enracinement territorial et la consolidation du caractère communautaire de la société québécoise' (Giguère 1995a, 100). Similarly, Jacques Boucher (1995a, 99–100) felt that participation by grassroots groups in the commissions had succeeded in widening the debate, moving it past the narrow confines of its original *économisme* and putting forth models of development based on social democratic ideals.[15]

Federalism and Neo-Conservatism

While the bishops criticized neo-conservative values without taking a position on the 1995 referendum question, certain Catholic groups argued that the Church's concern for social justice demanded a 'Yes' vote.[16] Most prominent among these groups were le Regroupement des religieuses et religieux pour le oui and the editorial team of *Relations*. They agreed that popular participation in the referendum debate itself was the first step in overcoming the fatalism engendered by the dominant *économisme* of Quebec political culture. But, beyond affirming the referendum process and the introduction of ethical debate into the public sphere of Quebec politics, they argued that sovereignty was a first, necessary, but not sufficient, step in opposing the neo-conservative agenda of the federal government.

Le Regroupement des religieuses et religieux pour le oui brought together some 400 nuns, brothers, and priests involved in social work to sign a strongly worded letter supporting a 'Yes' vote.[17] The letter stated that, while the Gospel did not dictate either political option, their own commitment to the poor led them to support a 'Yes' vote. The alternative to sovereignty, they argued, was an acceptance of the dominant neo-conservative discourse which contributed to the desperate social conditions they faced in their daily work. Since the government of Jean Chrétien had abandoned its commitment to the welfare state, Quebeckers were better off on their own. The Regroupement presented their open letter to the press at a brunch and press conference attended by approximately 120 of the signatories in a working-class area of Montreal. The event was attended by two PQ ministers, the local MLA and MP (Baillargeon 1995) and was covered by *Le Devoir, le Journal de Montréal, Radio Canada*, television news outlets, and the regional press.[18]

In its letter, the Regroupement lamented the fact that the referendum debate had been dominated by a pro-business agenda that focused solely on the economic risks associated with sovereignty. Totally absent from this discourse was any concern for social solidarity, any worry about the growing division between the wealthy and the poor, and any reference to the fight against exclusion and poverty (Regroupement des religieuses et religieux pour le oui 1995). Its analysis of the federal government and Canadian society was even more pessimistic. Pointing to the weakening of unemployment insurance protection, the abolition of federal transfer payments for welfare programs, the abandonment of social housing programs, and cuts to the budgets of the Canadian International Development Agency (CIDA), they argued that Chrétien's government had committed itself to dismantling the social safety net. The position of the Regroupement was not just a short-term defence of social programs but rather a stance against what they saw as the ideological foundation of a new Canada. They interpreted a 'Yes' vote as a rejection of the economic fatalism of the neo-conservatism promoted by the federal government that would allow the progressive forces in Quebec 'un nouvel espace de liberté et de responsabilité' in which to express their solidarity and compassion in new and creative social structures. For the Regroupement, a 'Yes' vote was the best way to build 'une société plus solidaire, sans violence, sans sexisme, sans discrimination.'

Another group which saw a 'Yes' vote as a step towards building a more just and participatory society was the editorial committee of the Jesuit journal *Relations*. The editorial committee also supported a 'Yes' vote for roughly the same reasons they did in 1980, but now their support for sovereignty was tied directly to their opposition to neo-conservatism. In an editorial published just before the 1995 referendum, the writers of *Relations* argued that the Chrétien government had a double agenda: to create a more centralized Canadian state and to submit the whole country to the imperatives of economic liberalism. Well aware that the PQ government of Parizeau had also adopted a neo-conservative agenda, they still supported sovereignty as a first step towards creating a more egalitarian, compassionate, and just society. They argued that the very structure of Confederation made Quebeckers' fight against neo-conservatism impossible since so many of the powers the people of Quebec needed to define their *projet de société* were monopolized by the federal government (Paiement 1995, 227). As well, federalism combined with neo-conservatism promoted feelings of powerlessness and apathy (Paiement 1995, 228). While sovereignty was no guarantee of a more democratic and just Quebec, federalism, recast in a neo-conservative model, virtually prohibited the development of such a society. Jacques Boucher (1995b, 164) noted that it was significant that the staunchest defenders of federalism in Quebec – such as the Conseil du patronat and the PLQ headed by Daniel Johnson – were at the same time the most enthusiastic promoters of the neo-conservative model of development.[19] Because of this connection, sovereignty became much more urgent.

Conclusion: Public Catholicism and Quebec Sovereignty

In both the 1980 and 1995 referenda, Catholic groups attempted to redefine a public role for the Church in Quebec society. In doing so, they have rejected both the old-style public Catholicism of the Duplessis era as well as the privatization of religion prescribed by liberalism. Such Catholics are a minority but, because they have the support of the bishops and several important religious communities and organizations, they are a significant one. Their attempts at the 'deprivatization' of religion take the form of resistance to the dominant political culture, which would relegate both religion and alternative ethical perspectives to the 'private' realm of subjective values and experiences. Informed by social scientists, such as Jacques Grand'Maison at the l'Université de Montréal and Fernand Dumont at l'Université Laval to name two, Church leaders have conscientiously adopted a modern posture: affirming the autonomy of political society, the liberty of individual consciences, *and* the Enlightenment agenda of the application of critical reason to the perfection of society. Moving beyond a simple instrumentalist definition of critical reason, Catholic leaders have sought to define a rational, ethical critique of the new secular nationalism, a critique which was, at the same time, identifiably Catholic.

The definition of this modern, public Catholicism was made possible only by the fact that the Catholic Church had come to redefine its relationship with Quebec society at a time when international Catholicism had come to accept the modern values of democracy, the rights of peoples to self-determination, and social justice. The Second Vatican Council and the emergence of a faith and justice movement within the Church allowed Catholics in Quebec to engage in the important debates of their societies *as Catholics*, without resorting to the premodern modes of public religion (see Baum 1991; Seljak 1995, 1996). It is an excellent example of a much broader phenomenon described so well by Casanova – an example which should lead us to rethink the categories of public and private, universal and particular, rational and ethical, which permeate our political culture and social-scientific models of secularization.

NOTES

1 A parallel system of education, health care, and social services for English-speaking Quebeckers was provided by the Protestant churches and by voluntary associations, but was funded largely by the state.

2 Martin shows that in those cases where a national enclave in a wider federation is united by religion (for example, Croatia, Slovakia, Brittany, the Basque country), national identity and claims-making is often medi-

ated by Catholicism. In cases of conquered people living in empires marked by a majority of a different ethnicity and religion (such as Poland and Ireland) the identification between religion and nationalism has often been complete. Such societies are marked by a high degree of clericalism, low tolerance of dissent and pluralism, and extraordinarily high levels of practice and Sunday observance (Martin 1978, 42–5). Baum (1991, 15–47) applies Martin's analysis to Quebec fruitfully.

3 Lemaire argues that the rise of instrumental reason over substantitive reason expressed itself in the intellectual world as a *néoscientisme technocratique*, an American-style positivistic approach to the study of society and the person defined against the humanities as 'value-free.' Continuing symptoms of the victory of technocratic reason in Quebec intellectual life include the abandonment of literary, philosophical, and historical studies; positivism in science; the ubiquitous faith in the cybernetic model under a veneer of cognitive science; and a runaway *'économisme,'* the dominance of economic determinism over political choice in public debates (Lemaire 1993, 18).

4 Gregory Baum discusses the importance of 'cultural Catholicism' in Quebec in his chapter of this volume.

5 Louis Balthazar (1986, 132–9) has argued that the idea that the Quebec state was the national state of all Quebeckers was the foundational idea behind the Quiet Revolution. Consequently, a shift away from the idea that the Quebec state should be the primary agent of the political, economic, and social development of Quebeckers represents a rejection of some of the founding principles of the Quiet Revolution.

6 Relying on the framework provided by David Martin, Gregory Baum (1991, 15–47) argues that this parallels the experience of the Catholic Church in Belgium.

7 For the limited but significant impact of the Dumont Commission's report, see Baum (1991, 49–65), and J. Harvey (1990). Gregory Baum deals with the significance of the commission in the context of the secularization of Quebec society in his chapter of this volume.

8 The press noted the efforts of the bishops to assure that neither sovereigntists nor federalists tied their political options directly to Christian values. See Martel (1980) and Béliveau (1980b).

9 Quebec Catholics frequently complained that English Canadian Christians were not so careful. They tended to identify federalism directly with the Christian virtues of unity, peace, and security. Even some Catholic bishops and parishes prayed for political unity as if it were God's will. In 1978, other Christians offered prayers for Canadian unity during the Week of

Prayer for Unity among Christians announced by Pope Paul VI (see Desrochers 1978a, 1978b). For a fascinating report on how English-speaking Christians in Canada continued to spontaneously and uncritically identify God's will for unity with Canadian federalism during the 1995 referendum, see Harry Hiller's chapter in this volume.

10 The Quebec bishops were following a position outlined by the Canadian Catholic Conference in a 1972 letter entitled, 'On Pastoral Implications of Political Choices,' in which the Canadian bishops wrote that when Quebeckers considered their political future – including independence – 'all options which respect the human person and the human community are a matter of free choice on the individual as well as the community level' (Canadian Catholic Conference 1987, 230). The Canadian bishops, in turn, were inspired by the 1971 document, *Justice in the World* (produced by the World Synod of Bishops), which sought to guarantee peoples the right to self-determination and freedom to develop according to their particular genius.

11 The World Synod of Bishops wrote that people had the right to development, that is, modernization, according to their own particular identity. Thus, the right to development was tied to the right to self-determination. See *Justice in the World* (nos. 13–19) in Gremillion (1976, 516–18).

12 The Catholic left's critical acceptance of the new nationalism is discussed at length in Chapter 6 of my doctoral dissertation (Seljak 1995, 367–513).

13 For a discussion of Catholic groups which have adopted these positions, see Vaillancourt (1984), and Baum (1992).

14 The French version reads: 'Les attitude évangéliques de respect et de dialogue, de recherche rigoureuse de la vérité et de la justice, d'accueil de nos différences, d'attention aux plus faibles de notre société.'

15 In fact, Giguère (1995b, 35) argued that Quebeckers' distinct identity was founded on their communitarian and democratic heritage and orientation. This heritage was expressed in Quebec's voluntary associations, popular movements, cooperatives, labour unions, chambers of commerce, and credit unions, as well as in its affirmation of local and regional identities, affirmation of popular education and mobilization, and promotion of a communitarian culture.

16 It is important to remember that such Catholics were in a strict minority. Polls since 1976 have consistently shown that church-going Catholics have been the least likely among all francophone Quebeckers to support independence, sovereignty association, or the PQ as a political party. See Nevitte and Gingras (1984), Grenville and Reid (1996), and Grenville, Reid, and Lewis (n.d.).

17 One of the instigators of the letter, Sister Thérèse Soucy, stated that those most likely to sign the letter were people most directly involved in providing services to workers and those on social assistance (Venne 1995). While its members came from some thirty different religious communities, and were very active in a number of Catholic and secular social justice groups, they signed the letter as individuals and not on behalf of any community or group.

18 The press conference included a modest brunch. The cost of the brunch and setting up the conference was covered by le Comité pour le oui, since all expenditures for the debate had to come under the umbrella of the official government-approved campaigns.

19 In a speech after the referendum, Ed Broadbent (1996) tied popular support for sovereignty to Bouchard's defence of the welfare state. While the federal government and the provincial governments of Ontario and Alberta all adopted the rhetoric of neo-conservatism, Bouchard has consistently rejected it in favour of a 'conservative' Keynesian liberalism. In an interview with this author on 23 May 1996, the editor of *Relations*, Carolyn Sharp, mentioned that she was not entirely comfortable with the tendency among progressive francophones in Quebec to identify federalism with 'neo-conservatism.' She worried that they often ignored progressive federalists who lamented the dismantling of the welfare state.

chapter eight

Catholicism and Secularization in Quebec

GREGORY BAUM

In the past many sociologists accepted the theory of secularization, according to which the spread of modernity would inevitably lead to the waning of religion. This theory was verified in several European societies, yet it never fitted the evidence gathered in the United States where religion continued to thrive. Whether the more recent spread of industrialization in parts of Asia, Africa, and Latin America will lead to the decline of religion is not at all certain. To the surprise of sociologists, religion has again, for better and for worse, become a social force in several parts of the world. In addition to this, fundamentalist movements have emerged in all the world religions. These recent developments persuade us that it would be rash to create a general theory to account for what happens to religion in the process of modernization. Since the place of religion in modern society depends on many historical factors, what we need are studies of religion in different social environments.

In this chapter I wish to examine the reaction of the Catholic Church to the rapid secularization that has taken place in Quebec society. I shall examine, in particular, two official reports commissioned by the Catholic bishops – the first published in 1971, the second in 1992 – that interpret the causes of this secularization in different ways and hence make recommendations that seem to contradict one another. Why has this intensely Catholic society in a period of less than two decades become the most secular province of Canada?

Quebec's Quiet Revolution

It is usually said, and rightly so, that Quebec moved rather late into cultural and political modernity. The provincial government, prior to 1960, protected traditional, premodern cultural ideals, restricted religious and political pluralism, and refused to regard the state as responsible for the social development of the population. The government had no ministry of education, no ministry of health, and no ministry of social welfare. Maurice Duplessis, the premier of Quebec during most of the years between 1936 and 1959, defended this tradition in unbending fashion. He wanted private societies to organize education, health services, and social assistance. The Catholic Church was pleased to fulfil this role. It assumed full responsibility for the organization of schools and colleges, hospitals and health care centres, and assistance to people in need. As a result the Church's organizational presence became ubiquitous. Let me add that English-speaking Quebeckers, about 20 per cent of the population, were not displeased with this policy of the government. Why? Because this policy allowed them to organize their own institutions without government interference.

In this situation the cultural power of the Church was enormous. It defined Quebec's cultural identity in opposition to the Protestant and secular culture of North America. It demanded unanimity within its own ranks and supported the government in its opposition to pluralism. The Church was sustained in its activities by the faith of the vast majority of the people. Their ardent piety produced a culture of solidarity and mutual aid. An intense faith inspired vast numbers of young people to become priests, sisters, and brothers dedicated to serve in their own society and the field of overseas missions.

This profound loyalty to the Church may seem like an anomaly in the middle of the twentieth century. Yet whenever a people has been conquered by empire and must struggle for its collective survival, the Church easily becomes a symbol of identity and resistance. This happened in Poland, Ireland, and Quebec.

There were signs in the 1940s and 1950s that the unanimity in the Catholic Church was being seriously challenged. Joseph Charbonneau, the Archbishop of Montreal, broke ranks with the other bishops in his support of non-confessional institutions and interventions in favour of workers' strikes (Hamelin 1984, 11). The review *Cité libre*, directed by intellectuals relying on liberal Catholic thought coming from France, criticized what it called the clerico-nationalist, corrupt, and undemocratic regime of Duplessis (Dion 1975, 55–60). Two priests, Gérard Dion and Louis O'Neil, published a book in 1956 that criticized Duplessis's reactionary policies and advocated democratic and egalitarian ideas

(Dion and O'Neil 1956). Examining activities and events in these two decades, historians have come to recognize the cultural and social currents that prepared the Quiet Revolution. Still, despite these moments of anticipation, when a Liberal government was elected on 22 June 1960, a cultural explosion took place that truly deserves the name Quiet Revolution (Gagnon and Sarra-Bournet 1997).

Quebeckers thought of themselves as a gifted and autonomous people with energy, ideas, and the will to construct their own society. If we follow Émile Durkheim's vocabulary designating as 'effervescence' the collective experience of peoples at dramatic turning-points of their history, we may say that for Quebeckers the Quiet Revolution was a time of effervescence. People wanted to catch up with modern society, be open to pluralism, participate in democratic decision making, express themselves in art and literature free of censorship, and create a modern educational system qualifying students to advance in the fields of science and technology. The agents of this cultural upheaval also wanted to free themselves from the economic domination of the English-Canadian elites and assume full political responsibility for their own society.

At the same time, the people acting in the Quiet Revolution wanted Quebec to remain faithful to its distinctive cultural tradition and not be assimilated into the other North American societies. They wanted Quebec to stand against the individualistic culture of these societies and preserve its own heritage of solidarity and cooperation. They used the word 'socialism' in a very wide sense ranging from cooperatism and social democracy to Marxist-inspired social reconstruction. Like many peoples caught in a premodern culture, Quebeckers wanted to catch up with modernity and yet remain a distinctive society.

Another consequence of the Quiet Revolution was that Quebeckers ceased to think of themselves in ethnic terms as part of the entire French-Canadian nation. They now thought of Quebec as their own nation, defined in terms of citizenship rather than ethnicity. While this altered self-perception disappointed French-Canadian minorities in other Canadian provinces, it opened Quebec society to ethnic and cultural pluralism, le Québec au pluriel.

The Quiet Revolution initiated a gradual process of secularization. The supporters of this revolution criticized the Catholic Church for having both defended the reactionary regime of Maurice Duplessis and impeded the entry of Quebec into North American modernity. They now referred to this regime as 'la grande noirceur.' Their intention was to secularize Quebec's self-perception and replace the religious myth or story that had defined Quebec's place and destiny in the past with the secular self-definition of a people eager to discover its power, talent, and originality.

Moreover, when the Liberal government eventually created ministries of education, health, and social assistance, and secularized the ecclesiastical institutions that had been serving these purposes, the Catholic Church lost a great deal of its power and influence in society. Only in the school system did the bishops retain a certain hold, even if it was no longer under their direct control.

✳   A significant number of Catholics welcomed these first two steps of secularization. At this time, the Second Vatican Council (1962–5) advocated a new openness to modernity, defended the autonomy of secular institutions, fostered ecumenical relations with Protestants, expressed its respect for religious pluralism, and urged lay people to become responsible actors in their society. Many Quebec Catholics rejoiced in this new teaching. They became ardent supports of the changes brought about by the Quiet Revolution.

David Seljak has recently examined in detail the reactions of Catholics to the Quiet Revolution by studying the positions adopted by Catholic papers, Catholic reviews, Catholic organizations, and important Catholics spokesmen, both clerical and lay (Seljak 1995). He has shown that while at first only a minority of Catholic activists supported the cultural transformation, by the end of the 1960s, the majority of Catholics, including priests and bishops, had reconciled themselves to the new society. Many actively supported the new Quebec. The conservative Catholic organizations that resisted these changes and hoped that the cultural revolution could be reversed became increasingly smaller and eventually disappeared.

At the same time the Church remained uncertain about its future. While it had lost its cultural power and institutional presence, the majority of its members still remained ardent believers, many of them eager for a quiet revolution in the Church itself. Catholic Action and other church organizations became involved in vehement controversies. It became evident, moreover, that by the end of the 1960s growing numbers of Catholics had become indifferent to their faith and disassociated themselves from their parishes. The first and second stages of secularization, which, as we saw, were welcomed by many Catholics, seemed to produce, in a manner that was not anticipated, a growing secularization of people's personal consciousness.

The Dumont Report[1]

At the end of the 1960s the Catholic bishops decided to set up a study commission, following the model of the royal commissions well known to Canadians, that was to examine the crisis of the Church, ascertain the aspirations of the Catholic people, and propose to the bishops directives and pastoral policies appropriate for the new situations. Fernand Dumont, a respected sociologist at Laval University, was asked to chair the commission, made up of twelve members, including one bishop and a few priests, with the remaining positions going to lay men and women, mainly activists associated with Catholic Action. The Dumont Commission, as it was called, held hearings in various parts of the province, received briefs written by persons and groups, and commissioned psycho-sociological research on the religious values of the Catholic population. Eventually in 1971 and 1972, the commission published the Dumont Report under the title *L'Église du Québec: Un héritage, un projet* (Commission d'étude 1971), accompanied by several smaller volumes that explored topics of the report in greater detail (Voisine, Beaulieu, and Hamelin 1971; Wener and Bernier 1971).

The briefs and recommendations the commission had received included a wide spectrum of opinions. At one extreme were the voices – a minority – that wanted a return to the discipline and unanimity of the old Church; at the other extreme were the voices – also a minority – that wanted the Church to abandon its hierarchical structure and become a popular democracy. The great majority of Catholics wanted to express their inherited faith and religious practice in new forms, more adapted to modern culture. The commission adopted two general principles for sorting out and synthesizing the aspirations of the Catholic people.

The first general principle was the judgment that the Quiet Revolution signalled a break with the past and was irreversible. In other words, it would be absurd to consider a return to the social and cultural conditions that had existed in the past. In fact, a fundamental recommendation of the Dumont Report, one which Quebec bishops have followed faithfully, was that there was no place in the Church for nostalgia, regret, or resentment. Laments over the loss of power were inappropriate. The new Quebec was here to stay, and the Church's task was to ask itself how it could best serve the people of Quebec.

The second general principle was theological in nature. Reflecting on the dynamic character of a collective identity, the Dumont Commission recognized that the social transformation of a society – or a Church –

must be faithful to the best in its history and, at the same time, respond creatively to the new conditions. By calling its report 'L'Église du Québec: Un héritage, un projet,' the commission wanted to emphasize that the Church must be both faithful to its inheritance and open to new developments. This principle allowed the commission to disregard the minority voices that advocated either conservative opposition to change or radical discontinuity with the past. The commission borrowed an idea from the advocates of the Quiet Revolution that looked upon society as 'a social project,' guided by a vision, led by a sympathetic government, and realized through the participation of all its members. The commission's report presented the Church as 'a project' – an idea previously unknown in Catholic ecclesiology – in which all Catholics, clergy and laity, were to take an active part. In the words of the Dumont Report, ecclesiastical arrangements and pastoral policies are always 'stratégies du provisoire.' The Church is like a group of people on a pilgrimage; it resembles a series of building sites; it is ever unfinished.

We note that the primary purpose of the Dumont Commission was not to mobilize the Church against the new, secularizing culture. The commission willingly accepted Quebec's secular self-definition as well the secularization of the network of social institutions previously operated by the Church. The commission also acknowledged that the Church could no longer speak for the whole of Quebec, that it had become one public voice among others. What the commission tried to do was to offer a synthesis of the convictions held by the practising Catholics regarding the role of the Church in the new situation. The commission probably thought that it did its work well and if the bishops accepted their proposals, then the members of the Catholic community, even if reduced in size, would thrive and communicate the meaning and power of the Gospel to their society.

Fidelity to Past, Openness to Future

What did the report mean by fidelity to the past? It mentioned three factors in particular: (1) the missionary orientation of the Quebec Church, (2) its commitment to 'les canadiens' and later to Quebec society, and (3) its character as a community of solidarity and shared values. The report then explained what fidelity to these three commitments entailed for contemporaries. First, to paraphrase the report, the Church's missionary orientation reveals the deep concern of Catholics for 'the world,' which manifests itself today in their engagement for justice and peace. The Church must now play a prophetic role in society. Second, the Church's commitment to Quebec reveals itself in the continued concern of the bishops for Quebec society as a whole. While the bishops only represent one community in this society, they must continue to speak to the urgent social issues from their Catholic ethical perspective, just as other communities and movements speak to the same issues from their point of view. A democratic society, the report argued, constructs itself out of the dialogue and interaction of its groups and communities. And third, the Church as a community of solidarity and shared values reveals itself in today's effort to make the Church into a more participatory and egalitarian society.[2]

The Dumont Report, here, offered a reinterpretation of the Church's tradition as a guide for its entry into modernity. It made two important recommendations. The Church, being faithful to its heritage, must now (1) assume a socio-critical function in society, and (2) become more democratic in its own self-organization. These recommendations deserve closer attention.

The Quebec bishops willingly received the first recommendation. Since they no longer represented the whole of society, they were no longer obliged to bless and legitimate it. They were now free to address themselves to social issues, guided by the Catholic understanding of social justice. They became critics of society.[3]

Following the recent evolution of Catholic social teaching, the bishops came to look upon Quebec society from the perspective of the poor and disadvantaged. Backed by the associations of the Catholic left, the bishops supported labour unions, cooperatives, and popular movements in their struggles for greater justice and in their efforts to transform society. Their Labour Day Statements on the first of May consistently dealt with controversial issues of social justice in a society that was increasingly shaped by the economic elites and their neo-liberal principles (Bergeron 1998). The bishops and many religious orders became participants in the movement 'Solidarité populaire Québec' which united labour unions, women's organizations and the popular associations in a common cause and which has articulated its programme in 'La charte d'un Québec populaire.'[4] As well, the bishops have supported 'les journées sociales,' a biennial assembly which brings together left-wing Catholic activists from all over the province.

It may be of interest to readers less familiar with the public debates in Quebec that the Catholic bishops have also addressed the national question from the perspective of social justice. They defend Quebec's right to political self-determination, which they regard as a human right, following the 1966 Covenant of the United Nations, signed by Canada and the other member states. According to Article 1 of this covenant, 'All peoples have the right to self-determination. By virtue of this right they freely determine their political status and freely pursue their economic, social and cultural development' (Laqueur 1989, 216). At the same time, the bishops insist that it is not their task to advise Quebeckers on how to define their collective future, whether within or without Canadian Confederation. In this context, the bishops argue that a nationalist movement is ethically acceptable only if it envisages cooperative relations with the neighbouring countries, if it protects the human rights of minority communities, and if it intends to create a more just and more open society (Baum 1991, 159–70).

Second, the Dumont Report recommended the democratization of the Church within the framework of the existing hierarchical structure. The three guiding principles were to be participation, pluralism, and the toleration of dissent. Let me first consider how the report presented the latter two principles. The report recognized that the Church's internal pluralism has three distinct causes. First, the present renewal movement would be more welcomed by some Catholics than by others and be realized more quickly in some regions than in others. The Catholic Church was, therefore, likely to become unevenly patterned for some time. Second, the urgent call that Catholics become committed to social justice would result in differing political engagements: some would prefer moderate reforms, while others would opt for more radical changes. Third, there existed in the Church different spiritual aspirations and different theological currents, all of which had a legitimate place in the Catholic tradition. On the difficult theological and ethical questions raised by the Church's encounter with modernity, there was not likely to be unanimity. There was room in the Church, however, for responsible dissent and respectful opposition.[5] It would be through patient wrestling with this internal pluralism that the Church would be taught by the Holy Spirit.

To facilitate the democratization of the Church, the report recommended the creation of both regional 'centres of decision making' that would formulate pastoral policies and regional 'common assemblies' that would allow the people affected by these policies to react to them and discuss their appropriateness. The reason why the report refers to 'regions' rather than 'parishes' is that the commission had entertained a lengthy debate on the continued usefulness of the parish. While parishes continue to fulfil an important role in villages and towns, in cities, especially Montreal with its mobile population and rapid secularization, parishes seemed to have lost their attraction. In the end, the commission defended the continued existence of parishes. 'Centres of decision making' and 'common assemblies' could be set up for the larger parishes or for wider regions embracing several parishes. The report recommended that these institutions be chaired by a lay person, not a priest, to avoid the tone of authority. These 'centres' were to elect members for a diocesan and a national pastoral council that would interact with the bishops of Quebec.

The Dumont Commission believed that the Church would thrive if it proclaimed and celebrated the Gospel in a manner that was open to the spirit of modernity. The members of the commission probably expected that the successful modernization of the Catholic Church would invite the lively participation of the practising Catholics and in this manner stem the tide of the ongoing secularization.

Let me add that the sociological imagination implicit in the Dumont Report was, in part at least, derived from Émile Durkheim. Durkheim assigned great importance to intermediary associations in the social and political life of modern democracies: they were to be schools of social solidarity and through dialogue and political debate they were to contribute to the promotion of the common good (Durkheim 1995, 183–8). The Dumont Commission interpreted the Church as one of these intermediary societies. It is also possible to detect in the commission's critique of the traditional Church, an allusion to Durkheim's concept of social pathology, that is, the deviation of a society from its declared principles (Durkheim 1995, 36–8, 252–3). The Church, which had forgotten that, as a community of God's people, it was meant to be a participatory community, was to be healed of this pathological trend by the reform of its structure. Both the Church and society as a whole are envisaged as organic societies.

What was the impact of the Dumont Report on the Quebec Church? While the bishops applied the recommendations of the Dumont Report only partially, its influence on the life of the Church was considerable. The bishops, as I mentioned above, willingly assumed a prophetic role in Quebec, calling for social justice, criticizing the dominant structures, and standing in solidarity with the poorer and weaker sectors of society. They acknowledged the Church's internal pluralism: they did not, on the whole, interfere with the critical movements in the Catholic community, and they tried to defend dissenting theologians from Roman censures. While the bishops did not institute regional centres of decision making and regional common assemblies, many bishops did introduce innovative team ministries involving lay people and priests and encouraged lay participation in the existing ecclesiastical structures.

To communicate its message to people in the parishes, the Dumont Commission prepared a booklet that summarized its findings (Côté 1972). While conservative Catholics were disturbed by the new orientation, Catholics who desired change, more participation, and greater freedom were confirmed in their spiritual option. The spirit of freedom and participation which characterized the Dumont Report remains strong in the Church of Quebec to this day.

Risquer l'avenir

Despite the Church's pastoral efforts inspired by the Dumont Report, the secularization of Quebec society continued. To this day the dominant culture, as revealed in novels, films, television plays, and newspaper stories, continues to associate the Church with 'la grande noirceur,' the imposed cultural conformism under the Duplessis regime. Still, there exists in Quebec no political anticlericalism, as it did exist in some of the Latin countries of Europe. It does not occur to Quebec politicians to make anticlerical remarks. Yet practising Catholics have become a smaller minority, and the survival of a good number of Catholic institutions is uncertain.

Twenty years after the Dumont Report, in 1990, the bishops of Quebec decided to created another commission, this time a smaller research team, chaired by a Dominican priest, Jean-Louis Larochelle, to investigate the decline of the Church and come up with new pastoral recommendations.[6] The Larochelle Report, entitled *Risquer l'avenir* (Larochelle Commission 1992), gives an account of the commission's methodology, which was quite different from the one used by the Dumont Commission. The empirical research drew upon the cooperation of a large number of parishes, carefully chosen to represent different regions of Quebec; different environments, urban and rural; and different economic conditions, affluent and indigent. The participating parishes were asked to set up committees to study the development of each of their parishes over the two decades between 1970 and 1990. The committees were requested to respond to a detailed questionnaire, after which they were interviewed by the commission. The members of the committees were drawn largely from parish workers, namely, lay people employed by the parish for a variety of pastoral tasks.

The radical conclusion of the Larochelle Report is that the Catholic Church in Quebec is dying. The report documents the continuing decline of membership in the parishes, the ageing of these communities, the almost complete disaffection of the young, the shrinking numbers of priests, the gradual disappearance of religious congregations, and the shattered self-image of the parishes overwhelmed by a feeling of powerlessness (Larochelle Commission 1992, 17–23). There is evidence that even the Catholics who continue to go to church have only a vague idea of what being a Catholic means and that they are unable to put into words what they really believe. The report concludes that unless the Quebec Church introduces a new pastoral approach, it will disappear altogether. With its back against the wall, the Church must 'risquer l'avenir,' risk its future by embarking upon a radically new path.

While the Dumont Report looked with favour upon the humanistic dimension of modernization – personal freedom, democratization, pluralism, and tolerance – the Larochelle Report analyses in critical fashion the secularizing consequences of modernization. This report accepts the sociological theory of secularization. It cites with approval the work of Peter Berger who has argued at length that the rational and scientific discourse dominant in modern society produces an approach to the world that leaves no room for divine transcendence. Berger echoes here the conclusion of Max Weber that the instrumental rationality dominant in modern society inevitably leads to the disenchantment of the world and thus the waning of religion. This is how the Larochelle Report puts it: 'Every type of society fashions the personality of its members. Through the process of secularization people interiorize the ways of doing, thinking and feeling proper to their society; thus the ways of their culture become their own personal way. When persons are socially integrated there is neither opposition nor rupture between them and their society, but rather continuity and interpenetration' (Larochelle Commission 1992, 76, my translation).

Even Christian believers in modern society, the report continues, discover that religion occupies a different place in their personal consciousness. From celebrating a total vision incarnate in society, religion becomes a freely chosen personal journey. The only religion that can survive, the report goes on, is one that is freely chosen and capable of defining its identity against society. The report recognizes the relative success in the modern world of 'the sects,' which emphasize personal conversion and opposition to the dominant culture and are willing to define themselves as marginal. The sects expose their members to counter-socialization. Catholics in Quebec, the report argues, will have to learn from them.

These sociological reflections guide the report in its positive recommendations. If the Catholic Church wants to survive in Quebec, it must communicate a voluntary, experiential, and well-informed Christian faith and adopt a counter-stance to society, not by bracketing society as do 'the sects,' but by critically engaging society in solidarity with the poor and the weak. These two points had already been made in the Dumont Report, which recommended both teaching religion to adults so that they could acquire a personal faith and urging Catholics to work for justice in society. Yet the Larochelle Report offers a more radical interpretation of these pastoral objectives. Three proposals are especially startling.

First, the Church should concentrate its teaching on adults. At present, great energy and resources are spent on the education of children. Behind this effort stands the idea that if children are brought up as well-catechized, practising Catholics, they will remain active members of the Church when they grow up. But this idea, the report argues, is an illusion. There is no empirical evidence whatsoever for the notion that Quebec children brought up as good Catholics remain Catholic as they enter adolescence and adulthood (Milot 1991, 63). Putting great effort into giving religious education to children is not a realistic pastoral policy. The Church should apply these resources, the report argues, to the education of adult Catholics, to improving their understanding of the Bible, to sustaining their personal engagement, and to teaching them the practical meaning of Christian faith in modern society. The Church should foster voluntaristic religion based on spiritual experience and profound conviction.

Second, the report suggests that the Church should abandon large parishes and instead organize Catholics in 'primary groups,' that is, groups small enough to allow members to enjoy face-to-face acquaintance. In such communities, the members could learn to speak to one another about their religious convictions and their doubts and could discuss the possible answers to their difficulties. Here also they could find support for their personal faith threatened as it is by secular society. Here they would also develop a critical sense in regard to the social order and discover how they can become agents of change in their society. While in large parishes priests teach the faith in doctrinal terms and the people remain silent, in small communities people learn to talk about what they believe in their own vocabulary and thus become capable of communicating their faith to others.

If primary groups are of the essence and secondary groups, such as large parishes are to be abandoned, then the giant church buildings that decorate Montreal and other cities in Quebec will lose their function. These great church buildings, the report maintains, impressive and beautiful though they be, should be relinquished and, if possible, sold. The financial resources put towards keeping these buildings in good repair and heating them in the winter could then be used to expand the Church's educational ministry and strengthen its social witness in society. These enormous churches, moreover, misrepresent the historical reality of today's Church. At one time these large edifices symbolized the spiritual and cultural unity of the local community and Quebec as a whole, in solidarity with worldwide Catholicism. Yet today, these massive buildings, largely empty on Sunday, confuse the parishioners and prevent them from accepting who they are, a small religious community in a secular society.

Third, the report recommends that the Church turn its back on cultural Catholicism. Catholicism can survive in Quebec only if it understands itself as a voluntaristic religion. In the New Testament, the report reminds the reader, the Church was a community of disciples. Repudiating cultural Catholicism means, in practical terms, that priests should refuse requests made by people to be married in church and have their babies baptized in church unless these people are active members of a Christian community. Similarly, priests should refuse to give Christian burial to people who had not been active Christians. This is a radical proposal since the majority of Quebeckers, while detached from their parish, still want to have a church wedding, have their babies baptized, and be buried in a church cemetery. The report regards this cultural Catholicism as a form of superstition that is damaging to the Church: it undermines the sense of Catholic identity and obscures the dividing line between the believing community and the secular society in which the former is situated. Cultural Catholicism tempts the Church to delude itself about its historical reality, to assume that it still represents society as a whole, and to cling to the illusion that its continued presence is guaranteed.

While the Dumont Report was guided by a Durkheimian imagination, the Larochelle Report has a certain affinity with Weberian thought. It accepted Weber's theory of secularization. For Weber, moreover,

society was conflictive, not organic: it was held together by a government with a big stick. Society shaped by the dominant institutions and
their cultural influence also included countervailing trends expressing the frustrations of people at the margins (Weber 1968, 929). The
Larochelle Report argues that the Church can only survive if it becomes
a countervailing movement. Weber also looked upon religion as
voluntaristic, rather than as the product of a community.[7]

The Larochelle Report provoked a lively debate in the Quebec Church.
After the publication of the report in 1992, a large assembly was held in
Montreal to discuss and vote on its recommendations. The assembly
gathered 570 people, among whom were 333 lay people, 51 religious
women, 2 deacons, 128 priests, and 25 bishops, plus representatives of
theological faculties and pastoral centres. The report was admired for
its brilliance, but its recommendations were on the whole not well
received. Many objections were raised to its conclusions.[8]

Some participants argued that the report was too pessimistic, that it
was not appreciative of the existing vitality in the Church, nor trusting
enough in the unpredictable power of the Holy Spirit. Others argued
that the report had an ecclesiocentric understanding of God's redemp-
tive presence in history. It presumed that divine grace is largely confined to the Church, while Catholic teaching after the Second Vatican
Council recognized that God is at work in the world, that all personal
manifestations of love and selflessness and all social transformations
towards greater justice and peace are signs of God's gracious presence,
and that it is the Church's task to read the sign of the times, discover
God's work in the world, and join its mission to the divine movement
in history. Still other participants complained that the report had an
excessively negative image of the modern world. Even the process of
secularization, it was argued, has a positive side: it dispenses the Church
from legitimating the established order and allows it to define itself as a
defender of the vulnerable and excluded. The Church, moreover, has
learnt a great deal from the modern world, beginning with the respect
for human rights.

Another objection argued that the report relied excessively on the
sociological theory of secularization, which has never been demonstrated, and in doing so overlooked the Church's own responsibility for
the loss of its members and its lack of attractiveness. The Church's
authoritarian structure, its triumphalist discourse and symbols, its in-
flexible sexual ethics, and its outmoded attitude towards women are all
at odds with the spirit of the Gospel and has persuaded many Catholics

to leave their parishes and turn their backs on the Church. The report, this objection argued, looks away from this disturbing phenomenon.

Another complaint dealt with the report's negative view of cultural Catholicism. People who are heirs of a Catholic culture retain, even if they are no longer practising Catholics, a good number of Catholic symbols, gestures, and virtues, such as a sense of the spiritual, resistance to materialism, loyalty to the family, engagement in charities, the cultivation of neighbourliness, and an extended social solidarity. When such people ask to be married in a Catholic church or to have their children baptized, they are not moved by sentimentality or superstition, but rather want to express in meaningful symbols the inherited values they continue to hold.

The radical proposals of the Larochelle Commission were rejected by the majority of the voters. Roman Catholics believe that the Church is the home of saints and sinners and hence hesitate to set up moral criteria for membership. Some participants at the assembly argued that the report was written by priests, based on the testimony of religious professionals working in the parishes, and hence reflected the perspective of highly motivated persons, people who made great demands on themselves and expected as much from others. In Weberian terms, the report reflected the perspective of religious virtuosi. The voters who rejected the bold proposals of the report believed that such exclusivism was not in keeping with the Catholic tradition. In my opinion, they were right. The existence of religious orders in the Catholic Church demonstrates that Catholicism makes room for several ways of being Christian, from saying a radical 'no' to the world chosen by the few, to various degrees of participation in society and its culture.

Rapid Secularization

Many observers of Quebec's Catholicism are puzzled by the speed with which the secular spirit has spread in this intensely religious society. I wish to argue that there are several historical reasons for this rapid secularization. Quebec's experience cannot be cited as a confirmation of the theory of secularization.

The coincidence of the Quiet Revolution and the Second Vatican Council in the early 1960s allowed engaged Catholics to support the modernization of Quebec society, including the secularization of its collective self-understanding and the ecclesiastical institutions that served education, health, and social welfare. These Catholics advocated, in accordance with the Vatican Council, the autonomy of society and its escape from the tutelage of the Church. Yet the sudden disappearance of the Church from people's collective identity and their social existence produced an unexpected secularization of personal consciousness.

Why did this happen so fast? Involved in this rejection of religion was undoubtedly a resentment against the Catholic Church which had enjoyed excessive power in the past and kept the people in cultural unanimity. This is a reaction commonly found in societies where the Catholic Church had been deeply intertwined with the government and the dominant culture. Quebeckers rejoiced in the new rationality that rescued them from the religious teaching that had controlled their lives, and they were now not willing to embrace a new religious teaching, even if it was more humanistic.

Another factor in the rapid secularization is the powerful impact of the Quiet Revolution on the self-understanding of French-speaking Quebeckers. I have described, at the beginning of this chapter, the experience of this cultural explosion in terms of Émile Durkheim's notion of 'effervescence,' an outburst of energies capable of transforming the self-perception of a tribe or a people. While most cultural changes are gradual and involve more than one generation, the Quiet Revolution, due to its effervescent character, transformed the consciousness of the generation involved in it.

Related to the observations made above is the fact the Quiet Revolution introduced the welfare state into Quebec society. The Quebec government saw itself as the principal agent of promoting the well-being of the citizens, their culture, their security, and their sense of identity, and hence fulfilled some of the functions formerly exercised by the Church. In my opinion, therefore, the rapid secularization of Quebec society is a singular event, for which it is difficult to find historical parallels. Still, the debates over the Church's pastoral and political orientation described in these pages clearly demonstrate that Quebec's Catholic Church is an interesting, lively, open, and pluralistic community.

NOTES

1 This section on the Dumont Report follows the more detailed analysis in Baum (1991, 49–65).
2 This new perception of the Church corresponds to José Casanova's analysis

of modern Catholicism as 'public religion.' See Casanova (1994).
3 The public role of the Catholic Church after the Quiet Revolution is examined in detail in David Seljak's chapter in this volume.
4 See 'La Charte d'un Québec populaire,' published by Solidarité Québec Populaire in 1994. Also see Baum (1992, 150).
5 As the report put it [my translation]: 'There exists in the Church a Christian ethic of dissent, criteria of Gospel authenticity permitting protest, in fact a pluralism inscribed in the Catholic tradition, marked as it is by tensions. It is important to remind those who cling to the "letter," – their "letter" – of the transcendent claim of the Holy Spirit' (Commission d'étude 1971, 112).
6 The discussion of the Larochelle Report here is based upon my article (Baum 1994).
7 How do Christian theologians choose the sociological approach that seems appropriate to them? This chapter is not the place to discuss this important topic. See Everett and Bachmeyer (1979).
8 The proceedings of the assembly were published in 1993 under the title *L'avenir des communautés chrétiennes* (Montreal: Fides).

chapter nine

Civil Religion and the Problem of National Unity: The 1995 Quebec Referendum Crisis

HARRY H. HILLER

It has often been said that, as a collectivity, Canadians have never been able to take their society for granted, and that, indeed, the primary characteristic of Canadian society has been the quest for survival. Repeated efforts have been made to enhance or develop consensus and manage conflict in the name of nation-building. Virtually in defiance of geography and diversity, the creation of a sense of society has been an arduous task in Canada (Bell 1992). Whether Canadian society is one nation (represented by Anglo-conformity), two nations (the French and English as the founding groups), three nations (adding First Nations), or polycentric and multicultural has always been a confounding reality that implied defects for those desiring to build a unitary state.

Postmodernism challenges the Canadian political community still further by pointing out that there is no single, integrative, transcendental, or hegemonic understanding of Canadian society, but that there are multiple de-centred discourses (defined by, say, region, race, or gender) that represent other experiences and meanings of Canada (Keohane 1997, 6). From this perspective, the search for a single hegemonic ideal is coercive, partial, and distorted. Postmodernism eschews the idea of a single 'master narrative' of Canadian history or common symbols as the basis for a mutual vision, and when such an ideal is proposed it is subject to a process of deconstructionism (Fulford 1993, 118). Globalization also threatens the Canadian political community through its minimization of traditional political boundaries. Instead, the postnational state replaces cultural distinctives with common economic interests and binds polities into a world community with its priorities of capitalist growth (Laxer 1991, 304). In both cases (postmodernism and globalization) the idea of a unitary Canadian society is increasingly problematic.

In spite of these postmodernist perspectives, nation-states continue to be important containers for personal identity and international relationships. They are clearly not static unchangeable containers, however, and competing forces reconstitute them and even minimize them. It is in this context that we must understand the 1995 Quebec Referendum, because it revealed the fragility and uncertainty of the Canadian nation-state as well as the inability of the countervailing forces of compromise and accommodation to preserve the political entity intact in the face of the threat of imminent dissolution.

The Referendum Crisis

The 1995 Quebec referendum began in a very uneventful way. Most non-Quebeckers saw the referendum campaign as essentially a Quebec issue in which they were not participants, and which represented the feelings of a minority of separatists in Quebec who would surely be defeated as voters, initially swayed by rhetoric and passion, were convinced by reason and logic. The experience of the first referendum in 1980 seemed to establish the precedent for defeat of the sovereigntist alternative, and many non-Quebeckers were both apathetic and irritated by the Québécois agenda and its implied rejection of Canada.

The expected passion-to-reason shift in Quebec opinion received a decided jolt over halfway through the campaign month of October, when polls were released indicating that the 'Yes' side was gaining ground. In fact, polls released from 17 to 19 October suggested a virtual tie, and, depending on how the 'Undecided' was configured, the 'Yes' vote even had a slight edge. This shift in poll support confronted Canadians elsewhere in Canada with the cold hard evidence for the first time that the fracturing of their society was an imminent possibility. By the weekend (21–2 October) distress signals began to be felt in the population at large. The Canadian dollar fell over one full cent, the Toronto Stock Exchange fell 122.8 points, and the Bank of Canada prime lending rate increased by almost a full percentage point. Suddenly, it was clear once again that Canada and Quebec could not be taken for granted.

Over the weekend, contemplation of the situation intensified in the 'rest of Canada,' and on Tuesday, 24 October, various forms of collective behaviour began to take place all over the country, which built to a crescendo over the next weekend in anticipation of the actual referendum scheduled for Monday, 30 October. A huge rally was held in Montreal on Friday, 27 October, and included many non-Quebeckers among the estimated 100,000 who attended. However, a flurry of other activity also took place outside of Quebec, such as rallies, letter/fax and telephone campaigns, petitions, and various group and individual acts. The purpose of these forms of collective behaviour was to send a message to Quebec based on emotion and sentiment, and often motivated by fear and anxiety, pleading with Quebeckers to reject the separatist alternative, and to vote to stay in Canada.

A research initiative was launched in the aftermath of the referendum whereby every major daily newspaper in Canada was scanned for the month of October for evidence of collective behaviour in the rest of Canada in relation to the Quebec referendum crisis. Telephone interviews were then conducted with named organizers for further information. All activities were then catalogued and classified. The data clearly demonstrated that the release of the poll results created a reaction of widespread concern outside of Quebec over the impending referendum, and a recognition of a potential victory for the sovereigntists. The assessment of the gravity of the situation clearly provoked some people to action in the face of what they considered to be a crisis. The question that emerges as far as this investigation is concerned is whether religion played any role at all during this period.

Civil Religion and Times of Crisis

The referendum crisis was essentially a crisis of societal unity or a threat to a polity with a bounded territory. Early analysts of the relationship between religion and society pointed out the integrating or binding nature of religion. Durkheim, for example, understood religious beliefs as shared meanings, and religious rituals as the experience of the transcendent force of society. It was Rousseau who coined the term 'civil religion' to refer to belief systems that legitimized societal bonding and the political order in order to ensure good citizenship (Gehrig 1979, 5). From these perspectives, religion was an important and necessary mechanism of social cohesion and integration.

In the 1960s Robert Bellah (1967) applied the concept of civil religion to the United States and began a continuing debate about the parameters and existence of such a phenomenon (Richey and Jones 1974; Fenn 1976; Gehrig 1979). According to Bellah, civil religion is related to institutional religion and yet transcends it. It is neither sectarian nor specifically Christian, yet borrows selectively from religious traditions, so that members of society feel an explicit continuity between institutional religion and civil religion. In that form, it is an institutionalized collection of beliefs about American society that somehow are made sacred. As the expression of the cohesion of a nation, civil religion has its own myths (America as the Promised Land), saints (Washington and Lincoln), and ceremonies (Independence Day or Memorial Day), all of which celebrate and legitimate national unity and the societal tradition. *Specific religions* are important to the *private sphere*, but *civil religion* is supposedly shared by all in the *public sphere*. Bellah felt that it was American civil religion that engendered and sanctioned a sense of collective destiny and provided integration among an otherwise diverse people.

The civil religion thesis has been applied with mixed success to many other countries of the world, for example, Mexico, Japan, and Italy (Bellah and Hammond 1980); South Africa (Moodie 1978); Japan (Takayama 1988); and the Soviet Union (Lane 1981). In most instances the American case appears to be quite unique. When comparing Canada with the United States, it is usually argued that Canada does not have a civil religion. Even Bellah himself notes this, although the assertion is made without discussion and analysis (Bellah and Hammond 1980, xiii). Most analysts base this conclusion on the fact that Canada does not have a revolutionary origin or the myths that surround such an event, which generated the national heroes and compelling mythologies so central to American civil religion (for example, see Lipset 1970). Furthermore, Kim (1993) points to other factors, such as the distinctiveness of Quebec society and societal dualism, bilingualism, regionalism, and political decentralization, among other reasons, to conclude that a civil religion has been absent if not an impossibility in Canadian society.

One of the key elements of Bellah's argument is that the American civil religion is particularly the product of 'times of trial.' Bellah argues that the first time of trial was the issue of independence from British imperialism, in which the themes of Exodus, Chosen People, Promised Land, and New Jerusalem emerged. The second time of trial was the Civil War, coupled with the issue of slavery, in which the themes of Sacrificial Death and Rebirth arose. The third time of trial was identified as the 1960s, when civil disobedience in relation to the Vietnam War and to the civil rights movement occurred, and in which issues of justice and order created an institutional crisis. Bellah understood that national myths and civil religion played a central role in reflecting its ideals back to the society, for the American civil religion provides transcendent ideals not only for the integration of the society but also for its judgment. The failure of the United States to live up to its ideals in this third time of trial produced what Bellah called a broken covenant, so that the civil religion 'is now an empty and broken shell' (Bellah 1975, 142). Bellah thus implies that American civil religion in the contemporary era may have lost its significance. Wuthnow (1988) has taken Bellah's ideas further and has pointed out that the old American civil religion has now been split into two factions (cf Davis 1997), one conservative and one liberal, and has therefore been considerably weakened. But it has also been challenged by alternative legitimating myths. In these analyses it is clear that societal legitimating apparatuses are not hegemonic and unchanging. They may decay, be transformed, or emerge under changing conditions.

National Unity as a Sociopolitical Problem

In many ways, civil religion is an outmoded concept in a postmodern world because it stresses a type of hegemonic unity rather than the realities of increasing pluralism and diversity typical of both Canada and the United States. Yet it is precisely this difficulty in dealing with diversity that has plagued the Canadian state and made societal unity a political problem. Conflict management is represented in a wide range of federal programs from bilingualism to equalization grants – all aimed at preserving the society intact and appeasing opposing groups whose agitation or protests have threatened the existing state. However, no action has been as directly confrontational as the election of the Parti Québécois in 1976 with its sovereignty platform, and the first referendum in 1980 on sovereignty-association. While the referendum was defeated, the sponsoring party was re-elected and eventually another party with separatist objectives, the Bloc Québécois, was elected federally to represent Quebec's interests in Canada's Parliament (Weaver 1992).

   The Canadian government had of course taken many initiatives since the Quiet Revolution in order to develop symbols of Canadian nationalism and to build commitment to the Canadian state (McRoberts 1997). These included a Task Force on Canadian Unity in 1979, the selection of a distinct flag, a bilingual national anthem, a bilingual civil service, and encouragement for bilingual education, among many other initiatives.

In some ways, these efforts had been alienating to both unilingual anglophones and francophones. Accommodations made were often viewed as weaknesses of the Canadian polity rather than accepted as distinctive Canadian strengths. The political divisions between Reform, the Liberals, and Conservatives, and the Parti Québécois/Bloc Québécois all represented competing visions of Canadian society which accentuated disunity. Each of these visions had their own legitimations. Virtually none of them drew on traditional religion and, while the government was trying to build some kind of transcendent loyalty and commitment among Canadians which would span these political divisions, it was clear that the Quebec issue had produced a strange mix of feelings in the rest of Canada from apathy to resentment to intolerance. Not all Canadians outside of Quebec became alarmed by the poll results that showed the distinct possibility of a 'Yes' vote, but it is clear that the flurry of actions in the last week of the campaign demonstrated that at least some Canadians were very worried and even in distress. While letter-writing, faxing, and telephone campaigns were carried out during the week preceding the referendum, the weekend prior to the referendum was the crescendo for public meetings. The apparent failure of the political process led to grassroots action to produce what Klandermans (1988) has called 'the mobilization of consensus' through largely spontaneous and uncoordinated actions identified as collective behaviour.

Given the parameters of an institutionally differentiated secular society, it would not be expected that religion would play any role in this effort. There is no significant body of evidence in the post–Second World War period that would lead one to expect that institutional religion in Canada would be involved in such matters of polity at all. Yet the evidence is that religious leaders and their institutions did become involved to an extent in this 'time of trial.' The purpose of this chapter is to describe and analyse that involvement, and to assess it in the light of the concept of civil religion.

The Prayer Vigil as Collective Behaviour

While spontaneous rallies were held from coast to coast on the final referendum campaign weekend, the most typical religious form of public involvement in the rest of Canada was the holding of prayer vigils on the weekend prior to the vote. Since the apparent crisis arose so quickly, the idea to hold a vigil was that of local religious leaders who spontaneously coordinated them in response to perceived needs of parishioners or as a personal desire to exert leadership in the community. In all cases the motivation was deep concern for the future of Canadian society as people had historically understood it.

A vigil is an ancient practice of prayer or devotional activity often occurring at night and held in response to some deep-seated concern. Within the Christian tradition vigils are related to the precedent of Christ's garden prayer experience prior to the crucifixion, as well as the Good Friday to Easter interregnum of watchfulness. Because of its association with devotional acts, and especially prayer, it is not a typical form of public behaviour except under the auspices of religion. However, in recent years vigils have been somewhat secularized by protest groups which have eliminated the overt reference to prayer and used them as a form of passive involvement in issues in which direct ideological debate is eschewed (Helman and Rapoport 1997).[1] In any case, vigils are not typically ongoing but are connected to specific concerns or crises. It follows from this that if churches were to become involved in an affair of the state, a natural and historically relevant way to participate would be through a prayer vigil. From a behaviourist perspective it is also the least confrontational and most passive form of involvement.

The data indicate that at least forty special event vigils were held across the country.[2] These were events that were explicitly called vigils or prayer vigils, but they ranged from quiet prayer with no formal program, to a formal service with planned speeches or pageantry, to something akin to a rally in a public place but sponsored by religious leaders. More communities held rallies rather than prayer vigils, but it is significant that even at some of these rallies religious leaders were called upon for an invocation or prayer.[3] The focus of this analysis, however, is those events identified as prayer vigils and which can be directly conceived as religious responses to the crisis. In a few locations, rallies were called vigils, for example, Victoria (Case 130–2), Ottawa (Case 133), and New Liskeard, Ontario (Case 135), because they took place at night and made use of candles. However, vigils that had no religious associations or overtones are not part of this analysis.

Approximately 10,000 people attended explicitly organized special event prayer vigils.[4] Many vigils were small and somewhat individualized, although large ones, such as those in Saint John (Case 84) or Calgary (Case 18), almost took on the character of a community rally, whether held in a park or in a church. Often it was impossible to coordinate all such activities in a community because of the spontaneous character of these events and the shortness of time, so in a few instances more than one vigil was held. Also, given the fact that Sunday services preceded the Monday referendum, it is highly likely that some kind of prayer activity occurred at many regular church services, and a number of reports of such activity were received (but no attempt was made to include them in the count). Furthermore, given the fact that such activity was part of regular programming, it seldom received much media coverage. A report in the *Winnipeg Free Press* on 31 October 1995 did suggest that 'O Canada' may have been sung in some churches at their regular Sunday services, as one woman claimed that she prayed for a 'No' victory and cried when the national anthem was sung in her church, illustrating the depth of the emotion that some people were feeling.

There were two types of vigils. One type virtually served as a nationalist rally in being a positive assertion of the need for national unity and the registering of that commitment with prayers in a public way. The second type was much more quietistic and sombre, and served to provide solace to those who were perplexed and troubled by the prospect of the referendum. The *rally-type vigil* tended to be larger, whereas the *quietistic vigil* was smaller and pensive.

Perhaps the best example of a rally-type vigil that was more celebrative was a mid-Sunday afternoon event at Rothesay Common, a park in Saint John, New Brunswick, entitled 'A Call to Prayer for Canada' (Case 84). Organized by a local Pentecostal pastor, who was also president of the ministerial association, and with the encouragement of the local Liberal MP, some 1,500 people attended on a sunny day, waving flags and cheering. With a choir and band providing the music, there was little sense of crisis as 'people were happy to be together and happy to be celebrating their country.' The appeal was to an emotional nationalism based on Canadians as a large family in which Quebec was viewed as a vital part.

There were four variants of the more quietistic vigil. One type was a *come-and-go vigil* held throughout referendum Monday. An Anglican church in Winnipeg opened its doors for prayer from 7 a.m. to 4 p.m. (Case 172). A United church in Brantford, Ontario, was open from 9 a.m. to 5 p.m. for a vigil, with no service or oral presentations for the twenty to twenty-five persons who came in at various times throughout the day (Case 48). A United church in Guelph, Ontario, had flipcharts with relevant Scriptures at the door, and suggestions for meditation in addition to time for discussion and prayer twice during the day (Case 50). Another type was an all-night vigil that began with a service in the early evening and with a service every three hours throughout the night, as in Ottawa-Hull where 600 attended in total (Case 38). The twenty-four-hour vigil was planned to conclude with the closing of the polls in Quebec at 8 p.m. on Monday evening. Another twenty-four-hour vigil was held in Kingston, Ontario, beginning at 4 p.m. on Sunday with public prayers every hour on the hour and private prayers on a come-and-go basis (Case 43).

Another vigil concept could be called a *dispersed vigil*, in which a leader called for people to pray wherever they were. Various Christian organizations – for example, Habitat for Humanity (Case 174) – spread the word through newsletters, and by telephone, fax, and e-mail, asking people to pray for the unity of the country. This concept was based on religious activity as a personal rather than a collective act – although there was some sense of mutuality in Christians joining together, if in a less-visible format. One Ottawa-area Catholic church urged its members to fast and pray all day on Monday (Case 134). Indeed, fasting on an individual basis was encouraged in a number of locations. Another innovative effort was a *continuous vigil* (when one vigil in one time zone ends, another vigil in another time zone begins) that was organized by a joint Anglican-Catholic parish in Winnipeg through the Internet, and eventually linked churches in New Brunswick, Vancouver, and perhaps elsewhere (Case 15).

A fourth vigil concept was the arrangement for a religious service in a church building – a *planned event vigil*. One of the more complex examples of this type of vigil was the linking of eleven United churches in ten provinces in a special simultaneous Sunday service labelled 'A Service of Prayer for Our Nation' (Case 40). Another variant of a planned event, but informally sponsored by the local ministerial association rather than merely the initiative of one church or religious leader, was the vigil held in Fredericton, New Brunswick, where the idea for the event came from a local clergyman and was held in his Baptist church, but was anticipated a month in advance as a significant time in Canadian history (Case 47). Letters were sent to all churches in the city and the press were informed. Participation in the service included representatives from other Protestant and Catholic churches in what was clearly intended as a community event. However, the focus of the event was a 'concert of prayer' rather than merely flag-waving.

As the province with a much larger population than other provinces (other than Quebec), it is not surprising that Ontario held more prayer vigils than any other province. It is unclear whether Ontario's geographical proximity or historical ties to Quebec may have been a factor, but vigils were more numerous in Ontario, although they did take place elsewhere as well. Not surprisingly, Ottawa was a key site for vigils as well as for other forms of collective behaviour. There were more reports of explicit church involvement there than in any other city. Just across the river from Quebec, and with Ottawa-Hull identified as the Canadian Capital Region, the population in Ottawa had the most to lose by a pro-sovereignty referendum result. From the data gathered it is also significant to note that Catholic churches were more explicitly involved here than in any other place. In one instance, three Catholic churches joined together for a three-hour vigil (Case 175). Almost all the other vigils held across the country were organized by Protestant groups, although a few were organized by Catholics or included Catholic participation. There were no records of prayer vigils organized by non-Christian groups, although one vigil included non-Christian representatives. Among Protestants, Anglicans were overrepresented as vigil sponsors, though United Church members, Baptists, and Pentecostals, as well as joint ministerials also organized vigils.

The Vigil and Church–State Relations

One of the issues that the vigils raised indirectly was whether national unity was necessarily divine or God's will. While there was some caution about assuming that Canadian unity was automatically religiously legitimated, and while reminders were often given that the example of the Lord's Prayer meant that prayer ultimately was for God's will to be done, there is no question that the dominant theme in prayer was for national unity. Another church–state issue was whether politicians should be involved in the vigils, for in some instances they were explicitly excluded to ensure it was a non-political event, as in Calgary (Case 18), while in other instances politicians were heavily involved and helped to legitimate the event in a public way, as in Fredericton (Case 47).

Perhaps the most relevant religious theme brought to the crisis was that of the need for reconciliation. Praying for a 'No' vote might be viewed as taking sides; praying for reconciliation was more neutral. Notions of forgiveness, understanding, goodwill, humility, and compassion were to be antidotes to the bitterness and intolerance which had been building in the country. Linguistic, ethnic, and racial differences needed to be put aside for the good of the nation. Thus, religious ideals attempted to play a role in transforming attitudes and in building better relationships between groups in the society.

Many of the vigils that were organized services of some kind used reconciliation as a theme. Perhaps the most dramatic of the vigils using a reconciliation theme was one organized by a pastor of a large Pentecostal Church in Hamilton, Ontario (Case 22). This pastor had strong patriotic leanings and also a very multiracial congregation. His experiences with this congregation sensitized him to the need for reconciliation that was both cross-denominational and cross-racial. Therefore, the service that he organized on Sunday afternoon (29 October) included not only prayers for repentance and against bigotry, but also featured flags from each province scattered across the sanctuary. The 350 people from sixteen denominations that were present were each asked to gather around one of the flags for prayer. Then the flags were brought together in a circle with the Quebec flag and people from Quebec in the middle while more prayers were said. This symbolic reconciliation ceremony included speeches from anglophones, francophones, Aboriginals, and new Canadians. Another application of the reconciliation theme at other vigils included prayers for healing, in acknowledgment of the animosities generated by the referendum campaign itself.

Were vigils viewed as churches getting involved in politics? It appears not, as no clergy reported any overt opposition. One Anglican priest who put up notices at public places and had the vigil announced on radio and TV remarked that many people said, 'O what a good idea! We're glad the church is doing something. No one considered it inappropriate. Two or three made a few snide comments about the Quebec situation, but that is as far as it went.' Probably the key here is that a prayer vigil was not viewed as a political act, even though it had political overtones. Maintaining the unity of the country was not perceived as politics. Second, while the vigil implied national unity, it was not offering anything particular to Quebec (except friendship), and certainly made no overt contribution to resolving the crisis. No promises were made to Quebec, and no new proposals for policy change were advocated. Thus, the vigils had neutral and passive overtones at the same time that they were squarely in support of national unity. While at some vigils there was tacit recognition that Quebec was free to choose, the emphasis at most vigils was on the need for unity and love for one's country as historically constituted.

The Sociopolitical Meaning of Vigils

In an institutionally differentiated society where religion has been both differentiated and privatized, the unity crisis provided a unique opportunity for religious participation outside of its own sphere. This kind of relationship of religion to polity was apparently not only received well by the community at large, but also caught the imagination of the media. Many members of the clergy were surprised that they could have such an impact and could arouse media interest for an activity which they had planned.

Vigils also provided an opportunity for community involvement by churches across denominational boundaries in a relevant national issue. Almost all events, even when held in a local church, were conceived as community events, and the appeal was made to the whole community. There is considerable evidence that the events broke denominational barriers as people attended vigils in churches with which they had no prior affiliation. In Sault Ste Marie, Ontario, organizers noted: 'We know that there were many people present from other churches but there were also many present that we did not know at all' (Case 137). The St Catharines, Ontario, United Church-sponsored vigil was the most unique in crossing non-Christian barriers, by including active participants from local Buddhist and Jewish groups (Case 71). Therefore, in some fashion vigils did provide a unique opportunity to bridge traditional organizational boundaries within communities. The use of the unity theme also brought non-church people into local churches as, for example, local school choirs were on occasion asked to participate. Thus, the vigils allowed some churches to reassert their roles as central community institutions.

Most people who went to prayer vigils had a strong belief in both Christianity and Canada. In most cases, these were people who bought the argument that Canada was truly to be God's dominion from sea to sea or, put another way, that faith in God and faith in Canada were in some sense yoked. Such persons were not bothered at all by the use of churches to support the interests of the Canadian state, because a united country was viewed as morally right, if not God-ordained. For example, the mayor of Fredericton, as reported in the *Fredericton Daily Gleaner* on 30 October 1995, challenged people to sing the national anthem 'with passion,' and to 'sing it loud enough so Lucien Bouchard can hear you in Quebec.' The use of a religious event to sing a song of patriotism may not be typical in Canada, but was justified on the grounds that the unity of Canada was a self-evident and righteous good.

There is some indication that people who came to vigils had ties to Quebec, either relatives or friends or colleagues, and had studied, worked, visited, or travelled there at some point in the past. For example, both St Catharines and Kingston, Ontario, were reported to have significant new 'in-migrants' from Quebec (Case 72 and 43). Sometimes even the clerical leaders had held a pastoral charge in Quebec in the past or had other collegial ties with clerics or churches in Quebec (for example, Case 71). These ties obviously heightened anxiety and concern. It was reported that when the media took notice of the prayer vigil in Kingston, people seemed to come in off the street, and about one hundred were present at the conclusion of the event on Monday afternoon, indicating that more people may have had ties to Quebec in that community (Case 43).

Regardless of whatever transcendent purposes the vigils may have had, sociologically they must be viewed as instrumental in providing people with a mechanism for participation in a situation in which they were powerless. Religious activity was clearly related to powerlessness. As one respondent in Kingston noted: 'People felt so helpless for there was nothing they could do. So the only thing left and the most important that they could do was to pray' (Case 43). From a religious perspective, the failure of the political process accentuated the need for prayer, which provided an opportunity for passive participation when active participation in the public order was either inappropriate or unavailable.

The concept of individual and collective prayer also had important sociological elements in that it implied a oneness of people whether they literally joined together or whether they were invisibly scattered across the country. At the Fredericton vigil the service concluded with what was called a 'concert of prayer,' as groups of six or seven huddled throughout the church in circles to share the prayer concern together (Case 47). Vigils, then, provided opportunities for social support among the concerned as well as creating invisible images of solidarity, much like Benedict Anderson's concept of nations as 'imagined communities' (1983). But vigils also created the image of solidarity even when unanimity may have been lacking. In their study of vigils as a mode of protest against Israeli-Palestinian violence, Helman and Rapoport (1997) found that vigils were particularly useful when individual interpretations of a situation varied and where direct ideological debate was to be avoided. In a similar fashion, the quietistic nature of some vigils allowed people to demonstrate their concern without anyone taking an explicit ideological position on the issue.

There is also evidence that churches played a cathartic role for those who were most distressed by the referendum prospects. For example, in Cambridge, Ontario, there was no formal program, but people were invited to break the silence as they desired by standing and then speaking whatever they had to say (Case 76). A candle was lit at the front and the organ played background music, and people shared their thoughts whenever they chose to do so. A United Church pastor in Guelph, Ontario, noted that 'some people got up in tears talking about their connections to Quebec. Sometimes people seemed quite distraught and sat there for considerable time.' A Catholic priest in Nova Scotia (Case 139) thought that some people were panic-stricken (at least partially supported by his total surprise at who attended the vigil), and it was for this reason that he thought that prayer was important. Another vigil in Nova Scotia was organized by a person who taught stress management (Case 140).

There were no overwhelming indicators from clergy about mass anxiety in the community over the referendum, but many did refer to the existence of at least some anxiety and the need for a peaceful presence. As one Ottawa Catholic official put it about their special noon mass attended by about five hundred: 'There was fear and terror in the hearts of people wanting to keep Canada together. Emotions were running very high. People said that something like this service was badly needed. There was even a standing ovation at the end' (Case 134). A respondent in St Catharines said: 'This was a point of anxiety for many people, and people needed a place and time to deal with their anxiety. It was not a service to tell God what to do, but an opportunity to deal with the reality and provide stability amid change' (Case 72). In addition to the general fear about what could happen, there was also the perceived need to prepare people for the outcome whatever it would be, and therefore healing and tolerance were sometimes stressed. 'This was something we needed to do as a sign or symbol of our support for Canadian unity,' one person commented, 'It was just a good feeling for coming together' (Case 78). In that sense, sanctuaries of churches conveyed their own messages of comfort and reassurance amidst the threat of change.

Did the vigils make any difference in Quebec, for example, to effect change in voting preferences? Since the vigils took place primarily on the weekend prior to referendum, it is not likely that Quebeckers knew about them. In fact, a review of all major daily newspapers in Quebec during this period indicated that not one of these vigils was reported in Quebec newspapers. In short, there is little evidence that the vigils were an overt instrument of influence or had any impact on voting Quebeckers.

Canadian Civil Religion and Times of Trial

Is there a civil religion in Canada? The rush to reject the comparability of American civil religion to the Canadian experience has in many ways ignored the historical record. Bellah (1975, 1) has pointed out that 'once in each of the last three centuries America has faced a time of trial, a time of testing so severe that not only the form but even the existence of our nation have been called in question.' In other words, when the existence of the nation as a collectivity was threatened, the need for legitimating myths was brought to the fore.[5] In the Canadian experience, there is evidence that the shift away from the attempt to build a state church in the pre-Confederation period to an alliance of Protestant denominations did produce a civil religion. The task of nation-building was indeed a daunting challenge among the original partners of Confederation, a task that was made even more difficult by westward expansion and by immigration. The surge of Quebec nationalism one century after Confederation and into the 1990s provoked a new sense of crisis, but at a time when the old legitimating myths have been far less prominent.

Both Canada and the United States at one time had religious establishments against which struggles occurred and which produced two variations of a denominational society in which Protestantism played a central role (Grant 1973a). The initial attempt to give the Church of England an official status in Canada was strengthened by the view that Loyalists were an exiled remnant suffering in the wilderness until their arrival in the Promised Land (Westfall 1989, 5). But pressure for disestablishment from Protestant dissenters or voluntarists produced church–state battles eventually symbolized by the secularization of the Clergy Reserves in 1854 (Moir 1959). Westfall has pointed out that, at least in Ontario, in the years leading to Confederation (1820–70), a distinctive Protestant culture took root as a consequence of disestablishment, which produced a block of four dominant Protestant bodies (Anglican, Presbyterian, Methodist, and Baptist) which became allies. If it was the state's responsibility to foster economic development through capitalist growth, it was the Protestant vision to ensure the moral character of the new society (Grant 1977).

It was in this era that the use of the term 'Dominion Of Canada' and its relationship to the Biblical reference in Psalm 72 ('He shall have dominion from sea to sea') developed. The expansionist enthusiasm of Protestant churches in the nineteenth century for participating in nation-building through missionizing was also powerful (Semple 1996). English-Canadian Protestants believed that they had a unique role to play in God's design in Canada, if not the world (Westfall 1989, 5). The linkage between religion and the Anglo dream for Canada was absolutely clear and conceptions of the role of religion in nation-building were very alive.[6]

This Protestant vision of Canada was always in some doubt because of the intransigence of Catholic Quebec, although eventual assimilation of Catholics was expected. But a challenge to that vision also came from the expansion and settlement of the west by immigrants from non-British source countries. Clifford (1973) has shown how the vision of the Canadian nation as 'His Dominion' through this Protestant consensus was threatened by the massive immigration from 1880 to the Second World War. The conception of the Dominion as a homogeneous population of evangelical Protestants was challenged by a western Canada populated by a wide range of persons with different backgrounds, such as the Chinese, Ukrainians, Mormons, Hutterites, and Doukhobors. The goal of Canadianizing and Christianizing was the immediate objective, but it became apparent by the Second World War that this Anglo-Saxon Protestant ideology no longer exerted its once powerful cultural hegemony.

It was in the interwar period, however, that the distinctive Canadian institution, the United Church of Canada, was born in 1925. The impulse to union, it has been argued, came not only from the efficiency rationale for churching new territory, but from the need to assimilate immigrants who threatened the nineteenth-century concept of His Dominion because 'Canadianization and Christianization were two sides of the same coin' (Vipond 1992, 168). The other macro-sociological impetus came from concern over the destructive potential of western regionalism/sectionalism in detracting from the national vision. Church union, then, was supported by the idea that Canada must be a united nation from sea to sea, and that a united church could play a role in nation-building. To that extent, the United Church was to become a symbol of national unity and also be 'the soul of the nation' (Silcox 1933; Grant 1967). Such lofty objectives may not have fit with eventual reality, but they certainly fit with the spirit of the times.[7]

The important thing to understand about civil religion is that it indeed is an ideology (Gehrig 1981; Blumstock 1993) or, put differently, a symbolic resource whose content may be contested (Williams and Alexander 1994, 4). It represents a legitimating myth, articulated by a particular group, which is then imposed on all members of a collectivity as a set of transcendent truths about the nature of the society. Bellah himself (1975, 107) admitted this early on in the debate by noting that from the 1960s onward, Natives and Blacks and members of other repressed cultures rejected the Anglo-Saxon image of American civil religion. He then raised the possibility of multiple civil religions. In deed, the concept of civil religion has gone into decline in the United States, at least partly because it appears as a form of 'cultural imperialism' (Moseley 1994, 18) in which a unified vision of America seemed 'out of touch, patriarchal, and condescending' to other groups (Porterfield 1994, 13). Increasing religious pluralism and ethnic diversity, in combination with a disillusionment with American society and the collapse of the Cold War, put the emphasis more on cultural conflict rather than solidarity and harmony and a universal civil religion.

There is nothing more postmodern than such a conclusion in admitting to the existence of a variety of civil religions. From this perspective, civil religions not only unite but they also divide. Instead of being inclusionary as it was once envisioned, a civil religion's rhetoric is now seen as exclusionary. In that sense, Bellah's third time of trial results in a societal problem with fragmentation replacing unity. Just as Wilson (1979) viewed American civil religion as the attempt to conserve the political culture of the Protestant establishment, and the breakdown of these legitimating myths reflected the breakdown of Protestant hegemony (cf Marty 1992), so the Protestant vision of Canada, as an attempt (primarily by Ontario) to shape the west, if not the entire country in its own likeness (Vipond 1992, 177), has been transformed by urbanization, increased pluralism, and globalization in post-Protestant Canada (Grant 1977, 19). Postmodernism renders even the search for a civil religion obsolete. In that sense, even the threatened disintegration of the state is a postmodern condition in which selective appeals to traditional institutions (such as religion) via piecemeal participation engender fragmented support (Flanagan 1996).

Religion and Social Continuity

Since political states still require and search for legitimations as a means to ensure compliance and unity, it is useful to inquire about how or whether religion can be drawn into such legitimations. This chapter has shown that in this third time of trial in Canada, religion, along with other societal institutions, did play a role in supporting the stability of the polity. In this regard Hammond (1980, 161) has argued that the courts and schools play a particular role in societal transcendence in the United States, meaning that public schools are the new Sunday Schools, and courts are the new pulpits for the collective good (cf Michaelson 1992, 366–86; Gamoran 1990). In the same way in Canada, courts define group rights, schools teach loyalty and pride in the state, multiculturalism and tolerance are taught as ideological ideals, and even a sport such as hockey is promoted as a national religion to bind Canadians together. In short, in spite of the postmodernist agenda the search for an elusive national unity prevails.

While the rationale behind such efforts may have changed in contemporary Canadian society, and while the old notions of a 'culture of order' based on conservative, hierarchical principles may have changed (Westfall 1989), religion has not lost its ability to provide social stability and to legitimate the political order. Its mobilizing potential, its ability to provide leadership and resources, and its structural location as a community institution allows religion to become available for uses promoting social solidarity as well as social conflict. As Juergensmayer (1993) has noted, secular nationalism is an ideological ally of the nation-state and often attempts to co-opt some aspects of religion to enhance consensus. In the case of the 1995 Quebec referendum, there is no evidence that denominational bureaucracies were either mobilized by political elites or that these bureaucracies attempted to mobilize their constituencies. For example, the *United Church Observer* did not even discuss the referendum and its implications – a strange omission given much of the rhetoric at the time of the creation of the United Church of Canada. However, the institutional differentiation of religion or the 'disenchantment of Canadian political life' (O'Toole 1984, 84) notwithstanding, it was action by laypersons and clergy in grassroots congregations that catalyzed religious involvement.

David Bromley (1997) uses the term 'crisis episode' to refer to times when social relations given high moral priority in a society generate structural contradictions which demand symbolic interpretations and organizational mobilization to address the condition of disorder. He notes that prophetic religious workers emerge when the goal is to restructure the social order, but that priestly religious authorization is energized by the threat of discontinuity and seeks to preserve the prevailing structure of social relations. Snow and Benford (1988) have observed that one of the core 'framing' tasks of social movements is to interpret and assign meaning to conditions and events. If we put these ideas together, it becomes clear that some churches responded to the polity crisis because of its threat to continuity, and thereby sought to provide meaning in the midst of conditions that threatened the social order.

The central role which Protestant churches played in this activity, and conversely the less central role which Catholic churches played (also see Seljak this volume), can be at least partly attributed to the historic role which Protestant churches have played in the national vision for Canada. Furthermore, the overwhelmingly pivotal leadership which Anglican churches provided should not only be related to a liturgical affinity with the concept of vigils, but also to their establishment heritage (O'Toole 1984) and to their symbolic role in national continuity. In spite of similar denominationalizing tendencies in Canada and the United States, Grant (1973a) has argued that Anglicanism has always been more directly allied with the state in Canada than the Episcopal Church has been to the American state. Note that the vigils did not evoke prophetic religious appeals for reform of the Canadian polity, but sought to preserve the status quo and the historic Anglo vision of the nation. Given its historic relationship to the Canadian dream, the comparative silence of the United Church in either the priestly or prophetic direction is also notable on this issue.

In conclusion, it needs to be pointed out that the response of religious organizations to this crisis of polity was not overwhelming. Nor have churches been involved in the ongoing problem of the inclusion of Quebec in the Canadian Constitution. Given the suddenness of the referendum 'scare,' yet also the long-standing nature of the 'Quebec problem,' it is conceivable that churches could have played a more active role than they did. From the perspective of postmodernity the question, then, is why they played a role at all. In cases of natural disasters or catastrophic events, religious organizations frequently play a key role in providing meaning and aid (Bradfield, Wylie, and Echterling 1989). Yet because this was not a natural disaster in which a meaningful void was created requiring explanations about 'Why did this happen?' there was little need for religious meaning.[8] Instead, to the extent that churches could be quickly activated, they became agents of societal continuity and reaffirmed the historic vision of the Canadian polity.

NOTES

The research support of Nika Karpinska and the advice of Norman Knowles and William Westfall are gratefully acknowledged.

1 There is one further notion of vigil that comes from care for a seriously ill person. Here medical specialists or close family engage in surveillance to support the person with technological assistance and as a gesture of love, generosity, and respect during a critical period (Fox 1995).

2 The number forty here refers only to specific special events designated as vigils and does not include regular services or calls for prayer on an individual basis.

3 Wuthnow (1994b, 136) discusses the use of religion in public rituals that are not in themselves organized by religious leaders as in some sense evidence of a civil religion.

4 These numbers are problematic and are purely estimates as there was no registry for participants. Estimating numbers in large crowds or keeping track of a 24-hour come-and-go vigil lacks exactness.

5 Hammond (1994) has recently argued that the term 'civil religion' be abolished in favour of the term 'legitimating myth' because it avoids the debate about whether a civil religion exists and instead focuses on the forces at work.

6 Despland (1977) makes an interesting point that clerical schools of historiography, such as represented in the work of Lionel Groulx or George M. Grant, tended to emphasize the religious contribution to nation-building but that, in contrast to the United States, non-religious conceptions of nation-building have been more dominant in Canada.

7 In the same way, John Simpson (1985a) has shown that the federal regulation of religious broadcasting has traditionally been to avoid criticism or divisiveness through cooperative programming and thereby to serve as an agent of the social system. The CBC, of course, was always mandated to promote national unity.

8 A study of a mine disaster in Pennsylvania (Kroll-Smith and Crouch 1987) found that there was little need for religious meaning in this context because the disaster was interpreted as a technical human engineering problem rather than as a natural disaster. In a similar way, it could be argued that in our case study religious meaning was less in demand because the crisis was viewed as 'man-made.' Religion's role was primarily to support or plead for a particular vision of the Canadian polity.

Part Four

BELIEVING AND BELONGING

Modern Forms of the Religious Life: Denomination, Church, and Invisible Religion in Canada, the United States, and Europe

PETER BEYER

I

One of the more constant and perplexing questions Canadians ask themselves is about Canadian 'national identity.' What is distinctive about 'us'? Part, but only part, of the inability to give a widely acceptable answer to this question is that a sizeable number of Canadians, in particular those who identify themselves as Québécois, already have a very clear idea of who 'we' are, but this collectivity specifically excludes three-quarters of those who live in Canada. Irrespective of whether one views Quebec nationalism as symptom or cause, its importance for the issue of Canadian identity is that it provides such an obvious contrast; or perhaps better, that it presents a clear model of how to answer such a question. And here we undoubtedly have one of the main reasons why the United States also provides a rather constant basis of comparison. Both the Québécois and the Americans somehow serve as 'norms' of what 'we' maybe *should* have, but do not. The norm and the model, of course, is that of the *nation*. Canada, and most especially what we often simply call the 'rest of Canada,' does not present itself as a clearly identified nation. Moreover, the question of nation in our world also seems to connect rather self-evidently with the idea of the *state*: nations and states go together. The United States is a nation-state. For many Quebec nationalists, the main problem is that the Québécois nation does not have a proper state; and Canada appears by contrast to be a state without a specifically overarching Canadian nation. There is something wrong here. Or is there?

Holding Canada up to the examples of the Québécois and the Americans in this fashion assumes a particular norm of collective identification called the nation. The operative question, however, is whether the nation is the only possibility. Must the answer to the question of what it means to be a Canadian take the *form of nation*? Rather than enter that debate directly (cf Gwyn 1996), in this chapter I approach it through what I hope to show is a very much related question: what typical forms does religion take in modern circumstances? Is there in this domain a putatively normative form parallel to that of the nation in the politico-cultural realm? And does Canada conform to such a pattern, if it exists? Historically, and even today, religion, state, and the nation have been closely, if not unambiguously, related; not only in Canada and the United States, but also in Europe, a third pole of comparison that I introduce to rid the question of its seeming bipolarity. My tasks in this chapter are, then, primarily to look at the question of the modern forms of religion; but also to see how such an analysis implicates the state and the nation; and in the process to situate Canada in that larger picture.

I take as my point of departure aspects of a rather standard discussion in the sociology of religion about modern religious forms, in particular forms of religious organization. In what has become a classic in the field, H. Richard Niebuhr, in his *Social Sources of Denominationalism* ([1929] 1957), lamented the sad state of a disunited Christianity in the United States. The argument was that the divisions among American Christians were not a reflection of real religious differences, but rather the expression of class, regional, and ethnic divisions. The denominational churches had compromised with the world; they had become more *secular* in the sense of more 'worldly.'

Niebuhr's work has attained near classic status in the sociology of religion because, in one stroke, it managed to expand into two directions the debate about the social forms of religion under modern conditions. Conceptually, it added the *denomination* to the more limited dichotomy of church/sect as introduced by Troeltsch and Weber; and geographically or culturally, it added the American situation to a discussion that had been focused more on Europe. Niebuhr, it must be said, favoured the *sect* as the pure, uncompromised form, lamented the accommodating *denomination*, but also rejected the established *churches* more typical of Europe: the close association of church and state made the former an even more 'worldly' form than were the American denominations. Ironically, however, once stripped of its theological motivation, Niebuhr's work had the effect of setting up the two 'compromised' forms as key concepts in a debate about the typical forms of religion under modern conditions. Since Niebuhr, both American and European contributors to the sociology of religion have, implicitly or explicitly, taken up this difference between the 'American' denomination and the 'European' church to argue about which region shows the more typical fate of religion in today's world; and, therefore, which is the exception. Moreover, almost the entire debate has been framed in terms of whether or not modern, contemporary societies are inherently secularizing, thus recalling Niebuhr's concern. Good examples of the contrasting conceptions are the work of Talcott Parsons (1974), Robert Bellah (1970), and, more recently and notably, Rodney Stark (see especially Stark and Iannaccone 1994) on the American side; and Peter Berger (1967), Thomas Luckmann (1967), and Bryan Wilson (1985) on the European side.

Parsons accepts that the churchly form has declined, but replaces it with privatized and voluntaristic denominationalism, on the one hand, and overarching and *national* civil religion on the other. The American and national model is key to the entire theoretical enterprise. One notes how the nation enters into this theory of modern religion. Bellah adopts roughly the same strategy, except that his evolutionary model gives a greater place to what Troeltsch called mysticism and his own later work discussed under such headings as 'Sheilaism' (Bellah et al. 1985) – that is, a highly individualized form of religion. Stark and his collaborators have gone significantly further than either Parsons or Bellah in that they virtually identify viable religion with its voluntaristic denominational form, the sect and the cult acting as derivative or inchoate 'feeder' categories (Stark and Bainbridge 1985). In their work, the overarching church does not disappear, but remains only as state-supported, *deformed* (monopolistic), and, be it noted, largely European religion.

By contrast, what unites the three European thinkers mentioned is an almost unquestioning acceptance of the churchly form as the model for socially significant religion. Wilson (1966) more or less dismisses the American denominational form as shallow religion, not, using Luckmann's term, religion *au sérieux*. Berger (1967), in his famous analysis from the 1960s,[1] also dismisses denominationalism as a symptom of secularization, and therefore as less than what religion could (should?) be. Luckmann (1967) in an important way completes the logic of this stance in that he focuses also on *un-formed*, namely, invisible religion, suggesting this latter, highly individualistic, type as the most representative of the shape of modern religion.

The differences between the American and European perspectives should not blind us to the strong similarities that also exist among them. Looking at the two sorts of vision schematically, we can represent them roughly like this:

American version: [civil religion] – denomination – sect – cult/ Sheilaism
European version: church – denomination – sect – invisible religion

Both American and European versions agree that the established and overarching churchly form has declined in power or disappeared in both Europe and the United States. With the partial exception of the

✳ civil religion thesis, all theorists also accept the shift of religion towards the individual, whether through the idea of voluntarism or invisibility. Both versions also recognize very similar sets of forms ranging on a continuum from the obligatory and overarching to the highly individualized, with the organized but voluntary in between. The main differences are in terms of the importance that each perspective assigns to these forms (indicated in bold). For the Europeans church is paradigmatic, and therefore modern society is a secularized one, meaning that religious institutions have lost most of their broad social influence. For the Americans church is not paradigmatic, and therefore it can disappear or be replaced in its supposedly erstwhile function by civil religion. To the degree that the denomination is paradigmatic for them, they do not see modern society as secularized, at least not in as strong a sense as do the Europeans.

To be sure, other notable contributors to the secularization debate in the sociology of religion, notably David Martin (1978) and more recently Steven Warner (1993), have tried to counteract the implicit regionalism by focusing expressly on national differences. These efforts seem not to have resolved the issue, in part because the stress on these differences does not address the root question, which is that of the *typical* social forms of religion under modern conditions. The search on the part of so many theorists involved in the discussion has been for a 'master trend,' a direction for the development of religion which *all* regions are following because they supposedly share a common context. What is becoming clear, however, is that the seeking of trends is itself the problem; that rather than seeking a *norm*, we should concentrate instead on the viable alternative responses to this situation.

The two models that I have just outlined point to, broadly speaking, four alternative religious forms: an overarching, state-influenced, and usually national one that subordinates or controls individual and group variation (church/civil religion); two organized and voluntaristic forms that differ in size but allow significant variation from group to group (denomination/sect); and a highly individualized religious form that carries with it few constraints on variation (invisible/individualized religion).[2] Together they represent a continuum from minimum to maximum variation and therefore from maximum to minimum centralized or convergent authority.

Looking at these types of form as alternatives, the question then becomes, not which will dominate – which represents the 'master trend' in the contemporary world – but rather what are the possibilities and consequences of each in that world. Quite obviously, thus formulated, this is a very broad question, and here cannot be the place for attempting anything like a complete answer. In keeping with my starting point, therefore, I limit myself to the discussion of this question with respect to three regions: the United States, Europe, and Canada (especially the last).

Following the dominant theories that I have just outlined, my focus in looking at these three regions is to assess the possibilities and consequences of only three of the forms: the church, the denomination, and invisible religion. The sectarian form, worthy of attention in its own right, is almost by definition not likely to dominate in any region, and therefore can be left aside for the time being. Although the churchly form is no longer strong or even present in most parts of these regions, such is not the case in certain countries of Europe, such as Poland or Ireland. Moreover, in many other European countries and in Quebec, the historical church is still very much present, but also seems to correlate with the dominance of invisible or even no religion. For both Europe and Canada, in fact, we can adopt and slightly adapt David Martin's formulation (in this volume) to the effect that these countries exhibit 'shadow establishments': either denominations that have or have had some of the features of establishment, or in the sense of established churches that have lost their erstwhile power but still retain a shadow of that influence. Beside the church and invisible religion, the denomination is also broadly present. In general, it seems, the denomination is strongest in the United States and still strong to some extent in Canada. The more invisible form, by contrast, appears to be particularly characteristic of many areas in present-day Europe, although it is also significant in the two North American countries.

Formulating the question of religious forms in terms of possibilities and consequences rather than dominant trends means, to some extent, following the strategy that David Martin adopted in his work on secularization theory (1978), namely, that we must take each region or country seriously in its own particularity. But that comparison demands some kind of overarching perspective that tells us how these regions and countries find themselves in the same context. For Martin, that overarching perspective was modernity/secularization; and it is a nuanced and globalized version of this that I adopt here. Such is not the only possibility, however. Stark and his collaborators, by contrast, find the common context in rational choice assumptions that apply in principle to all times and places (see Stark and Bainbridge 1987). This perspective, however, because it places individual choices so much at the centre, contains an inherent bias towards forms of religion structured along these lines, significantly eliminating the overarching churchly form from serious consideration. It is, therefore, as inappropriate for the present purposes as those versions of the secularization thesis that effectively recognize only this latter form as serious religion.

The remaining bulk of this chapter, therefore, proceeds as follows: in the second section I outline very briefly how I see the broad social context which the three regions under scrutiny share. Here I present a rather Luhmannian version of what constitutes the modern condition and how secularization fits into that context. The third section considers statistical evidence from the three regions which shows the relative dominance of the three religious forms in question. Using various sources, but above all the 1990 European Values Survey that included Canada and the United States, I show the degree to which at present Europe shows a dominance of church and invisible religion, the United States denominationalism, and how Canada lies in between. The last section then seeks to interpret these differences in terms of the specific history of each region, above all with relation to the question of religion and state. Thus rounded out, the discussion will have arrived back at its starting point.

II

The view of the modern societal context that I wish to put forward owes a great deal to the work of Niklas Luhmann, but it is thereby also quite similar in many of its basic positions to the hitherto dominant view in sociology as represented by thinkers ranging from Durkheim, Weber, and Simmel to Parsons, Wilson, and Luckmann. Stated briefly in its Luhmannian terms, modern, and indeed by now global, society has come about as the result of the rising dominance of societal systems based on instrumentality, technical rationality, or function. It is not only the dominance of such institutional spheres as economy, state, science, art, health, law, and mass media that characterizes the contemporary world, but the relative independence of these spheres in terms of the norms, values, and structures that govern each. The wealth-generating power of a capitalist economy, the surveillance power of the modern state, the information capacity of mass media, the knowledge and technological power of modern science, and so forth, are all in part dependent on the pursuit of these types of activity in terms of their separate and particular rationalities; and on the fact of their mutual interdependence. Religion in this modern circumstance is not necessarily, and certainly not historically, some sort of general residue that the other function systems leave behind. It is rather one of the function systems and, in the West, one of the earliest such systems to develop.

The questions of secularization and religious forms flow from this fundamentally modern, and by now global, structural situation. Secularization means simply that the other systems reproduce themselves without direct or explicit religious legitimation and reference; it is the other systems that are secularized. This secularization challenges religious instances to respond, to decide how religion fits into this modern world; how religion will go about its business and thrive in such a world. It does not mean the automatic and inevitable disappearance of religion, but it has historically meant that the hitherto dominant forms of religion are no longer nearly as socially influential. Here cannot be the place to analyse these anterior forms, except to say that they corresponded to societal contexts in which functional system formation did not dominate. The most important implication of this statement for the present purposes is that we must look upon *all four* of the forms under consideration here – that is, church, denomination, sect, and invisible – as modern forms: they represent different ways of institutionalizing differentiated religion in a context of functional system dominance. Whether invisible religion constitutes a form in this sense or expressly the absence of differentiated religion is a question that, for the time being, I leave open. More significant is the idea that the church, especially, is to be considered as a response to modern circumstances and not just as the typical religious form of 'traditional' societies. When I refer to church, therefore, I do not have in mind so much the Roman church of the European Middle Ages as the post-Reformation national Lutheran or the nineteenth-century Roman Catholic Church of the Syllabus and the devotional revolution. The critical distinguishing feature of the 'modern' church is that its purview is specifically national or state-centred, even when, as with the Roman Catholic church, the national church is part of a larger international organization. For this church, then, the close relation of state, nation, and religion is essential. The denomination, by contrast, moves away from such a close relation to the state and the nation, grounding itself instead in the concerted and deliberate incorporation of its adherents into the orthodox practices and beliefs that characterize it, and this not necessarily at all on a 'national' basis but either on a subnational or transnational one (cf Casanova 1997). The distinction is, admittedly, a subtle one, but one whose usefulness will become evident in what follows.

The four forms thus distinguished should not, however, be seen as mutually exclusive possibilities. As Niebuhr and virtually every other contributor to this vast debate in the sociology of religion has emphasized, religious subunits can change among these forms. The most commonly discussed transformation has been between sect and denomination or church (see, for example, Clark 1948; Mann 1955), and to some extent between church and denomination. Here the latter receives more attention. Equally as important for the present purposes, however, is the dynamic relation between denomination/church and invisible religion. Moreover, just as the sect can coexist with the other forms, so we should see the possibility of the other three coexisting with one another. Not only can church or denomination coexist with invisible religion, but we should also be open to the possibility of the church and denomination being present at the same time; not, be it emphasized, as a situation of inherent instability or transition, but as precisely a viable possibility.

These theoretical statements translate into the three regions under scrutiny as follows: Europe has historically been the centre of churches, denominations playing a secondary role. Rather than a historic switch from church to denominational dominance, this region has rather, by and large, maintained its emphasis on churches; the transformations have instead expressed themselves in terms of a rise of invisible religion *as a complement to the continued presence of churches*. The United States, by contrast, while exhibiting some church orientation in the colonial period, has, since independence, been a region of denominational dominance with a consistently significant co-presence of invisible religion. Canada, the hybrid in between, has seen various combinations. Historically, the English-speaking parts of the country had churches until the middle of the nineteenth century, but these coexisted with rising denominations, two or three of which became in the twentieth century for a time something like 'shadow' establishments (Martin this volume). Quebec strengthened and maintained churchly dominance until the 1960s, when it began switching rapidly to the co-presence of church and invisible religion in a fashion similar to the European experience. The rest of Canada went through a long period of about a century of denominational dominance, but has since the 1960s switched to a combination of denomination and invisible religion (see Beyer 1997). The three regions together, therefore, represent almost all the possibilities, at least if we look at them historically. At present the striking feature is that invisible religion has a strong presence everywhere, but there seems to be an option between denomination and church as far as the dominant alternative is concerned.

This said, we can now move on to consider the empirical data on these three regions. The purpose of this presentation is to show how and to what extent the three regions currently exhibit different possibilities for the coexistence of religious forms.

III

The theoretical starting points outlined in the previous two sections require operationalization if we are to use statistical data to illustrate them. The comparative task also demands at least one data set that allows this. For the latter, I rely on the results of the 1990 European Values Survey, which included Canada and the United States. I supplement this with other recent comparative efforts and some select Canadian data. As concerns the operationalization, certain questions that are routinely asked in censuses and surveys, along with known formal characteristics and statuses of religious organizations in different countries, can serve as approximations for the presence of the religious forms at issue.

I begin with the church. As I am styling it here, this form requires the presence of an established religion, and therefore we are looking for some measures of state sponsorship or regulation such that one or two religions or religious organizations receive clear favour. Alternatively, we can look for overwhelming national dominance that amounts to roughly the same thing. In either case, relatively high rates of at least subjective affiliation with these churches would be a requirement. We can therefore use measures of state regulation, subjective affiliation, and religious concentration as operational proxies for the presence of the churchly form (see especially Chaves and Cann 1992).

Denominations, by contrast, are organizations of some size which receive no state sponsorship and exist in a context of meaningful religious pluralism. Significantly lower religious concentration, less or no state regulation, and relatively high levels of subjective affiliation with denominations would be the prime measures here. I should note that measures of religious participation, above all church attendance, would not be an indicator of denominational (or churchly) presence, but rather one of dominance. Participation rates, in the present analysis, relate to the dominance of these forms but equally to the relative presence of invisible religion.

Invisible religion operates in this context less like a clear alternative religious form than what we call religious identity that is neither churchly nor denominational (or sectarian). One, but only one, measure of its presence would be the existence of people who claim no religious affiliation, membership, or identification. Another important variable, however, would be the rate of people who claim some link to a church or denomination but who do not participate in the activities of this organization. These are, in effect, the people who perhaps believe but do not belong/participate; or people who are formal members or affiliates, but who limit their participation to rare occasions such as rites of passage. This portion of a population is religious in a clear sense in that they believe and identify. Their religiosity is, however, by and large invisible in and for the churches/denominations.

Among the implications of dividing the standard religious measures in this way are the following. First, religiosity is not an all-or-nothing affair: one can be occasionally religious, lukewarmly religious, or partially religious. And this can be as relatively stable a condition as any other. In fact, individual religiosity can vary infinitely along whatever continuum one chooses to construct. The more significant question as concerns forms of religion is more usefully conceived as a question about convergent or authoritative forms of religion, ones that show more or less stable patterns of religious communication as the aggregate result of the participation in that communication by a large number of variable individuals; or ones that reflect the power of that authority over such large numbers. It is because I am asking the question of religious forms in the modern (Western) context at this level of authoritative or convergent social forms that the operationalized categorization I am using focuses more clearly on churches and denominations – the larger versions of such authoritative forms – than on the search for observable patterns in sectarian, cultic, invisible, individualized, implicit, civil, or no religion. This latter task is also important, but requires a different approach using categories that make distinctions more along the lines of variation in personal religiosity. It is just such an analysis that Andrew Grenville has undertaken in his contribution to this volume, where he generates relevant categories by cross-tabulating degree of religiosity with institutional or individualistic orientation.

Apportioning the available empirical measures as I have outlined lends a renewed status to measures that are more often considered problematic or even irrelevant. Thus, rates of subjective affiliation, belief, rites of passage, and passive membership become indicators not of, for instance, 'unfulfilled religious demand,' but rather evidence of ways of being religious that avail themselves of churchly or denominational religious resources, but not or only marginally within the authoritative purview of those forms. I begin the presentation of the empirical data by looking at the relative presence of this option in Europe, Canada, and the United States.

In his report on the European Values Survey, Loek Halman (Ester, Halman, and de Moor 1994) makes distinctions between different kinds of 'members' of religious organizations and those he classifies as the unchurched. Combining what he calls core and modal members, we get roughly what I would call those who believe, belong, and participate. By contrast, the marginal members, those who rarely participate but still declare subjective affiliation, and the unchurched, who have abandoned both, together constitute those who would fall in the invisible religion category as I have delimited it here. Table 10.1 summarizes the results for the United States, Canada, and several countries of Western Europe.[3]

Several observations flow from the data in Table 10.1. First, they are obviously quite crude measures of people's religiosity, but I report others below which more or less confirm this pattern (but see Grenville this volume). Second, I have included a separate column for 'affiliated only' to show the specific portion of those I am classifying as invisibly religious who still identify with a church or denomination. They are a significant proportion in most regions; the clear to overwhelming majority in the Nordic countries and Germany; and the largest group in

TABLE 10.1
Degrees of participation/affiliation (%)

Country	Churched 1981	1990	Invisible 1981	1990	Affiliated only 1981	1990
United States	59	54	41	46	35	23
Canada	46	39	54	61	43	35
Ireland	88	87	12	13	11	9
Italy	51	52	48	48	42	33
Spain	54	43	47	57	38	44
France	18	17	82	84	56	45
Belgium	42	30	58	70	42	38
Germany (W)	37	34	63	67	54	56
Netherlands	40	29	61	70	24	21
Britain	23	22	76	77	67	35
Denmark	12	10	88	89	82	81
Norway	15	12	85	88	81	78
Sweden	13	10	88	90	81	71

Source: Ester, Halman, and de Moor (1994, 44).

Britain, France, and Spain. Nonetheless, over the past decade there also seems to have been a movement away from this category, notably, in favour of the unchurched – even in the United States – not back towards the churched. This may or may not be a significant trend. Third, invisible religion can be seen as the dominant religious form in Canada and Western Europe, with the exception of Ireland and Italy. Fourth, comparison of the 1990 results with those of the 1981 survey shows an overall strengthening of the invisible religion category *in all regions*, albeit in general only marginally. It is probably safe to say that, for the time being, given the categories I am using, the religious orientations in these Western countries are stable, with perhaps some slight move in the direction of invisible religion; and within that category towards the genuinely unchurched.

The European Value Survey also gives data for what is called 'religious orthodoxy' and 'religiosity,' which reflect how orthodox people's beliefs are and how important religion is in daily personal life. These represent the intellectual and emotional dimensions, as it were. Table 10.2 presents the results. Here, while there is some variation that would indicate that these are not measuring exactly the same variable, as far as the three regions of comparison are concerned, we again find the same relation: Western Europe is least orthodox and least religious, with Ireland as the only real exception; the United States rates highest on

TABLE 10.2
Orthodoxy and religiosity by country

Country	Orthodoxy mean score (0–6)	Religiosity mean factor score (-1 to 1)
United States	4.83	.58
Canada	3.75	.22
Ireland	4.59	.53
Italy	3.85	.40
Spain	3.08	.07
France	2.08	-.52
Belgium	2.22	-.20
Germany (W)	2.74	-.12
Netherlands	2.20	-.28
Britain	2.92	-.25
Denmark	1.55	-.56
Norway	2.27	-.37
Sweden	1.42	-.72

Source: Verweij, Ester, and Nauta (1997, 315).

both counts; and Canada finds itself in between on both scores. Halman (Ester, Halman, and de Moor 1994, 48) notes as well that there is a clear difference on these two measures between the churched and the unchurched: although the differences between the two categories of regular participators is quite small, that between these and the two marginal classifications is by contrast very significant. The measures of orthodoxy and religiosity thus provide further evidence for the difference between churched (or denominational) and unchurched religious forms. They also support the inclusion of the marginally religious under the latter, that is, within the category of invisible religion.

If we can thus take the indicators in Table 10.1 and Table 10.2 as operational proxies for the relative presence or dominance of invisible religion in the three regions, religious concentration indexes and measures of state regulation can give us approximations for the relative presence of churches and denominations. Here, following data presented by Chaves and Cann (1992), we note the high number of European countries that are either highly concentrated, significantly regulated, or both. Table 10.3 summarizes the results from Chaves and Cann and the European Values Survey of 1990. Following these, and taking the score of 3 out of 6 on state regulation as a minimum for the existence of an established church, the church form is seen to dominate in virtually all European countries with the exception of the Nether-

TABLE 10.3
Religious concentration and religious regulation by country

Country	Degree of concentration	Degree of regulation
United States	.395	0
Canada	.466	0
Ireland	.939	0
Italy	.967	3
Spain	.979	2
France	.884	1
Belgium	.925	3
Germany (W)	.491	3
Netherlands	.456	0
Britain	.699	3
Denmark	.953	5
Norway	.941	5
Sweden	.929	6

Source: Verweij, Ester, and Nauta (1997, 317).

lands.[4] Overall, these data indicate quite clearly that the church form, and not the denomination, is the prevailing organized form of religion in Western Europe. It does not dominate in the sense that invisible religion dominates; but it is still very much present. Again, adapting Martin's term, in most European countries invisible religion dominates, but it does so in the *shadow* of church establishment.

By the same measures, Canada and the United States are just as clearly countries of denominationalism. Neither has any state regulation, both have low concentration indexes. Comparing Canada and the United States alone, we also note the significant contrast between these two countries. Canada shows a dominance of invisible religion on a scale more similar to Germany or Italy than to the United States. On orthodoxy and religiosity, Italy is again the closest comparison. The 'in-between' status of Canada thus seems clear. Nonetheless, it is probably unsafe to leave the observation there without at least attempting to take into consideration the fact that Canada includes Quebec.

Relying in this instance on Bibby's 1990 (1993) and Statistics Canada's 1991 (1993a) data, and using subjective claims to weekly attendance and affiliation as measures, we get the results portrayed in Table 10.4. Although these figures are as such not strictly comparable to those of the European Values Survey, they do indicate that, while Quebec varies from the national average on percentage unchurched, it is fairly close on weekly attendance. More importantly, other regions, notably,

TABLE 10.4
Attendance and membership in Canada and Quebec, 1990–1 (% of total population)

	Weekly attenders	Affliators	No religion
Canada	23	64.5	12.5
Quebec	23	73	4
Ontario	21	66.5	12.5
Maritimes	41	54	5
British Columbia	22	48	30

Source: Bibby (1993, 10); Statistics Canada (1993a).

the Atlantic Provinces and British Columbia are in their own ways as far away from the national average as Quebec. Where there is notable difference is between Roman Catholics in Quebec and those in the other provinces. Here, looking at weekly attendance rates, Bibby's 1990 figures show 29 per cent for the former and 43 per cent for the latter (1993, 6). Yet such Catholic differences between different regions are also evident in Western Europe (see Table 10.1). We can thus understand that the Canadian results on the European Values Survey hide within them important regional variation, but not of such a clear and consistent sort as to undermine the central observation that Canada exhibits an in-between status.

If we can accept that the data thus presented indicate three Western regions with rather different overall characteristics – internal variations understood and notwithstanding – then the task before us is to seek to understand the origins and consequences of these differences: where they come from and what they indicate about religion under these modern circumstances. This analysis brings us back to the question asked at the beginning of this chapter, namely, what is the role of the state in these scenarios, and how is Canada particular in this regard?

IV

I begin these considerations by looking at the United States. In this country, the institutional differentiation between religion and the state has a rather clear history, being expressed especially in the constitutional separation of church and state. What happened in the religious domain since independence can be summarized as the more or less steady rise of religious denominations, including Methodist, Baptist, Episcopalian, Roman Catholic, Congregational, and a large number of others. The exact number is not as important as the variety and the fact that none of them could receive state support. If we follow Finke and Stark's more recent reconstruction of American religious history (1992), then these denominations have been growing steadily, some over the long run more successfully than others. Moreover, sectarian, cultic, and invisible sorts of religion have always also been present and in many senses have been quite strong.

It is neither necessary nor justified by the empirical evidence that this historical development is simply and straightforwardly the result of supposedly universal factors operating, in principle, everywhere. I think, above all, of the idea of 'competitiveness under conditions of religious deregulation.' In fact, what is at least as likely and probably a good deal more so is that the structural conditions of modernization and secularization combined with cultural factors characteristic of the United States to make this result possible. We do not have to speculate as to the nature of these cultural factors. Different observers have made diverse suggestions as to what these might be. They include a high degree of stress on individual responsibility and on instrumental activism. There is the distrust of the state and the reluctance to invest this institution with the responsibility for the common good, meaning that the centre of gravity for collective action may lie elsewhere. It is in this light that religious patterns that emphasize individual experience, revivalism, and an evangelical style make a great deal of sense; as does the valorization of religious belonging as a mark of the proper and moral citizen (see Herberg 1955; Lipset 1990; Reimer 1995; Simpson and MacLeod 1985). In a similar vein, what Verweij, Ester, and Nauta (1997) have measured as a high stress on 'masculinity' dovetails well with these various items in that it values achievement, competitiveness, and individual independence over mutuality and agency within a collectivity. Together these can be seen to have discouraged both antireligiousness and the notion that overarching institutions, above all the church and / or the state, are to be trusted implicitly and entrusted explicitly with the responsibility of seeing to the moral and material welfare of the nation. And, be it noted, the lack of a 'providential' church or state specifically includes the possibility and reality of a strong cultural sense of nation.

However we look at and analyse such cultural factors in detail, together they point to a particular confluence of historical circumstances that expressed itself in, among other ways, the rise and prominence of American denominationalism. This became a specifically American way of re-embedding religion under modern structural conditions. Denominations in religion, like the political system with its stress on competitive interest-group mobilization and government by negotiated alliances, suited the cultural styles that came to characterize society in this country. To the degree, therefore, that society in the United States maintains these characteristic cultural emphases, to that degree we should expect the corresponding religious forms to continue to dominate as they have. This is most decidedly not to say that American society is determined in its future course only by what happens within that country. Global currents will, as in the past, continue to play critical roles. Using Roland Robertson's (1992) language, American denominationalism is therefore a prime indicator of the way that the globalized universal of structural differentiation and resultant secularization has particularized itself in the American context.

The corresponding history of Western Europe contrasts significantly with the American. Here the state, in modern times, has occupied a far more central position as the repository and instrument of the common good; and, not at all coincidentally, state-supported churches have been the rule rather than the exception. Of the Western countries, only France deviated significantly from this model after 1789; and even here, Roman Catholicism maintained its status as the religion and religious identity of the vast majority, other religious organizations not succeeding in displacing it to any significant degree. In all other countries, even as religious tolerance spread in the twentieth century, marking an increased differentiation of religion and politics, state churches have been maintained. They continue to be the prime centres of religious identification and, such as it currently is, of religious practice. When it comes to religion, these churches are still far more what Europeans look to for selected beliefs and practices, than alternative sectarian, denominational, and cultic groups and sources (see Campiche et al. 1992). The reasons for this state of affairs, as with the United States, likely lie in the particular cultural directions of the various countries in this region.

A prime one of these directions has already been mentioned: the degree to which Europeans trust the state to provide for, if not also manage, various institutional domains, above all health, education, and social welfare, but also to a lesser degree the arts and mass media, scientific development, and aspects of the economy. Without exception, European states spend a much higher proportion of their countries' gross national product (GNP) on social welfare than does the United States (see Verweij, Ester, and Nauta 1997). Their taxation rates are correspondingly higher than in North America. European countries have state-financed health systems and educational systems. Most of them still have state-controlled mass media. That churches should be included in this mix of institutions is not surprising. If we are therefore asking why Europeans in so many countries do not go to church, then a partial answer may be that, for them, the state is there to provide. Here may be a reason why level of state regulation correlates well and negatively with level of religious practice: the state, in these European countries does not so much suppress vital religion as fulfil and provide for a sense of embeddedness and security that religious organizations, in other circumstances, can also supply. In this context, churches can reduce their presence to 'shadows,' comforting presences that one can ignore for the most part, but that are also there when and if the need arises.

In addition, we should not forget the Catholic factor. The countries with relatively high church attendance in Western Europe are all Catholic, even though France and Belgium are Catholic, but not highly practising. Although the reasons for this are somewhat speculative, again the Catholic cultural stress on belonging to a greater collectivity may be at play, much as it is for the European sense of the role of the nation-state. The exceptions to the Catholic rule, however, should alert us to the fact that, by itself, Catholicism is only one factor among many that must be taken into consideration when attempting to understand the situation in any particular country.

The idea that religion and religious identity are bound up with the role of the state also points to the closely parallel association of religion and nation. If, as Will Herberg (1955) suggested, being American means being either Protestant, Catholic, or Jew, then the de facto establishment of churches in almost all Western European countries indicates a similar relation here: Swedes are Lutheran, the republican Irish are Catholic, as are the Italians and Spanish; the Germans are either Lutheran/Reform or Catholic, the English are (to a somewhat lesser extent) Church of England. These associations, while they do not explain differing levels of practice, do help to account for the persistence of particular identities, and for the striking differences between countries in Western Europe.

If we turn now to Canada, then, beside the common observation that this country lies 'between Europe and the United States,' we can also use this case to further understand European and American peculiarities. In other words, Canada is not just a mix of European and American factors, it has its own particularities that show again just how varied the possibilities for religious form are under modern circumstances.

The Canadian story has to be divided into, at the very least, English-speaking and French-speaking components. Nonetheless, there are important parallels between the two, and therefore they should not be seen strictly as two solitudes developing separately and in different directions. I begin with the English-speaking side.

Like the United States, established churches did not thrive or survive in Canada. By the mid-nineteenth century, official privileges for the Church of England and the Church of Scotland had been abolished, largely under the pressure from voluntary bodies such as the Methodists. At least in English-speaking Canada, denominationalism was the prevailing form by this time. In its various bodies, it shared the American stress on voluntarism and evangelical styles of worship and theology. Yet unlike their neighbours to the south, the main and increasingly dominant Canadian denominations cultivated a much closer relation to the gradually forming Canadian state. Indeed, the rough simultaneity of Confederation and disestablishment were indicative of the parallel development of both the religious and political institutions. Rather than becoming spheres with different missions and different cultural roles, the Canadian state and churches came to see themselves as largely cooperating in the same enterprise of building a *Christian* society in *British* North America. Unlike in the United States, the denominations that came to dominate the Canadian scene by the end of the nineteenth century were those that identified with this project, and not the more 'sectarian' churches, the ones that maintained a critical distance from the state. Once again using Martin's apt term, we can say that Canada was a country of plural shadow establishments or denominations. English-speaking Canadian society shared much of the trust of the state with the Europeans, but came to form its religious sector along more fragmented denominational lines. Among the consequences was that belonging to churches and belonging to the nation-state were less coordinated than in European countries, including Britain; but more so than in the United States. Therefore, by the end of the nineteenth century, Canadian denominations, while fewer than their American counterparts, had become relatively much stronger, incorporating a larger percentage of the population than in the United States (Beyer 1997). The Methodist, Presbyterian, Anglican, and Roman Catholic churches held the allegiance of the vast majority of the population; and participation rates were by all accounts quite high.

This situation continued well into the twentieth century, finally changing only in the post–Second World War period when the Canadian welfare state took over most of the broader social functions (health, education, welfare) that the churches had helped it to fulfil until that time. Once this shift took place, Canadians on the whole began adopting the more invisible pattern. Unlike in Europe, however, the state has not continued to support the churches because it had not been doing this for quite some time. In addition, unlike in the United States, where denominations continue to play the roles in distinction from the state that they had always played, the Canadian denominational reality did not respond by shifting meaningfully to a new set of denominations. The result has been that, while Canadians still go to church more often than Europeans, they do not go that much more often, and much of the difference can be accounted for by the relatively greater strength of the conservative/evangelical sector (see Bibby 1993).

The shift away from the shadow establishments represented as well the abandonment of the Canadian national project as specifically Christian. The post–Second World War era, however, also marked a similar shift away from the British component of the old national identity. Thus, while the welfare state rose, the hallmarks of the old cultural vision, such as it was, faded, leaving various pieces of an idea of nation, but little that is coherent. Indeed, it is only in times of crisis, such as the 1995 Quebec referendum (see Hiller this volume), that these pieces even give a hint of the possibility of an integrated vision (see Katerberg this volume). In this way, the particular path Canada has followed in the domain of religious forms has its reflection in the area of culture as well, here the lack of an overarching Canadian nation that coincides with a strong state.

A critical aspect of this difficulty is, of course, that such a vision would have to include Quebec. In this regard, the French Canadian story is different, but also has its parallels, especially as concerns the role of the state and the consequences of this for religion. Throughout much of the nineteenth century and in the twentieth century up until the Quiet Revolution, the Roman Catholic Church was the premier national institution among French-speaking Canadians. In Quebec especially, the state played an almost American role as an important, but ultimately not trustworthy institution, and certainly not one that represented the nation the way that states typically did in Europe. The reasons for this distrust, however, were not the American reasons: French Canadians were not radical voluntarists concerned to preserve their freedom from large, potentially overpowering institutions. It was rather that, as in Ireland and Poland, the church was the institution of choice rather than the state, because the state was deemed to be the indirect instrument of that and of those that threatened the nation with extinction. Accordingly, the nineteenth-century 'devotional revolution' became particularly effective in French Canada, such that, as the twentieth century wore on, French Canadians became more and more incorporated in the religious institution, becoming among the most 'believing and belonging' in the Western world.

As in Europe and English-speaking Canada, and unlike in the United States, the rise of the state in the post–Second World War period spelled the end of this era. The Quiet Revolution of the 1960s entailed effectively the transfer of the now Québécois national project from the church to the state. Not that the control of French-speakers over this state became greater, for we are dealing with the same provincial government throughout this story, but rather the level of identification of French Quebeckers with this state changed. The Roman church was not thereby so much rejected as put into the background, allowing French Catholics to transform themselves into typically European believers who do not participate and belong as well.

What is, in sum, different about Canada is the relative and changing cultural status of the denominations and the state, and with those, the different visions of nation. In both segments of this country, the two have been much more closely related and seen to serve complementary and, to a significant degree, interchangeable roles. Religious power and political power have thereby been variably but importantly linked. In the United States, that link at the level of culture and cultural/national identity has never existed in a similar fashion. American denominationalism has, therefore, followed a different route which serves to maintain and perhaps even to increase the social presence of the churches well beyond the levels of Canada and, with the exception of Ireland, all Western European countries.

In light of this conclusion, we do not have to decide whether Canada, Europe, or the United States represents the most typical fate of religion in modern Western circumstances, and certainly not which portrays the most typical relation between religion and state. None of them does and all of them do. The key factor is to keep in mind the cultural location of the most important collective institutions, here the church(es)/ denominations and the state(s). Effectively, the European and Canadian situations allow for periods of overwhelming religious presence in some periods, and a shift to 'low-demand' religion during others. As long as American society develops no substitute for the denominations as prime collective institutions, their strength is likely to continue. All three situations are thereby subject to change over historical periods, and to the relative stability of their patterns over long periods as well. There have been transitions and there will likely be more in the future. But nothing indicates the precise direction of those transitions, neither the factors that have been operative in Europe, in the United States, nor, for that matter, in Canada.

NOTES

1 In his more recent writings, Berger has opted for the more central position of the denomination reflecting a rather fundamental change of heart that may well be influenced by the situation in the United States where denominationalism is stronger than anywhere else in the world (see Berger 1986).

2 The question of what we should call this final 'form' is a difficult one. I do not consider any of the available formulations adequate, but in the rest of this chapter I will use 'invisible' religion as the least problematic of the alternatives. One option that I avoid in particular is 'implicit' religion, since this term raises even more acutely the question of what counts as religion beside its institutionalized and socially authoritative forms.

3 These results and those reported below are more or less duplicated by other multinational research, such as that of the World Values Survey of 1983 and the more recent project by the Angus Reid Group. See Campbell and Curtis (1994) and Grenville (this volume).

4 The European Values Survey measure of concentration is not all that reliable since it makes no distinctions among Protestant denominations. Yet following Chaves and Cann (1992), who used a Herfindahl index, the results for all the countries are relatively the same in the sense that they do not indicate a different conclusion than that drawn in the text.

chapter eleven

'For by Him All Things Were Created ... Visible and Invisible': Sketching the Contours of Public and Private Religion in North America

ANDREW S. GRENVILLE

Invisible religion.[1] Privatized faith. Believers not belongers. These phrases all describe religious belief that is more individual than institutional, more private than public. This chapter reports on a preliminary probe of the landscape of both private and public religious faith in North America and describes a cluster analysis-based segmentation of North Americans. This classification scheme arrays people into six distinct families based on their level of beliefs, behaviours, and the degree of privatization of faith.

Numerous sociological and theological paradigms clash over the cause and significance of public and private religion. These skirmishes all too often take the form of straw-man scraps between rational choice theory and some form of secularization theory.[2] Unfortunately, the 'new paradigm' (Warner 1993) of rational choice tends to be delivered in blustering proclamations of an analogy-based master trend that is blinkered in a 'gloriously American' manner (Simpson 1990, 371; Carroll 1996). And 'secularization,' a term most parties seem quite happy to agree to disagree on the meaning of, is a moving target that comes packaged in a variety of bewildering but stylishly ever-changing forms, both old-school and neo (Tschannen 1991). Almost invariably, empirical analysis pertaining to these theories focuses on organized religion, with measures of church attendance typically serving as the staff that separates the sheep from the goats.

This focus on organized religion and church attendance is unfortunate. It overlooks the complexity that qualitative investigations often uncover (for example, see Bellah et al. 1985; Roof 1993), and it blindly strolls past Robert Wuthnow's (1992, 4) provocative proposition that 'religious sentiment does not wax and wane, it changes clothes and appears in garb to which we are sometimes unaccustomed.' I agree with Nancy Ammerman (1997c) that, rather than focusing on 'either/or categories like sect/church, member/non-member, believer/skeptic, accommodation/resistance, or tradition/modernity,' we instead should 'begin to imagine ways of describing the much more complicated reality we encounter in a world where actors are constantly choosing their ways of being religious.'

Unfortunately, relatively little empirical work has been done recently that explores both the public and private 'ways of being religious' that we currently observe. For example, I reviewed a total of 261 articles published between 1994 and 1997 in the *Journal for the Scientific Study of Religion*, the *Review of Religious Research*, and *Sociology of Religion*.[3] Of these, only two dealt with both public and private faith, and then relatively tangentially. Ironically, one article was on Ireland (Carroll 1995) and the other concerned Northern Ireland (Hayes and McAllister 1995) – currently two of the most churched nations in the world. It is hoped that this preliminary probe will contribute to a greater understanding of the complicated reality of faith in North America and provide some small compensate for the dearth of scholarship in this area.

This probe has three prongs. The first provides some international context on the prevalence of private and public faith. These data come from a 1997 Angus Reid Group World Poll. The main focus of the second section is on the results of a cluster analysis – providing a typology of private and public faith in North America. The data in this section come from *God and Society in North America*, a study conducted by the Angus Reid Group, in conjunction with the Queen's University Unit on Religion and Society, the Institute for the Study of American Evangelicals, and political scientists John Green, Lyman Kellstedt, Corwin Smidt, and Jim Guth.[4] The final section sets forth some conclusions and thoughts for further research.

Phrases such as public and private religion and privatized faith are used in a variety of different manners, and so it is worth specifying my use of them here.[5] When there is reference to religion, faith, or beliefs, it is almost invariably to theological beliefs or behaviours that are explicitly Christian.[6] For example, the statement 'I believe the life, death, and resurrection of Jesus Christ provided a way for the forgiveness of my sins' is one of the measures of Christian belief or faith. The behavioural measures include subjective reports of church attendance, prayer outside of church, and reading of religious material.

Private religion, in usage here, has the general meaning of religious beliefs and behaviours that the individual *perceives* to be independent or separate from groups they have or had interaction with. In other words, it is private if you think it is yours and not part of someone or something else's. In our enquiry here, the concept of private religion has two substreams: whether one's faith apparently and reportedly exists apart from organized religion and whether one's theological outlook is said to have a personal rather than an organizational locus.

Faith is considered to be apart from organized religion if a person does not regularly attend church yet engages in religious behaviours or holds religious beliefs. Theological outlook is measured through responses to such statements as: 'My private beliefs about Christianity are more important than what is taught by any church.'

It should be noted that we are measuring *relatively* private and *relatively* public faith. Strictly speaking, private Christianity is an oxymoron. No one would hold Christian beliefs or engage in Christian devotions unless he or she learned of them from someone else. Likewise, no one holds beliefs that are entirely in accord with the church he or she attends (if indeed, a truly comprehensive system of beliefs exists within a church or denomination). The attempt here is to explore the types of relatively public or private faith that exist in North America.

Public and Private Religion in International Context

A study conducted by the Angus Reid Group in thirty-three countries around the world reveals that most nations have sizeable numbers of both public and private monotheists.[7] The investigation of faith in this international study was limited in scope, necessitating the use of relatively crude characterizations of public and private religion among monotheists.[8] Weekly attendance at religious services is a stand-in for public religion, and prayer (weekly or more often) *without* weekly attendance is the gauge of private religion or belief.[9]

Private believers clearly outnumber public belongers in nine of the countries, including such culturally diverse places as the Philippines, Finland, Indonesia, Ukraine, and Switzerland. Public belongers are more numerous in eight countries, including Poland, the United States, South Korea, Malaysia, and Italy. The remaining countries, including Canada, Argentina, France, and Australia, have roughly equal numbers of both.

Some notable differences emerge when we consider Canada and the United States in this context. The United States is a highly religious nation – with a large number of public belongers (40 per cent) and a quite sizeable group of private believers (27 per cent). Canada, relative to the other nations surveyed, is neither particularly religious nor irreligious. It stands apart from the United States in that it has half the number of public believers (church attenders), while the ratio of private to public believers is roughly 1:1 in Canada, and closer to 1:1.5 in the United States. This analysis, albeit crude, indicates that the two nations we are focusing on have some interesting and important differences in both overall religiosity and the relative degree of privatization.

It is intriguing to note that intracontinental variation is not limited to North America. There is also little consistency in either the prevalence or balance of size of these groups within Europe or Asia. Some small clusters of nations such as the Netherlands, Norway, and Sweden do show tendencies towards low levels of both public and private religion, but their neighbour Finland, with a high level of private belief, stands out as quite distinct. Public believers account for only 4 per cent of the population. There is likewise considerable divergence among European nations with a Catholic heritage. While Italy, Poland, Belgium, and Spain share a tendency towards more public than private religion, there is ample variation in the prevalence of belief overall and in each type of religiosity. Further, France is clearly different from these four in that neither public nor private religiosity is particularly prevalent and there is an equal balance between the two. One geographical grouping that does show consistency is the Catholic-colonized trio of Brazil, Mexico, and Argentina. In these three countries, the level of overall belief is similar and there tends to be a fairly even split between public and private faith, accounting for only one-third each.

Notably, the one nation to which Canada is very similar is Australia, its cultural cousin. Here we see a striking likeness both in the levels of belief and in the balance between public and private religion, each a little lower than in Canada, at around one-fifth. David Martin's chapter in this volume provides some penetrating insight into the reasons for the similarities observed in Canada and Australia.

In summary, this international analysis reveals tremendous variation in the levels and balances of public and private religiosity between nations. This is in keeping with an earlier analysis of World Values Study data (Campbell and Curtis 1994). One conclusion of that dissection was that 'the evidence of large national differences in church attendance and subscription to religious beliefs suggests ... that the relevant explanatory mechanisms for religious involvement vary considerably across societies.' Reviewing this variation underscores Ammerman's call to 'begin to imagine ways of describing the much more complicated reality we encounter.' It also raises questions as to the value of speaking about a common European situation.

A Typology of Public and Private Religion in North America

Most people in Canada and the United States assent to standard Christian creeds, and many agree with the items measuring privatization.[10] Frequent participation in religious activities is, however, less common – particularly in Canada. But just looking at these surface figures can be misleading in that there is much more variation than meets the eye. The segmentation brings this variation and the patterns therein to light.

Developing the Segmentation

Cluster analysis-based segmentation is perhaps best understood as a technique for identifying schools of thought. The statistical technique known as cluster analysis sifts through the data and comes to a solution that minimizes differences within groups and maximizes differences between groups. When a segmentation is created using cluster analysis, it is the patterns in the data that dictate the composition of the groups or segments. This makes it an ideal tool for uncovering new patterns, but it also means that the decision about which data to include in the segmentation is the most critical factor in its creation.

This segmentation is based on three streams of information: Christian doctrines, religious behaviours, and attitudes towards the church. The measures of Christian doctrine used were:

- 'The concept of God is an old superstition that is no longer needed to explain things in these modern times.'
- 'I feel that through the life, death, and resurrection of Jesus, God provided a way for the forgiveness of my sins.'
- 'I believe the Bible is the inspired word of God.'
- 'I believe the Bible is God's word and is to be taken literally, word for word.'
- 'I have committed my life to Christ and consider myself to be a converted Christian.'
- 'I feel it is very important to encourage non-Christians to become Christians.'

These first three beliefs are quite prevalent. But the evangelically oriented items measuring biblical literalism, conversion, and sharing the faith are more divisive.[11] The religious behaviours were frequency of church attendance, prayer, and the reading of the Bible or other religious material. There is considerable variation in the frequency with which people engage in these behaviours, with prayer being the most common.[12] The statements used to measure the privatization of faith are:

- 'My private beliefs about Christianity are more important that what is taught by any church.'
- 'I don't think you need to go to church in order to be a good Christian.'

The first item taps into a kind of theological independence, and agreement with it indicates the church's authority over an individual is minimal. The second statement complements the first, but explicitly questions the need for belonging to a faith community. Responses to these items should indicate very high levels of privatized faith – in both Canada and the United States.

These eleven items (eight attitude statements and three self-reports of behaviour) served as the raw material for constructing the segmentations.[13] When we connect the dots between these questions there emerges a clear picture of the state(s) of faith in North America.

The Segments' Silhouettes

The first stage of the segmentation cuts a bold swath through the population, dividing it into churchgoers, private believers, and nominal and non-Christians. While these groups are intriguing, it is the more nuanced sub-segments that richly reward detailed study.[14] Before painting a portrait of each group, I sketch out their silhouettes.

There are two types of committed churchgoers: the church-centred and privatistic churchgoers. They split over the degree of privatization of their faith. The church-centred place high value on church attendance and the church's teachings. Privatistic churchgoers, on the other hand, attend services weekly and take the Bible very seriously, but place higher value on their personal beliefs than on church teachings. Many are not convinced church attendance is required of 'good' Christians.

Private believers unravel into two strands: independent believers and occasional christians. Independent believers are the poster children for privatized faith. While maintaining a prayerful relationship with their God and attending church semi-regularly, they are not terribly orthodox and are resolutely convinced that church attendance is unnecessary and that their private beliefs are more important than what any church teaches. Occasional Christians, the other strand of private Christians, fill the pews at Christmas and Easter but otherwise tend to give little thought to either organized religion or their loosely held beliefs.

Nominal and non-Christians partition into private theists and atheists and agnostics. Private theists believe in God and pray, at least on occasion. But they neither feel religion is particularly important to them, nor do they ascribe to orthodox Christian beliefs about Christ, the Bible, or the value of belonging to a community of faith. Nonetheless, half describe themselves as Christians, and some do attend religious services, on occasion. Atheists and Agnostics are set apart by their ambiguity towards, or rejection of, the concept of God and other Christian doctrines.

Portraits of the Segments

In the following section I describe each of the segments in some detail, dwelling mainly on the nature of their faith (or lack thereof), as well as their demographic and geographical characteristics. A subsequent section compares and contrasts the groups in terms of levels of social involvement and social values.

The Church-Centred
Comprising 9 per cent of the Canadian and 20 per cent of the American adult population, the church-centred are pillars of the church, upholding its authority in their lives. The church-centred attend regularly, with four in ten at church a number of times during the week. And they take their church very seriously – the vast majority of the church-centred disagree with the notion that 'private beliefs about Christianity are more important than what is taught by any church.' This polarizes them from almost all other North Americans, who typically strongly agree with this statement of privatized faith. Nigh upon eight in ten also go so far as to set attendance at church as a minimum standard for 'good' Christians.

The church-centred also frequently engage in private devotions. Prayer is an everyday occurrence for most, and three-quarters read the Bible and other religious literature once a week or more. As one might expect, the church-centred are doctrinally very orthodox. There is universal agreement that Christ is their God and saviour. All see the Bible as the inspired word of God, with three-quarters receiving it as God's literal word. Nine in ten of this 'no-holds-barred' group describe themselves as has having 'committed their life to Christ.'

One-quarter (26 per cent) of the church-centred describe themselves as Roman Catholics, 37 per cent identify as Evangelical Christians (including 20 per cent of Catholics), and 41 per cent are comfortable with the label of 'liberal or progressive Christian.' Regionally, they are slightly underrepresented in Quebec (versus the rest of Canada) and slightly overrepresented in the southern United States.[15] Demographically, there is nothing starkly different about the church-centred. Just over half (56 per cent) are women, they are slightly older (though 30 per cent are 18–34), and their levels of education basically follow the pattern seen in the adult population.

Privatistic Churchgoers

Privatistic churchgoers are similar to the church-centred in their level of devotion and participation. Where they differ is in their attitudes towards the role of the church. All agree that their private beliefs about Christianity are more important than what is taught by any church. In this they are more adamant than the majority of North Americans. Despite the fact that they are regular attenders (33 per cent going at least twice a week), two-thirds do not think you need to go to church in order to be a 'good' Christian.

Prayer is a part of everyday life for most privatistic churchgoers and three-quarters read the Bible or other religious magazines and books on a regular basis. Though privatistic, they are still deeply orthodox in their adherence to Christian creeds. These evangelically oriented people feel it is important to spread the word. Like their church-centred compatriots, almost all privatistic churchgoers have committed their lives to Christ and feel it is important to encourage non-Christians to become Christians.

Equal numbers of this group (42 per cent each) describe themselves as evangelical Christians and liberal or progressive Christians. Catholics comprise just 20 per cent of this group. A total of 28 per cent of Americans and 11 per cent of Canadians are privatistic churchgoers and, as with the church-centred, they are slightly underrepresented in

Quebec and overrepresented in the southern states. Six in ten are women, and they tend to be somewhat older and less educated. They are also slightly more likely to be black or Hispanic.

Independent Believers
Independent believers think there is no need to go to church in order to be a 'good' Christian, and they are firmly of the opinion that their private beliefs about Christianity are more important than what any church teaches. Church attendance and reading of the Bible and other religious material tend to be occasional for these independent believers. But prayer is an everyday part of life for most, and their faith tends to be an important guide in their day-to-day existence. In an ironic twist on 'do unto others as you would have them do unto you,' independent believers do not feel it important to share their faith.

Independent believers assent to basic Christian doctrine but, in keeping with their independent character, their level of accord is sometimes not as intense as that observed with the churchgoer segments. For example, while almost all affirm Christ as God and saviour, a third agree only moderately with the statement 'through the life, death, and resurrection of Jesus, God provided a way for the forgiveness of my sins.' Likewise, while almost all agree that 'the Bible is the inspired word of God,' nearly half (44 per cent) agree only moderately. And unlike their churchgoer cousins, just a quarter of independent believers take the Bible as the literal word of God, with many of those holding this stance in a lukewarm manner.

Catholics account for 43 per cent of all independent believers, and 61 per cent describe themselves as liberal or progressive Christians, while just 10 per cent characterize themselves as evangelicals. One in five Canadians (22 per cent) and Americans (20 per cent) are independent believers, with citizens of the Southern States being a pinch less likely to fall into this category. Their age and education levels are indistinguishable from the average, and 60 per cent are women.

Occasional Christians
Occasional Christians tend to pray, go to church, or read religious material on occasion – perhaps a few times a year. While most report religion is important to them, they also offer that it tends to provide only 'some' guidance to how they live. They do not think you need to go to church in order to be a 'good' Christian. In keeping with their less-committal approach, the faith of occasional Christians is not passion-

ately individual in comparison to privatistic churchgoers and independent believers. Fewer (68 per cent) agree that their private beliefs are more important to them than are church teachings, and half of these (35 per cent) agree only moderately.

Doctrinally, occasional Christians are fairly orthodox in their concordance with statements regarding the divinity of Christ, forgiveness through Jesus, and the inspiration of the Bible. However, like the independent believers, some are not completely convinced and soften their answers with moderate levels of agreement. Less than half feel it important to share the faith, and most of these agree only moderately.

Occasional Christians represent 19 per cent of the Canadian and 16 per cent of the American adult population, with 59 per cent being male. Three in ten (30 per cent) are Catholic and half (52 per cent) call themselves liberal or progressive Christians, while just 10 per cent would think of themselves as evangelicals. They have slightly lower levels of education and there is also a slender skew towards the younger age group.

Private Theists

Private theists do not think the concept of God is an old superstition, and they do pray on occasion, but few feel religion is important to their lives. Private theists generally strongly agree that their private beliefs come first. Attendance at religious services is uncommon. Most do not feel they have forgiveness through Christ, though four in ten (38 per cent) do conceive of Christ as God. Non-Christian monotheists are a small but notable subgroup with the private theists. While they account for only 7 per cent of all private theists, half (50 per cent) of the people who described themselves as Jews and Muslims fall into this category by default, being believers in a God but not Christ.[16] However, these Jewish and Muslim private theists, like their Christian colleagues, tend not to be terribly devout.[17]

One in five (19 per cent) Canadians and 10 per cent of Americans are private theists, with slightly fewer being found in Quebec or the American South. They split quite evenly between men and women, are somewhat more likely to have a university degree, and a slightly higher proportion are under 35 years of age. One in five (21 per cent) describe themselves as Catholics, and 59 per cent accept the label of liberal or progressive Christian.

Atheists and Agnostics

The final group, atheists and agnostics, are set apart by the fact that eight in ten agree that 'the concept of God is an old superstition that is no longer needed to explain things in these modern times.'[18] As one might expect, there is no or little participation in religious activity by these atheists and agnostics. The fact that 19 per cent describe themselves as Catholics and 50 per cent as liberal and progressive Christians highlights that these labels are sometimes better indications of cultural identity than religious belief. Also, for some, membership in this group is more about ambiguity and ambivalence towards faith than complete rejection of the concept.

One in five Canadians (20 per cent) and just 6 per cent of Americans fall into the atheist and agnostic group, with the highest prevalence being in Quebec (27 per cent) and the lowest in the Southern States (3 per cent). There is nothing that distinguishes atheists and agnostics educationally, but those aged 18–34 are somewhat overrepresented and those over 55 are correspondingly underrepresented.

Social Involvement and Social Values

The six different segments vary not only in the nature and depth of their religious belief, but also in their degree of social involvement and social values. The greatest differences come in the realm of social involvement, as measured by participation in volunteer organizations. The church-centred are the most socially involved, seemingly group oriented in all respects. Over six in ten are members of a voluntary social group – excluding religious or church-related organizations – and 55 per cent volunteer their time to work for these groups.[19] At the other end of the scale are the occasional Christians. They have half the level of involvement of the church-centred, both in the prevalence of involvement and the number of groups they belong to. Atheists and agnostics also show low levels of social involvement. Between these two poles lay privatistic churchgoers, independent christians, and private theists – each coming in around the North American average. The variation observed here supports and expands upon previous observations (Wilson and Janoski 1995) that both depth and type of religiosity are linked to varying degrees of volunteer activity. These findings also add some nuance to the social capital debate (for example, see J. Coleman 1993; Fukuyama 1995: Ladd 1996: Putnam 1995a, 1995b) in that they point out that *how* one is religious can be as important as whether one *is* religious.

In terms of social values, the church-centred and the privatistic churchgoers are more likely to place highest priority on such ethical issues as promoting and preserving the family and raising moral standards. The private theists and atheists and agnostics tended to focus on more temporal concerns, such as building a healthy economy or, to a lesser degree, preserving the environment. The independent and occasional Christians fall in the middle, rolling with the North American average.

On the political front, it is not surprising that eight in ten of the church-centred and privatistic churchgoers agreed that 'it is essential that traditional Christian values play a major role in [Canadian/American] politics.' Just half of the independent and occasional Christians endorse that sentiment, as do a predictably small portion of the private theist and atheist and agnostic groups.

The data for this analysis were collected just prior to the American 1996 presidential election. A question was included regarding voting intentions.[20] Clinton led in all groups, but Dole was proportionately stronger in the church-centred and privatistic churchgoer groups. Clinton was much stronger in the less or non-religious segments. What is particularly interesting is that groups whose faith was most salient to them were least likely to vote for Ross Perot, a finding that confirms some previous work on third-party candidates (Gilbert, Johnson, and Peterson 1995).

Discussion

These analyses, both the international and North American, underscore the tremendous variation that exists in both the degree and manner of being religious – even with the predominantly Christian context of these samples. As I noted at the beginning of this chapter, Wuthnow (1992) suggested that 'religious sentiment does not wax and wane, it changes clothes and appears in garb to which we are sometimes unaccustomed.' With this segmentation we have a glimpse of some of the different religious 'outfits' people are wearing this season. We can imagine the committed churchgoers clad in their Sunday best, while the private theists are wearing shorts and T-shirts, as they sit out on a summer evening and ponder the majesty of the stars.

It is hoped that this analysis provides one reply to Ammerman's (1997c) call for new ways of describing the 'complicated reality' of religiosity. This analysis is, of course, not without its limitations. For example, the international inquiry utilizes quite crude categorizations of public and private faith. One result is an underestimation of the prevalence of both types of faith. The bluntness of these measures also robs one of the ability to identify finer patterns of variation in both public and private faith. In other words, the tremendous differences we observed fail to do justice to the truly bewildering patterns of variation that exist around the globe.

Another key limitation is the paucity of items on the privatization of faith that were available to be included in the cluster analysis. Had we a more comprehensive set of items, it may have been possible to identify more subtle distinctions between groups, and perhaps extract additional sub-segments. Likewise, had the sample been larger it would have been more feasible to explore the similarities and differences between such groups as Roman Catholics and Southern Baptists who apparently peacefully coexist in all the segments.

As it stands, this attempt to describe the contours of public and private faith in North America at least throws a spotlight on the limitations of viewing people's faith primarily through the oft-used dual lenses of denominationalism and church attendance. This cluster-based analysis of beliefs supports Italian scholar Antonio Gramsci's assertion that 'every religion, even Catholicism (in fact especially Catholicism ...) is really a multiplicity of religions that are distinct and often contradictory' (quoted in Carroll 1996). The lenses of denominationalism and church attendance have their blind spots – chiefly that they impose artificial homogenizing effects within a denomination while drawing attention away from private faith. The effect is the creation of false distinctions between people of different religious traditions. This analysis provides a corrective to this, but we must not throw the baby out with the bath water. This type of analysis could be enhanced by the addition of denominational filtering.

Given the similarities in culture and religious make-up, the striking differences between Canada and the United States in the prevalence of the different segments are heartening for Canadian nationalists like myself. But more importantly, they also lend support to Peter Beyer's (1997) suggestion that Canada can serve as a useful grindstone for the sharpening of rational choice theory. I would also hope that the variation in the nature and degree of the privatization of faith that we have observed in both would spur further refinement of (neo)secularization theory, with a greater focus on privatization. Reimer's (1995) look at cultural effects on religiosity through a comparison of Canada and the United States is a positive step in this direction, but there is still much to be explored.

As we rethink church, state, and modernity, it is my hope that the cast of characters we met through this analysis – the church-centred, privatistic churchgoers, independent believers, occasional Christians, private theists, and atheists and agnostics – will encourage us to move beyond such reductionist dichotomies as member/non-member and more fully explore the remarkable diversity of public and private religiosity.

NOTES

1 The title is from Colossians 1:16 (NIV, New International Version).
2 At the heart of rational choice or 'supply side' theory is the thought that faith is a necessary compensation for the sufferings of the human condition. Assuming that suffering is constant, rational choice theorists postulate that the demand for religion is constant. Thus, the variation among nations in the level of religious behaviour (most often measured as church attendance) becomes a function of the degree of competition between suppliers of religious 'services.' In nations where there is only one supplier (typically the Catholic Church) religion can be expected to be less vital, whereas in nations with many suppliers competing for attention religion ought to be flourishing. See Warner (1993) for more on rational choice theory, and Yamane (1997) and Tschannen (1991) for a useful discussion of secularization theory.
3 This analysis included volumes 36–8 of the *Journal for the Scientific Study of Religion*, volumes 36–8 of *Review of Religious Research*, and volumes 56–8 of *Sociology of Religion* (formerly *Sociological Analysis*). It is by no means a comprehensive review, but it does serve to underscore the point that this type of analysis is rarely undertaken.
4 Other contributors who must be cited include Rob Burbach, Mag Burns, Angus Reid, Kevin Christiano and – in spirit – the project's initiator, George Rawlyk. Many others, too numerous to name here, also made useful contributions.
5 There is also the important issue of biases: first, I am a Christian. One result of this is that I take faith seriously and see it as having a source in God. Second, I am a pollster. This means I take what people say fairly seriously – albeit with a vigilant eye for measurement error. Third, I am one of the most disreputable brands of pollsters: I am a market researcher. Market researchers focus on what each individual says because you sell products (or beliefs) to individuals and because experience has shown that social, economic, or political factors explain relatively little variance in

why people buy what they buy. Fourth, as my last statement would suggest, I am an empiricist. I believe quantitative methods can shed useful light on insight and perception. Fifth, I am a Canadian who grew up in Kingston, Ontario – a town whose historic sites revolve around fending off American aggression. And I take this too seriously. That means even my three-year-old knows he can get a rise out of me by saying 'w, x, y, zee.' It also means I tend to view the Canadian position on anything as inherently superior to the American one – without glorying in it of course, because that would be an American thing to do. Mea culpa.

6 The focus is on Christianity largely because no other religious group is prevalent enough in Canada or the United States to study with random samples of the population. In the international data there are two nations – Indonesia and Malaysia – which are predominantly Muslim. It is interesting to note that there is quite a difference between these nations in terms of the prevalence of public and private religion.

7 The study was conducted in May/June 1997 with samples of at least 500 adults per country. National probability samples were used in most nations. However, in Brazil, Mexico, India, and Indonesia the samples were limited to urban areas and intentionally skewed towards more affluent socioeconomic strata – reflecting an urban elite. In China, Russia, South Africa, and Thailand, the sample was limited to urban areas only, but respondent selection was designed to be representative of the urban areas sampled. For further information see *Angus Reid World Monitor*, no. 1, January 1998.

8 This investigation was limited to those describing themselves as Christians, Moslems, or Jews. This was done because of difficulties in deriving comparable measures for people of non-monotheistic faiths. People of other monotheistic groups were excluded because of their low incidence in the sample and subsequent difficulties in making meaningful conclusions about them.

9 Those respondents who indicated they are Christians, Moslems, or Jews were asked about frequency of attendance at religious services and frequency of prayer. The prevalence figures here are calculated for the entire population surveyed and not just the monotheists who were asked about these features of faith.

10 For more information on basic beliefs from the *God and Society in North America* study see the 4 November 1996 edition of *Maclean's* magazine.

11 In Canada, 28 per cent agree that the Bible is God's literal word, while 55 per cent of Americans feel the same way. Four in ten Canadians (37 per cent) consider themselves converted Christians, as do 62 per cent of

Americans. The item measuring the importance of converting non-Christians is interesting because it also brushes the border of the public/private divide. The levels of agreement with this item indicate a deep divide between Canada and the United States: 27 per cent of Canadians feel it is important to spread the faith – while twice as many (54 per cent) Americans feel the same way.

12 Fully 35 per cent in Canada and 58 per cent in the United States pray on a daily basis. The reading of religious material is less common, with just 21 per cent of Canadians and 44 per cent of Americans doing so once a week or more.

13 Different subsets of these eleven items were used depending upon the segmentation. In each case only items that were conceptually important and which provided statistically meaningful input into the cluster formation were chosen for inclusion. For the first broad categorization, ten of these eleven items were included in the cluster analysis, with the exception being the item measuring belief in God. It was not included because relatively few people agree that the concept of God is an old superstition. It therefore failed to be useful in differentiating between broad groupings of society. These same ten items were used to subdivide the private Christians. In order to differentiate between committed churchgoers we used five items: the three evangelically oriented items (measuring conversion and commitment, biblical literalism, and the importance of evangelism), as well as the two items measuring the privatization of belief. In subdividing the non-Christians just three items were employed: belief in God, frequency of prayer, and the relative importance of private beliefs versus church teachings. In each case a two-segment solution proved optimal, both in terms of reproducibility and face validity.

14 While our focus is on the six-segment solution, the three-cluster segmentation deserves a thumbnail sketch. The churchgoers are committed believers who pray and attend church regularly and believe it is important to encourage non-Christians to become Christians. Close to half the American population, but just one in five Canadians, fall into this broad category. Private believers tend to believe but not belong. While many regularly pray, church attendance tends to be occasional for they do not think it necessary to go to church in order to be a good Christian and strongly feel their personal beliefs are more important than what is taught by any church. Approximately four in ten Canadians and Americans are private believers. The nominal and non-Christian group contains the remainder of the population. In this segment there are some who believe, but commitment and participation tend to be very low with 58 per cent

never attending religious services. Four in ten Canadians and just one in six Americans are nominal or non-Christians.

15 The incidence of the church-centred is 6 per cent in Quebec and 10 per cent in the rest of Canada. In the southern United States it is 26 per cent versus 17 per cent in the rest of America. States considered southern include Alabama, Arkansas, Delaware, Florida, Georgia, Kentucky, Louisiana, Maryland, Mississippi, North Carolina, Oklahoma, Tennessee, Texas, Virginia, Washington DC, and West Virginia.

16 A very few Jews and Muslims do end up falling into the explicitly Christian segments, driven there by having similar patterns of behaviour and belief, outside of those pertaining explicitly to Christianity. Three in ten (29 per cent) of those who describe themselves as Jews hold beliefs that place them into the agnostic and atheist category.

17 For example, 53 per cent of the Jewish or Muslim private theists pray occasionally or never, and just 16 per cent attend religious services weekly.

18 It is noteworthy that 39 per cent of atheists and agnostics agree only moderately with the statement on the concept of God being an old superstition.

19 The study measured involvement in the following groups: professional or job related, social service, environmental, youth groups/clubs, community/neighbourhood, health-related, recreational, senior citizens', women's, political, veterans', support/small groups, and educational or cultural. Also measured was involvement in religious or church-related groups, but it was excluded from this measurement of social involvement. It is notable that very few of those who belong to a religious or church group are involved only in that one type of group.

20 Questions were also asked regarding voting intentions in Canada. The data are not shown here because the regionalization of political parties within Canada necessitates a split of the results between Quebec and English Canada. With six segments the sample sizes become too small to allow for meaningful analysis.

chapter twelve

A Generic Evangelicalism?
Comparing Evangelical Subcultures in
Canada and the United States

SAM REIMER

Possibly the most significant change in North American religion in the past few decades has been the resurgence of evangelicalism. With the decline of mainline Protestantism in both Canada and the United States, conservative Protestants have outgrown mainline Protestantism in America, and in both countries, conservative Protestant churches have more people in the pews on any given Sunday than mainline Protestant churches (Motz 1990; Bibby 1993; Kellstedt and Green 1993). Presently, evangelicals (as defined below) account for roughly one-quarter of the American population and about 10 per cent of the Canadian population (Kellstedt et al. 1993; Angus Reid 1996b). Their significant presence in both countries allows for international comparisons that illuminate both the convergence and divergence of evangelicalism in the two countries, and their vitality in light of secularizing forces has focused attention on the interaction between this religious tradition and modernity (cf Hunter 1987). In this chapter, I compare active evangelicals in Canada and United States by examining national and regional similarities and differences, with particular attention to broader cultural explanations.

Defining Evangelicalism

In a study of this nature, a definition of evangelicalism is necessary. Many definitions have been proposed in the literature, and can be placed into two basic categories. Some definitions are based on *belonging*, which places individuals in the evangelical category if they affiliate with conservative Protestant denominations or identify themselves as evangelicals (or fundamentalists, Pentecostals, and so on). Other definitions are based on *belief or behaviour*, where distinctive orthodox beliefs (for example, the inerrancy of the Bible) or behaviours (for example, conversion) are emphasized. However, there is no consensus on which criteria to use, or how to use them (Guth et al. 1988).

As I have argued elsewhere (Reimer 1996), different defining strategies should be used depending on the purposes at hand. In this study, I focus on evangelicalism as a *subculture*, limiting the term to those who participate in conservative Protestant denominations. Since I study the effect of the evangelical subculture on individual evangelicals, it is necessary to study those who actively participate in the subculture. Alternatively, one could study evangelicalism as a *movement*, which would include all those who meet a certain set of evangelical believing and/or behaving criteria, regardless of their denominational affiliation or religious identity. In other words, belief and behaving definitions will include conservative mainline Protestants and Roman Catholics in the evangelical category. These conservatives meet evangelical criteria but are not embedded in the evangelical subculture.[1]

Examining National Differences

It is natural to assume that Canadian and American evangelicals differ in the same ways as Canadians and Americans differ more broadly. This assumption itself contains two debatable assumptions. The first is that Canadians differ culturally from Americans, and that these differences are substantial enough to make for a measurable difference. The second assumption is that the evangelical subculture in both countries (or at least one of the countries, but presumably both) is influenced by the larger national cultures in substantial ways. That is, the cultural influences that shape evangelicals are not only internal (from within evangelicalism), but also external (from national or regional secular culture), and that the external influences are substantial enough to create a measurable difference.

Arguments for a distinctive national culture in Canada *vis-à-vis* the United States have been made most notably by Lipset in *Continental Divide* (1990). While Lipset suggests that Canada–U.S. cultural differences may be diminishing, he maintains that the two countries are still culturally distinct. He gives historical evidence to show that Canadians have avoided much U.S. extremism by deferring to authority, rejecting revolutionary tendencies, emphasizing peaceable foreign relations, keeping a tighter rein on excessive individualism and criminal deviance, celebrating tolerance and ethnic diversity, and offering more assistance to the less fortunate. In addition, the tendency towards church union and ecumenism is stronger in Canada, just as the tendency towards sectarian fundamentalism and schism is stronger in the United States (Noll 1997; Stackhouse 1993; Bibby 1987; Lipset 1990). The sweeping cultural generalization that Canada is a mosaic and the United States is a melting pot is evidence of perceived differences, at least in the minds of Canadians who concern themselves with maintaining a unique identity. Based on this line of argument, one would predict a distinctive Canadian evangelicalism.

Several arguments suggest disappearing or diminishing cultural differences between the two countries and thus the evangelicals in each country. The first is related to a growing globalization of organizations and culture. The close geographical proximity and the significant media, religious, political, and economic influences between the two North American countries in the past half century, indicate a greater tendency towards a global North American culture. Coupled with the tendency for increased U.S. influences are the diminishing British influences in the past fifty years (Noll 1997). Historically, the forty-ninth parallel has been at least as permeable to evangelicalism as to other cultural influences. While cross-border evangelical influences have been significant from both directions, south-to-north influences have been greater (Noll 1997; Rawlyk 1984, 1990a; Stackhouse 1994; Elliot 1994). Many evangelical denominations (for example, Lutheran Church-Canada, Pentecostal Assemblies of Canada) and parachurch organizations (for example, Focus on the Family, Promise Keepers), not to mention evangelical spokespersons and media influences, have been imported into Canada from the United States. These factors lead one to predict transnational uniformity.

Second, do secular external influences infiltrate North American evangelicalism to a significant degree? The question relates to whether or not evangelicalism as a subculture is maintaining its orthodoxy and orthopraxy under significant secular pressure to accommodate. Hunter (1983, 1987; see also Quebedeaux 1978) finds evidence of significant secularization within American evangelicals as beliefs and morals have softened, while others (Schmaltzbauer and Wheeler 1996) have argued for cycles of 'resacralization.'[2] Minimal external influences are at least plausible in many areas of North America because of the growing infrastructure of evangelical institutions that have led to the formation of a distinct subculture (Hunter 1987; Wuthnow 1988; Marsden 1980). In sum, then, the link between national culture and evangelical subculture is not clear. The purpose of this chapter is to examine this link and to try to make sense of it in light of institutional analysis and globalizing forces.

Method

In 1995 I surveyed core (or committed) evangelicals in two locales in Canada and two in the United States. This included 120 in-depth, face-to-face interviews. Respondents came from four denominations (representing the Baptist, Lutheran, Pentecostal, and Nazarene traditions) in four diverse locales (Minneapolis, Minnesota; Jackson, Mississippi; Winnipeg, Manitoba; and Saint John/Moncton, New Brunswick).[3] I then compared these data with national and international survey data, the best survey for my purposes being the 1996 Angus Reid/Pew survey which I use here. The poll involved phone interviews with roughly 3,000 randomly selected adults in the United States and 3,000 in Canada. Overall, the greatest surprise in the findings was the uniformity across the regions and across the forty-ninth parallel, from which I conclude that *there exists a transdenominational and transnational evangelical subculture in North America*. Similarities include evangelical identity and boundary maintenance, religious experience, beliefs, practices, and moral attitudes, as well as levels of encapsulation, tension with the world, and privatization.

Similarities

All the North American evangelicals I interviewed share a common understanding of their central identity as evangelicals and agree on the boundaries that separate evangelicals from non-evangelicals. In all regions, they used similar words to speak of their conversion and their relationship with God, and their central beliefs – salvation through Christ alone, the deity of Christ, and the authority of the Bible. I probed the 'scope' of their identity, that is, whether they identify themselves most narrowly by denomination, by religious tradition (for example, evangelical), or broadly as Christians. In all regions, a majority identify themselves foremost as Christians, and they are also equally likely to choose an 'evangelical' label in each region. In addition, all of the committed evangelicals I talked with felt that a Christian (as they defined it, based on orthodox beliefs and conversion) included individuals of other denominations, even non-Protestants. The 'content' – or the central tenets – of this identity is uniform as well. In response to open questions like, 'How would you identify yourself religiously?' consistent emphasis was placed on what Bebbington (1989) considers the four emphases of historic evangelicalism: conversionism (a born-again experience), crucicentrism (the centrality of the death and resurrection of Christ), biblicism (the authority of the Bible), and, to a lesser extent for my respondents, activism (evangelism, service, church attendance).

Further, evangelicals are in agreement on what groups they considered 'ingroups' (which they felt close to, such as Right to Life) and which are considered 'outgroups' (which they felt far from, such as the ACLU); see Conover (1988, 54). This agreement indicates that core evangelicals share subcultural boundaries and have a clear picture of their own distinctiveness *vis-à-vis* groups in the larger environment.[4]

In the main, I found only minor regional and national differences in their central religious beliefs, religious experience, orthodoxy, or orthopraxy. In all locations studied, the majority of active evangelicals chose their conversion as their most significant religious experience. Also, no regional differences appear in how often they experience God's presence or if they receive answers to their prayers. Regional differences in moral orthodoxy were minimal, and variation is better explained by age than by region. All evangelicals I studied agree on strict sexual mores (regarding abortion, pornography, homosexual sex, and premarital sex), but were looser on dancing, drinking, divorce, and viewing movies. Against my previous predictions, evangelicals that I talked with were not consistently more conservative in Mississippi and New Brunswick than in Minnesota and Manitoba, as indicated by similar levels of moral orthodoxy shown in Table 12.1. Nor did core evangelicals differ substantially on levels of private devotional or public ritual practice. All these findings are supported by national data sets as well.

Finally, evangelicals showed similar levels of encapsulation, tension with the 'world,' and privatization of faith. Encapsulation refers to the degree to which evangelicals interact primarily or exclusively with other evangelicals. Core evangelicals are encapsulated to a significant degree, since nearly 60 per cent of my respondents had no 'non-Christians' among their five closest friends. About 60 per cent of evangelicals in all regions could recall an example of being 'ridiculed for

TABLE 12.1
Moral values – core evangelical sample

	% saying the activity is 'always wrong'					
	Total sample	Minnesota	Mississippi	Manitoba	New Brunswick
Hitting a spouse	93.6	94.4	91.3	96.2	91.5
Homosexual activity	93.5	96.2	96.8	87.9	93.1
Sex before marriage	89.1	93.5	89.4	85.6	87.5
Buying and looking at pornography	88.8	86.9	91.4	87.5	90.3
Not claiming all income on income tax returns	85.3	84.8	81.7	85.4	90.3
Littering	72.7	76.2	74.2	68.9	70.8
Smoking	66.7	54.8	67	71.6	76.8
Gambling	63	52.8	64.4	59.8	81.4
Viewing x-rated movies at a theatre	50.3	32.1	53.8	53.8	67.6
Working in a bar	42.5	43.7	48.3	29	52.9
Overeating	36.5	40.4	40.7	27.9	38.2
Drinking alcohol	34.5	19.8	48.4	22.1	56.3
Divorce	22.1	24.5	22.8	13.7	29.6
Viewing a PG-rated movie at a theatre	14.6	4.8	18.9	13.7	25.4
Dancing	14.1	7.6	14.6	13	25
Participating in a protest that could lead to arrest	11.2	6.9	14.8	10	14.9
Buying a very expensive car	4.9	4.9	4.9	1	10.9

their faith,' and the moral disintegration of society was the greatest evangelical concern in all regions, which I used as indicators of tension. Regarding privatization, I found that committed evangelicals in all regions had difficulty verbalizing how their religiosity applied in two areas: with regard to the behavioural requirements for evangelicals and with regard to the how their faith affected their public lives.

Regarding the former, core evangelicals hedged on behavioural requirements for inclusion in the evangelical category. Many suggested that there should be some behavioural evidence of conversion, on the one hand, but were uncomfortable about compromising their belief that salvation was 'by grace through faith alone, not by works,' on the other. In other words, interviewees suggested the need for a vague 'lifestyle' change as evidence of salvation, but specific requirements suggested a legalism that made them uncomfortable. This ambiguity is brought out in my interview responses, as in this definition of a Christian: 'I would say someone [is a Christian] who has identified Jesus as the true son of God, who has given their life to Him and yielded their will and has asked God to be their Lord and Savior, and, um, I think that if that is true you will see a change, that their lives will be changed for the good' (Baptist woman, Minneapolis).

In addition, evangelicals had difficulty applying religious meanings and symbols in their work sphere. While 65 per cent of those respondents who work outside the home considered their job a 'calling,' and nearly all (94 per cent) respondents said that their faith had 'a great deal' or 'quite a bit' of an effect on their work, application of faith at work was mostly private. Although I pressed respondents for specific answers relating to, for example, evangelism at work, policy or structural elements implemented, job choice, or refusing contracts, a third of the most committed evangelicals could only point to private applications of faith (such as honesty or a positive attitude). Twenty-five per cent showed some public application (usually witnessing), and about 20 per cent stated that they made a (usually moral) stand that they thought was detrimental to their work. However, all the responses were limited to relational, not structural application of faith at work.

While 85 per cent of the evangelicals I interviewed said it was 'very important' for Christians to try to change the world around them, responses to how that could be done were vague, and there was little agreement. Answers like 'love people' or 'emulate Christ' were the common responses to this question. Responses further indicated that there was no 'one way' to change the world and that was subjectively determined. As one Pentecostal man from Winnipeg put it, '[We don't need] an agenda to change the world, I think an effective Christian will change the world just because of Christ who lives in them. [It's] just the effect of the Christian life.' In sum, then, evangelicals in all regions found it difficult to verbalize public application of their privatized faith.

Differences

However, some national differences appeared. In my interviews, the most consistent areas of divergence were in the areas of political views and tolerance, broadly defined. That is, there is not the same degree of alignment between religious and political conservatism in Canada as there is in the United States, a finding supported by national representative samples (Rawlyk 1994). Further, regardless of whether one looks at racial, political, religious, or moral tolerance, Canadian evangelicals are more tolerant.[5]

Using the Angus Reid/Pew international poll, I demonstrate that evangelicals show uniformity on central religious beliefs, but diverge in areas of tolerance and politics. In Figure 12.1, I show the total absolute differences between the Canadian and American response averages (mean differences) for religious, political, and tolerance measures (see the Appendix for more detail). A tendency of convergence (less total difference) indicates the minimized effect of the national boundaries.

Religious beliefs show notable convergence. Committed evangelicals (those who belong to conservative Protestant denominations) in the United States closely match the responses of their Canadian counterparts, with a small total difference, whereas American and Canadian evangelicals differ more, and all Americans and Canadians differ even more (see Table 12.2 in the Appendix for more detail). However, political beliefs show no convergence as we move from the general population to committed evangelicals, and U.S. evangelicals are consistently more conservative. Tolerance also shows minimal convergence, and Canadian evangelicals are consistently more tolerant. These findings – that there are national differences between American and Canadian active evangelicals in politics and tolerance, and rarely elsewhere – is consistent in hundreds of items on beliefs, attitudes, and practices in my research which I am unable to present here because of space limitations. Through regression analysis, it can also be demonstrated that these differences are better explained by national cultural explanations, not by denominational, regional, or demographic differences. This

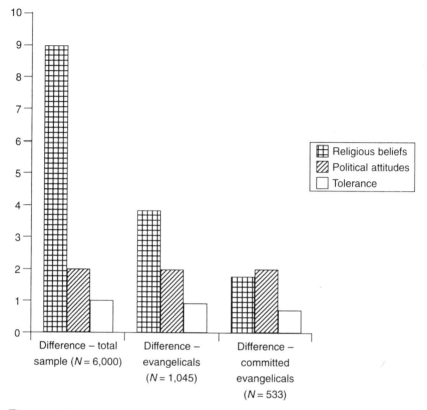

Figure 12.1
Mean differences for religious beliefs, political attitudes, and tolerance.
(Angus Reid/Pew II Survey, 1996).

finding suggests that national cultural distinctions between the countries remain – shown in political and tolerance attitudes – though they may be decreasing.

Discussion

I have demonstrated through the use of both qualitative and quantitative data that evangelicals show substantial uniformity transnationally in North America. The few differences that do remain are primarily related to two main differences: the coupling of conservative faith and politics in the United States, and higher tolerance in Canada. I look first at these differences.

The correlation between American evangelicals and conservative (republican) politics has a long history in the United States (Liebman and Wuthnow 1983; Green et al. 1996; Leege and Kellstedt 1993). It has only been recently demonstrated that this coupling is weaker in Canada (Rawlyk 1994; Angus Reid 1996b). According to the Angus Reid/Pew 1996 poll, a higher percentage of committed evangelicals (and all evangelicals) planned to vote Liberal rather than Reform in the 1996 federal election. Why this difference? American historian Mark Noll quotes English historian Richard Cawardine and Canadian historian Michael Gauvreau who suggest a mixture of theological and historical reasons. The 'optimistic postmillennialism, the Manichaean perception of the world as a battleground between good and evil, their moral absolutism, and their weak sense of institutional loyalty' were nineteenth-century roots of the evangelical tendency towards political extremes, while Canada's greater British influences, including a deference to authority, the notion of responsible government, and the significant historical involvement of evangelicals in left-leaning politics (notably Aberhardt and Douglas), resulted in a less polarized and less extreme political expression among Canadian evangelicals (Noll 1997, 15ff).

In Canada, tolerance, particularly ethnic tolerance, is celebrated, and is a fundamental part of what it means to be Canadian, according to former Prime Minister Pierre Trudeau (Bibby 1990). Lipset (1990), Berton (1987), and Malcohm (1985) suggest that tolerance of differences is an area of distinction between the two countries. This tolerance, along with the greater tendency to defer to traditional authority in Canada, makes the Canadian religious environment more ecumenical and less competitive (Bibby 1987), which enhances Canadian religion's civil, tolerant tone. Among other things, historians point to the fundamentalist-modernist divide, which was much more significant in the United States, leaving a residue of intolerance among present-day American evangelicals (Noll 1997). Similarities, on the other hand, make geographical boundaries seem arbitrary. I find two theoretical lenses helpful in illuminating these similarities: globalization and 'new institutionalism.'

Globalization theorists emphasize the increased international flow of goods, communication, and people that transcends geographical, cultural, and political boundaries (S. Coleman 1993; King 1991; Robertson 1989, 1992; Featherstone 1990; Wallerstein 1991; Waters 1995), by which

the 'constraints of geography on social and cultural arrangements re-
cede' (Waters 1995, 3). The process of globalization results in increased
global consciousness coupled with a universalized expectation of 'identity declarations' (Robertson 1992, 27), and the internationalization of
economic, political, religious, and other organizations and movements
(S. Coleman 1993). While global explanations are not necessary to explain similarities between two countries, nor does globalization predict
which similarities or differences will exist, globalization does help to
explain how these similarities came about.

Consistent with the salient and uniform identity I found among
evangelicals, Robertson (1992, 100) notes that globalization is a 'two-
fold process involving the interpenetration of universalization of
particularism and the particularization of universalism.' By this he
means that particularistic identities are maintained (though challenged)
in globalized societies and that ways of identification become shared.
For this reason globalization theory does not necessarily predict an
undermining of evangelical identity, since Robertson (1992) notes that
an international emphasis on individual self-identity is embedded in
the globalization process.

With increased flow of people, communication, goods, and organizations across the Canada–U.S. border and within each country, one
would expect to find less national distinctiveness in religiosity and thus
considerable convergence in areas of belief, attitudes, and practice among
evangelicals across North America. Specifically, those aspects considered centrally important to evangelical identity are expected to show
little variation by region. However, differences may appear in those
areas that are not central to the evangelical identity. As Hexham and
Poewe (1997, 43; and Poewe 1994, 17) have argued, international religious movements maintain the minimum of elements – an 'ecology of
tradition' – which are uniform across countries, while other elements
'take on local colour.' Thus, we find variation in political attitudes and
tolerance.

Beyer (1994) argues that globalization is the spread of specialized
social systems that follow functional lines. These systems (for example,
capitalist economy, scientific/technological), while totalizing in their
areas of specific function, leave people 'underdetermined' in mainly
private areas of life. It is these 'residual,' private areas where religion
informs. If this is the case, one would predict that evangelicals have
privatized faith, as I have delineated above.

While clearly not an exhaustive list of connections between my findings and globalization theory, these connections seem to indicate 'external' global influences within the evangelical subculture. While evangelicals have embraced the methods of popular culture (Myers 1989), they are also known for their resistance to worldly influences by creating alternative institutions that sustain their subculture. In fact, proponents of globalization argue that the worldwide spread of religious fundamentalisms is a result of the globalization process (Waters 1995; Beyer 1994), and creation of a viable evangelical subculture can be seen as a reaction to these external forces.

Evidence from my interviews suggests that 'internal' forces, particularly among core evangelicals, would have a substantial effect on their uniformity. Evangelicalism's 'culture producers' – particularly its churches, private schools, non-profit organizations, special interest groups, and so on – provide the institutional basis for this uniformity. That is, the similarities in my individual level data reflect a matching similarity in the churches and denominations through which the viability of evangelical subculture is maintained and transmitted.

Institutional similarity has been observed in other institutional spheres. The result has been a new paradigm in organizational thought, called the 'new institutionalism' (Powell and DiMaggio 1991). In a nutshell, proponents of new institutionalism argue that organizations now rationalize and bureaucratize less for reasons of efficiency and competition (as the 'old institutionalism' within organizational theory purported) and more for reasons related to the 'structuration of organizational fields' (DiMaggio and Powell 1991, 64). Organizational fields – or recognized areas of institutional life (for example, schools, hospitals, or car manufacturing plants) – pressure organizations to orient or adapt themselves towards the 'structure' (the taken-for-granted scripts and prescriptions for action) that defines the organizational field, leading to homogeneity within the field, which they refer to as 'isomorphism' (DiMaggio and Powell 1991, 66; Meyer and Rowan 1991, 50). New institutionalists focus their attention on the environments that shape the organization, not so much on the inner dynamics of the organizations themselves. In doing so, they emphasize that the norms and scripts that shape organizations are super-organizational, and that organizational fields are often national and international in scope. The boundaries of a field are defined by function, not by geography (Scott and Meyer 1991, 117f).

On the organizational level, I suggest that evangelical institutions form an 'organizational field.' According to DiMaggio (1983), an organizational field is defined by:

1 Increased interaction between organizations in the field
2 The emergence of interorganizational structures of domination and patterns of coalition
3 An increase in the information load in the field
4 The development of mutual awareness among participants in the organizations that they are involved in a common enterprise.

All of these aspects are true of evangelicalism in North America. As many have noted, evangelicals are prolific producers and disseminators of popular religious culture (Balmer 1993; Moore 1995; Myers 1989; Wheeler 1996). In the United States in 1995, some 2,500 Christian bookstores sold over $3 billion in evangelical literature, music, videos, T-shirts, greeting cards, and a host of other items (Christopherson 1997). The prominence of evangelical organizations such as the National Association of Evangelicals, the Christian Coalition, Focus on the Family (now in Canada as well), the Evangelical Fellowship of Canada, and other groups have created new patterns of coalition and domination within evangelicalism. Ecumenical efforts such as Promise Keepers, March for Jesus, Vision 2000, concerts of prayer, Billy Graham Crusades, and many other national and international organizations bring evangelicals of every stripe together in increasing frequency and numbers. The result has been an increased awareness among evangelicals that they are involved in a common enterprise, which, in turn, increases cooperation between them.

In addition, others have noticed a generic evangelicalism promoted by evangelical institutions. Wagner (1997), for instance, finds a 'generic' pan-conservative Christianity in the Christian schools she studied. With the proliferation of religious special interest groups (Wuthnow 1988), Wagner suggests that denominational differences are honed down because the support base from one denomination is too small, and curriculum and teachers need to be drawn from the wider evangelical pool.

An increased interaction between evangelical organizations is evident as well. Poewe demonstrates that international networks of interaction among Pentecostal organizations are increasing. In fact, she notes some mega-churches function much like international corporations in the exporting of religious products (Poewe 1994, 5). Simon Coleman (1993) shows how one aspect of conservative Protestant ideology was imported from the United States and diffused by an organization in Sweden. Hunter (1987, 172f) has documented the dissemination of (less orthodox) evangelical beliefs and attitudes through evangelical colleges and universities,[6] while Shibley (1996) has demonstrated that evangelicalism in the United States has been 'southernized' by the spread of southern-style evangelicalism into the north.

In sum, the evidence suggests that evangelical Christians are influenced by a 'structured' evangelical 'organizational field' that is supraregional and international in scope. As a result, core evangelicals show surprising similarity throughout North America. Of course, these organizations have also been significantly shaped by globalizing systems, and organizational conformity to these systems relates to globalizing tendencies. Thus, a globalization and organizational approach points to overlapping influences. In light of these modern influences, I end with a few comments about the study of religion and culture.

Conclusion

In the contemporary world, the interaction between religious particularisms and their cultural milieu is increasingly complex. Global forces have transformed the religious landscape by making conceptions of identity, organization, and tradition more fluid (Ammerman 1997c). As a result, previously clearly bounded religious groupings such as denominations and traditions are increasingly hard to delineate. It is for this reason that studying a religious subculture at its core makes sense. As one nears the periphery, the boundaries of the religious group become increasingly blurred. It is also at the core where the distinctiveness and effects of the subculture on its constituents are clearest.

Second, in societies that offer a plurality of religious choices with no social ramifications for 'mixing and matching' options within or between religious groups – a religious 'smorgasbord,' to use Bibby's (1987) term – either/or conceptualizations of the relationship between a religious group and its cultural milieu are increasingly inadequate. Old notions that conservatives 'resist' and liberals 'accommodate' are too simplistic when both are happening at the same time, and are often mutually supporting (Beyer 1994). For instance, evangelical churches are finding the mixing of secular media and Christian language increasingly rewarding for attracting members (using staging, music, and the like).

Third, studying the culture–religion link only within traditional geographical boundaries misses the increasing volume of influences that cross-cut these boundaries. As the world 'shrinks,' geographical boundaries are increasingly porous.

This study has compared evangelicals in Canada and the United States, and has given explanations for similarities and differences. I have shown evidence of globalizing effects on evangelicals in North America and of an evangelical 'organizational field,' both of which produce a transnational generic evangelicalism. I have attempted to show that both 'internal' organizational forces and 'external' globalization forces affect isomorphic tendencies within the evangelical subculture.

Appendix

In tables 12.2–12.4, I present the survey items and the mean differences which form the basis of Figure 12.1. The items for Tables 12.2 and 12.3 are measured on a four-point scale, from 'strongly agree' to 'strongly disagree.' Table 12.4 includes two items measured on a five-point 'very close' to 'very far' scale, and the three final items ask for a 'yes/no' response. For each item, I subtract the U.S. mean from the Canadian mean and then total the absolute differences. Evangelicals are defined as those who affiliate with conservative Protestant churches, and committed evangelicals are those who pray daily, attend church at least a few times a month, and say their faith is important to them. For a more detailed explanation of these measures, see Green et al. (1996).

TABLE 12.2
Mean differences, religious beliefs – Angus Reid/Pew Survey, 1996

Item	Difference – total sample (N = 6,000)	Difference – evangelicals (N = 1,045)	Difference – committed evangelicals (N = 533)
Concept of God is an old superstition	0.57**	0.2**	0
Human beings not made in God's image, but developed through evolution	0.74**	0.12	0.01
Jesus provides forgiveness of sins	0.81**	0.19**	-0.02
Jesus is divine son of God	0.46**	0.11	-0.03
Bible is inspired	0.7**	0.23**	0.02
Bible is literal	0.94**	0.47**	0.05
Committed life to God, consider myself a converted Christian	0.89**	0.26**	0
Good to encourage non-Christians to become Christians	0.92**	0.45**	0.15
Don't need to go to church to be a good Christian	0.52**	0.34**	0.41**
My private beliefs more important than what's taught in church	0.07	0.06	0.11
All the great religions of the world are equally true	0.39**	0.14	-0.23
World will end in battle of Armageddon	0.95**	0.52**	0.09
I want spiritual life more than riches	0.67**	0.18**	0.01
People who love God and work hard will always have enough money	0.5**	0.28**	0.21
Churches should spend more on poor	0.05	0.12	0.12
Churches should return illegal money	-0.09	-0.23**	-0.29
TOTAL	9.27	3.9**	1.75

Note: Item wording has been abbreviated. A positive number means a more orthodox response in the United States.
Significance: *0.05; **0.01. Totals are absolute-value totals.

TABLE 12.3
Political beliefs – Angus Reid/Pew Survey 1996

Item	Difference – total sample (N = 6,000)	Difference – evangelicals (N = 1,045)	Difference – committed evangelicals (N = 533)
Number of immigrants should be reduced	0.32**	0.43**	0.47**
Government should spend more on fighting poverty	0.03	0.26**	0.31**
Rich/poor gap is a significant problem	0.03	0.07	0.14**
Government and politics are sometimes too complex	0.02	0.05	−0.02
Voting is my only say in government	0.1**	0.3**	0.41**
Christians should get involved in politics to protect values	0.64**	0.34**	0.29**
Traditional Christian values should play a role in politics	0.32**	−0.02	−0.05
Church/religious organizations should be required to pay taxes	0.5**	0.36**	0.2**
Strict rules to protect environment are necessary	0.26**	0.28**	0.23**
Homosexuals should have the same rights as others	0.07	−0.01	0.1
Government regulation of abortion is infringement on women's rights	0.01	0.2**	0.13*
TOTAL	2.3	2.32	2.35

Note: Item wording has been abbreviated. A positive number means a more conservative response in the United States.
Significance: *0.05; **0.01. Totals are absolute-value totals.

TABLE 12.4
Tolerance attitudes – Angus Reid/Pew Survey, 1996

Item	Difference – total sample (N = 6,000)	Difference – evangelicals (N = 1,045)	Difference – committed evangelicals (N = 533)
I would rather have neighbours of my own colour	0.19**	0.27**	0.25*
How close do you feel to Roman Catholics?	0.11**	0.01	0.01
How close do you feel to the Christian right?	–0.48**	–0.2**	–0.01
Would you vote for an evangelical political leader?	0.04*	0.08*	0.06
Would you vote for a political leader who is an atheist?	0.29**	0.31**	0.24**
Would you vote for a Muslim political leader?	0.12**	0.21**	0.19**
Total	1.23	1.08	0.76

Note: Item wording has been abbreviated. A positive difference means a more tolerant response in Canada.
Significance: *0.05; **0.01. Totals are absolute-value totals.

NOTES

1 Rawlyk (1996) used belief/behaving criteria and found that one-third of his Canadian evangelical sample were Catholics. Since a higher percentage of believing and behaving evangelicals affiliate with mainline denominations in Canada than in the United States, using belief/behaving criteria in this study would make cross-national comparisons tenuous.

2 As I have noted elsewhere (Reimer forthcoming), whether evangelicals appear to significantly accommodate in survey research depends on two aspects. First, the commitment level of the evangelicals studied, or how narrowly evangelicalism is defined, makes a difference, since committed evangelicals show less accommodation. In this study I use committed evangelicals to control variation in responses based on commitment level. Second, it depends on what measures of beliefs, attitudes, and practices are used, since evangelicals remain orthodox in some areas (for example, sexual mores), while they have softened their stance on others (for example, playing cards, dancing) (Hunter 1984, 1987).

3 For defence of the survey methodology, see Reimer (1996).

4 Evangelicals were able to place a negative or positive valence on groups they were unfamiliar with, such as the ability of most Canadian evangelicals to express their feelings toward the ACLU. One interviewee stated, 'I don't know what a secular humanist is, but I am probably against it.' Clearly, group boundaries are shared. A paper on the distinctiveness of evangelical identity and boundary maintenance is available from the author.

5 There is one exception to this rule. American evangelicals are more tolerant of conservative groups which appear intolerant to Canadians, including 'fundamentalists' and Right to Life. In general, I conclude that Americans are more tolerant of intolerance and incivility, while Canadians are otherwise more tolerant (see Reimer forthcoming).

6 For example, of the twenty-two pastors in Canada that I interviewed, five were Americans and fifteen received some or all of their education in the United States.

Part Five

IDENTITY, GENDER, BODY

The Steeple or the Shelter? Family Violence and Church-and-State Relations in Contemporary Canada

NANCY NASON-CLARK

Wife abuse is a prevalent social phenomenon. From the rugged shores of Newfoundland to the pristine British Columbia coastline, Canadian women experience violence at the hands of the men who purport to love them. While the nature and frequency of the violence differ, the journey towards health and wholeness is always long and arduous. The question of whether religion augments or thwarts the healing process of abuse victims has been a central theme in my research for many years. The story of what happens when an abused religious woman seeks solace and support from her faith community is multifaceted, and it can be told from a variety of perspectives – that of women victims, clergy, women's groups, congregations, transition-house workers, and the individual experiences of people of faith. As we might expect, not everyone has the same story to tell.

In this chapter we will consider whether old paradigms of religion and modernity can help us to understand the vitality and empowerment that a woman's spiritual journey can offer her at the time of crisis. We will also explore how emerging definitions of family and faith within women's religious experience challenge both the secularization thesis and prevailing notions of feminist empowerment. Finally, we will investigate both the challenges to collaborative efforts between church and community resources and the economic and social forces that make partnerships between the sacred and the secular more desirable than in the recent past. Implicit within this discussion is the notion that the boundaries between the sacred and the secular are more porous in women's experiences than they are in our social-scientific theories. The implication for scholars of religion is that we must think anew about the complex web of church, state, and modernity in the lives of ordinary people and the communities they inhabit.

At first glance, churches and transition houses appear to be on an ideological collision course. While churches offer space to worship the sacred, transition houses provide safe shelter for women (and their dependent children) fleeing violent relationships. Churches claim ownership of the phrase *family values*, and feminists who lobby on behalf of transition houses claim to speak on behalf of *women victims of abuse*. In a sense each group is staking out its turf: religious elites choose the family; feminists choose women. Both groups want to stop violence in the homes of our nation. Both groups want to support healing and recovery. Both groups believe that their framework offers the most efficacious response to the pain, brokenness, and despair created by the long-term consequences of abuse. With cultural sensitivity to issues of battery in the domestic realm increasing, religious and community resources have been challenged to stem the tide of violence and to support the victims left in its wake.

Churches and transition houses support two dramatically opposed paradigms for understanding the major social problem of wife abuse. As a result, they offer us a window, as it were, to investigate the relationship between the sacred and the secular in contemporary culture. In this way, domestic violence provides a concrete example of the interaction between explicitly religious and non-religious forces in community life. The issue – and our response to it – has both private and public dimensions, replete with both religious and secular overtones.

Secularization Theory

Whether the secularization debate among social scientists of religion has reached a point of intellectual crisis is arguable (Hadden 1995), but clearly there are several empirical signs in North America that are 'highly inconvenient to secularization theory' (Warner 1993; McGuire 1985). In his critique of the 'old paradigm,' R. Stephen Warner rejects the notion that secularization is 'the master historical process' that inexorably pushes advanced societies to reject the sacred on the path to embrace modernity.

Jeffrey Hadden argues that among the factors posing the greatest challenge to the secularization thesis are the growth and influence of Christian fundamentalism and the ability of liberation theology to in-

spire and motivate those striving for change in the social and political
order of modern societies (Hadden 1995; cf Hunter 1985). Others point
to the prominence of healing groups, both within and outside of traditional religious structures (McGuire 1985), the strength and vitality of
new religious movements (Barker 1985) or countermovements (Shupe
and Bromley 1985), and the persistence of and increase in personal
religiosity in American culture (Dekker, Luidens, and Rice 1997).

Central to the secularization thesis have been two core concepts: (1)
the *replacement* of religious faith with faith in other secular principles,
such as science, or other ideologies, such as Marxism or feminism; and
(2) increasing *differentiation* or separation between secular and sacred
spheres of life. Implicit within the secularization model was the belief
that modernity and religion were incompatible: that the forces and
beliefs that gave rise to modern culture would lead to a marked decline
and shrinking potency of religious belief and practice (Dobbelaere 1985,
1987; Wilson 1985; cf Demerath and Williams 1992b).

Reflecting on the classics, Bryan Wilson (1985, 9, 18) has declared that
sociology documents 'a secularizing process,' where the intellectual,
scientific, technical, and practical take precedence over the emotional
and the moral. Claiming that secularization is the 'inherited model'
(Wilson 1985, 9–20), it is not surprising that a generation or more of
scholars have simply assumed the reliability, validity, and gener-
alizability of the secularization model (cf Hadden 1995; Warner 1993).

The secularization thesis was born and nurtured in the European
experience, and David Martin (1991) proposes that its unilinear pattern
may be cloudy at best in other geographical contexts. There is accu-
mulating evidence that modernity both augments the process of
secularization and thwarts its development by creating niches for the
rise of new religious movements or renewed connectedness with established religions (Stark and Bainbridge 1985). In the American context,
the conservative Protestant example shows that survival in the modern
world may not directly threaten its numeric representation, though it
does exact costs in terms of movement away from orthodoxy and
accommodation to secular influences (Hunter 1985).

As social scientists of religion have argued for a long time, the religious group meets not only the spiritual or religious needs of its members (for example, with the promise of salvation, a context to validate
personal experiences of God, and the enactment of rituals empowered
with religious significance), but religious groups also satisfy a myriad
of their members' secular needs (for example, offering a sense of

community and belonging, personal identity, direction, and hope) (Barker 1985). In the conservative Protestant context, several researchers have documented the all-encompassing nature of involvement within the faith community (Ammerman 1987). Hunter (1985) contends that conservative Protestants offer secularism's greatest challenge, since they actively promote an attempt to integrate orthodox Christianity with everyday life experiences in a cultural context presumed hostile to such integration.

Some theorists see secularization as a loss of the influence of the religious elite, rather than a sharp decline in individual religiosity (Kleiman, Ramsey, and Palazzo 1996; Chaves 1989). In a study of the response of Newfoundland Roman Catholic women in the aftermath of sexual scandal perpetrated by parish priests, it was revealed that women of faith reported a loss of confidence in their spiritual leaders, coupled with anger and resentment directed towards the religious hierarchy. Yet there was surprisingly little impact upon their own spiritual journey in terms of beliefs, religious practices, or personal piety (Nason-Clark 1998a).

Demerath and Williams (1992b) employ a community case study to explore how secularization and sacralization are linked in a local context. They argue that secularization needs to be viewed as an 'abridging of faith,' the gradual diminishment of the sacred into the hands of the secular. Through this process other-worldly ideas and objects once set apart for special veneration compete with this-worldly claims and, as a result, their power and status are altered in both nature and degree.

This chapter focuses on the issue of wife battery and examines the relationship between secular and sacred strategies in their response to a social issue that has been framed by modern feminist consciousness. We will explore the boundaries around church and community responses to abuse victims and analyse how new partnerships have been created among the caring professions to respond to a problem that is beyond the grasp of any one profession or discipline to reduce or eliminate.

Wife Abuse in the Canadian Context

Each Sunday morning, over two million Canadian women attend a worship service that is Christian in perspective.[1] Within these religious congregations are approximately 700,000 victims of abuse,[2] women who know all too well the pain and despair that violence has brought into their lives, their homes, and their spiritual journeys (Nason-Clark 1996). Epidemiological research demonstrates that violence knows no social class, ethnic, or religious boundaries (Straus, Gelles, and Steinmetz 1980), although it may be more difficult to detect among the most affluent or within particular communities where interaction with the outside host culture is discouraged (Timmins 1995). Since violence tends to disregard the differences between women – such as age, culture, religion, race, ethnicity, and social class (Fiorenza 1994) – all women live with the fear or reality of abuse (Copeland 1994). Typically, victimized women suffer 'behind closed doors' (Straus, Gelles, and Steinmetz 1980), in a social context where shame and secrecy have been carefully constructed (*Fire in the Rose Project* 1994). While clearly some women are more vulnerable than others, pervasive societal norms about the sanctity and privacy of family life deter women from disclosing their abuse. And economic dependency and fear keeps them in domestic situations where their emotional and physical health cannot be assured.

Within the past seven years, Statistics Canada (1993b) conducted a national survey of women aged eighteen years and older that focused on female experiences of physical and sexual violence. According to the data collected from over 12,000 women, three in every ten Canadian women have experienced at least one incident of physical or sexual abuse in a current or previous marital relationship that was consistent with legal definitions of these offences. The majority of women who had been assaulted were victimized on several occasions, with 32 per cent reporting more than ten incidents. Women with a violent father-in-law were at much greater risk of abuse, as were women who lived with men who drank regularly. One-third of victimized women reported that at some point they feared for their own lives. In 40 per cent of violent households, children witness the violence perpetrated against their mothers.

Just under half (45 per cent) of woman abuse incidents resulted in physical injury, although most of these women reported that they did not seek medical attention. Weapons were employed by 44 per cent of violent partners, with 16 per cent of the women interviewed by Statistics Canada indicating that their husbands had used a gun or knife against them. Few wife assault victims reported the abusive incidents to the police (26 per cent) or sought help from a social agency (24 per cent) or respite from a transition house (6 per cent). Rather, most victimized women relied on their informal network of support – friends and neighbours (51 per cent) and family (42 per cent) – to help them through the personal crisis. One in five victims had never disclosed the violence to anyone prior to revealing it to a Statistics Canada telephone interviewer. These data reveal that repeated incidents of violence far outnumber isolated acts of aggression in the life of a victimized woman.

The Response of the Feminist Community to Wife Abuse

The feminist wake-up call to the seriousness and pervasiveness of violence in the lives of ordinary women followed on the second wave of feminist consciousness that spread throughout North America, beginning in the 1960s and gaining strength in the ensuing decades (Currie 1990; DeKeseredy and Hinch 1991; Walker 1990). It is predicated on the notion that women who live in fear need a place where they can seek refuge apart from the unrestrained aggression of their partner. Transition houses offer temporary shelter to victimized women and their children, and volunteer workers and staff provide both information and counselling to house residents. Activist in orientation, the shelter movement seeks to transpose the private fear of an abused woman into a public issue of male violence against women (Loseke 1992). In this way, what happens in the bedrooms of the nation is reconstructed into political strategies for social change.

Feminists do not regard violence as a family issue (Martin 1981). Rather, they believe that violent men need restraint, and victims need safety and supportive services. Accordingly, woman abuse is conceptualized as a specific example of the pervasive problem of gender inequity and continuing evidence of the power imbalance between men and women within marriage and the broader culture (Timmins 1995). Central to any feminist analysis of violence is the issue of male anger and control, which is understood as a form of male privilege in a society that values men more than women (Dobash and Dobash 1979).

Violence includes any action that violates a woman's physical, emotional, sexual, or financial well-being, as well as threats of such intended behaviour (DeKeseredy and MacLeod 1997). In essence, woman abuse is any behaviour that seeks to shame, hurt, or humiliate a woman within the boundaries of an intimate relationship (Family Violence Prevention Initiative 1994; MacLeod 1987). Defining the issue, naming the victims, and charting the healing journey have political, clinical, and humanitarian dimensions, and implications for the transformation in a woman's life from victim to survivor (Nason-Clark 1998c).

The Response of the Conservative Protestant Faith Community to Wife Abuse

Conservative Protestants endorse enthusiastically the phrases *family life* and *family values*. In fact, the celebration of the traditional family has become a multimillion dollar business, with Dr James Dobson (1996, 1995) and his Focus on the Family organization exhibiting tremendous popular appeal, and dominating both the religious market-place through the sale of books, cassettes, videos, magazines and the religious media through radio broadcasts and regular newspaper columns. (See the chapter by John G. Stackhouse, Jr, elsewhere in this volume.)

While much of the message would be familiar to women of the post–Second World War era, it has been repackaged in some interesting ways to make it more palatable to a contemporary audience (Nason-Clark 1997). Women have a unique, but not exclusive, role as care-givers, but their heartstrings are tied to the domestic sphere where they are to watch the home fires carefully, for secularism, individualism, and materialism can invade the family context like a virus. Women, then, protect the inside of the home, serving as emotional thermostats (Nason-Clark 1995) and tension managers (Luxton 1980), as men wage war with the forces of evil in the external world. Hierarchy and submission are central constructs in the organization of the family (see LaHaye and LaHaye 1995, 1982; Smalley 1996, 1988), and divorce as well as gay rights are evidence that families have abandoned God and spiritual values. Within this perspective, 'happy family living' resides in strong male leadership and supportive, nurturant women. Groups like the Promise Keepers, who attract more than one million North American men to their rallies each year, are ample proof of the power and pervasiveness, not to mention appeal, of the concept of spiritual leadership in the family context (Elmore 1992; Janssen 1994; Lockhart 1996). Since family unity is God's plan, men and women are to strive for marital bliss at almost any cost.

As a result, conservative Protestant ideology regards violent acts in marriage as a function of misconceptions about God's design for marital harmony (see Dobson 1996). The issue is placed firmly within the family unit, to be resolved at that level: both partners are believed to be responsible to address the malaise they feel and to work in tandem to restore the marital relationship (Nason-Clark 1997). Consequently, clergy name the abuse as *family violence*, reluctant to lay blame or responsibility for the violence primarily in the hands of the abusive husband.

Moreover, pastoral counsellors tend to equate reconciliation with recovery, overly optimistic that reunification of an abusive man and his victimized wife is evidence that the marital relationship has been restored. The reluctance of many evangelical clergy to refer parishioners to secular sources of help, coupled with their reluctance to preach against violence in the family from the pulpit, can be construed as part of the conspiracy of silence related to wife abuse in conservative religious contexts (Nason-Clark 1998c). In essence, abused religious women and abusive religious men pose a direct challenge to the message of marital bliss and 'happy family living' so enthusiastically endorsed by contemporary evangelicals. As a result, many clergy find themselves caught between the rhetoric of the family they are meant to uphold and the reality of the pain and suffering presented to them in counselling contexts with parishioners (Nason-Clark 1996).

Yet, despite evidences of a *holy hush* related to the issue of wife abuse in communities of faith, there are a plethora of examples of *shattered silence*, created in large measure as a by-product of the gendered nature of church life (Nason-Clark 1998c). Church women's knowledge of abuse is framed by both the religious elite and feminist forces, and it is contextualized and interpreted through the experiences of women they know – friends, sisters, mothers, co-workers, or their own life stories – who have been personal victims of abuse (Nason-Clark 1995). Consequently religious women believe the family is *sacred*, but they know all too well that it may not be *safe*. Their response to both victims of abuse and to the transition-house movement is supportive and reinforced by the myriad of practical forms of assistance that they offer to abused women both within and outside of their faith community. An abused woman's safety is given priority, and the intervention strategy offers a victimized woman choices (for example, to remain or to leave her abusive husband) over her life and destiny.

Challenges to the Old Paradigm: Separation of Church and Community

Since the 1960s there has been a growing awareness of the extent and severity of wife abuse, together with an increasing recognition of the longer term implications for women victims suffering its pain and accompanying despair (Martin 1981). The literature on violence within the family unit has grown exponentially within this time frame (Gelles

1985), although few have considered the spiritual dimensions, or the role of religious belief or practice in the life of a victim or perpetrator (Fortune 1991; Horton and Williamson 1988). What was once considered a private issue, a domestic disturbance, has been moved from the bedrooms of the nation to the public arena by grassroots feminists. One man's abusive acts towards his wife within the confines of his own home are not his own private affair: rather, they represent a political issue of unrestrained male aggression in a culture that privileges male experience and promotes male power. In publicizing woman abuse, feminists challenged the notion that violence against women be conceptualized as a family issue, an emotional problem of one unhappy couple, where the solution rested with the man and the woman to resolve their differences or part company.

As interest and debate concerning violence against women have grown, the issue has been removed from the private sphere, but it has developed in ways both unanticipated and unwelcomed by some of its feminist founders (Walker 1990; Loseke 1992). Many grassroots women's organizations and feminist lobbyists charge that the movement to stop violence against women – and to promote transition houses for temporary refuge – has been marginalized and silenced when it attempts to politicize male anger and control (Barnsley 1995). From this vantage point, the state, the churches, and the powerful professions have hijacked the woman battery movement and watered down its feminist analysis (Quinby 1995). As a consequence, any challenge to cultural values and institutions that perpetuate male privilege has been lost. Feminists charge that the voices of the care-givers have drowned out the voices of the victims.

The old paradigm of sociology, motivated in large measure by functionalism, claimed that the family was private, removed from the domain of the public or political sphere. The issue of violence contextualized in the home environment challenges this view. By spotlighting the issue of woman abuse, feminists have challenged, in part, the boundaries between the personal and the political. Of course, this has been a central component to the feminist challenge in contemporary society. Women's private experiences have political implications. As such, then, feminism has been largely responsible for the direction and focus of contemporary thinking about violence, gender, and the family.

These notions of empowerment have had an impact on religious women in general and evangelical church women in particular in three distinct ways: the woman-centred circle of support; the context of religious women's care; and the role of clergy as empathic counsellor (Nason-Clark 1998c).

Woman-Centred Circle of Support

From our focus group research with almost 250 church women throughout Atlantic Canada, we have learned that the average church woman has offered personal support to another woman in her church, while the same proportion have been the recipient of another woman's care. This women-directed form of religious empowerment addresses the pressing practical needs of congregants, even as it bolsters their beliefs and sense of community togetherness. Because their knowledge of violence is linked to the women victims they know, evangelical women are both inclusive in their understanding of abuse and helpful in their response. By these beliefs and actions, more disclosures are encouraged. The kitchen table of a woman of faith is a safe place to admit violence. In fact, 60 per cent of the church women who participated in our research have offered an abused woman some form of emotional support, one in five had sheltered a woman overnight, and 12 per cent had given money. Smaller numbers had cared for children, provided transportation, or accompanied a victimized woman to court.

The form of empowerment practised by women of faith has both secular and religious overtones. It does not demand that an abused woman sever all ties with her violent partner, nor does it recommend that she remain in a family environment that threatened her emotional or physical safety. By appropriating selected features of both feminism and the conservative evangelical worldview, conservative church women offered choices, a form of agency whereby a victimized woman is encouraged to take control of her life, the lives of her children, and to resist the controlling behaviour of her partner, perhaps for the first time in her life (Beaman-Hall and Nason-Clark 1997a). The stories we have been told by abused religious women reinforce the fact that there are a myriad of ways that women exercise agency in their journey towards healing and wholeness.

The Context of Religious Women's Care

Through telephone interviews with shelter workers, we learned that the strongest link between churches and transition houses occurred not through professional contacts with clergy, but through the lives of church women. Groups of church women would support the local shelter through the provision of goods, funds, or by volunteering their time. As a group, church women interpreted their relationship with the transition house as a form of 'ministry,' a specific example of social action motivated by religious belief. Since their knowledge of violence was framed by knowing victims, and mediated by a history of receiving care themselves under the umbrella of Christian love, church women showed little sign of condemning women who left abusive partners. In fact, their work with the local shelter built a bridge between the sacred and the secular. Once that link was established, church women felt more at ease with referring other women to the transition house, and the shelter workers, in turn, were offered opportunities to speak during church services or to distribute pamphlets.

Church women themselves were aware that there were some challenges to be overcome in working collaboratively with transition houses, not least in terms of finding the right words to name the violent experience and to chart the healing journey. But their resolve to act with compassion outweighed their fears about having their worldview ridiculed. In essence the magnitude of the problem of abuse and the inability of any one theoretical perspective to meet all the accompanying needs of abuse victims ensured that there was ample work for all to do.

Clergy as Empathic Counsellor

In the current economic climate of fiscal restraint and close scrutiny of public funds, coupled with a shrinking social support net, churches and ministers are experiencing some unprecedented new challenges to their personal time and ministry resources. Some have argued that pastoral counselling is the new growth industry of the contemporary evangelical church. As I have argued elsewhere, long waiting lists for secular counsellors, increasing fees for private therapists, and very few professional resources in rural areas make the 'free' advice of the pastoral counsellor almost irresistible (Nason-Clark 1998c).

Our research program has involved almost 1,000 clergy from a variety of denominations across the Atlantic region. Consistently among evangelical pastors – and to a lesser extent in mainstream denominations as well – we have been told of the dramatic increase in the demand for pastoral counselling, coupled with the very real limitations for the average pastor. In our interview study of 100 evangelical ministers, we have learned that the average pastor spends two afternoons a week providing relationship or marital counselling, and most have counselled the following situations within the past year: an abused woman, an abusive man, and a couple where violence is common in the relationship (see Nason-Clark 1997, 57–82). Although ministers sometimes find themselves in the compromised setting of offering assistance to both victim and perpetrator, the clergy is one of the few community resources available to assist male batterers.

While members of the clergy tend to see reconciliation as one of, if not *the* main goal of clerical intervention in cases of wife abuse (Nason-Clark 1996), they do not discourage (and most encourage) an abused woman from temporarily separating from her abusive partner. When therapeutic intervention with the pastoral counsellor has been unable to stop the violence, or when abused men are unwilling to seek help, ministers usually advise permanent separation and the initiation of divorce proceedings. Since often some cleric was involved in the couple's wedding ceremony, the failure to reform the abusive man and to revitalize the relationship is considered to be a pastor's failure too. While the rhetoric of the Christian family literature would suggest that clergy may give unhelpful or even harmful advice to battered wives (Brown and Bohn 1989; Horton and Williamson 1988), our data reveal that members of the clergy are caught between an ideology of the family they want to uphold and the reality of parishioner counselling needs.

The Challenge to Secularization Theory

Appropriating feminist principles into their lives does not detract evangelical church women from their spiritual journey. In fact, in some ways it reinforces their quest for meaningful personal ministry in a world they perceive as hurting, but rather hostile, to their belief system. In reference to the issue of wife abuse, church women talked about earning the right to share their faith, or establishing credibility, through the example of their practical support of abuse victims, their *listening ear*, and their personal empathy with women who are suffering. Collectively, church women felt that their ongoing support of the local transition house, forged often by one woman from their church who exhibited a particular passion for the shelter movement, had created a climate where the sacred and the secular could be regarded as partners. Single-sex ministries within most evangelical churches have created spaces for women-only initiatives, and thus provided fertile ground for women-centred empowerment. Since the perceived hallmark of many conservative faith communities is personal service to others, this has provided an impetus for women to reach out to secular women who have been victimized by their husbands. Abused religious women themselves consider their faith an asset, not a liability, in their struggle to leave abusive partners and to begin a life free from the violence of the past (Beaman-Hall and Nason-Clark 1997b; Whipple 1987).

Church women's experience with wife abuse has not compromised their enthusiasm for the family; rather, problems with the family have nurtured their commitment to the faith perspective. It has had a sacralizing rather than a secularizing effect. As church women have appropriated select feminist principles into their everyday lives, they have not weakened in their Christian beliefs or practices. While they sometimes report growing impatience with the slow pace of change among their clerical leaders on this issue, including the apparent reluctance of clergy to condemn wife abuse from the pulpit (Nason-Clark 1998b), their involvement with women-centred small groups serves to counter their disappointment with the religious elite (see Wuthnow 1994a). From women's missionary societies to evangelical exercise classes, small groups are powerful forces within the local church setting, encouraging lay leadership and making religion increasingly relevant to an individual's daily experience (Searle 1994). In fact, the challenge of modernity has fostered the small-group experience, the need to find a place where 'everyone knows your name.'

Moreover, by examining the experiences of transition-house workers, clergy, and church women, we have found ample evidence of new or renewed links between churches and the community. To be sure, some of these bridges have been constructed during a time of fiscal restraint and shrinking government budgets. The links forged within these new economic realities have also highlighted churches' four major strengths useful to secular agencies involved in responding to the needs of abused women: physical space, community-based mission, infrastructural support, and volunteers (Nason-Clark 1997). The overwhelming numbers of women who have been victims of abuse combined with the fragile economic funding available to transition houses have produced within faith communities a greater willingness to cooperate and collaborate with other groups in order to survive the current economic and political climate. Perhaps they are partners by chance, but bridges between the steeple and the shelter challenge the secularization thesis which argues that within modernity the secular and the sacred must part company.

NOTES

I would like to gratefully acknowledge financial support from the following sources for my research and that of the Religion and Violence Research Team, of the Muriel McQueen Fergusson Centre for Family Violence Research at the University of New Brunswick, which I coordinate: The Louisville Institute for the Study of Protestantism and American Culture, the Social Sciences and Humanities Research Council, the Department of the Solicitor General, the Lawson Foundation, the Constant Jacquet Research Award of the Religious Research Association, the Secretary of State, the Muriel McQueen Fergusson Centre for Family Violence Research, and the UNB Research Fund. The following denominations have also contributed financially to this research program: the Atlantic District of the Wesleyan Church, the United Baptist Convention of the Atlantic Provinces, the Maritime Conference of the United Church of Canada, the Diocese of Fredericton of the Anglican Church, the Partners in Mission Initiative of the Anglican Church, and the Maritime Division of the Salvation Army. Members of the Religion and Violence Research Team include: Lori Beaman, Lois Mitchell, Sheila McCrea, Terry Atkinson, Christy Hoyt, and several graduate student assistants (Amanda Henry, Michelle Spencer, and Lisa Hanson).

1 The population of Canada exceeds twenty-seven million, of which over half are female (Statistics Canada, 1991 Census). Over 10 per cent of Canadians attend a Christian-based church service on a weekly basis, with women's attendance rates higher than their male counterparts (cf Bibby 1987, 1993).
2 Statistics Canada (1993b) reports that three in ten Canadian women have experienced physical or sexual violence from a current or previous partner.

chapter fourteen

The Politics of the Body in Canada and the United States

JOHN H. SIMPSON

I

In recent years a number of issues, controversies, and popular discourses bearing on the control, use, display, and maintenance of the body have entered public arenas. In some cases matters pertaining to the body sustain social continuity by intensifying the link between traditional values and practices (Ellison and Sherkat 1993). In other cases they signal new social directions by challenging established institutions (Schneirov and Geczik 1997). Occasionally body-related matters are implicated in conflicts in the global system of action.[1]

Where the body is now a subject of public attention and controversy especially in the West, it has also become an object of wide-ranging theoretical speculation (Bell 1972; Butler 1993; Foucault 1979, 1981, 1988; Frank 1991; Giddens 1992; Mellor and Shilling 1997; O'Neill 1985, 1989; Shilling 1993; Synnott 1993; Turner 1984, 1992, 1996). This development stands in marked contrast to the near absence of the body as a thematized unit of analysis in classic sociological theory and the variable but generally persistent suppression of the 'mode of desire' (Turner 1984) during the period of industrial capitalism and high modernity (Simpson 1993).

High modernity (c 1800–1965) was marked by the enactment of an ascetic ideology summarized in the Cartesian slogan, 'I think, therefore I am.' The conceptual separation of mind and body, the subordination of the body to the mind, and the dominance of reason in action were the principle elements of the Cartesian myth. 'Practical' Cartesianism in the form of instrumental means–ends rationalization subordinated nature and people to Western technology and civilization (Turner 1996, 10). The need to control bodies and reproduce them in order to sustain the entrepreneurial/industrial capitalist mode of production was undergirded by the ideologies and practices of ascetic Protestantism and those of Roman Catholicism as well in some circumstances (Simpson 1993). They were joined by the tendency in scientific medicine to treat the body as a stimulus–response 'machine' (thus, reinforcing high modernity's separation of mind and body), the use of the state's powers of organization, surveillance, and repression to form and control bodies as social units (Foucault 1979; cf. Lyon 1994a), and the rise of the patriarchal nuclear family – a unit separate but integral to the workplace and 'designed' for the reproduction and socialization of bodies and their maintenance through consumption (Shorter 1977; cf. Garrett 1998).[2]

The decade of the 1960s marked a definitive behavioural and ideological move against the restrictive cultural and institutional patterns of high modernity (Gitlin 1987; Levitt 1984; Roszak 1969). There was a turn that deconstructed the repressed body and increased tension between embodied and 'minded' forms of modern action. The dominance of the mind over the body was relaxed. The moral apparatus of bourgeois industrial capitalism seemed to lose its grip (Simpson 1998a; Turner 1996, 2). A visible counterculture of sexual permissiveness, the use of mind-altering substances, new forms of popular musical expression, and a rejection of the regimented industrial order of work was embraced by youth in the West. Sex, drugs, and rock and roll became the talismans of the post–Second World War baby-boom generation.

At the same time various social movements sought to advance the economic, political, and social rights of students, minorities, and the marginalized, including women, gays, and lesbians, and the disabled (Buechler and Cylke 1997; Herzog 1998; Eiesland and Saliers 1998). These movements also promoted nuclear disarmament, an end to the cold war and the halt of the American (and Soviet) sponsored 'hot' conflict in Vietnam. Together the counterculture and the sociopolitical movements of the 1960s formed a metonymous complex that combined progressive – often utopian – social and moral purposes with free expression of the body in a symbolic 'package' that was widely disseminated in the media. The modern sensibility of duty and suppression of the body gave way to a postmodern mood of right and expression of the body. The modern emphasis on the immanence of the mind and self in action was joined and countered by a new emphasis on embodied forms of action. The body became part of the self project (Mellor and Shilling 1997). The 'somatic' society was born (Turner 1996).

No single factor accounts for the body-oriented sociocultural shifts in the West that took off in the 1960s and worked themselves out in subsequent decades, often in interaction with new developments such as the advent of AIDS. Multiple causes and multiple outcomes are entwined in complex patterns where causes and outcomes are interchangeable. Factors implicated in the changing times include new forms of work focused on services, information, communication and transportation, an increase in the participation of women in the workforce, the development of highly reliable methods of birth control, second- and third-wave feminist social analysis, critiques of the patriarchal model of family and work, and the rise of consumer capitalism.

The changes of the 1960s are encoded in the shift across the West from a strong emphasis on economic and political security or material values to a recognition of postmaterialist values that foreground individual expression, participation in decision making, and the preservation and enhancement of nature rather than its domination and exploitation (Englehart 1990). At the most general level of interpretation this shift can be viewed as a new moment in the construction, meaning, and relationship between what Talcott Parsons (1979) writing late in his life described as the 'hot spots' of civilization: the institutions that embed economic and reproductive exchanges and their media – money and sex. The enactment of postmaterialist values and the concomitant rise of body-oriented action are consistent with Parsons's analysis of the reconfiguration of norms pertaining to work and the family that have occurred at crucial junctures in the evolution of Western civilization. However, as Englehart (1990) observes – and as Parsons, no doubt, would have agreed – general trends and movements are subject to national particularisms and peculiarities. Cross-national differences in the configuration of institutions and variations in the cultural resources embedded in the social systems of nation-states can act as 'filters' or gates that shape the flow of movements in ways that produce 'local' versions and responses to general trends (cf Simpson 1996, 1998b). Thus, while there has been a culture shift in the West that is traceable to the events and the generational sensibility of the 1960s, there are variations across the nation-states of the West in terms of such matters as the impact of consumer culture and the political expression of body-related issues.[3]

The purpose of this chapter is to 'tease out' comparisons between

Canada and the United States regarding the impact of the somatic
society in North America. Where the shift to postindustrialism in the
context of economic globalization has generated a diffuse set of work-
related social problems (Barlow 1990, 1995), the mitigation and solution
of these problems tends to proceed within the established frameworks
of the welfare state and its reconfiguration in late capitalism. Body
matters, on the other hand – especially abortion and homosexuality –
have become sources of sharp division and ongoing unsettled, intense,
bitter conflicts in the public arenas of North America (Jelen and Chandler 1994; Rayside 1998). These conflicts are implicated in relations
between the institutions of church and state where law, ethics, and
morals may collide. Furthermore they are implicated in controversies
and practices within denominations (O'Toole et al. 1991) and in the
expression of religion and morals in the everyday lives of ordinary
citizens (Simpson 1998a). Arguably, then, body matters are 'leading
indicators' of social tensions and changes in late modernity. The right to
work and a fair wage – the central domestic concerns of the parents of
the baby-boom generation – have been supplemented (if not replaced)
by body-oriented issues in the public arenas of North America.

Data discussed below provide a base for a consideration of the emergent relations between church, state, and the body in the somatized
societies of North America. In the first instance attention is directed to
the demographic roots of controversy over body matters. Consideration of attitudes towards a variety of body issues in the Canadian and
American populations follows. Third, general attitudes are examined
in Canada and the United States regarding linkages between religion
and politics, that is, the nexus where battles over the body tend to be
joined.

II

Religious demography provides the baseline indicator of the likelihood
that controversies pertaining to the body will arise in a national jurisdiction. Although patterns of church–state relations and the organization of politics (Martin 1978) may affect the intensity of body-oriented
controversies, the number of carriers of the ingredients for body-oriented conflicts is the best initial estimate of the likelihood that body
politics will occur in a population. Since the mid-1970s concerns regarding abortion, sexual orientation, personal 'purity,' and the control
of the body have been expressed and pursued as political issues by

some within the domain of sectarian Protestantism (Simpson 1983).[4] A supporting hand has been lent by some Roman Catholics where Roman Catholicism lacks a determinative majority and where the issue of abortion has become publicly salient (Cuneo 1989).

No European nation-state has the provocative population character-istics that have led to politicized body controversies: a sizeable compo-nent of sectarian Protestants with Roman Catholics in a minority position. A comparison of the American and Canadian populations in that re-gard is instructive. Canada is a near-majority Catholic country (46 per cent) at the aggregate national level. America, on the other hand, is a Protestant country (57 per cent). Proportionately, there are nearly twice as many Catholics in Canada as there are in the United States, and for every Baptist in Canada there are nearly eight in the United States. About 13 per cent of the American population and 20 per cent of the Canadian population is mainline Protestant and there are about twice as many Protestant others (neither Baptist nor mainline) in the United States as there are in Canada.

Not every Baptist or other sectarian Protestant is a carrier of the ingredients of a body-oriented politics or so-called moral majority–type politics (Simpson 1983). Furthermore, some mainline Protestants are carriers of body-oriented politics and the category of Protestant other contains both carriers and non-carriers. Nevertheless, the religious de-mography of America underwrites body-oriented public controversy, but the religious composition of the Canadian population does not support politically oriented body conflicts to the same degree.[5]

Some interesting comparisons can be drawn between the foregoing remarks and results from the Canada/U.S. Religion and Politics Survey (CUSRPS) (Angus Reid 1996a).[6] Earlier surveys by the American Na-tional Survey of Religious Identification (NSRI, see Kosmin and Lachman 1993) and Statistics Canada (1991 Census) elicited religious identity or affiliation as a response to a set of unfiltered alternatives to the ques-tion, 'What is your religious identity/affiliation?' CUSRPS, on the other hand, posed the following filter question to respondents: 'Do you ever think of yourself as part of a religious tradition? For example, do you consider yourself as Christian, Jewish, Muslim, other non-Christian, agnostic or atheist, nothing in particular, or something else?' Only those who answered 'Christian' were probed for a specific denomina-tional response. The figures from NSRI and the 1991 Census of Canada indicate the proportion of Christians in the American (86 per cent) and Canadian (83 per cent) populations. The percentage of respondents in each country who said they were Christian in response to the CUSRPS filter is 76 per cent in the United States and 68 per cent in Canada. Also, there are estimates based on the CUSRPS survey for the percentage of Catholics in the Canadian population (33 per cent) and the American population (21 per cent) and the percentage of Baptists in the two populations as well (Canada, 1.4 per cent; United States, 16 per cent).

There are differences – in some cases substantial differences – between the CUSRPS estimates and estimates from the Census of Canada and NSRI. According to CUSRPS both Canada and the United States are less Christian and less Catholic than indicated by the other sources. Also, CUSRPS provides an estimate of fewer Baptists in Canada and the United States than the other sources do. However, the estimated proportion of sectarian Protestants in each country – using Baptists as a rough indicator – adheres to the familiar pattern of fewer sectarian Protestants in Canada than in the United States.[7]

The religious demography of a country is a baseline indicator of its capacity for body-oriented politics. An exploration of the distribution of orientations and attitudes towards body-oriented matters sharpens the assessment of the likelihood of such politics. Writing in the wake of Ronald Reagan's election in 1980, George Marsden (1980) noted that American fundamentalism had re-emerged as a political force in the United States. Many themes and causes were the same as during the first fundamentalist era, according to Marsden, including a call to return to evangelical-Victorian mores with an emphasis on 'personal holiness as evidenced especially by avoidance of barroom vices' (p. 228). Marsden also recognized that there were new issues, including opposition to the women's movement and abortion, that had drawn some sectarian Protestants into the public arena.

In the context of the rise of the new Christian right as a force in the American public arena in the late 1970s, Marsden's references to both 'barroom vices' and new issues such as abortion raise the question of support in the American population for old and new body-oriented issues. Barroom vices encompass drinking alcoholic beverages and the use of tobacco. Viewed from within the frame of the conservative Protestant interpretation of Romans 12:1 ('I beseech you therefore, brethren, by the mercies of God, that ye present your bodies a living sacrifice, holy, acceptable unto God'), drinking and smoking pollute the body, thereby rendering it unholy and unacceptable to God. Thus, smoking and drinking are – at least from a sectarian Protestant perspective –

religiously implicated body-oriented matters. They are the old body issues in the public arenas of North America.

How do the old body issues fare, today, in the American population as a basis for politics? Changing American attitudes towards barroom vices are instructive. According to the NORC General Social Survey (GSS) (see <http=//www.norc.uchicago.edu/homepage.htm>) there is clearly no basis in the American population for a politics of prohibition. What was killed in 1933 remains dead. In 1993 only 28 per cent of the respondents indicate that they are abstainers. Even among those re-spondents classified as fundamentalists, 53 per cent say that they use alcohol; 72 per cent of religious liberals say that they drink.

While the American population is not 'on side' in terms of the 'clas-sic' Protestant body issue of abstention from alcohol, tobacco use presents a somewhat different picture. Only 27 per cent of the respondents indicated that they are smokers. Among those classified as fundamen-talists, 26 per cent say that they smoke. Among religious liberals the figure is 31 per cent. The most reasonable interpretation of these find-ings is that smoking has ceased to be a 'spiritually focused' body issue in America and has become a consensual health-related matter. A barroom vice has been transformed into a health risk factor.

Where barroom vices have lost their once formidable public clout as signifiers of religious practice and Protestant respectability (Gusfield 1963), new body issues have taken their place. However, these issues have little if anything to do with the use of practices to mark distinc-tions, differences, status levels, and mobility patterns in the society (Simpson 1985b). Rather, at the heart of the issues is a concern regard-ing the moral strength and continuity of American society. That con-cern has been precipitated in such issues as prayer in the schools, abortion, homosexuality, and controversies regarding women in the labour force.

The focus in this chapter is on the explicitly body-oriented issues that are part of the complex of concern: sexual orientation and abortion. But extramarital sex is also relevant, a matter that has contemporary sali-ency in the American public arena in light of allegations regarding the extramarital sexual behaviour of President Bill Clinton. In 1977 about 60 per cent of Americans rejected abortion on demand (Simpson 1983). That figure drops to 55 per cent in 1993, with sampling error (probably) accounting for most of the difference. Clearly, the American population is divided on the issue of abortion on demand, with a small majority siding with the politicized Protestant sectarian position.

In 1977 about 68 per cent of the NORC GSS respondents took the view that homosexual relations between consenting adults were 'always wrong' (Simpson 1983). In 1993 the figure is virtually the same: 66 per cent. Again, the American population sides with the politicized new Christian right position on the issue.

In 1993 77 per cent of the GSS sample indicated that extramarital sex is 'always wrong.' That represents a slight increase (again, probably attributable to sampling error) over the 1977 figure of 73 per cent (Davis 1982). Americans are less conflicted in their attitudes towards extramarital sex (77 per cent strongly disapprove) than they are regarding either abortion on demand (55 per cent reject it) or homosexual relations (66 per cent strongly disapprove).

There is a bi-modal pattern in the distribution of attitudes towards homosexual relations (66 per cent say that they are 'always wrong,' 22 per cent say that they are 'not wrong at all') and abortion on demand (45 per cent approve, 55 per cent disapprove). On the other hand, the distribution of attitudes towards extramarital sex is highly skewed in the direction of disapproval. There is no sizeable 'rump' at the approval end of the distribution. All other things being equal, bi-modal distributions of attitudes in populations underwrite conflict. Because there is no division in the population that provides a basis for conflict (most Americans disapprove of extramarital sex), the skewed distribution of attitudes towards extramarital sex, paradoxically, may have strengthened President Clinton's hand in the controversy regarding his extramarital sexual behaviour. There is no sizeable response rate at the approval end of the scale to underwrite a plausibility structure for conflict.

The fact that a new body-oriented politics entered the American public arena in the late 1970s in reaction to social somatization is consistent with the religious demography of the United States and patterns of orientation in its population to abortion and homosexuality. The religious demography of Canada does not favour an American-style politics of body issues. Is it the case that attitudes in the Canadian population to body issues also discourage body-oriented public controversies?

Data for assessing that question are not available in a Canadian equivalent of the NORC General Social Survey. Estimates provided here are taken from Bibby's (1993) Project Can90, the 1984 Canadian National Election Survey (Lambert et al.), and CUSRPS. Of the three sources of data, only Project Can90 has items that match the NORC GSS questions pertaining to abortion on demand and homosexual relations between consenting adults. Cross-tabulations (truncated) of those items with the self-reported importance of religion appear in Bibby (1993, 87). Bibby's cross-tabulations can be compared with cross-tabulations of the abortion and homosexual relations items in the NORC GSS with the self-reported strength of religion.

Among the Project Can90 respondents indicating that religion is very important in their lives, 15 per cent approve of abortion on demand, and 17 per cent approve of homosexual relations. Among the respondents reporting that religion is not important at all in their lives, 46 per cent approve of abortion on demand and 40 per cent approve of homosexual relations. Among American respondents reporting high religious strength, 30 per cent approve of abortion on demand and 23 per cent say that homosexual relations are not wrong at all. Among those who report low religious strength, 54 per cent approve of abortion on demand and 27 per cent approve of homosexual relations.

While caution should be exercised in interpreting the figures, it would appear that Canadians tend to be more conservative than Americans regarding abortion on demand and somewhat more liberal regarding homosexual relations. These patterns are consistent with general differences in the religious demography of the countries. Canada is more Catholic than the United States. The United States is more Protestant and has more sectarian Protestants in its population than Canada. As a rule Catholics are more conservative regarding abortion and somewhat more liberal in their views of homosexuality than sectarian Protestants.

The homosexuality items in the surveys mentioned above elicited judgments from respondents regarding the moral status of homosexual behaviour. Where question wording shifts to the performance of public roles, interesting differences emerge between Canada and the United States. In 1984, Canadians' attitudes towards homosexuals in the school classroom and Americans' attitudes towards homosexuals teaching in postsecondary institutions of learning suggested that Canadians are more 'edgy' than Americans regarding the presence of homosexuals in teaching roles.

In deciding whether that conclusion is justified it should be borne in mind that the 1984 NORC General Social Survey question can be interpreted as an indicator of attitudes towards civil rights and, specifically, the desirability of freedom of expression in a venue (the postsecondary classroom) where ideas are supposed to receive free rein. While the question may evoke some thoughts about the risk of corrupting the morals of youth, it is more likely – given the marked emphasis on the norm of free speech in American society – to raise the question of the extent to which limits should be imposed on the expression of 'dangerous ideas.' The question in the 1984 Canadian National Election Survey, on the other hand, may have evoked the putative risks involved in exposing school-age children to homosexuals. In that case the emphasis is not on free speech but rather on the potential for child abuse and the recruitment of 'innocent youngsters' to a deviant lifestyle.

The best direct evidence for differences between Canada and the United States in the matter of body issues is found in the CUSRPS data obtained in response to an open-ended question regarding issues that should receive the greatest attention of leaders. As Table 14.1 indicates, no Canadian respondents mentioned either abortion or moral issues and pornography as matters that should receive 'first call' on leaders' attention. Only 1 per cent of Canadian respondents mentioned moral issues and pornography at all. On the other hand, both abortion and moral issues were each mentioned by 3 per cent of the American sample as the most important issue facing leaders, and 6 per cent and 5 per cent, respectively, thought that leaders should pay attention to those matters.

Table 14.1 also provides figures regarding the issues that Canadian and Americans thought were most important in 1996. For Canadians it was jobs and unemployment. For Americans it was crime/violence and education/schools. Comparisons between these figures and the numbers for abortion and moral issues are instructive. Clearly, abortion and moral issues were hardly on the public agenda in Canada at all in 1996. Jobs and unemployment were. In the United States, on the other hand, there was less consensus regarding what was important, and abortion and moral issues were reasonably close in importance to those issues that were deemed to be the most important (crime and education). In general theoretical terms, the numbers in Table 14.1 indicate that social control or system maintenance (crime/violence/education/schools/abortion/moral issues) were perceived by the American public as problematic in 1996. In Canada, on the other hand, adaptation or survival in the form of jobs and the reduction of unemployment were significant public concerns.

CUSURPS respondents were also asked to indicate the importance of different public goals arranged in two sets of three priorities each. The priorities in each set tap orientations towards a social control goal (raising moral standards; preserving and promoting the family), a ma-

Table 14.1
Issues that should receive greatest attention from leaders in 1996 –
First Mention (+), Total Mentions (++)

Issue	Canada (%) +	Canada (%) ++	United States (%) +	United States (%) ++
Jobs / unemployment	27	46	–	–
National unity / Quebec's future	18	41	–	
Economy / recession	14	24	–	–
Deficit / debt / gov't spending	12	23	–	–
Healthcare / medicare	6	16		
Crime / violence	–	–	9	20
Education / schools	–	–	9	20
Deficit / debt / govt. spending	–	–	8	15
Defence	–	–	8	17
Economy / recession	–	–	8	15
Drugs	–	–	7	15
Health care		–	6	14
Abortion	*	*	3	6
Moral issues / pornography	*	1	3	5

* Less than 1%
Source: CUSRPS

terialist goal (maintaining law and order; building a healthy economy), and a postmaterialist goal (giving people more say in government; protecting the environment).

In each set of priorities, the social control goal was chosen more often by Americans, with the materialist goal second and the postmaterialist goal third. The pattern of choices among Canadians is more complex. In the first set, the postmaterialist and materialist goals were chosen at virtually the same rate, with the social control priority ranking third. In the second set of priorities, the materialist goal ranks first, the social control goal second, and the postmaterialist goal third. In both sets of priorities, Canadians were less likely to endorse social control goals than Americans.

Where matters pertaining to social control or system maintenance can be thematized in public arenas in terms of personal morality, they can also be thematized in terms of the discourse of rights. The responses of Canadians and Americans to items in the CUSRPS survey pertaining to the rights of gays and lesbians and the regulation of abortion are as follows. A majority of respondents in both countries endorse the proposition that gays and lesbians should have the same rights as other citizens and that the government regulation of abortion infringes the rights of women. The pattern of implication in the discourse of rights – at least in the cases of homosexuality and abortion – is virtually the same in Canada and the United States. Why?

The idea of human rights has been interpreted as a fundamental element in the 'social ontology' of the West (Thomas et al. 1987; cf Huntington 1996, 220–50). The idea of human rights, in other words, is an institutionalized element in the culture of the West. It is a taken-for-granted feature of Western civilization and, as such, is endorsed and valued throughout the West. That, of course, does not mean that practices with respect to rights are necessarily the same across nation-state jurisdictions within Western civilization. However, it does mean that the idea of human rights tends to be accepted by at least substantial pluralities of citizens in nation-states across the West. It is not surprising, then, that Canadians and Americans are similar in terms of their willingness to recognize and endorse the idea of human rights in the case of abortion and homosexuality.

Notwithstanding the institutionalization of the idea of human rights in the West there are differences across national jurisdictions in the enactment of human rights in everyday practices and orientations. In the matter of body issues these differences are mediated in part by religion, religiosity, and linkages between religion and politics. As a rule, variation across jurisdictions in the level of tension and conflict regarding abortion and homosexuality is directly proportional to the level of religiosity and the linkages between religion and politics: the higher the level of religiosity and the stronger the links between religion and politics, the higher the level of tension where abortion and homosexuality are thematized as matters of public concern.

The CUSURPS study also shows that, compared with Americans, Canadians consider religion to be less important in their lives. Fewer indicate that they are affiliated or active in religious organizations, there is a lower rate of activism in religious organizations in Canada, and more Canadians than Americans indicate that one need not go to church to be a 'good Christian.' In general, religion is somewhat less important to people in Canada than it is in the United States, and Canadians are less involved in religion than Americans.

Regarding linkages between religion and politics, fewer Canadians than Americans indicate that religion is important to their thinking about politics. Fewer Canadians believe that it is essential that traditional Christian values play a role in politics and that Christians should get involved in politics to protect their values. More Americans than Canadians feel close to the Christian right.

III

The data adduced above constitute a sketch of certain responses in Canada and the United States to the rise of the somatic society, responses that can be framed in the first instance within demographic contrasts. With proportionately more Roman Catholics and mainline Protestants than the United States, Canada is a 'churchly' society. America, on the other hand, with its large proportion of non-mainline Protestants is a sectarian society. The strident politicization of abortion and homosexuality in the American political arena that began in the late 1970s is, ultimately, attributable to the sectarian Protestant emphasis on individual moral purity linked to an ideology associating national strength with individual beliefs and behaviour (Falwell 1980). That, of course, does not mean that Roman Catholics and others, as well, were not 'on side' particularly on the matter of abortion. Nevertheless, the emergent body-oriented sociomoral politics of the late 1970s and its development in the 1980s had its base in Protestant sectarianism (Nesmith 1994). Furthermore, apart from the presence in the American public arena of the sensibility of sectarian Protestant personal moral purity (assuredly not uncontested), it is difficult to imagine that the extramarital adventures of President Clinton would have become a public and political affair in the 1990s.

Where the American response to the somatic society can be characterized as a grassroots reorganization of politics that brought Protestant sectarians back into the public arena, the responses in Canada have been different and more complex. In the first place, a sectarian Protestant sensibility has never had a hegemonic position in the Canadian public arena (Grant 1973a). There have, of course, been sectarian Protestants who have played prominent roles in Canadian public life: Tommy Douglas, John Diefenbaker, Ernest Manning, and, currently, Preston Manning, the leader of the Reform Party of Canada. In each case, however, an emphasis on individual responsibility and personal purity remained a taken-for-granted private affair (the Mannings) or was expressed within a Tory (Diefenbaker) or socialist (Douglas) context championing social justice and collective integrity (Lipset 1990).

Preston Manning, who is, perhaps, as close to an American-type sectarian Protestant politician as any Canadian has ever been, nevertheless does not thematize such issues as abortion, homosexuality, and capital punishment in terms of policy positions that would be implemented were the Reform party to form the government of Canada. His own views are clear on these matters. He opposes abortion and homosexuality and favours capital punishment. Were the Reform party to come to power, Manning would seek advice on body issues via national referenda, with choices between policy options referred to the electorate of Canada for assessment. That is as close (and it is not very close) as Canada has come, so far, to a contemporary American-style politics of body issues at the federal level.

Canada lacks the strident political voices and hard-bitten absolutism on body issues that have characterized America's public arena since the late 1970s. In fact, the Canadian response to the advent of the somatic society has been significantly more positive than the American response. While demography plays a role in differentiating the two countries in that regard, differences in relations between institutions and modes of political action are important as well.

Since its foundation as a nation-state, the United States has been a secularized country by virtue of the non-establishment clause in its Constitution. Secularization in this case refers to the relationship between church and state. Canada in that regard is not secularized to the same degree. There never has been a constitutional provision prohibiting the state's supporting presence in religious institutions and organizations in Canada. By the same token, the dominant church traditions in Canada have tended to be something other than centres of voluntary action playing roles in grassroots, interest-oriented politics. Rather, churches have laid claims on governments via elite accommodation. Thus, the leaders of governments and the leaders of churches have recognized and served each other's needs within the communicative circle of elite accommodation (Simpson and MacLeod 1985; Hagan forthcoming).

Prior to the Quiet Revolution, the 'tightest' fit between church and government elites was found in Quebec, where there was not only a codetermination of the public agenda but also the presence of the Roman Catholic Church as a major agent in the provincially funded sectors of health, education, and social services. In the Quiet Revolution, Quebec was rapidly and thoroughly secularized in an institutional sense. The politics of accommodation shifted from a religious to a linguistic base (Simpson 1988).

In terms of body issues and the advent of the somatic society, Quebec has underwritten non-discrimination with respect to sexual orientation and publicly thematized the need for social benefits for same-sex couples. Abortion is available as it is elsewhere in Canada, too. Quebec francophones have the lowest birth rate in Canada. Thus, the move of the Roman Catholic Church in Quebec from quasi-established to denominational status (cf Greeley 1972) has not only entailed the diminution of its role as a provider of health, education, and social services, but it has also transformed the church's teachings on body matters into voluntaristic norms that no longer have a determinative role in public space. The link between the everyday private practices of individuals and a public sense of normative requirements has been compromised as it invariably is where the Roman Catholic Church moves from a church-type status into denominationalism (cf Swatos 1979).

Where the Roman Catholic Church in Quebec is, clearly, not an advocate of a liberal position on body-oriented issues, it has not engaged in a vociferous politics of opposition to change. Ironically, its own 'children,' the political elites of Quebec, secularized the institutions of the province. The Church has not mobilized in any massive public way against them. On the other hand, Canada's largest Protestant denomination – the United Church of Canada – became proactive in response to the advent of the somatic society when it moved to allow the ordination of sexually active gays and lesbians in 1988. Viewed in the lens of history, there is some irony here.

As the bearer of the Methodist tradition, the United Church of Canada carried the norms of strict Protestant individual morality. The control of the sale of liquor still has the marks in many provinces of the Methodist or Protestant sectarian sensibility regarding drinking: a human weakness that should not be condoned and only barely tolerated where necessary. The Methodist stamp on Canadian society (outside Quebec) was pointedly symbolized and summed up in the ironic pejorative label 'Toronto the Good,' a city of churches where it was not possible to have 'fun' on Sundays until long after the end of the Second World War (Morton 1973).

Why did a bastion of 'Toronto the Good' – the United Church of Canada – become the only large and nationally influential Christian church in the world to ordain sexually active gays and lesbians? A key element was the earlier response of political elites to the advent of the somatic society. As Pierre Elliott Trudeau put it in his well-known quip, 'The state has no place in the nation's bedrooms' (Christiano 1994, 83). Trudeau's remark put the government on record as generally accepting of the implications of the somatic society. Trudeau's own lifestyle, as well, was publicly perceived as consistent with the sensibility of the 1960s, embodying as it did the outward signs of the permissive counterculture (Christiano 1994, 87–8). That brought a new element into play on the field of elite accommodation.

In the second place, while the United Church of Canada historically opposed the secular 'fun' agenda of modernity including drinking and gambling, it was the major Protestant church sponsor of the social gospel in Canada – the movement to mitigate the worst human effects of industrial capitalism and the commodification of agricultural production (Allen 1971). It was a party, in effect, to the founding of the Canadian welfare state through the political process of elite accommodation wherein the United Church of Canada was (and remains) a significant advocate for economic justice. As a 'justice church,' the United Church of Canada contains a rhetorical frame that allows it to respond to and assimilate new directions in the advocacy of justice.

The somatization of society in the wake of the 1960s was accompanied by a heightened global sense of right that underwrote the enlargement of justice in the Western ontology to include the 'righting' of the bodies of the marginalized: women, gays, and lesbians, people of colour, and the disabled. In that regard, the United Church of Canada expanded the scope of its justice mission when it 'righted' and, thereby, 'normalized' the bodies of gays and lesbians by extending ordination to them. That act was not only consistent with the history of the United Church of Canada as an advocate of justice, but it was also consistent with the accommodation of political and church elites that is still characteristic of the public sphere in Canada even though religion is no longer as publicly important as it was before the Quiet Revolution and the secularizing trends that affected English Canada after the Second World War (Simpson 1988).

IV

Clearly, body politics are alive and well, today, in the United States and in Canada. The furor in the United States regarding the extramarital affairs of President Bill Clinton and the recent rage in Alberta over the Supreme Court of Canada's decision calling for the revision of the Alberta Human Rights Code to eliminate discrimination on the basis of sexual orientation underscore the presence of body politics. I have argued that contemporary body politics can be traced to the deconstruction of the disembodied mind – the turn against Cartesian dualism – that was enacted and symbolized by the generational revolt of the 1960s.

Although the generational revolt of the 1960s was an event that swept across the broad plain of Western civilization, it has worked itself out in various ways within the nation-states of the West. Religious demography, individual opinions and attitudes, and the extent and intensity of religious practice provide a different resource base for the politics of the body in Canada and in the United States. Furthermore, differences in the institutional and organizational features of the societies have an impact on political behaviour and agitation focused on body-oriented issues as well.

Both Canada and the United States have responded to the advent of the somatic society. Canada has moved in the direction of liberalization in a quieter and smoother way than the United States and it has moved further than the United States in institutionalizing rights at the state level for gays and lesbians. While abortion has been decriminalized in both countries, access to abortion has been limited in the United States by restrictions imposed through the welfare system. Abortion has also been subjected to intense protest accompanied by hostile – sometimes lethal – behaviour in the United States. Although there has been some collective agitation against abortion in Canada, it has not been as widespread nor as conflicted as in the United States (Ginsberg 1993).

The institutions of religion in Canada and the United States have responded differently in mediating the impact of the somatic society. The response in the United States runs from civil, considered rejection of the ordination of gays and lesbians by most mainline Protestant churches to intense hostility to both abortion and homosexuality within the precincts of the new Christian right. In Canada, on the other hand, the response to the somatic society has been one of quiescence, isolated disapproval, or brave endorsement in the case of the United Church of Canada. Which of these directions will prevail in the twenty-first century remains to be seen.

NOTES

1 The Western press recently reported that in certain fundamentalist circles in Egypt 'eggplants and gourds have been declared "un-Islamic" since these

vegetables can be stuffed, and the act of stuffing them might make women think of sex' (Roberts 1998, D14). One imagines secular, Western cosmopolitans muttering, 'And what do they think minarets symbolize?'

The body has its uses in national arenas, too. The late Diana, Princess of Wales, arguably, found her body to be her best weapon in her 'war' against the House of Windsor (Morton 1995). Her 'confession' on national television of infidelity as a response to the Prince of Wales's adultery aroused public sympathy. Her use of alternative therapies – herbal medicine, reflexology, acupuncture, colon irrigation – can be framed as a counter-systemic allegory of disdain for the restrictive conventions of the royal house. Alternative therapies challenge the authority of established medicine. Diana not only entered her body in the fray against the royal house via a public confession of her adultery, but she also provided a sense of metonymic protest by subjecting her body to unconventional types of care. Her own well-publicized embodied ordeal, the affliction of bulimia, bolstered the body as a unit of action and site of problems in late capitalism.

2 Where the body was an object of positive action in high modernity, it tended to be treated as either a sexual force within a counter-systemic, collective context controlled by religious adepts or secular utopians, or an object to be cultivated and, perhaps, even sacrificed in accord with rigid, politicized aesthetic ideals. It was also viewed as a machine-like apparatus that required proper maintenance and repair.

Thus, forms of free love were practised in the highly regimented Oneida community in America (Stark and Bainbridge 1997) and in avant-garde circles of the left as well (E. Wilson 1982). The physical education movement followed an aesthetic ideal that, arguably, reached its apogee in the Third Reich's obsession with 'perfect' bodies and its destruction of 'grotesque' bodies (Segal 1998). The ordered 'disorder' of modern ballet occasionally evoked dramatic images of human sacrifice (Eksteins 1989). The maintenance of the body-as-machine found expression among elites in the dietary and cleansing rituals of exclusive spas and sanatoria (Boyle 1993). In all of the 'revolts' against modernity's general tendency to sublate and forget the body there was a distinct, paradoxical element of suppressive control and a marshalling of the body in order to achieve an ideal, define a social boundary, or mobilize for a cause. In high modernity the body was not a unit of voluntaristic expression.

3 Late capitalism produces a surfeit of goods and services serving wants that stretch far beyond the putative needs of populations at least as far as those needs were defined when industrial/entrepreneurial capitalism 'reigned.' The shift from an emphasis on production to consumption as the driving

force of an economy has a somewhat different meaning where the memory and reality of class dominance in postfeudal societies persists as opposed to the circumstance where differences between classes tend to be only loosely connected at least in a popular sense with status and power differences. Thus, both the timing of the advent of relative affluence and increased consumption within a society and whether a society is postfeudal or liberal (in the Whig sense) affect the meaning of consumerism. For generations, Americans have had a sense of being a 'people of plenty' (Potter 1954). Furthermore, as Veblen (1908) pointed out long ago, consumption in America is a sign of, simply, having the means to consume. On the other hand, in postfeudal societies consumption occurs within the memories of sumptuary, class-bounded exchange. Consumption not only represents the possession of the means to consume, but it also marks residual boundaries between classes that can be traced to historical differences in the possession and use of the means of violence. Consumption in postfeudal societies is not, simply, a sign of the possession of the means to consume. These differences, then, may explain the ambivalent fascination of British (Featherstone 1991) and continental theorists (Bourdieu 1984) with the relatively recent advent of mass consumption in the United Kingdom and Europe and its links to perceived and constructed social differences and boundaries. The masses are now told via advertising that 'It's *Your* Choice!' One imbued with the Whig sensibility and comfortably located 'upscale' might respond: 'So, what else is new? Isn't that the way it's always been?'

4 The term 'sectarian Protestantism' as used herein refers to those Protestant traditions that have never had an established relationship with any state. In this usage Anglican, Episcopalian, Lutheran, and Presbyterian are not sectarian Protestant traditions. Baptist, Pentecostal, Assembly of God, and the like are sectarian Protestant traditions.

5 Differences between Canada and the United States in religious demography and other social features pertaining to religion were extensively explored in the *Canadian Journal of Sociology* 3, no. 2 (1978).

6 See Andrew Grenville's chapter in this volume for details regarding the design and sampling frames for the survey.

7 What is unusual and, perhaps, groundbreaking in the Angus Reid survey is the provision of the response categories 'nothing in particular' and 'something else' in filtering respondents to determine religious tradition. These categories usually do not appear in the range of responses to a query about religious identity or affiliation in a survey. A substantial proportion of respondents in both Canada (21 per cent) and the United States (16 per cent) chose one or the other of the categories. Thus, some of the 'leakage'

out of the Christian and Catholic categories detected by the CUSRPS survey can, probably, be accounted for by the provision of 'nothing in particular' and 'something else' as response categories. 'Nothing in particular,' especially, deserves further exploration as, perhaps, an indicator of diffuse, non-specific religiosity particularly where it is offered alongside 'no religion' as a response alternative.

chapter fifteen

Consumers and Citizens: Religion, Identity, and Politics in Canada and the United States

WILLIAM H. KATERBERG

Borders make for differences, even if they signify only 'imagined communities' (Anderson 1983). According to a 1996 *Maclean's* report, 19 per cent of Canadians say 'religion is important to their political thinking,' compared with 41 per cent of Americans (Corelli 1996, 40). Recent elections confirm this difference. News stories rarely note the religious beliefs of Canadian politicians, and religious organizations seldom have a significant impact on Canadian elections. For example, the Reform party's Preston Manning downplays his evangelical faith. By contrast, in the 1970s and 1980s in the United States, Jimmy Carter's 'born-again' testimony, Ronald Reagan's endorsement of Southern evangelicals, and George Bush's courting of the religious right made headlines. So too in the 1990s did evangelical mistrust of Bill Clinton rate front-page coverage, as did the political trench work of Ralph Reed's Christian Coalition.

But exactly what differences borders make is not always so clear. In *The Culture of Disbelief* (1993, 3), Stephen Carter criticized American intellectuals and politicians for creating 'a political and legal culture that presses the religiously faithful to be other than themselves, to act publicly, and sometimes privately as well, as though their faith does not matter.' In Canada in the 1990s, meanwhile, conflicts over Newfoundland's denominational school system raised constitutional questions and a political ruckus (Sweet 1997); Alberta Premier Ralph Klein feuded with a Roman Catholic bishop and church groups over video lottery terminals; and the *Globe and Mail*'s editors preached to politicians and clergy in British Columbia about the virtues of keeping church and state separate (Politics Gets Religion 1998).

Generalizations about religious identity and politics are thus tenuous. The 1996 *Maclean's* report suggests that religion is more privatized north of the border; other examples may not nullify this generalization but do confuse it. So does history. During the early twentieth century religion was pervasive in Canadian politics and public life; indeed, according to Mark Noll (1992, 546), Canada once had a stronger case for being a 'Christian nation' than the United States. How should this be understood?

This essay compares the evolution of religious identity in politics and public life in Canada and the United States, focusing on such themes as citizenship, consumer-cultural markets, modernity, and postmodernity. It does so not to reach definitive conclusions, but to reflect on frameworks in which to think about these issues. Although religion plays a greater role today in American politics than in Canada, where identities are relatively more fragmented and postmodern, religious identity has become increasingly a matter of consumption in both countries, as cultural markets increasingly define the public role of religion. These trends have clear implications for civic life. The changing place of religion in public life in North America indicates that civic values and citizenship are undergoing a fundamental transformation (Mouffe 1992; Turner 1990).

The modern 'problem of identity,' Zygmunt Bauman contended in *Life in Fragments* (1995, 81), 'was how to construct an identity and keep it solid and stable' (also see Taylor 1989). Amidst modernity's centrifugal, fragmenting currents (for example, industrialization, globalizing markets, urbanization, national and international migration, democratic and socialist revolutions, associated intellectual and cultural changes, and religious competition) the 'modern project' was to construct universalizing institutions and stable populations. The significance of cultural identities, religious or otherwise, was legitimating the social order and nation-state (Giddens 1991, 1990). Religious institutions, communities, and movements in North America from the 1800s to the mid-1900s cannot be reduced to legitimization (they also existed in pluralist cultural markets and served believers' irreducible religious needs), neither can they be separated from politics. For example, religious affiliation remains a reliable predictor of voting patterns. The Liberals in Canada and Democrats in the United States consistently have won the votes of Roman Catholics and immigrants, groups long outside what were middle-class white, Anglo-Saxon, Protestant (WASP) establishments (Noll 1990; Wearing 1991; Kelley 1990).

Religion's legitimating function was evident in Canada after the American Revolution. British North America's political architects bolstered the colonial Anglican Church as a bulwark against further revolution. This effort failed, as evangelicals and other dissenters effectively challenged the Anglican quasi-establishment for the souls of people in the colonies and then disestablished Anglicanism in the 1830s and 1840s. Nevertheless, religion became a powerful source of legitimation, as an informal Protestant cultural establishment coalesced in English Canada and a Roman Catholic one in Quebec (Murphy and Perin 1996; Westfall 1989; Fingard 1972).

Protestantism also served as an informal religious-cultural establishment in the United States. The American Constitution formally separated religious institutions from the state, but republican ideologues insisted that for democracy to work, and for citizens to be trustworthy, morality and religion were essential. Advocates of republicanism emphasized that women (as 'naturally' pious and moral persons) needed to nurture in their husbands and sons the values necessary for a stable democracy. Temperance advocates, abolitionists, and other antebellum reformers took inspiration from Revolutionary idealism and religious revivals and worked to make America a Protestant 'righteous empire' (Marty 1977). All of this happened despite greater religious pluralism than existed in Canada.

Well into the twentieth century in North America these kinds of legitimating relationships between religious, cultural, and political establishments continued. In the name of Protestant piety, racial/ethnic purity, and democratic stability, nativists opposed unrestricted immigration and emphasized the assimilating task of churches, schools, and other civic groups (Katerberg 1995a, 1995b). Prohibitionists hoped to restrict the use of alcohol to aid piety, morality, public health, economic efficiency, and clear-headed politics. As a 'social gospel,' Prohibition was about progress, nationalism, the search for modern order, and building the 'Kingdom of God.' These overlapping goals linked the middle-class WASP institutions and subcommunities of the establishment in English Canada and the United States (Valverde 1991; Wiebe 1967). Social gospel movements helped to legitimate liberal democracy, but in their radical expressions they also played a prophetic, subversive role, attacking injustices in modernizing North America. An even closer, but not uncontested, relationship developed in French Canada between Roman Catholicism and the political establishment (Trofimenkoff 1983).

Perhaps the most obvious place where religious identities, social order, and politics overlapped was in public schools. Besides academic subjects, English Canadian and American public schools promoted progress, capitalism, individualism, good citizenship, and consensus Protestantism. Predictably, Roman Catholics and other critics of establishment Protestantism opposed this last goal. American Catholics funded their own parish schools; in most Canadian provinces, reflecting greater numbers, particularly in Quebec, Catholics won public funding. Indeed, throughout most of the twentieth century Newfoundland and Quebec have had school systems based on denominational lines (Sweet 1997; Tyack and Hansot 1982).

Despite significant common ground, reflecting an imperative in modern nation-states to use the cultural legitimation that religion can provide, religious and national identities in Canada and the United States followed distinct patterns. Links between religion, social order, and nationalism remained more tenuous in Canada than in the United States. French-English linguistic cleavages and regional conflicts made it difficult to identify the 'Kingdom of God' with Canada as a whole. This was less a result of consensus Protestantism's fragility or conflicts with Roman Catholics than a consequence of Canada's fragmented national identity. In the United States a more coherent civil religion evolved. 'Manifest destiny' blended notions of progress, conquest, democratic experimentation, God's 'New Israel,' and America's exemplary mission to the world. Until the 1900s this mission typically was defined in Protestant terms; by the mid-twentieth century it had expanded into a more ecumenical Judaeo-Christian civil religion. And yet, *within particular regions*, relations between religious, social, and political establishments may have been tighter in Canada.[1] Most obvious in this vein was Roman Catholicism in Quebec; close behind were the culturally powerful mainline Protestant denominations of Ontario (Grant 1988b; Stephanson 1995).[2]

The point here is that there were multiple and sometimes contradictory ways that religious identities intertwined with social, economic, and political establishments in North America until the mid-1900s. As a public phenomenon, religious identity was partly about cultural legitimation, reflecting a modern drive to encourage dependable citizens, social stability, efficient workers, faith in national progress, and fixed identities. Even counter-hegemonic, prophetic religions championed alternative forms of legitimation and citizenship. The problem was balance – managing modernity's centrifugal forces (Berman 1988). During the 1960s, in both Canada and the United States, multicultural ideology, the welfare state, and consumer capitalism further encouraged diversity, fragmenting identities and legitimation strategies. In the process, identity became less a matter of legitimation and citizenship and more about consumer choices. It shifted from rooting people in various overlapping communities, with rights and obligations, to a consumer ethic of therapeutic self-realization and personal development (Lears 1981). The fragile balance between rights and obligations, and individuals and communities, moved towards individualism and rights (Bauman 1995).

Although partial and inconsistent, these shifts are crucial elements of the so-called postmodern condition. 'Postmodern' signifies many things – most obviously, an era of transition in which the ideals and institutions of the modern project have not disappeared but have been fundamentally challenged (D. Harvey 1990). Constructing universalizing institutions and fixed identities especially seems less possible and desirable. Faith in progress and in using reason to manage and control modernity's turbulent effects also seems naive and even imperialistic. Consequently, modern structures such as multinational corporations continue to shape social relations, culture, and politics; but centralizing forces like nation-states, civic cultures, and citizenship suffer fragmentation. They are increasingly incapable of countering centrifugal trends with effective universalizing measures or compelling fixed identities. For that matter, voting patterns suggest that many politically active citizens want this pattern to continue. The growing number of citizens not voting in effect passively accepts these trends, likely expressing pessimism about resisting them. As Zygmunt Bauman (1995, 81) put it, if modernity 'built in steel and concrete,' to establish fixed identities, postmodernity uses 'bio-degradable plastic.' The 'postmodern problem of identity' is 'how to avoid fixation and keep the options open' (also see Sarup 1996).

For religious and cultural identities this 'postmodern problem' reflects fragmentation and diversity *and* homogenizing trends. As Mike Featherstone has emphasized in *Undoing Culture* (1995, 118), globalizing corporations promote universal production and consumption but market to local cultures. 'I'd like to buy the world a Coke,' company commercials declared in the 1970s; but 'Coca-colonization' requires the marketing of products in diverse cultural locales around the globe. 'We are not a multi-national, we are a multi-local,' one company statement claimed in this vein. Religious movements also reflect both universal (or global) trends and local diversities. 'Fundamentalism' originated in conservative Protestantism, but the word signifies movements in religions varying from Islam to Hinduism. Also on a large scale, globalization seems to offer the Roman Catholic Church new opportunities as an international institution, in ways reminiscent of its premodern role in medieval Europe (Lyon 1994b). In terms of religious identities, then, postmodern fragmentation and consumerism are universalizing *and* parochial. Postmodernity is transitional in its globalism *and* its pluralism, a shift in balance rather than a complete break from modernity. Some observers thus depict it as 'hypermodernity' (Borgmann 1992).[3]

The complex character of postmodernity also accounts for the ambiguity of contemporary identity questions. Spiritual, ethnic, national, political, sexual, class-based, and more, identities address existential dilemmas, individually and collectively. Who are we? Where are we? What is wrong? What is the solution? These questions are irreducibly religious (Middleton and Walsh 1995). Consumerism itself perhaps is a form of spiritual longing, with people constructing identities using choices found in the market (Lyon 1996; Clapp 1998). Do amusement parks, department stores, casinos, and shopping malls serve as churches, temples, meccas, and synagogues? Is Las Vegas a 'New Jerusalem'? In a 1997 song the pop group U2 noticed these spiritual connections, observing: 'when you get through the gates of the playboy mansion,'

> then will there be no more time of sorrow
> then will there be no time for pain
> then will there be no time of sorrow
> then will there be no time for shame.[4]

The playboy mansion serves as a telling, sexist[5] metaphor for consumerism and longing, for a heavenly kingdom and the hope of transcendence, however illusory. As such, it hints at crucial aspects of the relationship between identities, religion, and consumer markets (Mouw 1994). The metaphor also is political; its sexism highlights the need for critiques of the commodification of women's bodies and identities, and for political analysis of consumerism generally. What, then, are the political implications of religious identities and consumerism? What is their public place? Indeed, what do 'public' and 'private' mean?

As these questions suggest, identities are personal *and* political, private *and* public, dilemmas *and* solutions. They can legitimate or repudiate communities, societies, and political regimes. Postmodernism recognizes the fragmented character of identities. Instead of autonomous, integrated, rational modern individuals, able to choose or construct an identity, postmodern individuals are disintegrated multiple personas, whose 'choices' are fabricated in diverse political and culture marketplaces. If so, what does it mean to be human? Or a citizen? These postmodern conditions and insights point to the challenges faced by prophetic religious movements. Their targets are diffuse, and they are themselves consumable identity choices (Lears 1981; Moore 1995). Religious identities and consumer markets thus are inextricably public in their implications and more than the sum of personal choices. They are frameworks which shape and limit the scope of the consumer choices that people make. Or is this a contested conclusion? Are markets and religious identities public? To better understand such concepts as 'public' and 'private,' the process of secularization needs examination. One key issue is the relationship between religion and social-political establishments. Another is the process of differentiation.

During the nineteenth and early twentieth centuries Canada and the United States both had pluralist religious cultures, especially the United States. Sects flourished in English Canada, especially in the west, but mainline Protestantism and Roman Catholicism predominated. In Quebec the Roman Catholic Church held almost complete sway, except among anglophones. The United States was a more open market. As in Canada, evangelical movements shaped Protestantism, mainline denominations included, but many more sectarian groups flourished (Martin 1978). Significantly, although neither the United States nor Canada had a true religious establishment, social and cultural links between religion, political culture, and social values were powerful. The American Constitution separated church and state formally as institutions. While ties existed between provincial governments and religious institutions in Canada (especially in education, health, and social welfare), there were no official state churches, only 'shadow' establishments (see David Martin's chapter in this volume). When various levels of the state in Canada and the United States secularized in this century, religious institutions and groups thus continued to evolve in the social-cultural market-place. Where institutional separation had been greater, as in the United States, secularization was more limited in terms of the health of religious institutions, the flexibility of civil religion, and the legitimating function of religious identities. Where 'shadow' establishments had been strongest, as in Quebec, secularization was much more thorough, as religious institutions such as the Roman Catholic Church had a difficult time adapting to a deregulated cultural market-place.

The central issue here is 'differentiation,' the process by which modernizing societies segment and separate social, cultural, and political spheres, institutionally and ideologically (Martin 1978). Two crucial sectors in this process are religion and the market-place. Sociological analysis generally has emphasized that religion has become privatized, losing its public-political role and devolving to personal choices (Lyon 1985). Liberal frameworks of analysis similarly view the cultural market-place as private (contrasting corporations, as private institutions, with the public nature of the state). While institutional and ideological segmentation clearly is evident in liberal-capitalist democracies such as Canada and the United States, this emphasis on differentiation and privatization in modern societies must be balanced with a focus on integration. Socialist political economy stresses linkages and power relationships between social, economic, cultural, and political spheres.[6] Modernization in North America meant the segmentation of economic, religious, and political institutions, but it also entailed 'nation-building' policies, using cultural identities to legitimate the nation and promoting economic policies to build a strong national economy. Distinctions between private/public and personal/political thus need to be made with care. They are as much ideological as descriptive (Offe 1984; Held 1989; D. Harvey 1990).[7] To view consumer culture, markets, and religion only as private is arguably to uncritically accept a liberal-capitalist view of culture and the economy.

If liberal assumptions are put aside, however, religion's place in public life during the modern era takes on a different cast. Even so, it is clear that the integrating forces of 'nation-building' have fragmented since the 1960s, and differentiation has increased. Religious identities, citizenship, civic values, and other aspects of culture are, as a result, undergoing a transformation. In the process what is happening to public life?

Numerous forces in the 1960s transformed the relationship between religious identities, public life, and politics in North America – notably, consumerism, secularism, the welfare state, and multiculturalism. None of these was new to the 1960s, but they came together at that time in terms of personal behaviour, cultural and political consciousness, transformed religious practices, the role of religion in politics, and the cultural market-place. The decade of decades for secularization in Canada and the United States was the 1960s.

During the early twentieth century, throughout North America, levels of religious membership and church attendance reached a plateau. Numbers did not fall precipitously in the 1920s or 1930s. Indeed, during the postwar years of the 1950s many denominations experienced growth, although some observers have contended that this was 'merely' a respectable, suburban, civic religiosity, rather than faith rooted deeply in personal commitments (Bibby 1987; Berton 1965). At the very least this growth suggests that the overlapping, reinforcing relationship between citizenship, social respectability, and religious identity continued to shape Canada and the United States.

The events and trends that overwhelmed this relationship in the 1960s can be grouped under the rubrics of multiculturalism and the welfare state. Immigration from new sources after 1945, Black civil rights, the New Left, the counterculture, fascination with Eastern religions and New Age spirituality, feminism, Native rights, interest in ethnicity, Vatican II, and other developments all increased the reality and awareness of social, ethnic, cultural, and religious pluralism in North America during the 1960s (Ellwood 1994; Farrell 1997). At the same time, under Lyndon Johnson in the United States and Pierre Trudeau in Canada, the welfare state expanded greatly. The impact of these trends on religion and politics can be seen clearly in Quebec.

In an astonishingly short time, the Quiet Revolution and separatist nationalism transformed the social and political establishment in Quebec, as the provincial government took over education, health, and social services long run by the Roman Catholic Church (Behiels 1985; McRoberts 1988, Baum this volume).[8] This effectively secularized Quebec in terms of the direct influence of religion on government institutions, cultural identity, and personal religious practice. As noted earlier, close ties between religious institutions and an establishment usually lead to thorough secularization when that establishment secularizes (Martin 1978). This clearly happened in Quebec, perhaps Canada's most secularized province since the 1960s (see Baum, and Seljak this volume).

The Quiet Revolution and Quebec separatism also helped to transform Canada more widely. A biculturalism and bilingualism commission ultimately led to a quasi-official redefinition of Canada as bilingual and multicultural. In this context the place of religious identity in politics and public life was recast. In a multicultural Canada people increasingly began to see religion as properly a private matter. Citizens should freely express their ethnic and religious identities, but no longer should citizenship be defined in terms of particular cultural heritages (such as, for example, a WASP identity for English Canada).[9] Multiculturalism did not become official policy in the United States, but similar values redefined expressions of national identity there, as 'melting pot' images successfully competed with pluralist ones (Palmer 1976; Gleason 1984; Hollinger 1995).

Multicultural ideologies have become common in Canada and the United States, but with different results. American pluralism has forced recognition of diversity; but multicultural policies remain a lightning rod in the 'culture wars,' along with racial issues and affirmative action (Hunter 1991). Canada also has experienced conflict, as separatists in Quebec and some English Canadians reject multiculturalism as a state policy. But relative to the United States, multiculturalism has become part of the 'common sense' of Canadians, assimilating a good deal of ethnic and religious diversity, and separating it from party politics. This does not mean that racism and ethnic conflict no longer exist in Canada; neo-conservatives, for example, regularly oppose state funding of multicultural projects. But multiculturalism is shifting the public place of ethnic and religious diversity from party politics to interest-group brokers and cultural markets (Bibby 1990; Pal 1993; Bissoondath 1994).

On the surface, this trend suggests that multiculturalism as a state policy has succeeded as Canada's legitimizing ideology. The reality is more complex. It has 'succeeded,' perhaps, by redirecting cultural identity from politics to the market-place and by fragmenting Canada as an imagined community. Can national identities and citizenship be based wholly on an abstract civic culture? one might ask. But multicultural policies cannot be judged in a vacuum; they must be considered in relation to regional conflicts and transnational economic trends, notably, American ownership of much of Canada's economy and culture. The North American Free Trade Act's potential impact on Canadian cultural policies is a good example. Canadians and Americans are assimilated at work, as consumers, by the popular media, and in leisure pursuits at least as much as by state policies, schools, churches, and other civic organizations. Similar concerns can be raised about the welfare state, which has had a profound impact on citizenship and political participation in general.

In both Canada and the United States, state management of the economy and society through Keynesian policies and health, education, and social programs undercut competitive politics, loosened citizens' identification with party combat, and discouraged civic life (Coleman 1996). Instead of public debate and participation, politics became defined more and more by government services provided for citizen clients by competent, consensus-oriented administrators. Even contentious religious, moral, and political problems (for example, abortion) usually were decided not by public debate or party policies but in the courts. In this sense, the Canadian and American stories are alike. Crucial differences remain, however. The American welfare state was never as complete as Canada's, and was dismantled already in the 1980s by Reaganomics and the cultural assaults of the so-called moral majority.

In this enigmatic story, what is noteworthy is the salience of religion for politics into the 1960s. For example, in Canada the Baptist preacher Tommy Douglas led the New Democratic party and regularly used social gospel imagery, speaking of building 'Jerusalem' in a green and pleasant land. By the 1970s overt social gospel language had faded. NDP policies continued to be influenced by the social gospel, but Christian identities faded into the background (Noll 1990). There was more continuity in the United States during the 1960s and 1970s, as civil rights leaders, New Left activists, and defenders of America's 'silent majority' regularly employed moralistic and specifically religious language. This continued into the 1980s and 1990s (Farrell 1997). Nevertheless, political use of religious categories and assertions of religious identities in American national life today encounters rising opposition, particularly by educated political and intellectual elites (Kramnick and Moore 1996; Carter 1993).[10] At the same time, scholars began to emphasize the value of religion in another public arena: North America's market-places.

In *Unknown Gods*, sociologist Reginald Bibby described the character of secularization in Canada today and pointed to its limits. Many Canadians continue benignly to neglect their churches, especially the mainline denominations; but they have not given up on spirituality or stopped asking religious questions and expressing religious needs. Bibby demonstrated that secularization has not meant a decline of religiosity so much as a failure of religious institutions to meet people's needs. There is out there a large, untapped market of spiritual desires. Among Christians, evangelicals and fundamentalists seem the least ineffective at meeting people's needs and marketing religion. Bibby's argument built on his analysis in *Fragmented Gods*, which showed that even deeply committed religious Canadians typically divorce faith and religious practices from other areas of their lives, politics included. Bibby echoed the work of scholars who study American religion in market terms by analysing which messages and methods have sold best in America's religious market-place. Furthermore, as Lawrence Moore has shown in *Selling God*, Christians and other religious groups, social gospellers included, have not been passive victims of this trend, but often actively promoted it (Bibby 1993, 1987; Moore 1995; Finke and Stark 1992).

In terms of identity, public life, and politics, this viewpoint suggests that the key question is not how much religion may have declined, but how its role in North America has changed. Religion's primary place increasingly seems to be multicultural consumer markets rather than civic life and party politics. Even ignoring TV preachers, Vision Television, and Christian Contemporary Music, the prevalence of religious themes and spiritual longing in mainstream TV, movies, and popular music indicates this (Moore 1995; McDannell 1995).[11] These examples of religious identities in the market-place are about public life, not privatization. The fundamental importance of this point cannot be overstated, since it often seems a truism that religion became privatized in the modern world. This viewpoint is closely tied to the question of whether (or how) the economy and markets are public or private. These issues are critical, even more, because they highlight broader transformations in public life and civic culture. The decline of religion's legitimation function in politics today has coincided with an erosion of civic cultures and commitments in general (Bellah et al. 1985).

This is no coincidence. At the heart of the relationship between religious identity and public life – and civic values and citizenship – is the meaning of 'public.' Changing patterns of religious identity, civic culture, and politics in North America today thus need to be creatively rethought in terms of consumer-cultural markets, challenges to the nation-state, and postmodern fragmentation. The welfare state helped to undercut public debate and civic culture by taking socioeconomic issues out of politics in the name of managerial expertise and consensus. Conservative ideologues as well as finance ministers dealing with budget deficits have attacked the welfare state, but these attacks have not led to a revitalized civic culture. Arguably, this is so for two reasons. First, multinational corporations, communications technology, and the consolidation of world markets have undercut the ability of nation-states to protect and promote their sovereignty and integrity. Second, seemingly ubiquitous consumerist values have contributed to the erosion of many people's commitments to civic life and communities beyond their immediate personal interests (Putnam 1995a; Clapp 1998). Not only have national and civic identities fragmented, along with religious ones, but democratic institutions, citizenship, and cultural legitimation seem less and less relevant to people's daily lives (Barber 1996). A sign of this is that more North Americans today use credit cards than vote. These points suggest avenues for further reflection.

The influence of religious-cultural markets in North America is not new. However, their predominance in public life, as civic values and associations and the nation-state itself fragment, is. Patriotism and citizenship have not disappeared but are waning, while markets, consumerism, and multinational corporations are growing in power. This gets to the crux of postmodernity – the erosion of unifying forces in public life, such as national and religious identities, the state, and civic commitments. The process is not linear. It has developed further in Canada, but also has had an impact on the United States. The aim here is not naively to defend centralized modern nation-states, but to emphasize the vacuum in public life that their fragmentation leaves. Without meaningful citizenship, what civic and democratic choices are left? Are people merely labourers, consumers, or stockholders?

A paradoxical example of these trends, which highlights Canadian-American differences, is the contradictory rhetoric of the religious right. In the United States religious conservatives are among the most highly mobilized of political voting blocks and civic organizers. The Moral Majority, Christian Coalition, and like-minded political candidates in the United States have promoted three broad goals: free-market economics, American patriotism and loyalty, and 'traditional' Christian and American values. But, as the late Christopher Lasch (1991) emphasized, these goals are incompatible in the end. Free markets disdain limits and promote possessive individualism and libertarianism. Meanwhile, patriotism and Christian values encourage community, balance, and continuity, that is, historical and traditional limits on individual freedom and self-interest. The religious right in the United States thus champions values and policies that foster legitimation and promote modern linkages between national, political, and religious identities. At the same time, it promotes national and global socioeconomic patterns that feed fragmentation and undercut communities, the state, and values rooted in historical traditions. Supporters of Canada's Reform party have similar goals. Compared with the United States, the critical difference is the reticence of Reform leaders such as Preston Manning to raise religious and moral issues in public (Harrison 1995). Finally, the religious right's policies are not a counterbalance to market-place religiosity so much as a sign of imbalance (notably, the odd idea, often held by supporters and critics, that religious politics in the 1980s and 1990s is something new). The relative, changing fortunes of the religious right in the United States and Canada thus highlight the extent and limits of secularization in politics and public life (Casanova 1994).

None of this means that religious identities and civic culture have disappeared from political debates. But as conflicts over religion in education suggest, citizens increasingly define themselves as political consumers. Defenders of religiously 'neutral' public schools emphasize the need to teach children in diverse societies common values, to encourage tolerance, and to produce loyal citizens (archetypal modern goals). Multiculturalism is about legitimation in this context. Yet the same multicultural values allow Christian, Jewish, Sikh, Muslim, and other groups to justify public funding of private religious schools to maintain their religious or culturally defined identities. Private schools do not necessarily threaten public life and citizenship, but they do presuppose more heterogeneous definitions of civic culture. It is difficult for schools and other civic institutions to promote the 'public good' when such notions are fragmented and more likely to lead to conflict than consensus (Sweet 1997).

While concerned with religion and spirituality, the debate over private religious schools also is often overtly consumerist. As taxpaying stockholders and consumers, citizens have a right to decide where their money is spent say defenders of public funding for private religious schools. The fiscal pot is too small, critics typically respond, emphasizing the need to protect public education's viability. Significantly, these divisive issues are generally decided in courts rather than in legislatures – in short, outside of direct public debate.[12]

Paradoxically, in Canada, where religious identities less often shape politics, several western provinces publicly fund private religious schools. In the United States, where religious identities are much more common in politics, such practices are virtually non-existent. Canada's pattern reflects a history in which it once could claim to be a 'Christian nation,' and indicates as well the greater fragmentation of Canadian identities today, relative to the United States. This fragmentation is apparent in the highly contested provincial policies regarding the place of religion and the state in public life and private education.

In the process, competing interest groups now struggle as consumer-citizens for access to and control of public money, trying to ascertain the meaning of multicultural values in civic life, religion, and education.

This essay's major theme is fragmentation. To use a market metaphor, since the 1960s religious identities and citizenship have been 'deregulated.' The consumer-cultural market-place may be an emerging centre, but a highly fluid, centrifugal one that is at the same time global. In this context religion has not become private; rather, the balance of its public place is moving from legitimation, politics, and citizenship to consumer-cultural markets. More broadly, citizenship and civic cultures themselves have become defined by consumerism. Public life today is cast not with 'consumers and citizens' so much as 'citizen consumers.' Indeed, it is difficult to define 'public' in such a context. This is not a linear, determined 'end of history.'[13] In May 1998 negotiations for the Multilateral Agreement on Investment (MAI) stalled partly because of public protest. Whether opposition to the MAI signifies a meaningful reassertion of democratic citizenship in North America and elsewhere remains to be seen (Barlow and Clarke 1997). The long-term implications for democracy, religion, and identity are murky at best, but the challenges for prophetic religious movements and radical politics are evident (Wallis 1994).[14]

This essay also suggests that however embattled, reified, defined, and limited, secularization might well be considered in broader terms than usual. It is no accident that North American civic cultures fragmented at the same time that Canada and the United States experienced religious secularization. Modern projects like the nation-state promoted centralization, universal rights and obligations, and differentiation to manage the centrifugal forces of modernity. The decline of citizenship, the foundering of the welfare state in the face of globalizing markets and diversity, and the shift of religious identities in public life from legitimating the nation-state to consumer-cultural markets suggest not only the failure of universal projects but a loss of faith in them. By trying to recognize, promote, *and contain* diversity, multiculturalism wrestles with but does not solve this conundrum (Katerberg 1995a; Mouffe 1992).

Finally, this essay suggests that scholars of religion in the modern and contemporary postmodern eras need to rethink concepts such as 'public' and 'differentiation.' Are nation-states, civic cultures, and citizenship in decline, or at least undergoing a significant transformation? Are transnational corporations and consumer-culture becoming society's predominant institutions and values? If so, what does this mean for public life? It certainly is becoming more diffuse, fluid, plural, and fragmented. Is it disappearing? Or do conceptions of the public need redefinition? Are corporations public institutions? Do shopping malls function as decentred social centres, like the literal 'market-place' of a premodern village green? Are the media, all media, not just the CBC, NPR, and PBS, public forums?[15] If so, what is the place of religious identities in public life in North America?[16]

Religion retains a greater overt presence today in party politics in the United States than in Canada, reflecting its more stable national identity and a historically more fluid, broadly established civic religion. Yet the differences between Canada and the United States should not be overstated; from a long-term viewpoint the similarities are greater. Throughout North America religion continues to move in public life from politics to the market, from civic culture and citizenship to consumer-cultural markets. Scholars of religion need to rethink their categories, take advantage of socialist and feminist categories to challenge dominant liberal conceptions of 'public,' 'private,' and 'civic,' and ask broader questions (Mouffe 1992). How are citizenship and the state changing, or declining? Is the market-place emerging as a decentred centre in public life? What is the place of religious movements in all of this, as consumable cultures, legitimating ideologies, and community organizations? Lastly, and perhaps most importantly, are religious movements and institutions merely reacting to these changes or playing a determinative role?[17]

Analysing religion in relation to consumerism and markets is risky business, much like the dangers of secularization theories. Are market and secularization models descriptive observations or prescriptive ideologies? How does scholarship affect the 'real' world? Is scholarship public or private? Do scholars contribute to religion's commodification today by reifying it as a marketed cultural product, enclosing even prophetic religions and radical traditions within the hegemony of consumable choices? Or, can consumerism and market ideology be subverted – 'consumed' – from within? At the very least, scholars should insist that religious identities and markets occupy public spaces and are not merely aggregates of personal, private choices. To say even that much is to 'rethink' and indeed challenge secularization and the market's relentless commodifying impulses.

NOTES

1 This is not to deny religious, ethnic, political, or class conflict, nationally or regionally, but to focus on the character and goal of establishments in Canada and the United States.

2 C.P. Stacey (1983) has referred to the 'Methodist aristocracy' of Toronto. Quebec and Ontario are two examples, not to deny regionalism in the United States, Atlantic Canada, and Canada's Northwest.

3 'Postmodern,' as a signifier of cultures in transition, could be replaced by 'late,' 'mature,' or 'hyper' modern.

4 'The Playboy Mansion,' from the CD *Pop* © 1997 Polygram.

5 Acknowledging *Playboy*'s sexism, the metaphor can work for both sexes and various sexual orientations. For example, parallel links between women's sexual liberation and consumerism, and identity themes, can be seen in the 1960s in Helen Gurley Brown's *Sex and the Single Girl*, and her editorial transformation of *Cosmopolitan* (D'Emilio and Freedman 1988). The sexism embedded in the metaphor highlights the inequalities of the sexual revolution, the commodification of sex, and the ongoing gendering of consumerism.

6 In his overview of sociology, as a discipline, and its treatment of religion in modern societies, James Beckford (1989) stresses the limited impact of Marxist categories on the sociology of religion.

7 A similar point could be made from feminist perspectives. Families and sexuality are not merely personal but also political. Family violence, for example, is not a private but a public matter (Adamson, Brisken, and McPhail 1988; Nason-Clarke this volume).

8 In retrospect, the 1940s and 1950s paved the way for the Quiet Revolution. The point, in terms of identity, is the experience of it as sudden – transforming people's consciousness. Trofimenkoff (1983) calls the Quiet Revolution 'noisy evolution.'

9 Pierre Trudeau's 1969 White Paper on Amerindian-government relations is an extreme example (Dickason 1992).

10 Christopher Lasch (1991) links the 'secularist' attitudes of elites to declining faith in democracy.

11 Canada's Vision Television broadcasts material from various faiths. For a popular take on religion and television, see 'God And Television,' *TV Guide* (U.S. edition), 29 March – 4 April 1997.

12 Newfoundland and Quebec, which historically had denominational systems, are exceptions. There, constitutional amendments have been necessary for change to take place. In Newfoundland there has been

considerable debate by religious, educational, and political leaders. The results of Newfoundland's two referenda have been ambiguous; it is likely that court cases and high-level negotiations will decide the shape of the province's future school system, which likely will continue to have a religious influence. Note also recent court cases in Ontario, where Jewish and Protestant groups tried to force the province to partially fund private schools (Sweet 1997).

13 In his controversial essay and subsequent book, Francis Fukuyama (1992) heralded the triumph of liberal capitalism and democracy, and the death of alternative political and social visions.

14 For the breakdown of negotiations, see stories and columns in the *Globe and Mail* for April and May 1998. It is noteworthy that American newspapers, even the *New York Times*, paid little attention to the MAI until its failure, whereas Canadian media showed an earlier interest in debating it. This suggests the greater Canadian awareness of contemporary threats to sovereign nation-states. Note also other social and political movements still defending and working within the civic/public sphere – for example, women's groups, shelters for the homeless, runaways, and battered women, environmental groups, co-ops, and peace activism (Boyte 1980; Epstein 1991; Holsworth 1989; Wallis 1994). These examples need to be balanced by the growth of 'self-interest groups' (Putnam 1995a).

15 I have not explored the transformation of civic-voluntary organizations. Are they in decline, in terms of volunteers and donations, or being transformed? Many of the voluntary associations flourishing today (little league sports, AA, therapeutic groups, and the like) provide services for their members rather than the broader public outside their self-interests (Putnam 1995a). What do public and private mean in American suburbs that are run not by municipal governments but by homeowner associations; voting power in these communities rests in property ownership, not citizenship. More than 130,000 such communities exist in the United States, with their 'shadow governments' and 'quasi-public' status (Garreau 1991).

16 These themes can be viewed under the rubric of civic or civil religion. Harry Hiller, in this volume, stresses that civic religions are contested (sources of repression, assimilation, and sometimes liberation) and perhaps multiple (in Canada clearly, but less so in the United States). My argument about religious identity and citizenship, and the decline of nation-states and civic cultures, stresses that civil religions may be disappearing, or at least fragmenting and declining, but that religions remain a part of public life, especially in the market-place.

17 This essay has tended to focus on religion's public place; the problem with this approach is its implied functionalism, reducing religion to a determined role, rather than recognizing religion as a significant and integral human impulse that can play a determinative role (Beckford 1989; Lyon 1996).

References

Adam, Marcel. 1980. Dieu, le Christ et le pape sollicités en faveur du oui? Editorial. *La Presse*, 12 April, A6.

Adamson, Nancy, Linda Brisken, and Margaret McPhail. 1988. *Feminist Organizing for Change: The Contemporary Women's Movement in Canada*. Toronto: Oxford University Press.

Airhart, Phyllis D. 1990. Ordering a New Nation and Reordering Protestantism. In *The Canadian Protestant Experience, 1760–1990*, ed. George A. Rawlyk. Burlington, ON: Welch.

Albrow, Martin. 1996. *The Global Age: State and Society beyond Modernity*. Cambridge: Polity Press.

Alexander, Jeffrey C. 1995. *Fin de Siècle Social Theory*. London: Verso.

Allen, Richard. 1971. *The Social Passion: Religion and Social Reform in Canada*. Toronto: University of Toronto Press.

Ammerman, Nancy. 1987. *Bible Believers: Fundamentalists in the Modern World*. New Brunswick, NJ: Rutgers University Press.

– 1997a. *Congregation and Community*. New Brunswick, NJ: Rutgers University Press.

– 1997b. Golden Rule Christianity: Lived Religion in the American Mainstream. In *Lived Religion in America: Toward a History of Practice*, ed. David D. Hall. Princeton: Princeton University Press.

– 1997c. Organized Religion in a Voluntaristic Society. *Sociology of Religion* 58, 3: 203–15.

– 1997d. Review of *Material Christianity: Religion and Popular Culture in America*, by Colleen McDannell. *Sociology of Religion* 58, 3: 289–90.

Anderson, Benedict. 1983. *Imagined Communities: Reflections on the Origin and Spread of Nationalism*. London: Verso.

Angus Reid Group. 1996a. *Canada/U.S. Religion and Politics Survey.* Toronto: Angus Reid Group.
- 1996b. *Dataset and Data Presentation by Andrew S. Grenville.* Toronto: Angus Reid Group.
- 1996c. *God and Society in North America.* Toronto: Angus Reid Group.
Appadurai, Arjun, ed. 1986. *The Social Life of Things: Commodities in Cultural Perspective.* Cambridge: Cambridge University Press.
Arès, Richard. 1948. Les droits de l'homme devant les Nations-Unies. *Relations* 8, 96: 348 51.
- 1949a. La déclaration universelle des droits de l'homme. *Relations* 9, 97: 9–13.
- 1949b. Quand les Nations Unies s'occupent de Dieu. *Relations* 9, 99: 63–6.
- 1949c. D'où viennent les droits de l'homme? *Relations* 9, 100: 96–9.
Assemblée des évêques du Québec (AÉC). 1984a. Construire ensemble une société meilleure: Deuxième message de l'Assemblée des évêques du Québec sur l'évolution politique de la société québécoise, le 9 janvier 1980. In *La justice sociale comme bonne nouvelle: Messages sociaux, économiques et politiques des évêques du Québec 1972–1983*, ed. Gérard Rochais. Montreal: Bellarmin.
- 1984b. Le peuple québécois et son avenir politique: Message de l'Assemblée des évêques du Québec, sur l'évolution de la société québécoise, le 15 août 1979. In *La justice sociale comme bonne nouvelle: Messages sociaux, économiques et politiques des évêques du Québec 1972–1983*, ed. Gérard Rochais. Montreal: Bellarmin.
- 1991. Les chemins de l'avenir. Mémoire à la Commission Bélanger-Campeau. *L'Église Canadienne* 24, 1 (3 January): 7–10.
- 1995. *Le référendum et l'évolution de la société québécoise.* Message du Comité exécutif de l'Assemblée des évêques du Québec à l'occasion du vote référendaire sur l'avenir du Québec, le premier novembre 1995. Montreal.
Baillargeon, S. 1995. Les religieuses répondent à l'appel du OUI. *Le Devoir*, 23 October, A3.
Balmer, Randall. 1993. *Mine Eyes Have Seen the Glory: A Journey into the Evangelical Subculture in America.* New York: Oxford University Press.
Balthazar, Louis. 1986. *Bilan du nationalisme au Québec.* Montreal: L'Hexagone.
Barber, Benjamin. 1996. *Jihad vs McWorld: How Globalism and Tribalism Are Reshaping the World.* New York: Ballantine.
Baril, Alain, and George Mori. 1991. Leaving the Fold: Declining Church Attendance. *Canadian Social Trends* 22: 21–4.
Barker, Eileen. 1985. New Religious Movements: Yet Another Great Awakening? In *The Sacred in a Secular Age: Toward Revision in the Scientific Study of Religion*, ed. Phillip E. Hammond. Berkeley: University of California Press.

Barlow, Maude. 1990. *Parcel of Rogues: How Free Trade Is Failing Canada*. Toronto: Key Porter.
– 1995. *Straight through the Heart: How the Liberals Abandoned the Just Society*. Toronto: Harper Collins.
– and Tony Clark. 1997. *MAI: The Multilateral Agreement on Investment and the Threat to Canadian Sovereignty*. Toronto: Stoddart.
Barnsley, Jan. 1995. Co-operation or Co-optation? The Partnership Trend of the Nineties. In *Listening to the Thunder: Advocates Talk about the Battered Women's Movement*, ed. Leslie Timmins. Vancouver: Women's Research Centre.
Baum, Gregory. 1986. Recent Roman Catholic Social Teaching: A Shift to the Left. In *Religion, Economics, and Social Thought*, ed. Walter Block and Irving Hexham. Vancouver: Fraser Institute.
– 1991. *The Church in Quebec*. Montreal: Novalis.
– 1992. The Catholic Left in Quebec. In *Culture and Social Change: Social Movements in Quebec and Ontario*, ed. Colin Leys and Marguerite Mendell. Montreal: Black Rose.
– 1994. A Church's Response to Secularization: Analysis of a Debate. *Ecumenist*, 2nd series, 1: 97–101.
– 1995. Christian Social Justice Statements on the Upcoming Referendum. *Socialist Studies Bulletin* 40: 11–21.
Bauman, Zygmunt. 1995. *Life in Fragments: Essays in Postmodern Morality*. Oxford: Blackwell.
Bazowski, Raymond, and Robert MacDermid. 1997. Constitutional Imaginings and the Nation-State. *American Review of Canadian Studies* 27, 2: 221–52.
Beaman-Hall, Lori, and Nancy Nason-Clark. 1997a. Partners or Protagonists? Exploring the Relationship between the Transition House Movement and Conservative Churches. *Affilia: Journal of Women and Social Work* 12, 2: 176–96.
– 1997b. Translating Spiritual Commitment into Service: The Response of Evangelical Women to Wife Abuse. *Canadian Woman Studies* 17, 1: 58–61.
Beatty, Jim. 1997. Clark Urges Political, Religious Union to Combat Social Woes: A Consultation with Spiritual Groups Touches Briefly on Specific Issues like Gambling. *Vancouver Sun*, 9 July, B3.
Beaudry, Albert. 1980. Le référendum: Un pas dans la bonne direction. *Relations* 40, 459: 131–3.
Bebbington, David W. 1989. *Evangelicalism in Modern Britain: A History from the 1730s to the 1980s*. London: Unwin Hyman.
Beckford, James A. 1989. *Religion and Advanced Industrial Society*. London: Unwin Hyman.

- 1992. Religion, Modernity and Post-Modernity. In *Religion: Contemporary Issues*, ed. Bryan R. Wilson. London: Bellew.
- 1996. Postmodernity, High Modernity and New Modernity: Three Concepts in Search of Religion. In *Postmodernity, Sociology and Religion*, ed. Kieran Flanagan and Peter C. Jupp. London: Macmillan.

Behiels, Michael. 1985. *Prelude to Quebec's Quiet Revolution: Liberalism versus Neo-Nationalism, 1945–1960*. Montreal: McGill-Queen's University Press.

Béliveau, J. 1980a. Les chrétiens pour le OUI demandent à Ryan de retirer ses paroles. *La Presse*, 23 April, A15.
- 1980b. Mgr Grégoire est satisfait de la discrétion des prêtres. *La Presse*, 9 May, A12.

Bell, Daniel. 1972. *The Cultural Contradictions of Capitalism*. 2nd ed. London: Heinemann.

Bell, David V.J. 1992. *The Roots of Disunity: A Study of Canadian Political Culture*. Toronto: Oxford.

Bellah, Robert N. 1967. Civil Religion in America. *Daedalus* 96, 1: 1–21.
- 1970. Religious Evolution. In *Beyond Belief: Essays on Religion in a Post-Traditional World*. New York: Harper and Row.
- 1975. *The Broken Covenant: American Religion in Time of Trial*. New York: Seabury.

Bellah, Robert N., and Phillip E. Hammond. 1980. *Varieties of Civil Religion*. San Francisco: Harper and Row.

Bellah, Robert N., Richard Madsen, William M. Sullivan, Ann Swidler, and Stephen M. Tipton. 1985. *Habits of the Heart: Individualism and Commitment in American Life*. San Francisco: Harper and Row.

Bender, Paul. 1983. The Canadian Charter of Rights and Freedoms and the United States Bill of Rights: A Comparison. *McGill Law Journal / Revue de droit de McGill* 28, 4: 811–66.

Benson, Iain T. n.d. Why the Centre Is Not 'Right' or 'Left.' *CentrePoint* 1, 2. Accessed at the website www.CentreForRenewal.ca.

Berger, Peter. 1967. *The Sacred Canopy: Elements of a Sociological Theory of Religion*. New York: Doubleday Anchor.
- 1974. *Pyramids of Sacrifice: Political Ethics and Social Change*. New York: Basic Books.
- 1977. *Facing Up to Modernity: Excursions in Society, Politics, and Religion*. New York: Basic Books.
- 1986. *The Capitalist Revolution: Fifty Propositions about Prosperity, Equality, and Liberty*. New York: Basic Books.
- 1997. Epistemological Modesty: An Interview with Peter Berger. *Christian Century*, 29 October, 972–8.

Bergeron, Yvonne. 1998. Paroles d'évêques à contre-courant: Les messages du 1er mai. In *Intervenir à contre-courant*, ed. Michel Beaudin et al., 63–88 Montreal: Fides.

Berman, Marshall. 1988. *All That Is Solid Melts into Air: The Experience of Modernity*. New York: Penguin.

Bernstein, Maurice André. 1994. *Foregone Conclusions: Against Apocalyptic History*. Berkeley: University of California Press.

Berton, Pierre. 1965. *The Comfortable Pew*. Toronto: McClelland and Stewart.

– 1987. *Why We Act like Canadians*. Toronto: Penguin.

Beyer, Peter. 1990. Privatization and the Public Influence of Religion in Global Society. In *Global Culture: Nationalism, Globalization, and Modernity*, ed. Mike Featherstone. London: Sage.

– 1994. *Religion and Globalization*. London: Sage.

– 1997. Religious Vitality in Canada: The Complementarity of Religious Market and Secularisation Perspectives. *Journal for the Scientific Study of Religion* 36, 2: 272–88.

Bibby, Reginald W. 1987. *Fragmented Gods: The Poverty and Potential of Religion in Canada*. Toronto: Irwin.

– 1990. *Mosaic Madness: The Poverty and Potential of Life in Canada*. Toronto: Stoddart.

– 1993. *Unknown Gods: The Ongoing Story of Religion in Canada*. Toronto: Stoddart.

– 1995. *There's Got to Be More! Connecting Churches and Canadians*. Winfield, BC: Wood Lake Books.

Biron, Jean-Marc. 1995. Les évêques et le référendum. *Relations* 611: 132–3.

Bissoondath, Neil. 1994. *Selling Illusions: The Cult of Multiculturalism in Canada*. Toronto: Penguin.

Black, Conrad. 1977. *Duplessis*. Toronto: McClelland and Stewart.

Black, Edwin R. 1975. *Divided Loyalties: Canadian Concepts of Federalism*. Montreal: McGill-Queen's University Press.

Blumstock, Robert. 1993. Canadian Civil Religion. In *The Sociology of Religion: A Canadian Focus*, ed. W.E. Hewitt. Toronto: Butterworths.

Borgmann, Albert. 1992. *Crossing the Postmodern Divide*. Chicago: University of Chicago Press.

Botting, Gary. 1993. *Fundamental Freedoms and Jehovah's Witnesses*. Calgary: University of Calgary Press.

Bouchard, P. 1980. Notre choix est légitime. *Le Devoir*, 23 April, 13, 14.

Boucher, Jacques. 1995a. Les commissions et l'avenir de la démocratie. *Relations* 610: 99–100.

– 1995b. La question nationale. *Relations* 612: 163–4.

Bourdieu, Pierre. 1984. *Distinction: A Social Critique of the Judgement of Taste.* Cambridge: Harvard University Press.

Boyle, T. Coraghessan. 1993. *The Road to Wellville.* New York: Viking.

Boyte, Harry C. 1980. *The Backyard Revolution: Understanding the New Citizen Movement.* Philadelphia: Temple University Press.

Bradfield, Cecil, Mary Lou Wylie, and Lennis G. Echterling. 1989. After the Flood: The Response of Ministers to a Natural Disaster. *Sociological Analysis* 49, 4: 397–407.

Broadbent, ed. 1996. Broadbent's Lament for a Nation. *Catholic New Times,* 18 February.

Bromley, David. 1997. Remembering the Future: A Sociological Narrative of Crisis Episodes, Collective Action, Culture Workers, and Countermovements. *Sociology of Religion* 58, 2: 105–40.

Brown, Joanne, and Carole Bohn, eds. 1989. *Christianity, Patriarchy and Abuse: A Feminist Critique.* Cleveland: Pilgrim Press.

Bruce, Steve. 1996. *Religion in the Modern World: From Cathedrals to Cults.* Oxford: Oxford University Press.

– 1992., ed. *Religion and Modernization: Sociologists and Historians Debate the Secularization Thesis.* Oxford: Clarendon.

Buechler, Steven, and F. Kurt Cylke, Jr., eds. 1997. *Social Movements: Perspectives and Issues.* Mountain View, CA: Mayfield.

Burkinshaw, Robert. 1995. *Pilgrims in Lotus Land: Conservative Protestantism in British Columbia, 1917–1981.* Montreal: McGill-Queen's University Press.

Butler, Judith. 1993. *Bodies That Matter.* London: Routledge.

Campbell, Ken. 1980. *No Small Stir: A Spiritual Strategy for Salting and Saving a Secular Society.* Burlington, ON: Welch.

– 1983. Interview by George Egerton. Milton, Ont., 13 June.

Campbell, Robert A., and James E. Curtis. 1994. Religious Involvement across Societies: Analyses of Alternative Measures in National Surveys. *Journal for the Scientific Study of Religion* 33, 3: 217–29.

Campiche, Roland, Alfred Dubach, Claude Bovay, Michael Kruggeler, and Peter Voll. 1992. *Croire en Suisse(s).* Geneva: L'Age de l'homme.

Canada. Canadian Intergovernmental Conference Secretariat. 1969. *The Constitution and the People of Canada.* Ottawa.

– Citizens' Forum on Canada's Future. 1991. *Report to the People and Government of Canada.* Ottawa: Minister of Supply and Services.

– Department of Foreign Affairs and International Trade. 1991. *Documents on Canadian External Relations,* ed. Hector Mackenzie. Vol. 14, *1948.* Ottawa: Minister of Supply and Services.

Canada. House of Commons. 1960. Special Committee on Human Rights and

Fundamental Freedoms. *Minutes of Proceedings and Evidence*. Ottawa: Queen's Printer.
- 1966–68. Standing Committee on Health and Welfare. *Minutes of Proceedings and Evidence*. Ottawa: Queen's Printer.
- 1967. *Debates*, 5 December. Ottawa: Queen's Printer.
- 1967–69. Standing Committee on Justice and Legal Affairs. *Minutes of Proceedings and Evidence*. Ottawa: Queen's Printer.
- 1969a. *Debates*, 23 January. Ottawa: Queen's Printer.
- 1969b. *Debates*, 11 February. Ottawa: Queen's Printer.
- 1969c. Standing Committee on Justice and Legal Affairs. *Minutes of Proceedings and Evidence*, 4 March. Ottawa: Queen's Printer.
- 1981. *Debates*, 22 April. Ottawa: Queen's Printer.
Canada. Parliament. 1948. Special Joint Committee of the Senate and the House of Commons on Human Rights and Fundamental Freedoms. *Minutes of Proceedings and Evidence*. Ottawa: King's Printer.
- 1966–7. *Proceedings of the Special Joint Committee of the Senate and the House of Commons on Divorce*. Ottawa: Queen's Printer.
- 1981. *Minutes of Proceedings and Evidence of the Special Joint Committee of the Senate and of the House of Commons on the Constitution of Canada*. Ottawa: Queen's Printer.
Canada. Senate. 1950. *Proceedings of the Special Committee on Human Rights and Fundamental Freedoms*. Ottawa: King's printer.
Canadian Catholic Conference. 1987. 'On Pastoral Implications of Political Choices,' 21 April 1972. In *Do Justice! The Social Teaching of the Canadian Catholic Bishops, 1945–1986*, ed. E.F. Sheridan, SJ. Sherbrooke and Toronto: Editions Paulines and Jesuit Centre for Social Faith and Justice.
Canadian Conference of Catholic Bishops, Episcopal Conference for Social Affairs, 1994. *Will the Poor Have the Most to Fear from Social Security Reforms?* Ottawa: Canadian Conference of Catholic Bishops.
Canadian Conference of Catholic Bishops. 1995. *Let Justice Flow Like a Mighty River*. Brief presented to the Royal Commission on Aboriginal Peoples. Ottawa: Canadian Conference of Catholic Bishops.
Carroll, Michael P. 1995. Rethinking Popular Catholicism in Pre-Famine Ireland. *Journal for the Scientific Study of Religion* 34, 5: 354–65.
Carroll, Michael P. 1996. Stark Realities and Eurocentric/Androcentric Bias in the Sociology of Religion. *Sociology of Religion* 57, 3: 225–39.
Carter, Stephen. 1993. *The Culture of Disbelief: How American Law and Politics Trivialize Religious Devotion*. New York: Basic Books.
Casanova, José. 1994. *Public Religions in the Modern World*. Chicago: University of Chicago Press.

- 1997. Globalizing Catholicism and the Return to a 'Universal' Church. In *Transnational Religion and Fading States*, ed. Susanne Hoeber Rudolph and James Piscatori. Boulder, CO: Westview.

Castells, Manuel. 1996, 1997, 1998. *The Information Age: Economy, Society and Culture.* 3 vols. Oxford: Blackwell.

Centre for Renewal of Public Policy. 1998. Statement of Activities and Budget. Photocopy in possession of John G. Stackhouse, Jr.

Champion, Françoise. 1993. Religieux flottant, éclectisme et syncrétismes. In *Le fait religieux*, by J. Delumeau. Paris. Fayard.

Chaves, Mark. 1989. Evidence from U.S. Church Attendance Rates, 1972–1986. *Journal for the Scientific Study of Religion* 28, 4: 464–77.

Chaves, Mark, and David E. Cann. 1992. Regulation, Pluralism, and Religious Market Structure. *Rationality and Society* 4, 3: 272–90.

Christiano, Kevin J. 1989. Federalism as a Canadian National Ideal: The Civic Rationalism of Pierre Elliott Trudeau. *Dalhousie Review* 69, 2: 248–69.

Christiano, Kevin J. 1994. *Pierre Elliott Trudeau: Reason before Passion.* Toronto: ECW.

Christie, Nancy, and Michael Gauvreau. 1996. *A Full-Orbed Christianity: The Protestant Churches and Social Welfare in Canada, 1900–1940.* Montreal: McGill-Queen's University Press.

Christopherson, Neal. 1997. Christian Fiction. Master's thesis, University of Notre Dame.

Citizens for Public Justice. 1996. *Public Justice and Human Rights.* Toronto: Citizens for Public Justice. Submission to the House of Commons on Bill C-33.

- 1997. CPJ's Public Policy Voice: A Proposal to Sustain, Strengthen, and Build the Capacity of CPJ. Toronto: Citizens for Public Justice (December). Pamphlet.

Clapp, Rodney, ed. 1998. *The Consuming Passion: Christianity and the Consumer Culture.* Downers Grove, IL: InterVarsity.

Clark, S.D. 1948. *Church and Sect in Canada.* Toronto: University of Toronto Press.

- 1968. *The Developing Canadian Community.* Toronto: University of Toronto Press.

Clarke, Brian. 1996. English-Speaking Canada from 1854. In *A Concise History of Christianity in Canada*, ed. Terrence Murphy and Roberto Perin. Toronto: Oxford University Press.

Clarkson, Stephen, and Christina McCall. 1991. *Trudeau and Our Times*, vol. 1, *The Magnificent Obsession.* Toronto: McClelland and Stewart.

Clifford, N. Keith. 1969. Religion and the Development of Canadian Society: An Historiographical Analysis. *Church History* 38: 506–23.

- 1973. His Dominion: A Vision in Crisis. *Studies in Religion / Sciences Religieuses* 2, 4: 315–26.

Coleman, James S. 1993. The Rational Reconstruction of Society. *American Sociological Review* 58, 1: 1–15.

- 1996. *Party Decline in America: Policy, Politics, and the Fiscal State.* Princeton: Princeton University Press.

Coleman, Simon. 1993. Conservative Protestantism and the World Order: The Faith Movement in the United States and Sweden. *Sociology of Religion* 54, 4: 353–73.

Comité exécutif de l'Assemblée des évêques du Québec. 1995. Le référendum sur l'avenir du Québec. *L'Église canadienne* 28, 4: 103–5.

Commission d'étude sur les laïcs et l'Église. 1971. *L'Église du Québec: Un héritage, un projet.* Montreal: Éditions Fides.

Conover, Pamela Johnston. 1988. The Role of Social Groups in Political Thinking. *British Journal of Political Science* 18, 1: 51–76.

'Constitution Finder.' 1998. Online database maintained by Robert H. Burger, T.C. Williams School of Law, University of Richmond. Available from http://www.urich.edu/~jpjones/confinder/const.htm.

Cook, Ramsay. 1985. *The Regenerators: Social Criticism in Late-Victorian Canada.* Toronto: University of Toronto Press.

- 1997. Salvation, Sociology, and Secularism. *Literary Review of Canada* 6, 1: 10–12.

Copeland, Mary Shawn. 1994. Reflections. In *Violence against Women*, ed. Elisabeth Schüssler Fiorenza and Mary Shawn Copeland. London: SCM.

Corelli, Rae. 1996. How Very Different We Are. *Maclean's*, 4 November, 36–40.

Cormie, Lee. 1991. Aspects of Catholic Social Teaching after Vatican II. In *Church and Canadian Culture*, ed. Robert E. VanderVennen. Lanham, MD: University Press of America.

Côté, Yves. 1972. *L'Église du Québec: Un héritage, un projet – Rapport synthèse.* Montreal: Fides.

Crysdale, Stewart, and Jean-Paul Montminy. 1974. *Religion au Canada / Religion in Canada ... 1945–1972.* Downsview and Quebec: York University and Presses de l'Université Laval.

Cuneo, Michael W. 1989. *Catholics against the Church: Anti-Abortion Protest in Toronto, 1965–1985.* Toronto: University of Toronto Press.

Currie, Dawn H. 1990. Battered Women and the State: From the Failure of a Theory to a Theory of Failure. *Journal of Human Justice* 1, 2: 77–86.

Davie, Grace. 1994. *Religion in Britain since 1945: Believing without Belonging.* Oxford: Blackwell.

- 1996. Religion and Modernity: The Work of Danièle Hervieu-Léger. In

Postmodernity, Sociology and Religion, ed. Kieran Flanagan and Peter C. Jupp. London: Macmillan.

Davis, Charles. 1980. *Theology and Political Society*. Cambridge: Cambridge University Press.

– 1994. *Religion and the Making of Society*. Cambridge: Cambridge University Press.

Davis, Derek. 1997. Law, Morals, and Civil Religions in America. *Journal of Church and State* 39: 411–25.

Davis, James A. 1982. *General Social Surveys, 1972–1982: Cumulative Codebook*. Chicago: National Opinions Research Center.

DeKeseredy, Walter, and Ronald Hinch. 1991. *Woman Abuse: Sociological Perspectives*. Toronto: Thompson Educational.

DeKeseredy, Walter, and Linda MacLeod. 1997. *Woman Abuse: A Sociological Story*. Toronto: Harcourt Brace.

Dekker, Gerard, Donald Luidens, and Rodger Rice. 1997. *Rethinking Secularization: Reformed Reactions to Modernity*. Lanham, MD: University Press of America.

de Lagrave, J.-P. 1979. Un message de liberté. Editorial. *Le Devoir*, 28 August, 4.

Demerath, N.J., and Rhys H. Williams. 1992a. *A Bridging of Faiths: Religion and Politics in a New England City*. Princeton: Princeton University Press.

– 1992b. Secularization in a Community Context: Tensions of Religion and Politics in a New England City. *Journal for the Scientific Study of Religion* 31, 2: 189–206.

D'Emilio, John, and Estelle B. Freedman. 1988. *Intimate Matters: A History of Sexuality in America*. New York: Harper and Row.

Despland, Michel. 1977. Religion and the Quest for National Identity: Problems and Perspectives. In *Religion and Culture in Canada / Religion et culture au Canada*, ed. Peter Slater. Waterloo, ON: Canadian Corporation for Studies in Religion.

Desrochers, Irénée. 1978a. La politique et les croyants au Canada: I. L'Église catholique et 'l'unité canadienne.' *Relations* 38, 436: 116–21.

– 1978b. La politique et les croyants au Canada: II. L'oecuménisme et 'l'unité canadienne.' *Relations* 38, 437: 131–5.

– 1978c. Québec-Canada: Self-reliance et solidarité des peuples. *Relations* 38, 440: 225, 238–40.

– 1979a. Le droit du Québec et les tactiques de M. Clark. *Relations* 39, 449: 167–72.

– 1979b. Les évêques du Québec et l'avenir du peuple en vue du référendum. *Relations* 39, 452: 264–8.

– 1979c. Jean-Paul II et les peuples qui ne siègent pas encore à l'ONU. *Relations* 39, 454: 326–8, 349.

de Valk, Alphonse. 1974. *Morality and Law in Canadian Politics: The Abortion Controversy*. Dorval, QC: Palm.

Devlin, Patrick. 1965. *The Enforcement of Morals*. London: Oxford University Press.

Dickason, Olive. 1992. *Canada's First Nations: A History of Founding Peoples*. Toronto: McClelland and Stewart.

DiMaggio, Paul J. 1983. State Expansion and Organizational Fields. In *Organizational Theory and Public Policy*, ed. Richard H. Hall and Robert E. Quinn. Beverly Hills: Sage.

– and Walter W. Powell. 1991. Introduction to *The New Institutionalism in Organizational Analysis*, ed. Walter W. Powell and Paul J. DiMaggio. Chicago: University of Chicago Press.

Dion, Gérard, and Louis O'Neil. 1956. *Les chrétiens et les élections*. Montreal: Éditions de l'Homme.

Dion, Léon. 1975. *Nationalisme et politique au Québec*. Montreal: Hurtibise HMH.

Djwa, Sandra. 1987. *The Politics of the Imagination: A Life of F.R. Scott*. Toronto: McClelland and Stewart.

Dobash, R.P., and R.E. Dobash. 1979. *Violence against Wives: A Case against the Patriarchy*. New York: Free Press.

Dobbelaere, Karel. 1985. Secularization Theories and Sociological Paradigms: A Reformulation of the Private-Public Dichotomy and the Problem of Societal Integration. *Sociological Analysis* 46, 4: 377–87.

– 1987. Some Trends in European Sociology of Religion. *Sociological Analysis* 48, 2: 107–37.

Dobson, James C. 1995. *Straight Talk: What Men Need to Know; What Women Should Understand*. Dallas: Word.

– 1996. *Love Must Be Tough: New Hope for Families in Crisis*. Dallas: Word.

Doyle, Denise J. 1984a. Religious Freedom and Canadian Church Privileges. *Journal of Church and State* 26: 293–311.

– 1984b. Religious Freedom in Canada. *Journal of Church and State* 26: 413–35.

Dupront, A. 1996. *Qu'est-ce que les Lumières?* Paris: Folio.

Durkheim, Émile. 1995. *Selected Writings*, ed. Anthony Giddens. Cambridge: Cambridge University Press.

Edwards, Bob, and Michael W. Foley, eds. 1997. Social Capital, Civil Society and Contemporary Democracy. Special issue of *American Behavioral Scientist* 40, 5.

Eiesland, Nancy L., and Don E. Saliers. 1998. Barriers and Bridges: Relating the Disability Rights Movement and Religious Organization. In *Human Disability and the Service of God*. Nashville: Abingdon.

Eksteins, Modris. 1989. *Rites of Spring: The Great War and the Birth of the Modern Age*. Toronto: Lester and Orpen Dennys.

Elliot, David. 1994. Knowing No Borders: Canadian Contributions to American Fundamentalism. In *Amazing Grace: Evangelicalism in Australia, Britain, Canada and the United States*, ed. George A. Rawlyk and Mark Noll. Montreal: McGill-Queen's University Press.

Ellison, Christopher E., and Darren E. Sherkat. 1993. Conservative Protestantism and Support for Corporal Punishment. *American Sociological Review* 58, 1: 131–44.

Ellwood, Robert. 1994. *The Sixties Spiritual Awakening: American Religion Moves from Modern to Postmodern*. New Brunswick, NJ: Rutgers University Press.

Elmore, Timothy. 1992. *Soul Provider*. San Bernardino: Here's Life.

Englehart, Ronald. 1990. *Culture Shift in Advanced Industrial Society*. Princeton: Princeton University Press.

Ens, Adolf. 1994. *Subjects or Citizens? The Mennonite Experience in Canada, 1870–1925*. Ottawa: University of Ottawa Press.

Epp, Frank H. 1974. *Mennonites in Canada, 1786–1920: The History of a Separate People*. Toronto: Macmillan.

Epp, Jake. 1981. Communication with George Egerton. 18 March.

Epstein, Barbara. 1991. *Political Protest and Cultural Revolution: Nonviolent Direct Action in the 1970s and 1980s*. Berkeley: University of California Press.

Ester, Peter, Loek Halman, and Ruud de Moor. 1994. *The Individualizing Society: Value Change in Europe and North America*. Tilburg: Tilburg University Press.

Everett, W.W., and T.J. Bachmeyer. 1979. *Disciplines in Transformation: A Guide to Theology and the Behavioral Sciences*. Washington: University Press of America.

Faith Today. 1986. Huntley Street Covers the Continent. *Faith Today* 4: 58.

Falwell, Jerry. 1980. *Listen America!* Garden City: Doubleday.

Family Violence Prevention Initiative, Province of Nova Scotia. 1994. Newsletters 1–5.

Farrell, James. 1997. *The Spirit of the Sixties: The Making of Postwar Radicalism*. New York: Routledge.

Faulkner, Charles Thompson Sinclair. 1975. For Christian Civilization: The Churches and Canada's War Effort, 1939–1942. PhD dissertation, University of Chicago.

Featherstone, Mike. 1990. *Global Culture: An Introduction*. London: Sage.

- 1991. *Consumer Culture and Postmodernism*. London: Sage.
- 1995. *Undoing Culture: Globalization, Postmodernism and Identity*. London: Sage.
Fenn, Richard K. 1976. Bellah and the New Orthodoxy. *Sociological Analysis* 37, 2: 160–6.
Fentress, James, and Chris Wickham, eds. 1992. *Social Memory*. Oxford: Blackwell.
Ferguson, Niall, ed. 1997. *Virtual History: Alternatives and Counterfactuals*. London: Picador.
Fieguth, Debra. 1997. Newfoundland Catholics, Pentecostals Lose Fight. *Christian Week*, 23 September, 1.
Fingard, Judith. 1972. *The Anglican Design in Loyalist Nova Scotia*. London: SPCK.
Finke, Roger, and Rodney Stark. 1992. *The Churching of America, 1776–1990*. New Brunswick, NJ: Rutgers University Press.
Fiorenza, Elisabeth Schüssler. 1994. Introduction to *Violence against Women*, ed. Elisabeth Schüssler Fiorenza and Mary Shawn Copeland. London: SCM.
Fire in the Rose Project. 1994. What Is Abuse?: Facts and Stories. Ottawa: Canadian Council on Justice and Corrections.
Flanagan, Kieran. 1996. Introduction to *Postmodernity, Sociology and Religion*, ed. Kieran Flanagan and Peter C. Jupp. London: Macmillan.
Fortune, Marie. 1991. *Violence in the Family: A Workshop Curriculum for Clergy and Other Helpers*. Cleveland: Pilgrim Press.
Fotheringham, Allan. 1998. Glen Clark Resorts to Leading B.C. on a Wing and a Prayer. *Financial Post* (Toronto), 25 February, 23.
Foucault, Michel. 1979. *Discipline and Punish: The Birth of the Prison*. Harmondsworth: Penguin.
- 1981. *The History of Sexuality*, vol. 1, *An Introduction*. Harmondsworth: Penguin.
- 1988. *The History of Sexuality*, vol. 2, *The Care of the Self*. Harmondsworth: Penguin.
Fox, Nick. 1995. Postmodern Perspectives on Care: The Vigil and the Gift. *Critical Social Policy* 15, 44–5: 107–25.
Francis, E.K. 1948. Mennonite Institutions in Early Manitoba: A Study of Their Origins. *Agricultural History* 22, 3: 144–55.
- 1955. *In Search of Utopia: The Mennonites in Manitoba*. Glencoe, IL.: Free Press.
Frank, Arthur. 1991. *At the Will of the Body*. Boston: Houghton Mifflin.
Frye, Northrop. 1976. Conclusion to *Literary History of Canada: Canadian Literature in English*. 2nd Ed. Vol. 3, ed. Carl F. Klinck, Alfred G. Bailey,

Claude Bissell, Roy Daniells, Northrop Frye, and Desmond Pacey. Toronto: University of Toronto Press.

– 1982. Sharing the Continent. In *Divisions on a Ground: Essays on Canadian Culture*, ed. James Polk. Toronto: Anansi.

Fukuyama, Francis. 1992. *The End of History and the Last Man*. New York: Free Press; Toronto: Maxwell Macmillan.

– 1995. Social Capital and the Global Economy. *Foreign Affairs* 74, 5: 89–103.

Fulford, Robert. 1993. A Post-Modern Dominion: The Changing Nature of Canadian Citizenship. In *Belonging: The Meaning and Future of Canadian Citizenship*, ed. William Kaplan. Montreal: McGill-Queen's University Press.

Fulton, Davie. 1983. Interview by George Egerton. Vancouver, 18 September.

Gadamer, Hans-Georg. 1985. *Truth and Method*. New York: Crossroad.

Gagnon, Alain G., and Michel Sarra-Bournet, eds. 1997. *Duplessis: Entre la grande noirceur et la société libérale*. Montreal: Éditions Québec Amérique.

Gamoran, Adam. 1990. Civil Religion in American Schools. *Sociological Analysis* 51, 3: 235–56.

Garreau, Joel. 1991. *Edge City: Life on the New Frontier*. New York: Doubleday.

Garrett, William R. 1998. The Protestant Ethic and the Spirit of the Modern Family. *Journal for the Scientific Study of Religion* 37, 2: 222–3.

Gauvreau, Michael. 1990. Protestantism Transformed: Personal Piety and the Evangelical Social Vision, 1815–1867. In *The Canadian Protestant Experience 1760–1990*, ed. George A. Rawlyk. Burlington, ON: Welch.

Gehrig, Gail. 1979. *American Civil Religion: An Assessment*. Storrs, CT: Society for the Scientific Study of Religion.

– 1981. The American Civil Religion Debate: A Source for Theory Construction. *Journal for the Scientific Study of Religion* 20, 1: 51–63.

Gelles, R.J. 1985. Family Violence. *Annual Review of Sociology* 11: 347–67.

Giddens, Anthony. 1976. *New Rules of Sociological Method*. London: Hutchinson.

– 1990. *The Consequences of Modernity*. Stanford: Stanford University Press.

– 1991. *Modernity and Self-Identity*. Cambridge: Polity Press.

– 1992. *The Transformation of Intimacy*. Cambridge: Polity Press.

– 1994. Living in a Post-Traditional Society. In *Reflexive Modernization: Politics, Tradition and Aesthetics in the Modern Social Order*, ed. Ulrich Beck, Anthony Giddens, and Scott Lash. Cambridge: Polity Press.

Giguère, Joseph. 1995a. La souveraineté et les frontières du possible. *Relations* 610: 100–1.

– 1995b. Souverains et communautaires. *Relations* 608: 35–6.

Gilbert, Christopher P., Timothy R. Johnson, and David A.M. Peterson. 1995. The Religious Roots of Third Candidate Voting: A Comparison of

Anderson, Perot and Wallace Voters. *Journal for the Scientific Study of Religion* 34, 4: 470–84.

Ginsberg, Faye. 1993. Saving America's Souls: Operation Rescue's Crusade against Abortion. In *Fundamentalism and the State: Remaking Polities, Economies, and Militance*, ed. Martin E. Marty and R. Scott Appleby. Chicago: University of Chicago Press.

Gitlin, Tod. 1987. *The Sixties: Years of Hope, Days of Rage.* New York: Bantam.

Gleason, Philip. 1984. Pluralism and Assimilation: A Conceptual History. In *Linguistic Minorities and Pluralism*, ed. John Edwards. London: Academic.

Glendon, Mary Ann. 1991. *Rights Talk: The Impoverishment of Political Discourse.* New York: Free Press.

Globe and Mail. 1998. 'Politics Gets Religion.' Editorial. *Globe and Mail,* 24 February, A22.

Grand'Maison, Jacques. 1979. *Une foi ensouchée dans ce pays.* Montreal: Leméac.

Grant, John Webster. 1955. Asking Questions of the Canadian Past. *Canadian Journal of Theology* 1, 2: 98–104.

– 1963. Blending Traditions: The United Church of Canada. In *The Churches and the Canadian Experience*, ed. John Webster Grant. Toronto: Ryerson.

– 1967. *The Canadian Experience of Church Union.* Richmond: John Knox.

– 1973a. 'At Least You Knew Where You Stood with Them': Reflections on Religious Pluralism in Canada and the United States. *Studies in Religion / Sciences Religieuses* 2, 4: 340–51.

– 1973b. Religion in Canada: A Historical Perspective. Paper presented to the Canadian Society for the Study of Religion.

– 1977. Religion and the Quest for a National Identity. In *Religion and Culture in Canada / Religion et culture au Canada*, ed. Peter Slater. Waterloo, ON: Canadian Corporation for Studies in Religion.

– 1988a. *The Church in the Canadian Era: The First Century of Confederation.* Rev. and expanded ed. Burlington, ON: Welch.

– 1988b. *A Profusion of Spires: Religion in Nineteenth-Century Ontario.* Toronto: University of Toronto Press.

– 1988c. Protestantism and Society in Canada. In *Encyclopedia of the American Religious Experience: Studies of Traditions and Movements*, vol. 1, ed. Charles H. Lippy and Peter W. Williams. New York: Charles Scribner's and Sons.

Great Britain. Parliament. 1957. Committee on Homosexual Offences and Prostitution. *Report of the Committee on Homosexual Offences and Prostitution.* London: Her Majesty's Stationery Office.

Greeley, Andrew M. 1972. *The Denominational Society.* Glenview, IL: Scott, Foresman.

Green, John C., James L. Guth, Corwin E. Smidt, and Lyman A. Kellstedt.

1996. *Religion and the Culture Wars: Dispatches from the Front.* Lanham, MD: Rowman and Littlefield.

Greene, Bonnie, ed. 1990. *Canadian Churches and Foreign Policy.* Toronto: James Lorimer.

Grégoire, P. 1980. Le référendum, avant et après. *L'Église de Montréal* 98, 19: 291–3.

Gremillion, Joseph. 1976. *The Gospel of Peace and Justice: Catholic Social Teaching since Pope John.* Maryknoll, NY: Orbis.

Grenville, Andrew S., and Angus E. Reid. 1996. Catholicism and Voting No. *Ottawa Citizen,* 2 January, A9.

– and D.C. Lewis. n.d. Quebec Nationalism and Catholic Communitarianism: An Analysis of the Catholic Vote in the 1995 Quebec Referendum. Unpublished paper.

Gusfield, Joseph R. 1963. *Symbolic Crusade: Status Politics and the American Temperance Movement.* Urbana: University of Illinois Press.

Guth, James L., Ted G. Jelen, Lyman A. Kellstedt, Corwin E. Smidt, and Kenneth D. Wald. 1988. The Politics of Religion in America: Issues for Investigation. *American Politics Quarterly* 16, 3: 357–97.

Gwyn, Richard. 1996. *Nationalism without Walls: The Unbearable Lightness of Being Canadian.* Rev. ed. Toronto: McClelland and Stewart.

Habermas, Jürgen. 1976. *Legitimation Crisis.* London: Heinemann.

– 1981. Modernity versus Postmodernity. *New German Critique* 22: 3–14.

– 1987. *The Philosophical Discourse of Modernity.* Cambridge: MIT Press.

Hadden, Jeffrey. 1995. Religion and the Quest for Meaning and Order: Old Paradigms, New Realities. *Sociological Focus* 28, 1: 83–100.

Hagan, John. Forthcoming. *Northern Passage: The Lives of American War Resisters in Canada.* Cambridge, MA, and London: Harvard University Press.

Halbwachs, Maurice. 1950. *The Collective Memory.* New York: Harper-Colophon.

– 1992. *On Collective Memory.* Chicago: University of Chicago Press.

Hamelin, Jean. 1984. *Histoire du catholicisme québécois. Le XXe siècle,* vol. 2, *De 1940 à nos jours,* ed. Nive Voisine. Montreal: Boréal Express.

Hammond, Phillip E. 1980. Pluralism and Law in the Formation of American Civil Religion. In *Varieties of Civil Religion,* ed. Robert N. Bellah and Phillip E. Hammond. San Francisco: Harper and Row.

Hammond, Phillip E. 1994. American Civil Religion Revisited. *Religion and American Culture* 4: 2–7.

Handy, Robert T. 1976. *A History of the Churches in the United States and Canada.* New York: Oxford University Press.

– 1987. The 'Lively Experiment' in Canada. In *The Lively Experiment Continued,* ed. Jerald C. Brauer. Macon: Mercer University Press.

Harrison, Trevor. 1995. *Of Passionate Intensity: Right Wing Populism and the Reform Party of Canada*. Toronto: University of Toronto Press.

Hart, H.L.A. 1963. *Law, Liberty, and Morality*. Stanford: Stanford University Press.

Harvey, Bob. 1997. Court Rejects Bid for Religion in Schools. *Ottawa Citizen*, 4 July, A6.

Harvey, David. 1990. *The Condition of Postmodernity*. Oxford: Blackwell.

Harvey, Julien. 1990. Le rapport Dumont, à court terme et à long terme. *Sociologie et Sociétés* 22, 2: 127–32.

Hayes, Bernadette C., and Ian McAllister. 1995. Religious Independents in Northern Ireland: Origins, Attitudes, and Significance. *Review of Religious Research* 37, 1: 65–83.

Head, Ivan. 1972. Foreword to Pierre Elliott Trudeau, *Conversation With Canadians*. Toronto: University of Toronto Press.

Heelas, Paul. 1996. *The New Age Movement*. London: Routledge.

Held, David. 1989. *Political Theory and the Modern State*. Stanford: Stanford University Press.

Helman, Sara, and Tamar Rapoport. 1997. Women in Black: Challenging Israel's Gender and Socio-Political Orders. *British Journal of Sociology* 48, 4: 681–96.

Herberg, Will. 1955. *Protestant–Catholic–Jew*. Garden City: Doubleday.

Hervieu-Léger, Danièle. 1986. *Vers un nouveau christianisme?* Paris: Cerf.

– 1990. Religion and Modernity in the French Context: For a New Approach to Secularization. *Sociological Analysis* 51: S15–S25.

– 1993a. Present-Day Emotional Renewals: The End of Secularization or the End of Religion? In *A Future for Religion? New Paradigms for Social Analysis*, ed. William H. Swatos. Newbury Park: Sage.

– 1993b. *La religion pour mémoire*. Paris: Cerf.

– 1994. Religion, Memory and Catholic Identity: Young People in France and the 'New Evangelization of Europe.' In *Religion in Contemporary Europe*, ed. John Fulton and Peter Gee. Lewiston, NY: Edwin Mellen Press.

– 2000. *Religion as a Chain of Memory*, trans. Simon Lee. Cambridge: Polity Press.

Herzog, Albert A., Jr. 1998. *An Analysis of the Disability Rights Movement within American Mainstream Protestantism at the Regional and Local Level*. Columbus, OH: Center for Persons with Disabilities in the Life of the Church.

Hewitt, W.E. 1993. The Quest for the Just Society: Canadian Catholicism in Transition. In *The Sociology of Religion: A Canadian Focus*, ed. W.E. Hewitt. Toronto: Butterworths.

Hexham, Irving, and Karla Poewe. 1997. *New Religions as Global Culture: Making the Human Sacred*. Boulder, CO: Westview.

Hiemstra, John L. 1983. *Trudeau's Political Philosophy*. Toronto: Institute for Christian Studies.

Hollinger, David. 1995. *Postethnic America: Beyond Multiculturalism*. New York: Basic Books.

Holsworth, Robert. 1989. *Let Your Life Speak: A Study of Politics, Religion, and Antinuclear Weapons Activism*. Madison: University of Wisconsin Press.

Horton, Anne, and Judith Williamson, eds. 1988. *Abuse and Religion: When Praying Isn't Enough*. New York: D.C. Heath.

Hunter, James Davison. 1983. *American Evangelicalism: Conservative Religion and the Quandary of Modernity*. New Brunswick, NJ: Rutgers University Press.

– 1984. Religion and Political Civility: The Coming Generation of Evangelicals. *Journal for the Scientific Study of Religion* 23, 4: 364–80.

– 1985. Conservative Protestantism. In *The Sacred in a Secular Age: Toward Revision in the Scientific Study of Religion*, ed. Phillip E. Hammond. Berkeley: University of California Press.

– 1987. *Evangelicalism: The Coming Generation*. Chicago: University of Chicago Press.

– 1991. *Culture Wars: The Struggle to Define America*. New York: Basic Books.

Huntington, Samuel P. 1996. *The Clash of Civilizations and the Remaking of World Order*. New York: Simon and Schuster.

Hutchinson, Roger. 1982. Ecumenical Witness in Canada: Social Action Coalitions. *International Review of Mission* 71: xx.

– 1992. *Prophets, Pastors and Public Choices: Canadian Churches and the Mackenzie Valley Pipeline Debate*. Waterloo, ON: Wilfrid Laurier University Press.

Irvine, William. 1985. Comment on 'The Reproduction of the Religious Cleavage in Canadian Elections.' *Canadian Journal of Political Science* 18, 1: 115–7.

Janssen, A., ed. 1994. *Seven Promises of a Promise Keeper*. Colorado Springs: Focus on the Family.

Janzen, William. 1990. *Limits on Liberty: The Experience of Mennonite, Hutterite, and Doukhobor Communities in Canada*. Toronto: University of Toronto Press.

Jefferson, Thomas. 1987. Jefferson's Letter to the Danbury Baptists (1 January 1802). In *Church and State in American History: The Burden of Religious Pluralism*. 2nd Ed., ed. John F. Wilson and Donald L. Drakeman. Boston: Beacon.

Jelen, Ted G., and Marthe A. Chandler, eds. 1994. *Abortion Politics in the United States and Canada*. Westport, CT: Praeger.

Jenkins, Thomas. 1997. *The Character of God*. Oxford: Oxford University Press.

Johnston, Maureen. 1981. Communication with George Egerton. 18 February.

Johnston, Richard. 1985. The Reproduction of the Religious Cleavage in Canadian Elections. *Canadian Journal of Political Science* 18, 1: 99–113.

Juergensmeyer, Mark. 1993. *The New Cold War? Religious Nationalism Confronts the Secular State.* Berkeley: University of California Press.

Juhnke, James C. 1989. *Vision, Doctrine, War: Mennonite Identity and Organization in America, 1890–1930,* vol. 3 of *The Mennonite Experience in America.* Scottdale, PA and Waterloo, ON: Herald.

Kaplan, William. 1989. *State and Salvation: The Jehovah's Witnesses and Their Fight for Civil Rights.* Toronto: University of Toronto Press.

Katerberg, William H. 1995a. The Irony of Identity: An Essay on Nativism, Liberal Democracy, and Parochial Identities in Canada and the United States. *American Quarterly* 47, 3: 493–524.

– 1995b. Protecting Christian Liberty: Mainline Protestantism, Racial Thought, and Political Culture in Canada, 1918–1939. In Canadian Society of Church History, *Historical Papers 1995.*

Kelley, Robert. 1990. *The Transatlantic Persuasion: The Liberal-Democratic Mind in the Age of Gladstone.* New Brunswick, NJ: Transaction.

Kellstedt, Lyman A., and John C. Green. 1993. Knowing God's People: Denominational Preference and Political Behavior. In *Rediscovering the Religious Factor in American Politics,* ed. David Leege and Lyman A. Kellstedt. Armonk: M.E. Sharpe.

Kellstedt, Lyman A., John C. Green, James L. Guth, and Corwin E. Smidt. 1993. Religious Traditions and Religious Commitments in the U.S.A. Paper presented at the 22nd International Conference of the International Society for the Sociology of Religion, Budapest, Hungary, 9–12 July.

Kenney, James F. 1933. Relations between Church and State in Canada since the Cession of 1763. *Catholic Historical Review* 18: 439–71.

Keohane, Kieran. 1997. *Symptoms of Canada: An Essay on the Canadian Identity.* Toronto: University of Toronto Press.

Kilbourn, William. 1968. The Past. In *Religion in Canada: The Spiritual Development of a Nation,* ed. William Kilbourn. Toronto: McClelland and Stewart.

Kim, Andrew. 1993. The Absence of Pan-Canadian Civil Religion: Plurality, Duality, and Conflict in Symbols of Canadian Culture. *Sociology of Religion* 54, 3: 257–75.

Kines, Lindsay. 1997. Clark Meets Religious Leaders to Discuss B.C. Jobs, Economy. *Vancouver Sun,* 7 July, A1.

King, Anthony D., ed. 1991. *Culture, Globalization and the World-System: Contemporary Conditions for the Representation of Identity.* New York: Macmillan.

Kits, Harry J. 1988. World Views and Social Involvement: A Proposal for Classification of Canadian Neo-Calvinist Social Involvement, 1945–1980. MPhilF. thesis, Institute for Christian Studies.

– 1989. Twenty-Five Years of Public Witness. *Catalyst* 12: 1, 11.

Klandermans, Bert. 1988. The Formation and Mobilization of Consensus. In *From Structure to Action: Comparing Social Movement Research across Cultures*, ed. Bert Klandermans, Hanspeter Kriesi, and Sidney Tarrow. Vol. 1 of *International Social Movement Research*. Greenwich, CT: JAI Press.

Kleiman, Michael, Nancy Ramsey, and Lorella Palazzo. 1996. Public Confidence in Religious Leaders: A Perspective from Secularization Theory. *Review of Religious Research* 38, 1: 79–87.

Knowles, David, ed. 1982. *Canada: Sharing Our Christian Heritage*. Toronto: Mainroads.

Kolakowski, Leszek. 1990. *Modernity on Endless Trial*. Chicago: University of Chicago Press.

Kosmin, Barry A., and Seymour P. Lachman. 1993. *One Nation under God: Religion in Contemporary American Society*. New York: Crown.

Kramnick, Isaac, and R. Laurence Moore. 1996. *The Godless Constitution: The Case against Religious Correctness*. New York: Norton.

Kroeker, P. Travis. 1986. Canada's Catholic Bishops and the Economy: A Theological Ethical Analysis. *Toronto Journal of Theology* 2: 3–18.

Kroll-Smith, J. Stephen, and Stephen Robert Couch. 1987. A Chronic Technical Disaster and the Irrelevance of Religious Meaning: The Case of Centralia Pennsylvania. *Journal for the Scientific Study of Religion* 26, 1: 25–37.

Kumar, Krishan. 1995. *From Post-Industrial to Post-Modern Society*. Oxford: Blackwell.

Küng, Hans. 1988. *Theology for the Third Millennium*. New York: Doubleday.

Lachance, P. 1980. L'Église au secours de la société. Editorial. *Le Soleil*, 17 January, A6.

Ladd, Everett C. 1996. The Data Just Don't Show Erosion of America's 'Social Capital.' *Public Perspective* June / July: 1–6.

LaHaye, Tim, and Beverley LaHaye. 1982. *The Battle for the Family*. Old Tappan, NJ: Fleming H. Revell.

– 1995. *The Spirit-Filled Family*. Eugene, OR: Harvest House.

Lambert, Ronald D., Steven D. Brown, James E. Curtis, Barry J. King, and John M. Wilson. *1984 Canadian National Election Survey*. See <http://www/icpsr.umich.edu:80/cgi-bin/archive.prl?path=ICPSR&num=8544>

Lane, Christel. 1981. *The Rights of Rulers: Ritual in Industrial Society – The Soviet Case*. Cambridge: Cambridge University Press.

Laqueur, Walter, ed. 1989. *The Human Rights Reader*. New York: New American Library.

Larochelle Commission. 1992. *Risquer l'avenir*. Montreal: Fides.

Lasch, Christopher. 1991. *The True and Only Heaven: Progress and Its Critics*. New York: Norton.

Laxer, James. 1991. *Inventing Europe: The Rise of a New World Power*. Toronto: Lester.

Lears, T.J. Jackson. 1981. *No Place of Grace: Antimodernism and the Transformation of American Culture, 1880–1920*. New York: Pantheon.

Leege, David, and Lyman A. Kellstedt, eds. 1993. *Rediscovering the Religious Factor in American Politics*. Armonk: M.E. Sharpe.

Lemaire, Paul-Marcel. 1993. *Nous Québécois*. Ottawa: Leméac.

Levin, Charles. 1998. Contribution to 'Symposium: Will the 21st Century Be an Age of Religious Revival?' ed. Gerald Owen. *Books in Canada* 27, 1: 12–3.

Levitt, Cyril. 1984. *Children of Privilege: Student Revolt in the Sixties: A Study of Movements in Canada*. Toronto: University of Toronto Press.

Liebman, Robert, and Robert Wuthnow. 1983. *The New Christian Right: Mobilization and Legitimation*. New York: Aldine.

Lind, Christopher, and Joe Mihevc. 1994. *Coalitions for Justice: The Story of Canada's Interchurch Coalitions*. Ottawa: Novalis.

Lipset, Seymour Martin. 1970. *Revolution and Counter-Revolution: Change and Persistence in Social Structures*. New York: Basic Books.

– 1990. *Continental Divide: The Values and Institutions of the United States and Canada*. New York: Routledge.

Lockhart, William H. 1996. Redefining the New Christian Man: An Investigation into Books Related to the Promise Keepers Movement. Paper presented at the Annual Meetings of the Association for the Sociology of Religion, 16–18 August, New York City.

Loewen, Royden K. 1993. *Family, Church, and Market: A Mennonite Community in the Old and the New Worlds, 1850–1930*. Urbana: University of Illinois Press.

Loseke, Donileen R. 1992. *The Battered Woman and Shelters: The Social Construction of Wife Abuse*. New York: State University of New York Press.

Luckmann, Thomas. 1967. *The Invisible Religion: The Problem of Religion in Modern Society*. New York: Macmillan.

Luellau, Frank. 1998. Letter to John G. Stackhouse, Jr. 1 May.

Luxton, Meg. 1980. *More Than a Labour of Love*. Toronto: Women's Press.

Lyon, David. 1985. *The Steeple's Shadow: On the Myths and Realities of Secularization*. London: SPCK.

– 1994a. *The Electronic Eye: The Rise of Surveillance Society*. Minneapolis: University of Minnesota Press.

– 1994b. *Postmodernity*. Minneapolis: University of Minnesota Press.

– 1996. Religion and the Postmodern: Old Problems, New Prospects. In *Postmodernity, Sociology and Religion*, ed. Kieran Flanagan and Peter C. Jupp. London: Macmillan.

– 2000. *Jesus in Disneyland: Religion in Postmodern Times*. Cambridge: Polity Press

Lyotard, Jean-François. 1984. *The Postmodern Condition*. Minneapolis: University of Minnesota Press.

Mackey, Lloyd. 1987. Christian Political Activist Launches a New Party. *Christianity Today*, 3 April, 36–7.

– 1997. B.C. Premier Consults Religious Leaders: Glen Clark Pauses to Consider the Soul. *Christian Week* (Winnipeg), 5 August.

Maclean's Special Report. 1993. God is Alive. *Maclean's*, 12 April.

MacLeod, Linda. 1987. *Battered But Not Beaten ... Preventing Wife Battering in Canada*. Ottawa: Canadian Advisory Council on the Status of Women.

Malcohm, Andrew. 1985. *The Canadians*. New York: Times Books.

Mann, William F. 1955. *Sect, Cult, and Church in Alberta*. Toronto: University of Toronto Press.

Marsden, George M. 1980. *Fundamentalism and American Culture: The Shaping of Twentieth Century Evangelicalism, 1870–1925*. New York: Oxford University Press.

Marshall, David. 1992. *Secularizing the Faith: Canadian Protestant Clergy and the Crisis of Belief, 1850–1940*. Toronto: University of Toronto Press.

Martel, J. 1980. L'Église se fera discrète. Editorial. *Le Soleil*, 26 April, B2.

Martin, David. 1965. Towards Eliminating the Concept of Secularization. In *Penguin Survey of the Social Sciences*, ed. Julius Gould. Harmondsworth: Penguin.

– 1978. *A General Theory of Secularization*. Oxford: Basil Blackwell.

– 1991. The Secularization Issue: Prospect and Retrospect. *British Journal of Sociology* 42, 3: 465–74.

– 1995. Sociology, Religion and Secularization: An Orientation. *Religion* 25: 295–303.

– 1996. The General Theory of Secularisation: Retrospect and Prospect in Europe. In *Identités religieuses en Europe*, ed. Grace Davie and Danièle Hervieu-Léger. Paris: Découverte.

Martin, Del. 1981. *Battered Wives*. Rev. ed. San Fransisco: Volcano Press; 1st ed. San Francisco: New Glide Publications, 1976.

Marty, Martin E. 1977. *Righteous Empire*. 2nd Ed. New York: Harper and Row.

– 1992. *Civil Religion, Church and State*. Munich: K.G. Saur.

Matas, Robert. 1998. Clark Seeks Religious Help. Poverty Not Part of God's Plan: Prelate. *Globe and Mail* (Toronto), 24 February, A3.

Matthews, Robert, and Cranford Pratt, eds. 1982(?). *Church and State: The Christian Churches and Canadian Foreign Policy*. Toronto: Canadian Institute of International Affairs.

McDannell, Colleen. 1995. *Material Christianity: Religion and Popular Culture in America*. New Haven: Yale University Press.

McDonald, Michael. 1988. Respect for Individuals versus Respect for Groups: Public Aid for Confessional Schools in the United States and Canada. In *Philosophical Dimensions of the Constitution*, ed. Diana T. Meyers and Kenneth Kipnis, with Emily R. Gill. Boulder, CO: Westview.

McGowan, Mark G. 1990. Coming Out of the Cloister: Some Reflections on Developments in the Study of Religion in Canada, 1980–1990. *International Journal of Canadian Studies* 1, 2: 175–202.

McGuire, Meredith. 1985. Religion and Healing. In *The Sacred in a Secular Age: Toward Revision in the Scientific Study of Religion*, ed. Phillip E. Hammond. Berkeley: University of California Press.

McKercher, William R. 1983a. The United States Bill of Rights: Implications for Canada. In *The U.S. Bill of Rights and the Canadian Charter of Rights and Freedoms*, ed. William R. McKercher. Toronto: Ontario Economic Council.

– ed. 1983b. *The U.S. Bill of Rights and the Canadian Charter of Rights and Freedoms*. Toronto: Ontario Economic Council.

McRoberts, Kenneth. 1988. *Quebec: Social Change and Political Crisis*. 3rd ed. Toronto: McClelland and Stewart.

– 1997. *Misconceiving Canada: The Struggle for National Unity*. Toronto: Oxford.

Mellor, Philip A., and Chris Shilling. 1997. *Re-Forming the Body: Religion, Community and Modernity*. London: Sage.

Mendelsohn, Matthew, and Richard Nadeau. 1997. The Religious Cleavage and the Media in Canada. *Canadian Journal of Political Science* 30, 1: 129–46.

Meyer, John W., and Brian Rowan. 1991. Institutionalized Organizations: Formal Structure as Myth and Ceremony. In *The New Institutionalism in Organizational Analysis*, ed. Walter W. Powell and Paul J. DiMaggio. Chicago: University of Chicago Press.

Michaelson, Robert. 1992. The Public Schools and America's Two Religions. In *Civil Religion, Church and State*, ed. Martin E. Marty. Munich: K.G. Saur.

Middleton, David, and Derek Edwards, eds. 1990. *Collective Remembering*. London: Sage.

Middleton, J. Richard, and Brian J. Walsh. 1995. *Truth Is Stranger Than It Used to Be: Biblical Faith in a Postmodern Age*. Downers Grove, IL: InterVarsity.

Milot, Micheline. 1991. Le catholicisme au creuset de la culture. *Studies in Religion / Sciences religieuses* 20, 1: 51–64.

Mitchell, Basil. 1967. *Law, Morality and Religion in a Secular Society*. London: Oxford University Press.

Moir, John S. 1959. *Church and State in Canada West: Three Studies in the Relation of Denominationalism and Nationalism, 1841–1867.* Toronto: University of Toronto Press.

– 1967. *Church and State in Canada, 1627–1867: Basic Documents.* Toronto: McClelland and Stewart.

– 1968. The Upper Canadian Roots of Church Disestablishment. *Ontario History* 60, 4: 247–58.

– 1983. Coming of Age, but Slowly: Aspects of Canadian Religious Historiography since Confederation. Canadian Church History Association, *Study Sessions* 50: 89–98.

Montreal Gazette. 1979. Le ton modéré des évêques. *Le Soleil,* 27 août, A4.

Mol, Hans. 1985. *Faith and Fragility: Religion and Identity in Canada.* Burlington, ON: Trinity.

Moodie, T. Dunbar. 1978. The Afrikaner Civil Religion. In *Identity and Religion: International Cross-Cultural Approaches,* ed. Hans Mol. London: Sage.

Moore, R. Laurence. 1995. *Selling God: American Religion in the Marketplace of Culture.* New York: Oxford University Press.

Morton, Andrew. 1995. *Diana: Her New Life.* New York: Simon and Schuster.

Morton, Desmond. 1973. *Mayor Howland: The Citizens' Candidate.* Toronto: Hakkert.

Moseley, James G. 1994. American Civil Religion Revisited. *Religion and American Culture* 4, 1: 13–18.

Motz, Arnell. 1990. The Condition of the Canadian Church. In *Reclaiming a Nation,* ed. Arnell Motz. Richmond, BC: Outreach Canada Ministries.

Mouffe, Chantal, ed. 1992. *Dimensions of Radical Democracy: Pluralism, Citizenship, Community.* Oxford: Blackwell.

Mouw, Richard. 1994. *Consulting the Faithful: What Christian Intellectuals Can Learn from Popular Culture.* Grand Rapids: Eerdmans.

Murphy, Terrence, and Roberto Perin, eds. 1996. *A Concise History of Christianity in Canada.* Toronto: Oxford University Press.

Myers, Kenneth. 1989. *All God's Children and Blue Suede Shoes: Christians and Popular Culture.* Wheaton: Crossway.

Nason-Clark, Nancy. 1995. Conservative Protestants and Violence against Women: Exploring the Rhetoric and the Response. In *Sex, Lies and Sanctity: Religion and Deviance in Modern America,* ed. Mary Jo Neitz and Marion Goldman. Greenwich, CT: JAI Press.

– 1996. Religion and Violence against Women: Exploring the Rhetoric and the Response of Evangelical Churches in Canada. *Social Compass* 43, 4: 515–36.

– 1997. *The Battered Wife: How Christians Confront Family Violence.* Louisville: Westminster John Knox Press.

– 1998a. Abuses of Clergy Trust: Exploring the Impact on Female Congregants' Faith and Practice. In *Wolves within the Fold: Religious Leadership and Abuses of Power*, ed. Anson Shupe. New York: Rutgers University Press.

- 1998b. Evangelical Church Women and the Fight to End Family Violence. In *Religion in a Changing World: Comparative Studies in Sociology*, ed. Madeleine Cousineau. Westport, CT: Greenwood.

- 1998c. Shattered Silence or Holy Hush: Emerging Definitions of Violence against Women in Sacred and Secular Contexts. Manuscript under review.

Nelson, Ralph. 1995. Ideologies. In *Introductory Readings in Canadian Government and Politics*. 2nd Ed., ed. Robert M. Krause and R.H. Wagenberg. Toronto: Copp Clark.

Nesmith, Bruce. 1994. *The New Republican Coalition: The Reagan Campaigns and White Evangelicals*. New York: Peter Lang.

Nevitte, Neil. 1978. Religion and the 'New Nationalisms': The Case of Quebec. PhD dissertation, Duke University.

Nevitte, Neil, and François-Pierre Gingras. 1984. An Empirical Analysis of Secular-Religious Bases of Quebec Nationalism. *Social Compass* 31, 4: 339–50.

Niebuhr, H. Richard. [1929] 1957. *The Social Sources of Denominationalism*. Reprint, New York: Meridian.

Nock, David. 1993. The Organization of Religious Life in Canada. In *The Sociology of Religion: A Canadian Focus*, ed. W.E. Hewitt. Toronto: Butterworths.

Noll, Mark. 1992. *A History of Christianity in the United States and Canada*. Grand Rapids: Eerdmans.

- 1997. Canadian Evangelicalism: A View from the United States. In *Aspects of the Canadian Evangelical Experience*, ed. George A. Rawlyk. Montreal: McGill-Queen's University Press.

- ed. 1990. *Religion and American Politics from the Colonial Period to the 1980s*. New York: Oxford University Press.

Nora, Pierre. 1996. *Realms of Memory*. New York: Columbia University Press.

Norman, E.R. 1968. *The Conscience of the State in North America*. Cambridge: Cambridge University Press.

Offe, Claus. 1984. *Contradictions of the Welfare State*, ed. John Keane. Cambridge: MIT Press.

O'Neill, John. 1985. *Five Bodies: The Human Shape of Modern Society*. Ithaca: Cornell University Press.

- 1989. *The Communicative Body*. Evanston: Northwestern University Press.

O'Toole, Roger. 1982. Some Good Purpose: Notes on Religion and Political Culture in Canada. *Annual Review of the Social Sciences of Religion* 6: 177–217.

- 1984. Some Good Purpose: Notes on Religion and Political Culture in

Canada. In *Models and Myths in Canadian Sociology*, ed. Stephen D. Berkowitz. Toronto: Butterworths.

- 1996. Religion in Canada: Its Development and Contemporary Situation. *Social Compass* 43, 1: 110–34.

O'Toole, Roger, D.F. Campbell, J.A. Hannigan, Peter Beyer, and John H. Simpson. 1991. The United Church in Crisis: A Sociological Perspective on the Dilemmas of a Mainstream Denomination. *Studies in Religion / Sciences Religieuses* 20, 2: 151–63.

Ontario Multi-Faith Coalition for Equity in Education. 1993. Equipping Students for Responsible Citizenship. Brief presented to the Ontario Royal Commission on Learning. Toronto: OMCEE.

- 1994. Ensuring Choice and Equity for All Students: An Alternative Governance Model for Ontario Education. Toronto (March).

Page, Donald. 1993a. Interview and correspondence with George Egerton. Langley, B.C., March–April 1993.

- 1993b. Interview by George Egerton. Vancouver, 29 March.

Paiement, Guy. 1995. Projet de société et souveraineté. *Relations* 614: 227–8.

Pal, Leslie. 1993. *Interests of State: The Politics of Language, Multiculturalism, and Feminism in Canada*. Montreal: McGill-Queen's University Press.

Palmer, Howard. 1976. Reluctant Hosts: Anglo-Canadian Views of Multiculturalism in the Twentieth Century. In *Multiculturalism as State Policy*. Ottawa: Minister of Supply and Services.

Palmer, Howard. 1990. Polygamy and Progress: The Reaction to Mormans in Canada, 1887–1923. In *The Morman Presence in Canada*, ed. Brigham Y. Card, Herbert C. Northcott, John E. Foster, Howard Palmer, and George K. Jarvis. Logan: Utah State University Press; Edmonton: University of Alberta Press.

Palmer, Vaughn. 1997. Let He Who Is without Sin ... The Day Glen Clark Found Religion. Editorial. *Vancouver Sun*, 9 July, A10.

Pangle, Thomas L. 1993. The Accommodation of Religion: A Tocquevillian Perspective. In *The Canadian and American Constitutions in Comparative Perspective*, ed. Marian C. McKenna. Calgary: University of Calgary Press.

Parsons, Talcott. 1951. *The Social System*. Glencoe, IL: Free Press.

- 1960. *Structure and Process in Modern Societies*. Glencoe, IL: Free Press.

- 1963. Christianity and Modern Industrial Society. In *Sociological Theory, Values, and Sociocultural Change*, ed. Edward Tiryakian. New York: Harper and Row.

- 1968. Christianity. In *International Encyclopedia of the Social Sciences*, ed. David L. Sills. Vol. 2. New York: Macmillan.

- 1974. Religion in Postindustrial America: The Problem of Secularization. *Social Research* 41, 2: 193–225.

– 1979. Religious and Economic Symbolism in the Western World. *Sociological Inquiry* 49, 2–3: 1–48.

Phillips, Paul K. 1996. *A Kingdom on Earth: Anglo-American Social Christianity, 1880–1940.* University Park: Pennsylvania State University Press.

Piché, Eric. 1999. Religion and Social Capital in Canada. MA thesis, Queen's University, Kingston, Ontario.

Poewe, Karla, ed. 1994. *Charismatic Christianity as a Global Culture.* Columbia: University of South Carolina Press.

Popper, Karl. 1957. *The Poverty of Historicism.* London: Routledge.

Porterfield, Amanda. 1994. American Civil Religion Revisited. *Religion and American Culture* 4: 7–13.

Post-Modernity Project. 1996. *The State of Disunion.* Charlottesville: University of Virginia.

Potter, David M. 1954. *People of Plenty: Economic Abundance and the American Character.* Chicago: University of Chicago Press.

Powell, Walter W., and Paul J. DiMaggio, eds. 1991. *The New Institutionalism in Organizational Analysis.* Chicago: University of Chicago Press.

Pratt, Renate. 1997. *In Good Faith: Canadian Churches against Apartheid.* Waterloo, ON: Wilfrid Laurier University Press.

Putnam, Robert D. 1995a. Bowling Alone: America's Declining Social Capital. *Journal of Democracy* 6, 1: 65–78.

– 1995b. Tuning In, Tuning Out: The Strange Disappearance of Social Capital in America. *PS: Political Science and Politics* 28, 4: 664–83.

Quebedeaux, Richard. 1978. *The Worldly Evangelicals.* San Francisco: Harper and Row.

Quinby, Ajax. 1995. Taking Back the Movement: Resisting Professionalization and Listening to Women. In *Listening to the Thunder: Advocates Talk about the Battered Women's Movement*, ed. Leslie Timmins. Vancouver: Women's Research Centre.

Rawlyk, George A. 1984. *Ravished by the Spirit: Religious Revivals, Baptists, and Henry Alline.* Montreal: McGill-Queen's University Press.

– 1990a. *Champions of the Truth: Fundamentalism, Modernism, and the Maritime Baptists.* Montreal: McGill-Queen's University Press.

– 1990b. Politics, Religion and the Canadian Experience: A Preliminary Probe. In *Religion and American Politics from the Colonial Period to the 1980s*, ed. Mark Noll. New York: Oxford University Press.

– 1994. Who Are These Canadians Who Call Themselves Evangelicals? *Christian Week*, 15 November.

– 1996. *Is Jesus Your Personal Saviour? In Search of Canadian Evangelicalism in the 1990s.* Montreal: McGill-Queen's University Press.

- ed. 1990c. *The Canadian Protestant Experience, 1760–1990*. Burlington, ON: Welch.
- 1997. Introduction to *Aspects of the Canadian Evangelical Experience*. Montreal: McGill-Queen's University Press.

Rayside, David. 1998. *On the Fringe: Gays and Lesbians in Politics*. Ithaca: Cornell University Press.

Regroupement des Religieuses et Religieux pour le 'Oui.' 1995. Regroupement des religieuses et religieux pour le 'Oui.' Open letter. Montreal.

Reimer, Sam. 1995. A Look at Cultural Effects on Religiosity: A Comparison between the United States and Canada. *Journal for the Scientific Study of Religion* 34, 4: 445–57.

- 1996. North American Evangelicalism: Cultural Influences on Religious Conservatives. PhD dissertation, University of Notre Dame.
- Forthcoming. 'A More Irenic Canadian Evangelicalism? Comparing American and Canadian Evangelicals.' In *Revivals, Baptists, and George Rawlyk: Essays in Memory of George A. Rawlyk*. Wolfville, NS: Gaspereau Press.

Remple, Henry David. 1975. The Practice and Theory of the Fragile State: Trudeau's Conception of Authority. *Journal of Canadian Studies* 10, 4: 24–39.

Resnick, Philip. 1984. *Parliament vs People: An Essay on Democracy and Canadian Political Culture*. Vancouver: New Star.

Resolution. 1981. Reprinted in *Thrust: The Quarterly News and Review Magazine of the Evangelical Fellowship of Canada* 13, 1: 2.

Revision for Canada's SCP, A. 1990. *Christian Century*, 5 December, 1129.

Richey, Russell E., and Donald G. Jones, eds. 1974. *American Civil Religion*. New York: Harper.

Rioux, Marcel. 1976. *La question du Québec*. Montreal: Parti Pris.

Roberts, Paul William. 1998. The Politics of Islam. *Globe and Mail*, 25 July, D14–12.

Robertson, Roland. 1989. Globalization, Politics, and Religion. In *The Changing Face of Religion*, ed. James A. Beckford and Thomas Luckmann. London: Sage.

Robertson, Roland. 1992. *Globalization: Social Theory and Global Culture*. London: Sage.

- 1995. Glocalization: Time-Space and Homogeneity-Heterogeneity. In *Global Modernities*, ed. Mike Featherstone, Scott Lash, and Roland Robertson. London: Sage.

Robinson, Svend. 1981. Communication with George Egerton. 9 March.

Rochais, Gérard, ed. 1984. *La justice sociale comme bonne nouvelle: Messages sociaux, économiques et politiques des évêques du Québec 1972–1983*. Montreal: Bellarmin.

Roof, Wade C. 1993. *A Generation of Seekers: The Spiritual Journeys of the Baby Boom Generation*. New York: HarperCollins.

Roszak, Theodore. 1969. *The Making of a Counter Culture: Reflections on the Technocratic Society and Its Youthful Opposition*. Garden City: Doubleday.

Ruttan, Brian. 1985. GATT-Fly and the Churches: Changing Public Policy. In *Justice as Mission: An Agenda for the Church*, ed. Terry Brown and Christopher Lind. Burlington, ON: Trinity.

Sarra-Bournet, Michel. 1986. *L'affaire Roncarelli: Duplessis contre les Témoins de Jéhovah*. Quebec: Institut québécois de recherche sur la culture.

Sarup, Madan. 1996. *Identity, Culture and the Postmodern World*. Athens: University of Georgia Press.

Schmalzbauer, John A., and C. Gray Wheeler. 1996. Between Fundamentalism and Secularization: Secularizing and Sacralizing Currents in the Evangelical Debate on Campus Lifestyle Codes. *Sociology of Religion* 57, 3: 241–57.

Schneirov, Mathew, and Jonathan Geezik. 1997. The Aesthetic of the Body and Public Life. Paper presented at the Annual Meeting of the American Sociological Association, Toronto, 9–13 August.

– 1998. Technologies of the self and the aesthetic project of alternative health. *The Sociological Quarterly*, 3,3: 435–451.

Schwartz, Mildred. 1974. Canadian Voting Behaviour. In *Electoral Behavior: A Comparative Handbook*, ed. Richard Rose. Glencoe, IL: Free Press.

Sclater, James A. 1998a. Affidavit filed in the Supreme Court of Canada's hearing of *Attorney General of Ontario v M and H*, court file no. 25838.

– 1998b. Electronic mail to John G. Stackhouse, Jr. 19 March.

– 1998c. Memorandum to John G. Stackhouse, Jr. 23 March.

Scott, F.R. 1977. *Essays on the Constitution: Aspects of Canadian Law and Politics*. Toronto: University of Toronto Press.

Scott, W. Richard, and John W. Meyer. 1991. The Organization of Societal Sectors: Propositions and Early Evidence. In *The New Institutionalism in Organizational Analysis*, ed. Walter W. Powell and Paul J. DiMaggio. Chicago: University of Chicago Press.

Searle, Natalie. 1994. The Women's Bible Study: A Thriving Evangelical Support Group. In *I Come Away Stronger: How Small Groups Are Changing American Religion*, ed. Robert Wuthnow. Grand Rapids: Eerdmans.

Segal, Harold B. 1998. *Body Ascendant: Modernism and the Physical Imperative*. Baltimore: Johns Hopkins University Press.

Seljak, David. 1995. The Catholic Church's Reaction to the Secularization of Nationalism in Quebec, 1960–1980. PhD dissertation, McGill University.

– 1996. Why the Quiet Revolution Was 'Quiet': The Catholic Church's Reaction to the Secularization of Nationalism in Quebec after 1960. Canadian Catholic Historical Association, *Historical Studies* 62: 109–24.

Semple, Neil. 1996. *The Lord's Dominion: The History of Canadian Methodism.* Montreal: McGill-Queen's University Press.

Sharp, Carolyn. 1995. Le mensonge néo-libéral: L'idolâtrie continue de nous appauvrir. *Relations* 614: 232.

Shibley, Mark. 1996. *Resurgent Evangelicalism in the United States: Mapping Cultural Change since 1970.* Columbia: University of South Carolina Press.

Shilling, Chris. 1993. *The Body and Social Theory.* London: Sage.

Shorter, Edward. 1977. *The Making of the Modern Family.* New York: Basic Books.

Shupe, Anson, and David Bromley. 1985. Social Responses to Cults. In *The Sacred in a Secular Age: Toward Revision in the Scientific Study of Religion,* ed. Phillip E. Hammond. Berkeley: University of California Press.

Silcox, C.E. 1933. *Church Union in Canada: Its Causes and Consequences.* New York: Institute of Social and Religious Research.

Simpson, John H. 1983. Moral Issues and Status Politics. In *The New Christian Right: Mobilization and Legitimation,* ed. Robert C. Liebman and Robert Wuthnow. New York: Aldine.

– 1985a. Federal Regulation and Religious Broadcasting in Canada and the United States: A Comparative Sociological Analysis. In *Religion / Culture: Comparative Canadian Studies,* ed. William Westfall, Fernand Harvey, and John H. Simpson. Ottawa: Association for Canadian Studies.

– 1985b. Status Inconsistency and Moral Issues. *Journal for the Scientific Study of Religion* 24, 2: 155–62.

– 1988. Religion and the Churches. In *Understanding Canadian Society,* ed. James Curtis and Lorne Tepperman. Toronto: McGraw-Hill Ryerson.

– 1990. The Stark-Bainbridge Theory of Religion. *Journal for the Scientific Study of Religion* 29, 3: 367–71.

– 1993. Religion and the Body: Sociological Themes and Prospects. In *A Future for Religion? New Paradigms for Social Analysis,* ed. William H. Swatos. Newbury Park, CA: Sage.

– 1996. 'The Great Reversal': Selves, Communities, and the Global System. *Sociology of Religion* 57, 2: 115–25.

– 1998a. Confessions, Outings, and Ordeals: Understanding Media in America. In *Religion, Mobilization, and Social Action,* ed. Anson Shupe and Bronislaw Misztal. Westport, CT: Praeger.

– 1998b. Selves and Stories: From Descartes to the Global Self. In *Character and Identity: The Philosophical Foundation of Political and Sociological Perspectives,* ed. Morton A. Kaplan. St Paul: Paragon House.

– and Henry MacLeod. 1985. The Politics of Morality in Canada. In *Religious Movements: Genesis, Exodus, and Numbers*, ed. Rodney Stark. New York: Paragon.

Small, Peter. 1998. Court Says No to Parents' Appeal. *Toronto Star*, 13 February, A17.

Smalley, Gary. 1988. *Hidden Keys of a Loving, Lasting Marriage*. Grand Rapids: Zondervan.

– 1996. *Making Love Last Forever*. Dallas: Word.

Smiley, Donald V. 1983a. Commentaries. In *The U.S. Bill of Rights and the Canadian Charter of Rights and Freedoms*, ed. William R. McKercher. Toronto: Ontario Economic Council.

– 1983b. The Canadian Charter of Rights and Freedoms with Special Emphasis on Quebec–Canada Relations. In *The U.S. Bill of Rights and the Canadian Charter of Rights and Freedoms*, ed. William R. McKercher. Toronto: Ontario Economic Council.

Smith, David. 1981. [The Evangelicals]. Loose-leaf Liberal briefing book. (Mid-April).

– 1982. Interview by George Egerton. Ottawa, 22 February.

Sniderman, Paul. 1988. Attitudes toward Civil Liberties and the Canadian Charter of Rights. Computer file available from the Institute for Social Research, York University.

Sniderman, Paul, Joseph Fletcher, Peter Russell, and Phillip Titlock. 1988. Liberty, Authority, and Community: Civil Liberties and the Canadian Political Culture. Paper delivered at the Annual Meetings of the Canadian Political Science Association, 9 June, at the University of Windsor.

Snow, David A., and Robert D. Benford. 1988. Ideology, Frame Resonance, and Participant Mobilization. In *From Structure to Action: Comparing Social Movement Research across Cultures*, ed. Bert Klandermans, Hans Peter Kriesi, and Sydney Tarrow. Vol. 1 of *International Social Movement Research*. Greenwich, CT: JAI Press.

Sortons le Québec de l'appauvrissement. 1994. Montreal: Secrétariat de l'Assemblée des évêques du Québec.

Stacey, C.P. 1983. *A Date with History*. Ottawa: Deneau.

Stackhouse, John G., Jr. 1990. The Protestant Experience in Canada since 1945. In *The Canadian Protestant Experience, 1760–1990*, ed. George A. Rawlyk. Burlington, ON: Welch.

– 1992. Whose Dominion? Christianity and Canadian Culture Historically Considered. *Crux* 28: 29–35.

– 1993. *Canadian Evangelicalism in the Twentieth Century: An Introduction to Its Character*. Toronto: University of Toronto Press.

– 1994. More Than a Hyphen: Twentieth-Century Canadian Evangelicalism in Anglo-American Context. In *Amazing Grace: Evangelicalism in Australia, Britain, Canada and the United States*, ed. George A. Rawlyk and Mark Noll. Montreal: McGill-Queen's University Press.

– 1995a. Mainline, Evangelical, Ecumenical: Terms, Stereotypes, and Realities in Canada. *Touchstone* 13: 14–23.

– 1995b. The National Association of Evangelicals, the Evangelical Fellowship of Canada, and the Limits of Evangelical Cooperation. *Christian Scholar's Review* 25: 157–79.

Stark, Rodney, and William S. Bainbridge. 1985. *The Future of Religion: Secularization, Revival, and Cult Formation*. Berkeley: University of California Press.

– 1987. *A Theory of Religion*. New York: Peter Lang.

– 1997. *Religion, Deviance, and Social Control*. New York: Routledge.

Stark, Rodney, and Laurence R. Iannaccone. 1994. A Supply-Side Reinterpretation of the 'Secularization' of Europe. *Journal for the Scientific Study of Religion* 33, 3: 230–52.

Statistics Canada. 1993a. *Religions in Canada*. Ottawa: Industry, Science and Technology Canada, catalogue number 93–319, Tables 1, 3, 6.

– 1993b. The Violence against Women Survey. *The Daily*, 18 November.

Stephanson, Anders. 1995. *Manifest Destiny: American Expansion and the Empire of the Right*. New York: Hill and Wang.

Stiller, Brian C. 1984. Interviews by George Egerton. Vancouver, January.

– 1994. *Don't Let Canada Die by Neglect and Other Essays*. Markham, ON: Faith Today.

Stiller, Brian C., with Bruce Guenther. 1997. *From the Tower of Babel to Parliament Hill: How to Be a Christian in Canada Today*. Toronto: HarperCollins.

Straus, M.A., R.J. Gelles, and S.K. Steinmetz. 1980. *Behind Closed Doors: Violence in the American Family*. New York: Doubleday Anchor.

Sumner, William Graham. 1933. The Bequests of the Nineteenth Century to the Twentieth. *Yale Review* 22: 732–54.

Swatos, William H. 1979. *Into Denominationalism: The Anglican Metamorphosis*. Storrs, CT: Society for the Scientific Study of Religion.

Sweet, Lois. 1997. *God in the Classroom: The Controversial Issue of Religion in Canada's Public Schools*. Toronto: McClelland and Stewart.

Synnott, Anthony. 1993. *The Body Social*. London: Routledge.

Takayama, K. Peter. 1988. Revitalization Movement of Modern Japanese Civil Religion. *Sociological Analysis* 48, 4: 328–41.

Taylor, Charles. 1989. *Sources of the Self: The Making of the Modern Identity*. Cambridge: Harvard University Press.

– 1991. *The Malaise of Modernity*. Concord, ON: Anansi.

– 1992. Can Canada Survive the Charter? *Alberta Law Review* 30, 2: 427–47.

Teichroew, Allan. 1971. World War I and the Mennonite Migration to Canada to Avoid the Draft. *Mennonite Quarterly Review* 45: 219–49.

Thomas, George, John W. Meyer, Francisco O. Ramirez, and John Boli. 1987. *Institutional Structure: Constituting State, Society, and the Individual.* Beverly Hills: Sage.

Timmins, Leslie, ed. 1995. *Listening to the Thunder: Advocates Talk about the Battered Women's Movement.* Vancouver: Women's Research Centre.

Tiryakian, Edward. 1991. Modernization: Exhumetur in Pace. *International Sociology* 6, 2: 165–80.

Todd, Douglas. 1998a. Religious Leaders to Focus on Poverty in Talks with Clark: A Cross-Section of Spiritual Paths Will Be Represented in the Private Session on Monday with the Premier. *Vancouver Sun*, 20 February, B6.

– 1998b. Clark Chides Churches over Stands on Social Issues: Premier Wants Wider Ethical Debate on Poverty. *Vancouver Sun*, 23 February, A1.

– 1998c. Religious Leaders Tell Premier of Fears of Poor Getting Poorer. *Vancouver Sun*, 24 February, B1.

Toulmin, Stephen. 1990. *Cosmopolis: The Hidden Agenda of Modernity.* New York: Free Press.

Troeltsch, Ernst. 1912. *Die Soziallehren der christlichen Kirchen und Gruppen.* Tubingen: Mohr.

Trofimenkoff, Susan Mann. 1983. *The Dream of Nation: A Social and Intellectual History of Quebec.* Toronto: Gage.

Trudeau, Pierre Elliott. 1965a. Federalism, Nationalism, and Reason. In *The Future of Canadian Federalism / L'avenir du fédéralisme canadien*, ed. Paul-A. Crépeau and C.B. Macpherson. Toronto: University of Toronto Press; Montreal: Les Press de l'Université de Montreal.

– 1965b. The Practice and Theory of Federalism. In *Social Purpose for Canada*, ed. Michael Oliver. Toronto: University of Toronto Press.

– 1968a. Constitutional Reform and Individual Freedoms. *Western Ontario Law Review* 8: 1–9.

– 1968b. *Federalism and the French Canadians.* Toronto: Macmillan.

– 1970. *Approaches to Politics.* Toronto: Oxford University Press.

Tschannen, Oliver. 1991. Sociological Controversies in Perspective. *Review of Religious Research* 36, 1: 70–86.

Turner, Bryan. 1984. *The Body and Society: Explorations in Social Theory.* Oxford: Blackwell.

– 1990. Outline of a Theory of Citizenship. *Sociology* 24, 2: 189–217.

– 1992. *Regulating Bodies: Essays in Medical Sociology.* London: Routledge.

– 1996. *The Body and Society: Explorations in Social Theory.* 2nd ed. London: Sage.

Turner, John. 1993. Interview by George Egerton. Vancouver, 19 May.

Tushnet, Mark. 1992. The Constitution of Religion. In *Civil Religion, Church and State*, ed. Martin E. Marty. Munich: K.G. Saur.

Tyack, David, and Elisabeth Hansot. 1982. *Managers of Virtue: Public School Leadership in America*. New York: Basic Books.

United Church of Canada. 1998. The Church and the Public Arena. Accessed through the United Church of Canada website: www.uccan.org, on 2 April.

Vaillancourt, Jean-Guy. 1984. Les groupes socio-politiques progressistes dans le catholicisme québécois contemporain. In *Les movements religieux aujourd'hui: Théories et pratiques*, ed. Jean-Paul Rouleau and Jacques Zylberberg. Montreal: Bellarmin.

Valverde, Mariana. 1991. *The Age of Light, Soap, and Water: Moral Reform in English Canada, 1885–1925*. Toronto: McClelland and Stewart.

VanderVennen, Robert E., ed. 1991. *Church and Canadian Culture*. Lanham, MD: University Press of America.

Van Ginkel, Aileen, ed. 1992. *Shaping a Christian Vision for Canada: Discussion Papers on Canada's Future*. Markham, ON: Faith Today.

Veblen, Thorstein. 1908. *The Theory of the Leisure Class: An Economic Study of Institutions*. New York: Macmillan.

Venne, M. 1995. Jésus aurait-il voté OUI? *Le Devoir*, 14 October, A12.

Verweij, Johan, Peter Ester, and Rein Nauta. 1997. Secularization as an Economic and Cultural Phenomenon: A Cross-National Analysis. *Journal for the Scientific Study of Religion* 36, 2: 309–24.

Vipond, Mary. 1992. Canadian National Consciousness and the Formation of the United Church of Canada. In *Prophets, Priests and Prodigals: Readings in Canadian Religious History, 1608 to Present*, ed. Mark G. McGowan and David B. Marshall. Toronto: McGraw Hill Ryerson.

Voisine, Nive, André Beaulieu, and Jean Hamelin. 1971. *Histoire de l'Église catholique au Québec, 1608–1970*. Montreal: Fides.

Wagner, Melinda. 1997. Generic Conservative Christianity: The Demise of Denominationalism in Christian Schools. *Journal for the Scientific Study of Religion* 36, 1: 13–24.

Walker, Gillian A. 1990. *Family Violence and the Women's Movement: The Conceptual Politics of Struggle*. Toronto: University of Toronto Press.

Wallace, Ruth A., and Alison Wolf. 1995. *Contemporary Sociological Theory*. Englewood Cliffs, NJ: Prentice-Hall.

Wallerstein, Immanuel. 1991. The National and the Universal: Can There Be Such a Thing as World Culture? In *Culture, Globalization and the World-System: Contemporary Conditions for the Representation of Identity*, ed. Anthony D. King. New York: Macmillan.

Wallis, Jim. 1994. *The Soul of Politics: Beyond 'Religious Right' and 'Secular Left.'* New York: New Press; Maryknoll, NY: Orbis.

Walsh, Gary, and Bruce Clemenger. 1998. Conversations with John G. Stackhouse, Jr. Kingston, ON, 14–16 May.

Walsh, H.H. 1954. Canada and the Church: A Job for Historians. *Queen's Quarterly* 61, 1: 71–9.

– 1956. *The Christian Church in Canada*. Toronto: Ryerson.

– 1963. A Canadian Christian Tradition. In *The Churches and the Canadian Experience*, ed. John Webster Grant. Toronto: Ryerson.

Warner, Stephen. 1993. Work in Progress toward a New Paradigm for the Sociological Study of Religion in the United States. *American Journal of Sociology* 98, 5: 1044–93.

Waters, Malcolm. 1995. *Globalization*. New York: Routledge.

Wearing, Joseph, ed. 1991. *The Ballot and Its Message: Voting in Canada*. Toronto: Copp Clark.

Weaver, R. Kent, ed. 1992. *The Collapse of Canada?* Washington: Brookings Institution.

Weber, Max. 1958. *The Protestant Ethic and the Spirit of Capitalism*. New York: Scribner.

– 1968. *Economy and Society: An Outline of Interpretive Sociology*, ed. Guenther Roth and Claus Wittich. New York: Bedminster.

– 1996. *Sociologie des Religions*. Paris: Gallimard.

Wener, Norman, and Jocelyne Bernier. 1971. *Croyants au Canada français: Recherches sur les attitudes et les modes d'appartenance*. Montreal: Fides.

Westfall, William. 1976. The Dominion of the Lord: An Introduction to the Cultural History of Protestant Ontario in the Victorian Period. *Queen's Quarterly* 83, 1: 47–70.

– 1989. *Two Worlds: The Protestant Culture of Nineteenth-Century Ontario*. Montreal: McGill-Queen's University Press.

– 1997. Voices from the Attic: The Canadian Border and the Writing of American Religious History. In *Retelling U.S. Religious History*, ed. Thomas A. Tweed. Berkeley: University of California Press.

Westhues, Kenneth. 1976a. The Adaptation of the Roman Catholic Church in Canadian Society. In *Religion in Canadian Society*, ed. Stewart Crysdale and Les Wheatcroft. Toronto: Macmillan and Maclean-Hunter.

– 1976b. Religious Organization in Canada and the United States. *International Journal of Comparative Studies* 17: 206–25.

Westin, Alan F. 1983. The United States Bill of Rights and the Canadian Charter: A Socio-Political Analysis. In *The U.S. Bill of Rights and the Canadian Charter of Rights and Freedoms*, ed. William R. McKercher. Toronto: Ontario Economic Council.

Wheeler, Barbara. 1996. You Who Were Far Off: Religious Divisions and the Role of Religious Research. *Review of Religious Research* 37, 4: 289–301.

Whipple, Vicky. 1987. Counselling Battered Women from Fundamentalist Churches. *Journal of Marital and Family Therapy* 13, 3: 251–8.

Whitaker, Reginald. 1980. Reason, Passion and Interest: Pierre Trudeau's Eternal Liberal Triangle. *Journal of Political and Social Theory* 4, 1: 5–31.

Wiebe, Robert. 1967. *The Search for Order, 1877–1920.* New York: Hill and Wang.

Williams, John R., ed. 1984. *Canadian Churches and Social Justice.* Toronto: Anglican Book Centre and James Lorimer.

Williams, Rhys H., and Susan M. Alexander. 1994. Religious Rhetoric in American Populism: Civil Religion as Movement Ideology. *Journal for the Scientific Study of Religion* 33, 1: 1–15.

Wilson, Bryan R. 1966. *Religion in Secular Society.* London: C.A. Watts.

– 1975. The Debate over 'Secularization.' *Encounter* 45, 10: 77–83.

– 1982. *Religion in Sociological Perspective.* Oxford: Oxford University Press.

– 1985. Secularization: The Inherited Model. In *The Sacred in a Secular Age: Toward Revision in the Scientific Study of Religion,* ed. Phillip E. Hammond. Berkeley: University of California Press.

– 1992. Reflections on a Many Sided Controversy. In *Religion and Modernization: Sociologists and Historians Debate the Secularization Thesis,* ed. Steve Bruce. Oxford: Clarendon.

Wilson, Edmund. 1982. *The Thirties: From Notebooks and Diaries of the Period.* New York: Washington Square Press.

Wilson, John F. 1979. *Public Religion in American Culture.* Philadelphia: Temple University Press.

Wilson, John, and Thomas Janoski. 1995. The Contribution of Religion to Volunteer Work. *Sociology of Religion* 56, 2: 137–52.

World Council of Churches, The First Assembly of the. 1949. London: SCM.

Wuthnow, Robert. 1988. *The Restructuring of American Religion: Society and Faith since World War II.* Princeton: Princeton University Press.

– 1992. *Rediscovering the Sacred: Perspectives on Religion in Contemporary Society.* Grand Rapids: Eerdmans.

– 1993. *Christianity in the Twenty-First Century: Reflections on the Challenge Ahead.* New York: Oxford University Press.

– 1994a. *I Come Away Stronger: How Small Groups Are Changing American Religion.* Grand Rapids: Eerdmans.

– 1994b. *Producing the Sacred: An Essay on Public Religion.* Urbana: University of Illinois Press.

Yamane, David. 1997. Secularization on Trial: In Defense of a Neosecularization Paradigm. *Journal for the Scientific Study of Religion* 36, 1: 109–22.

Zylberberg, Jacques, and Pauline Côté. 1993. Les balises étatiques de la religion au Canada. *Social Compass* 40, 4: 529–53.

Index